THE
SURVEYOR
AND THE
SILVERSMITH

Land Speculation on the Frontier
of Western Pennsylvania

C. Prentiss Orr

Explorditions
Pittsburgh, PA

Dedication

To my "Root" and to roots.
That is,
to the love of my life, our families, our very own family,
and the first of a next generation.

Contents

Preface

Any writer of narrative history would not think of tackling an authoritative account of his subject unless presented with boxes of sequential diaries, decades of daily journals, or steamer trunks filled with long lost letters from long lost lovers. It's not hard to understand why. No honest writer of history wants to hedge reasonable conjectures with a bunch of "likely"s, "might-have"s, or "there-can-be-little-doubt-that"s. David McCullough never suggested that John Adams *probably* feared Hamilton. Erik Larson did not write that Marconi *might* have been inspired by Heinrich Hertz. And Walter Isaacson never *doubted* that Benjamin Franklin had a healthy libido. Isaacson had no doubt. He had most all of the man's letters (and those of his confidants, too.)

Which is to confess that, although informed by decades of business correspondence written by a meticulous merchant, given ledger books (dating from 1775) recording every sale and expense from a young artisan's workshop, and having discovered endless maps, plats and patents of America's frontier then surveyed in territories yet not governed by white men, the narrative you are about to read comes from ample and, indeed, reliable sources, but, alas, from dozens of dusty tin boxes, assorted bundles of nonsequential letters, scads of clipping files saved in scores of historical societies, and, thankfully, hundreds of digitized books now available online. No one treasure trove of primary resource deemed this project possible, but literally hundreds of seemingly disparate clues and far flung facts suggested I could boil a strong broth if not simmer a hearty soup. For this reason, I have provided many a reference and footnote.

I have also quoted letters extensively. If I have included too many, or too much content of any one letter, it is because I am charmed by the language, logic, and idioms of the 18ᵗʰ century. Our first president may have had issues with spelling, but he had none in turning a phrase to argue his point. I have inserted brackets to clarify meaning or context only when necessary and I have left all organic punctuation intact.

A word about interpreting Native American culture and religion. Most cultural anthropologists willingly admit to knowing embarrassingly little about tribal rituals and, even less so, the spirituality of indigenous people. Of what scant knowledge we have, a preponderance of doubt must apply to the white man's Judeo-Christian interpretation of the same. Further, I confess to using terms like *injun*, *redskin* or *savage*, but only in contexts I alone think permissible.

Finally, this narrative is about people and legacy. I have often thought, like the novels of Charles Dickens, society long ago was populated with a much wider spectrum of human character; that, since the advent of popular drama—since the universal evolution of radio sitcoms and television talk shows and mass-market novels—we are all, sadly (and perversely,) much more alike. We all strive to respect one another. We all mean to be socially aware. We all hope to relish family. In the end, of course, we all just want to belong. But, yes, "back when," there were characters who didn't "belong," who didn't fit in, who had their own notions of self-importance or self-awareness. There were those who kept unimaginable secrets, those who fell prey to preposterous schemes or impossible dreams, and those who, despite desperate odds, dared to do the unthinkable.

And most everyone carried a gun.

It was, after all, the wild west. The funny thing is, then, the wild west was western Pennsylvania.

Introduction

When one lives in a house that is 200 years old (as I do now) built on property that was acquired some 235 years ago, there is a sense of history permeating a place whenever one is present. For me, my curiosity is constantly prodded by some stone that has been turned or relocated, some magnificent tree that has withstood centuries of weather events and environmental change, or some smell from a chimney that has vented years of smoke and dust from inside to outside. Most often, I observe the creativity and care with which some historical advancement in technology was applied to the house or land. Human ingenuity and perseverance is abundantly evident.

Imagine the early years if you will. A creek flows through the property and empties into the Ohio River. It is lined with plentiful clay soil. So, to improve upon primitive living structures (log cabins), a decision is made to construct a grand house from brick such as exist in Philadelphia after the War of 1812. The new house must be located above the flood plain of the creek; experience has already shown the disastrous effects of the Ohio River when engorged by rainwater or melting snow. First an audacious foundation is laid in a large rectangular hole all dug by hand. One end of the foundation hole terminates at an extensive granite ledge serving as the anchor support for the principle chimney of the house. The walls of the hole are then lined with very large boulders of sandstone dragged by horse-drawn wagon from a nearby quarry on the property. The position of the foundation is set so that one longwise side of the house will be bathed in sunlight; during winter months this will warm the house. In summer the leaves of hundreds of deciduous trees will provide cooling shade. It is evident that thoughtful planning has occurred in siting this house. The structure is framed with huge hand-hewn timbers meted together in mortise and tenon fashion and stabilized with wood pegs (because nails are just not available.) To complete the house structure requires molding by hand and baking in ovens thousands upon thousands upon thousands of bricks made from the clay in the creek. No small task.

The house is built laboriously and with precision. The exterior and interior walls are layered two bricks thick with a fresh batch of mortar concocted from scratch every day. Each room on the first story, as well as the second, is designed with a wood-burning fireplace, each serviced by a separate flue to exhaust smoke up a chimney. In all, eleven working Rumford-design fireplaces with hearths are built precisely to deliver heat safely and efficiently. The engineering to prevent downdrafts and backdrafts of smoke into the house has been cleverly calculated.

The tongue-in-groove wooden flooring are made from indigenous white oak sawn by a water-powered sawmill constructed on the property's creek. Not to be overlooked wood-box piping is laid a long distance to carry fresh water to a spring house adjacent to the residence.

Such were a few of the myriad considerations involved in the construction of this house over a period of at least seven years. Slowly, tediously, did the structure take shape. First a two-story section was completed (and inhabited,) and then a larger three-story body was added to the early house and finished.

I am awed by the effort, energy and time devoted to constructing the house. Most certainly there were many problems and obstacles to be resolved by ingenuity. (I suppose I am grateful not to know them all!) So it was that by 1823, almost forty years after the purchase of the property did a grand house suitable for comfortable, civil habitation become occupied by a hearty and energetic family of eight persons. Thus my curiosity of how they endured and what they accomplished became a subject of great interest.

This house of the early nineteenth century was built at the dawn of an era introduced by the steam engine. Serving initially as a trading post and post-office on the principal road going west from Pittsburgh, the activity around it—whether by foot, horseback, wagon or stagecoach—was a continual semi-chaotic condition at the house. Soon, however, the steam engine promoted commercial use of the Ohio River by means of paddlewheel boats. This innovation diverted some activity from the use of the road. Eventually, the steam engine on railroad tracks marked a major technological change by the 1850's. This change ended the trading post and post-office activities, and the house became only a residential domicile.

Over time the wood-burning fireplaces were supplemented by a coal-burning hot air convection furnace, which required hot air ducts to be ingeniously installed. Later, natural gas lighting was introduced to supplant the use of candles, requiring gas pipes to be cleverly concealed. Then along came indoor plumbing with many more pipes to be configured into the house but which graciously eliminated the outdoor privy. Then electricity was introduced with wires connected to outlets and switches running throughout the house. Oh, the agony of fishing thick-gaged wire!

All the foregoing description is based on material evidence revealed by living in this house which has endured for two centuries. Imagine what daily living was like: keeping fires burning in cold weather, hauling water in buckets from the spring house, reading by candle light and cleaning up wax drippings, cooking, sleeping, washing, using the privy.

Yet what fascinates me more is discerning the story—truly, a narrative history—of the people who acquired the land and built the house and promoted reading, writing, and "doing sums," and who invited itinerant preachers and complete strangers to spend time on a cool porch or by a warm fire. To uncover the personal history of the Leet/Shields family and to link these personal histories to the broader settlement of western Pennsylvania, I had to call on someone willing to dig through it all. He has rumbled and tumbled and bumped through doors, drawers, and archives to read copious letters, diaries and newspaper accounts of the people and events that are described in this book. So rather than me continuing to dwell on this old house, I invite you to learn about the stalwart surveyor, Daniel Leet, and the intrepid silversmith, Thomas Shields, who joined forces, fortunes and family in western Pennsylvania.

Enjoy the journey.

—Jay Brooks

Dearest wounds of Jesus,
> Whoever does not love you, and does not give his
> whole heart to you, holds nothing dear.

Wondrous wounds of Jesus,
> Holy fissures, you make sinners holy, and thieves
> from saints. How amazing!

Powerful wounds of Jesus,
> So moist, so gory, bleed on my heart so that I may
> remain brave and like the wounds.

Juicy wounds of Jesus,
> Whoever sharpens the pen and with it pierces you
> just a little, licks and tastes it.

Prologue

Like the sickle moon hanging over the Ohio River outside, Daniel Leet's hours waned. He sweated under hand-sewn quilts, his breathing shallow and labored. A lone bedside candle cast a lumpy silhouette across papered walls.

At Daniel's side, Eliza—his only child—clasped her hands in devout prayer, reading psalms from a well-worn Bible laying on her lap. Dressed in black, she mourned the inevitable. Whether she feared her father's soul would not meet the full embrace of a forgiving savior or that his time might linger in torment surely justified for sins he never confessed, she could do nothing more than pray. Pray for redeeming grace. Pray for eternal rest. Pray for peace.

On Thursday, June 17, in the year 1830, Daniel Leet died in his bed at "Newington," a once 1,400-acre plantation in southwestern Pennsylvania. Not just twenty miles west of Pittsburgh, he had taken residence there only ten months earlier. An earlier gift to his daughter and son-in-law, Newington, including its several barns, mills, a schoolhouse, and summer home, was then attended by stable hands, gardeners, and more than a few kitchen maids.

The *Washington (Pennsylvania) Examiner* reported his demise nine days later.[1] "For many years before his death, he had retired from the active scenes of life, and now has descended to the grave, ripe in years, and after, it is humbly hoped, having made his peace with God and all mankind. 'Peace be to his ashes.'"

Daniel Leet was 82.

---

[1] *The Examiner and Farmers' and Mechanics' Repositor*, Vol. XIV, No. 7, Washington, PA, June 26, 1830

His was an unusually long life, even by standards his great-great grand-children would not come to expect.[2] He outlived his many close friends and compatriots, gentlemen known to American history by the names William Crawford, Levi Hollingsworth, Robert Morris, John Nicholson, Alexander Hamilton, and George Washington. In fact, he outlived his wife by sixteen years, a woman who, in her own time, was as famous as they.

A licensed surveyor of America's earliest expansion west, he was a true frontiersman. Well beyond the Allegheny mountains, deep into Ohio terri-tory, his fearless expeditions into Indian country, and his wild ventures in land speculation, challenged the morals upon which America's earliest citi-zens—indeed, its founding fathers, too—settled a country in times of right-eous faith and brazen greed. Lauded as a hero most of his adult life, he es-chewed answering questions about bravery, military life, or the thousand-mile expeditions he travelled with two conspiring Virginians, one of whom died a most horrific death, and the other who became president. Present at the slaughter of hundreds of Natives, ambushed and attacked by scalping warriors, yet friend to once benevolent sachems whose names and good deeds were never recognized in white men's books, Daniel Leet, too, shared few words. But of his successes, triumphs, and virtues, the frontier was well aware; he seemed to have been present at every turn of early American history.

Experiencing much of the same history, too, was an early acquaintance, an artisan, Philadelphia-born, who cast his wealth upon the rivers of the north and into the wilds of the far west. A devout Baptist, steeped in the politics of church and city, he showed early on a vision that America's for-tunes were not to be created by the gentry, but by the farmer—not by the statesman, but by the settler—not by specie, but by sweat. Thomas Shields, still one of the most prized colonial silversmiths, whose works adorn the collec-tions of dozens of American museums, forged his passion for progress in the most remarkable ways.

Let it be known, near Sewickley, Pennsylvania, there is a lone church, once an integral part of life at Newington that honors Daniel Leet. Not sur-prisingly there was also a church Thomas Shields built in Northampton County. A Baptist who wore his faith on his sleeve, Shields channeled Amer-ica's rampant religiosity while Leet was seemingly dismissive of it. Yet it is the

---

[2] https://ourworldindata.org/life-expectancy

latter's church that still stands. And perhaps for good reason. It may be the one lasting proof of Daniel Leet's redemption.

This is the story of two pioneers, one a surveyor, the other a silversmith, both land speculators who found success never before realized. And, until now, never before told.

PART ONE
(1748-1775)

*In which world powers and pioneers
pierce America's wild frontier while
trying to keep peace with the Natives.*

Hanna's Town

Like most newspapers of its time, the front page of the *Daily Pittsburgh Gazette* for July 15, 1836, was emblazoned with ads. Among solicitations to purchase Ward's Vegetable Hair Oil, Orris Tooth Wash, containing "neither chlorine or alkalies," or India Rubber Clothes for "firemen, stage drivers, or steamboat men," appeared a recounting of an unspeakable incident fifty years earlier.

The story was prefaced by a notice to the Gazette's subscribers. "In the absence of news of interest or importance, we present our readers to-day with an account of the burning of Hanna's Town by the Indians in the year 1782. Many of the characters mentioned were well known at a period long subsequent to that occurrence, and this event having taken place in our immediate neighborhood, will, on that account alone, be interesting to many readers."

It is no less interesting today than it was then to the residents of Pittsburgh in 1836, or to the hapless community of Hanna's Town in 1782. News of a far greater threat—of horrendous bloodshed on the Sandusky plains—had not yet reached the tiny settlement in Westmoreland County, when this story first unfolded.

"On the 13th day of July, 1782, a party of the townsfolk went to O'Connor's fields, about a mile and half north of the village, to cut down the harvest of Michael Huffnagle. No person resided on the premises where the grain was growing, nor indeed was there at that period resident inhabitants, except in few instances, upon any of the improvements, or settlements northwest of the town.

"There was, therefore, little impediment to the Indians, either by way of resistance, or even of giving warning of their approach. When the party of reapers had cut down one field, and were about to commence at another, one of the number who had for some purpose crossed to the side next to the woods, returned in great alarm, and reported that he had seen a number of Indians in the act of approaching them. The whole reaping party took the alarm and ran for the town, each one intent upon his own safety. They arrived successively out of breath, and each one by his own alarm, added to that of the people of the village. The scene which then presented itself, may more readily be conceived than described. Fathers seeking for their wives and children, and children calling upon their parents and friends, and all hurrying in consternation to the Fort. After some time had passed for reflection, it was proposed… that some persons should reconnoitre… Four young men… pursued a direct course towards Connor's fields; whilst Capt. J [Matthew Jack], who happened to be in the town, pursued a more circuitous rout on horseback.

"The captain was the first to arrive at the fields, and his eye was not long in doubt, for the whole force of the savages was there mustered, and just in the act of moving forward. It may be supposed the hum and rustle of their moving made his pulse beat quick. He turned his horse to fly, but was observed and pursued. When he proceeded a short distance, he met the four on foot—told them to fly for their lives, that the savages were coming in great force, that there was no safety but in the fort… he would take a circuitous rout and alarm the settlements. The four made all speed to the town, but the foremost Indian obtained sight of them, and gave them hot pursuit. By the time they had reached the crab-tree creek, … he turned and saw the savages, with their tufts of hair flying in the wind, and their brandished tomahawks, for they had emerged into the open space around the town, and commenced the war whoop. He resolved to make one of them give his death halloo, and raising his rifle to his eye, his bullet whizzed true, for the stout savage at whom he aimed, bounded into the air and fell upon his face. Then, with the speed of an arrow, he fled [f]or the fort, which he entered in safety, where he found his comrades.

"The Indians were exasperated when they found the town deserted, and after pillaging the houses, they set them on fire. One savage, who had put on the military coat of one of the inhabitants, paraded himself so ostentatiously, that he was shot down.—A maiden, by name Jennet Shaw, was killed in the fort—a child having ran opposite the gate, in which there were some apertures through which a bullet from the Indians occasionally whistled, she followed it, and as she stooped to pick it up, a bullet entered her bosom—she thus fell a victim to her kindness of heart. The savages, with their wild yells and hidious gesticulations, exulted as the flames spread, and looked like demoniacs rejoicing over the lost hope of mortals."

Outside the village, where word of the attack spread more quickly than wild fire, parties of women and children fled for their safety to distant homesteads, while their men rode to the rescue of those besieged at the fort. The Indians took full advantage.

"Heavy were the hearts of the women and maidens as they were led into captivity. Who can tell the bitterness of their sorrow? They looked, as they thought, for the last time upon the dear fields of their country, and of civilized life; they thought of their fathers, their husbands, their brothers; and as their eyes streamed with tears, the cruelty and uncertainty which hung over their fate as prisoners of the savages, overwhelmed them in despair."

Back at the fort, the lone standing defense against certain death, the surviving villagers schemed to save their skins.

"After some consultation, it was the general opinion that the Indians intended to make an attack the next morning, and as there was about forty-five or sixty men, the contest was considered extremely doubtful, considering the great superiority of numbers on the part of the savages. It became therefore a matter of the first importance, to impress the enemy with a belief that large reinforcements were arriving. For that purpose the horses were mounted by active men, and brought full trot over the bridge of plank, that was across the ditch which surrounded the stockading. This was frequently repeated; two old drums were found in the fort, which were new braced, and music on the fife and drum was kept occasionally going during the night. Whilst marching and counter-marching, the bridge was frequently crossed on foot by the whole garrison. These measures had the desired effect... the sounds carried terror into the bosoms of the cowardly savages. They feared the retribution which they deserved, and fled ...

"The little community, which had now no homes but what the fort supplied, looked out on the ruins of the town with the deepest sorrow. It had been to them the scene of heartfelt joys. Embracing the intensity and tenderness of all which renders the domestic hearth and family altar sacred..."

What remained of Hanna's Town after the raid of July, 1782, was the stockade fort and a single log courthouse. It had been the first seat of government west of the Alleghenies. Ever a threat to the sanctity of Native lands, Hanna's Town, founded just nine years earlier, was never resettled.

Bordentown, New Jersey

Today, Bordentown, New Jersey, is a small city of approximately 4,000 residents, encompassing only about a square mile, defined as much by its bedroom economy as by the concrete barriers of I-295 to the west and I-95 a little farther east. A half-hour's drive southwest will get you into the heart of Philadelphia. New York City is another forty minutes north. Only the interstate system and Delaware River separate the city from Pennsylvania. Crosswicks Street, its major thoroughfare named after the creek bordering its northern limits, features clean rows of Georgian brick townhouses and grass-lined blocks of white clapboard homes reminiscent of the town's colonial past. A Friends Meetinghouse, built in 1740, still stands on Farnsworth Street. The town also distinguishes itself in claiming the sometime residency of Thomas Paine who, during cooler Revolutionary months, may have found restful comfort away from Philadelphia's more hotheaded citizens.

Eighteen years before *Common Sense* incited independent thinking, Daniel Leet was born in Bordentown on June 11, 1748. The second child of Isaac Leet and Rebecca Vaughn and the eldest of four sons and five daughters more to come, Daniel must have learned early the familial duties to which a first-born son was entrusted. For more than 52 years, he seemingly never left his brothers' sides.

In 1750, and for several years before and many after, Bordentown served as a convenient layover for travelers between America's two greatest cities. Only a morning's carriage ride up the Delaware, Trenton was also home to a growing economy. In Hunterdon County, just north of Trenton, Isaac tended to a small farm he owned.[1] In the parlance of the time, he was "a yeoman there."

Yet, the Leet family removed themselves altogether from New Jersey to the more rural Prince William County, Virginia, around 1760. Vast farms along the banks of the Potomac were growing plentiful tobacco at the time, suggesting the Leet family might have been drawn to tend larger fields. Besides native corn, tobacco was the one crop colonists were allowed to trade. Even with steady exports to London, it was not a lucrative business.[2] For a brief period of about twenty years, until the intense nutrient demands of tobacco exhausted the soil, the area attracted merchants and farmers alike seeking fortunes larger than were to be earned in more competitive markets like Philadelphia. Certainly, Isaac Leet was not among the successful, because he moved his growing family again, this time to Augusta County.

Which is to say, the Leets moved to America's wild frontier.

*   *   *   *   *

Virginians today might recognize Augusta as their state's second-largest county. It encompasses the cities of Waynesboro and Staunton, situated in the lush Shenandoah Valley. But, as early as 1740, Augusta County was something much, much larger. It was truly an amorphous blob of untold square miles—hundreds of thousands of square miles—loosely defined by geologic formations like the Allegheny Mountains or the Susquehanna River, or by the Appalachian foothills and tributaries that would not be mapped accurately for years to come. Think of this vast terrain as if it were West Virginia today. It mostly is. Yet, a good part of what Virginia then claimed was also part of what Pennsylvania claimed. Blur any further definition of Augusta County by what Maryland also might have claimed; these three provinces reached far west to the wilds known then only as Ken-Tuk-Kee, Monongalia, and the much feared "Ohio country." Until 1744, there was little reason to sort any of it out because, really, this was all impenetrable Indian territory, anyhow.

Of course it always had been. No white man, venturing west beyond the Allegheny mountains, or decades earlier, hunting along the Susquehanna

---

[1] New Jersey, U.S., Abstract of Wills, William Vaughn, pg. 492.

[2] Sakolski, *The Great American Land Bubble*, pg. 14

River, or even hundreds of years before that, first stepping ashore, did not know that the land on which he trod had long been inhabited by a people of countless generations and of many cultures. But the audacity of European caste and the promise of a singularly omnipotent god gave the white man authority to do as he wished. Ever-itinerant trappers and traders were able to create posts at the mouths of major tributaries west—notably at Logstown on the Ohio River or Venango at the mouth of French Creek—but pioneers who wished to settle permanently faced horrendous odds. A single family rarely survived the grueling process of clearing land, feeding livestock, fending off wolves and mountain lions, or most importantly, raising healthy children. Even tight-knit communes of many families could barely make do. Natives were as curious about the white man's determination to settle on one particular spot as they were his efforts to create farm land from dense forests. Survival required the regular assistance of others—trader, Indian or neighbor—to replenish tools, lead and gunpowder. And in exchange for these necessities pioneers needed to produce goods of ready value—commodities like tallow, cloth or moonshine. Of course, in making a trade, a settler might "confuse" the ambitious Native who, perhaps enticed by a few cordial cups of whiskey, misunderstood the value of a recent transaction. Settling up a few days later, now sober, the parties might exhibit defiant behaviors. Keeping the peace was sometimes a less delicate process than building mutual trust.

And now, native tribes who may have traded with early English colonists were also trading with the French, increasingly in numbers and goods, as they descended from far northern wilds. Unlike the Brits, the French were primarily interested in the many resources available just for the taking. Tall sturdy lumber was of immense value to their fleets, and furs of beaver, otter, and ermine were prized by their royal courts. The fact that Cartier, Champlain and LaSalle "first" explored the St. Lawrence River rooted French interests in all that could be traded from raw forests north of the great seaway. That LaSalle "discovered" the access the Great Lakes gave to rivers flowing south—especially to New Orleans—only piqued French curiosity. Perhaps there were other more expedient routes back to the Atlantic. And along such routes would come the discovery of ever more bountiful forests and the necessity to play fairly with the Natives whose assistance they so much relied upon.

The strength of alliances between, say, the tribal Senecas and the French, or the Delawares and the British, were as much predicated on the favors they bestowed as on the quality of the guns, tomahawks or liquor they bartered. The French often had superior goods; the British could afford to be more generous. They constantly competed for the favor of confused and fickle Natives. Meanwhile, of course, adding to tensions, the French and British were at war thousands of miles across the Atlantic. For the pioneer who sought more and better land, the times became increasingly unsettling. Certainly, there was endemic fear that, unless the Natives were mollified by some universal agreement, the lands might fall to French interests, especially if those much-hated *étrangers* should make peace with the Natives first.

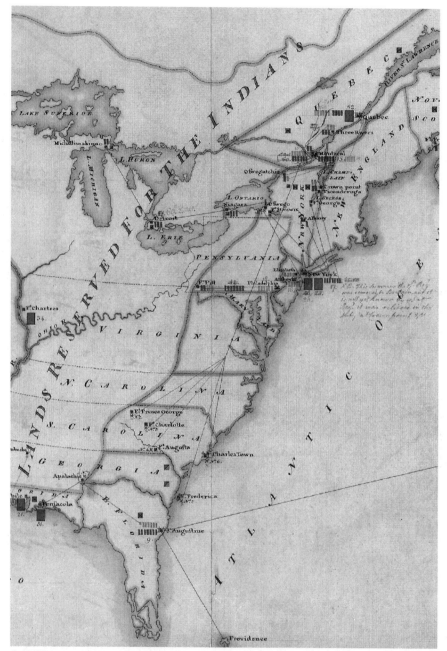

A 1767 map suggesting the western extent of lands claimed by the colonies and otherwise identifying the strength of British forces. *Paterson, Daniel. Cantonment of His Majesty's forces in N. America according to the disposition now made & to be compleated as soon as practicable taken from the general distribution dated at New York 29th. March. [1767] Map. Library of Congress.*

The Treaty of Lancaster

And so, in 1744, in the village of Lancaster, Pennsylvania, a handful of men representing each of Pennsylvania, Maryland and Virginia met with Canassatego, a leader of the Iroquois people, representing the Six Nations. More than just a peaceable alliance among the Mohawks, Oneidas, Onondogas, Cayugas, Senecas, and, (by 1720) the Tuscaroras, the Six Nations was a confederacy of tribal government over which as many as fifty sachems held sway and who would meet in times of internal strife, war or famine. It was a centralized government of a very like-minded, yet diverse people.

Lt. Governor George Thomas represented Pennsylvania. A member of the Virginia Council of State, Thomas Lee, represented his province. Maryland presented itself with not one, but three commissioners. Legend portends that Benjamin Franklin was there, too. (Fascinated by native culture, he had begun publishing tracts of Indian agreements beginning in 1736. The concept of a confederation of self-governing councils, the very construct of the Six Nations, so intrigued Benjamin Franklin that he would later incorporate the notion of a centralized government of colonies into his Albany Plan in 1754.) Franklin, however, did not attend the meeting, but he did publish the events of the "pow-wow" in 1748.

The Treaty of Lancaster would be interpreted by the several convening parties as having very different meanings. The Virginians believed the treaty entitled them to the very claim they had always made, principally that their King was entitled to all lands west to the Pacific. The Pennsylvanians believed the treaty would eventually remove the Shawnees and Delawares from the Lehigh and Wyoming Valleys. The Maryland Commissioners believed that the Indians, who were extorting payment from squatting settlers, had simply agreed to "bury their hatchets." In a speech of brotherly love, one Maryland commissioner was given an honorary Indian name. Many other speeches assured the Natives that the colonists were there "but to strengthen the chains of friendship" or to "keep our fires burning brightly" in the "warmth" of their sincere friendship. Most speeches were punctuated with the presentation of wampum—strings or belts of polished mussel beads—to which the Indians would chant hearty approval.

By all accounts, the meeting was a great success. Essentially, after three days of sharing tobacco and standing around the proverbial punchbowl, it was commonly understood that Canassatego had ceded all lands west to the Ohio River. For this accession to well more than 30,000 square miles, the representatives of the Six Nations received 200 shirts, four duffle blankets, 47 guns, 1,000 flints, 200 bars of lead, two half-barrels of gun powder, and four dozen Jew's harps.[3]

Never mind that the Delawares, Shawnees or Wyandots were not invited to the party. Never mind that the lands ceded were as much theirs as any of the six Iroquois tribes (who lived much farther north in New York.) Never mind that the treaty was a document that none of 24 sachems who signed it could read.

Of course, the French were no party to the Lancaster Treaty. It's not certain they even learned about it until years later. Indeed, longtime frontiersmen like George Croghan and Christopher Gist, whose trading grounds were on the Ohio and other posts west, did not learn about the Treaty of Lancaster until 1752.

In short order, Thomas Lee ascended to the office of President of the Virginia Council of State and then organized the Ohio Company of Virginia to appraise the incalculable resources of Augusta County. Included were the Appalachian range and lands extending far west to the Ohio River and north to the Monongahela. He would make land claims for himself and many prospective investors.

Lee then organized his venture in partnership with two well-respected and well-connected gentlemen, brothers Lawrence and Augustine Washington, both wealthy landowners, Virginia officers, and skilled surveyors. Virginia Governor Robert Dinwiddie became a major investor in the Ohio

---

[3] Marshe, *Journal of the Treaty at Lancaster*, pg. 18

Company, as did many other officers of his military, including George Mercer who, within the year, petitioned King George II for more than 500,000 acres, of which 200,000 were instantly granted. (The remaining 300,000 acres would be granted within seven years if the new company could successfully settle a minimum of 100 families willing to inhabit any of these first 200,000 acres.)

The Ohio Land Company, as it became known, would require the services of many surveyors. Fortunately, the brothers Washington had ready and able associates, not to mention a younger half-brother who was keen to learn the art. That young man earned his surveyor's license from William and Mary College in 1749, the very same year.

Washington and Crawford

Born in Berkley County, Virginia, William Crawford was just four years old when his father died.[4] Fortunately, his mother, Honora, had help with her small family. Richard Stephenson was the family's farmhand. He had been indentured to William's father for a period of seven years. At the time of his patron's death however, Stephenson had more or less fulfilled his obligations. If there was time he still owed, it would matter not; Stephenson married Honora within the year and became William's and his baby brother, Valentine's, stepfather. The following year, 1727, the Crawford-Stephenson family moved farther west to Frederick County, Virginia, and settled on land they claimed—without warrant, survey or deed—on Bullskin Creek, nestled in a northern valley of the Shenandoah.

William, like most children of the colonial frontier, learned the essential skills of survival. And more. To grow hearty crops of green vegetables, corn or barley, they built up mounds of soil to create raised gardens which were less subject to crippling early frosts. He and his brothers stripped rings of bark from maple trees and "deadened" others they wished to fell; when the spring sap could not rise, the leaves would wither and the tree would die. Once "girdled," deadened limbs then were piled around the tree trunk, and burned. A year later, the charred, rotting trunk could be hacked from the ground, helping to clear out more farm land. The process took a full eighteen months. With younger trees, William and Valentine learned how to build a log cabin, learned the art of hewing split logs for floor boards (or

---

[4] Butterfield, *Expedition Against Sandusky*, pg. 81

"puncheons,") learned to measure openings for doors and windows, learned basic geometry, and, in fact, basic algebra, too.

They became expert riflemen, loading a musket with gun powder, then a lead ball, cocking the arm to strike the flint to fire a shot. And they learned to do all of this while running—a difficult, but necessary feat—in case a bear attacked, or "injuns" were in pursuit.

Even in the wilds, without any book other than a Bible, William Crawford earned an education of some unlikely promise. For, in or about 1740, he was received into the family of John Vance, a pioneer surveyor, to take up the trade. That Honora Crawford or Richard Stephenson—neither of whom could read or write themselves—would have foreseen that the applied science of surveying might have inordinate and lasting value beyond the convenience of distinguishing one's property from another, is prescient if not clairvoyant. How they compensated Vance for the education William would receive, or why they would carry on without the support of their eldest teen son, is not known. But William left his family and moved in with the Vances some distance away.

Clearly, he learned much. Four years later, he married the Vances' daughter, Hanna, and, then, blessed with three children within the next six years, William moved his young family to property he was able to purchase, legally, for £1 an acre. Then known as Cattail Run, the property abutted vast land owned by Lord Fairfax, descendant of Lord Culpepper, royal heir to the northern neck of the Shenadoah Valley, and who, in short time, happened to rent some 128 acres from William. They became good friends.

And, so it was, that in 1750, Lord Fairfax, father-in-law to Lawrence Washington, and a generous mentor to Lawrence's younger half-brother, introduced William Crawford to George Washington, Virginia's newly commissioned surveyor of Culpepper County. George was then 18. William was 28. Over the course of that fall, Washington and Crawford would become trusted friends, surveying land belonging to Lord Fairfax, Lawrence Washington, John Vance and even William's stepfather, Richard Stephenson. Of course, they would explore many other properties, too—lands they would wish to own themselves, lands for which they needed no authority to survey, lands owned since the dawn of humanity by no other claim than that granted solely by the Great Spirit to those who shared it freely.

George and William created a bond that would last decades.

The Forks of the Ohio

By 1752 Governor Dinwiddie learned of a clear and present threat in "the Ohios." The French, stationed on the Riviére Le Boeuf (near present-day Waterford, Pennsylvania) and supplied with 1,500 men and sufficient canoes to descend south, intended to build forts encroaching on lands otherwise claimed by the British throne. Dinwiddie would have nothing to do with such arrogant provocation (not to mention one that could jeopardize his personal investment in the Ohio Land Company.) Whatever forests the French might have thought to trespass were very clearly under his King's domain. Dinwiddie needed them to know that. And so he sought the aid of an eager 21 year-old adjutant major, willing and able to make a journey 500 miles northwest, to deliver a single letter to the French commander stationed there.

Enter young George. Now a fearless frontiersman whose survival skills he would credit to William Crawford, and now a practiced surveyor familiar with forested lands he had mapped with Lord Fairfax as well as Crawford, Washington led an expedition in the company of Christopher Gist, also then employed by the Ohio Land Company. Along with them rode Jacob Van Braam, Washington's erstwhile fencing instructor and a French interpreter, and "four Indian traders and baggage-men."

Embarking from Williamsburg on October 31, 1753, with a letter addressed to the Commandant of the French forces at Fort Le Boeuf, young George first stopped in Fredericksburg, Virginia, and then Wills Creek (near Cumberland, Maryland) where the Ohio Company had already built a trading post. From there, marching on, a week later, he described in his journal:

"The excessive Rains and vast Quantity of Snow that had fallen, prevented our reaching Mr. Frazier's an Indian Trader, at the Mouth of Turtle-Creek, on Monongahela, till Thursday the 22d.

"The Waters were quite impassable, without swimming our Horses; which obliged us to get the Loan of a Canoe from Frazier, and to send Barnaby Currin, and Henry Steward [aides], down Mononga-hela, with our Baggage, to meet us at the Forks of Ohio, about 10 Miles, to cross Aligany...

"As I got down before the Canoe, I spent some Time in viewing the Rivers, and the Land in the Fork, which I think extremely well situated for a Fort, as it has the absolut Command of both Rivers. The Land at the Point is 20 or 25 Feet above the common Surface of the Water, and a considerable Bottom of flat, well-timbered Land all around it, very convenient for Building... "

Evident in Washington's narrative is the knowledge that the Ohio Company had already made plans for the area.

"About two Miles from this, on the South East Side of the River, at the Place where the Ohio Company intended to erect a Fort..."

Indeed, George Mercer, the man who had requested from King George the 500,000 acres for the Ohio Land Company, had the location already mapped out.

"It is a Plain about 3/4 of a Mile in Length, and 1/2 Mile in Breadth, bounded on the North by a very high Hill (where the fort is to be built) on the Southward and East by Shurtees Creek on Eastward and West by the Ohio River which runs around this Hill."[5]

But Washington had other ideas and expressed them in his journal:

---

[5] Schwartz, *The French and Indian War*, pg. 13

"As I had taken a good deal of Notice Yesterday of the Situation at the Forks, my Curiosity led me to examine this more particularly, and I think it [the Ohio Company's proposed site] greatly inferior, either for Defence or Advantages; especially the latter; for a Fort at the Forks would be equally well situated on Ohio, and have the entire Command of Monongahela, which runs up to our Settlements and is extremely well design'd for Water Carriage, as it is of a deep still Nature; besides, a Fort at the Fork might be built at a much less Expence, than at the other Place."

Along this journey, Washington saw many sites which, to his surveyor's eye, he considered ideal for homesteading. That he knew the Ohio Company had first considered the mouth of Shurtee's Creek an ideal location for a fort doesn't suggest he agreed with its promise. Few did. (Perhaps not even the earlier French trader Pierre Chartiers for whom it was named.) But Washington would soon "run it out" the very next year when, upon subsequent orders of Governor Dinwiddie, he returned to the Forks of the Ohio to build a "strong house" and, by doing so, secure the confluence of the three rivers for the construction of a true fort.

The strong house, around which bastions would rise, was first called Fort Prince George. A larger fort, in four years' time, will give Pittsburgh its name.

Militia Law

In December of 1753, Governor Dinwiddie reported back to his Virginia House of Burgesses the consequence of Washington's expedition to Fort Le Boeuf, declaring in the *Pennsylvania Gazette* of December 13, that he had "sent several considerable Presents to the Indians, that are our Allies, and in Friendship with us. These people seem much surprised at the Conduct of the French, and appear full of Resentment; and have assured the Commissioners, sent from me, of their sincere Attachment to the British Interest, and to the English Colonies on this Continent."[6]

"These people"—collectively, yet dismissively meaning the "Indians"— were a constant subject of both the intelligentsia of Williamsburg and, of course, settlers in the west. The only thing that a growing colony feared more than the indifference of the American Native was the influence another civilized society might have on them. It was one thing for the British loyalist to constantly appease the Native's resentment of the white man building homesteads along once virgin waterways, it was something else to assuage the fear of conflict when goaded on by other foreign white men. In essence, British colonialists were as racially insensitive to the plight of the Native as, for centuries still, modern white society is to accepting cultural diversity. That the British were already fighting the French well across the Atlantic was not a secondary issue. That the Natives could be used as mere pawns in this battle on American soil was just less obvious. Except for the pious humility of a few rare missionary movements, the colonists had no capacity to meet Natives as equals. They could never quite grasp the irony

---

[6] "Address to the House of Burgesses," *The Pennsylvania Gazette*, December 13, 1753

of the intolerance they bred in the new world, one they had come to to escape the intolerance of the old. To them, the Indians were heathens. They had no documented religion. They dressed strangely. They smelled. They drank themselves into frenzies so as to commit heinous acts of plunder—and, worse, murder—just for the sport of it. Clearly, and commonly accepted, the Indians were unreasoning savages, a pestilent people that even "considerable Presents" could not come to please.

Almost singularly for this reason did the colonies create militia law. Back in England, militias had been assembled since as early as 1660, but none was regularly active unless in training, an annual event lasting just several weeks. British militia had no cavalry and no artillery. Rarely were they "called up" until, ironically, King George assembled his royal forces to sail to the colonies. Then, because the more able soldier and experienced officer were across the Atlantic, militias on British soil were necessary to keep local peace.

Of course, that was not the case in America. Long before any Continental soldier was enjoined to America's defense, all regions, all counties and every town had an organized and ready militia. They were the one and only means by which towns could defend themselves from marauding "savages." For the most part they were self-funded, self-armed and self-assembled by democratic vote. Indeed, the Governors of the many provinces appointed officers to ranks of authority under which men would assemble for expeditions deemed necessary by their "command." But there was no lawful military command for militia who, separate from British, French or Continental armies, were left to their own devices to protect their own people. Militias were regulated only by their collective moral compass.

Beginning in the 1770s, when the talk of independence divided the colonial gentry into Tories and Whigs, when as yet a citizen was subject to a system of laws having no more integrity than the unreasonable taxation and ever crueler punishments for which the system was seemingly built, there was no "common law." Of course, there was no Constitution, yet. And, as such, there was no Federal law. Consider then, too, that towns like Pittsburgh—whether in Virginia or Pennsylvania, who was to say?—could rest on no provincial law.

Yet, provincial Governors appointed judges as a first order of lawfulness in regions like West Augusta. These very same judges, esteemed as they were in their communities, became the leaders of their own militias.

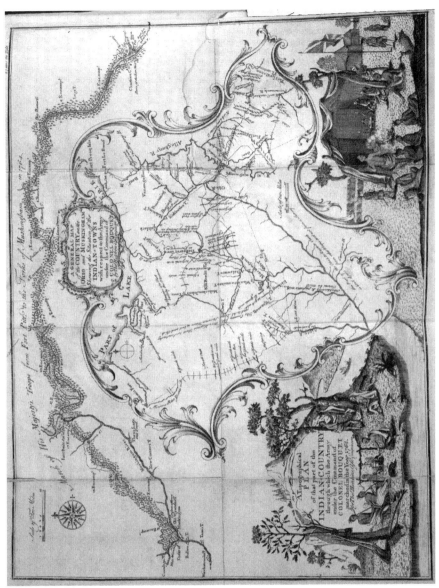

A 1764 map attributed to Thomas Hutchins depicting the notorious Ohio Country as visited by Colonel Henry Bouquet in his early, failed campaign. Uncharacteristically for its time, the illustrations depict Natives as peaceful and sociable. Wikipedia Commons.

And so, local law amounted to nothing much more than honor among men. And honor—separate from that which might have been substantiated by military rank—meant approbation of a moral code steeped in and defended by Judeo-Christian ideals of fairness, dignity and peace.

If the Native was considered, at best, to be heathen, then what allegiance could be expected of him to the white man's law? No man—no militia—could bring him to trial in any legitimate way to give oath to any American sense of jurisprudence. And if the pioneer could settle on land for which he had no authority, then the Native had no reason to obey the white man's "way."

Without a common ground, without "common law," without recourse to a higher authority, there could be no justice. And there was none. There was only survival. Or death.

Shurtees Creek

First embarking from God-knows-where, William Huston, in 1770, paddled his loaded canoe forty miles up Shurtees Creek, then stroked another mile or so farther up a promising, yet unnamed tributary, where, hungry for dinner, he tossed in a fishing line. Legend says he caught a 60-pound yellow catfish. Satisfied with his meal, he claimed the very site as his homestead. He named it Catfish Camp.[7]

Landowners in colonial America, like most British gentry, named their property whatever they pleased.

Yet, in fact, the property had already been known to other settlers as the hunting camp for a Delaware Chief whose name, Tingooqua, was said to mean Catfish.[8] Tingooqua's presence in the area was recorded by Charles Mason (of Mason-Dixon fame) in 1767, and the French had marked the same tributary on which Huston fished as Wissameking, the Shawnee word for catfish. Whichever origin is more accurate, the story of William Huston's prize catch is typical evidence of the appropriation of Native history by imperious Europeans.

However, the notion that a lucky fisherman could just stake a claim for any land he desired along any accessible water source is true. On lands far removed from the law, possession was surely nine-tenths of it.

Adventurous early pioneers could simply mark a claim by hatcheting away at four easily identifiable trees, one situated at each corner of his claim. Once marked, the settler could move on to a trading post for heavy axes and

---

[7] Eckert, *That Dark and Bloody River*, pg. 18

[8] Oyler, *Tribune-Review*, Jan. 5, 2017

pull-saws, or go back home to fetch the wife and youngin's. Returning to claimed, yet unsettled sites even two years later was common. There was so much land, so many waterways and streams, so many deer, buffalo, squirrels, and turkeys—and, of course, catfish weighed in the tens of pounds—any other settler could find land as promising as the next. No early pioneer had to worry about another taking his claim. Hatchet marks were there for all to see, indelible for years to come, just as good as any deed.

And therein reared the problem.

While the markings might defend one's claim against other settlers later paddling up the same creek, they were visible proof to Natives that a white man had assumed rights for which he had no authority. Where there were no laws to be enforced—and if so, by whom or with what immediacy?—there was blatant arrogance and, at the very least, chest-thumping bravado for all to see. Especially the Native. Perhaps, selflessness and moral integrity were ideals not well served by white men seeking their fortunes in the wilds.

The pioneer's dream was owning free, fertile land on which to grow corn for meal, rye for whisky, oats for horses, and, once truly settled, hay for cattle; not to mention potatoes for the Sunday stew. That was all. Settlers eventually might dream of selling excess crops for trade—for wash tubs, gingham, and tools. The more productive land could be made, the more one could trade.

As such, in early America, the one commodity that could generate lasting wealth was land. And there was plenty to be had.

Unless, of course, you lived in a city.

Indentured Servitude

In the bustling town of Philadelphia, Thomas Shields was apprenticed to become an artisan. In the Fall of 1758, his father James paid a princely sum of £50 to "John Bayley, Goldsmith." The indenture was for a term of four years and six months, by which time, Thomas Shields would turn 21 years and nine months.

Born in June of 1743, Thomas Shields was the third son of four boys and four daughters of James and Mary Chalfant Shields, of Newlin, Chester County, Pennsylvania. Like Isaac Leet, James Shields is recorded in tax documents as a yeoman; that is, by then-common use of the term, he was a landowner and a farmer thereon. How James knew to indenture his son to John Bayley, or how it was Thomas might have expressed interest in metal smithing, is not known. What is certain is that Thomas excelled in his craft and, by 1765, he opened his own shop located on Front Street, "the third door above the Drawbridge." An advertisement in *The Pennsylvania Gazette*, dated July 4, 1765, promoted both his inventory and good character: "A Neat Assortment of Gold, Silver and Jewelry Ware, [he] intends carrying on his Business in all its Branches, and will be greatly obliged to all Gentlemen and Ladies, that will please to favor him with their Custom; may depend on having their Work done in the best and neatest Manner, at the lowest Rates, and with the greatest Dispatch."

Addended to the notice, he further announced, "Said Shields gives the highest Price for old Gold."

The ad survives today on microfilm. It is a remarkable testament to early American artisans; Thomas Shields silverware would become much prized by collectors. Today, the Winterthur Museum boasts having more than 14

Shields artifacts, mostly silver spoons, but also a snuffer tray, sugar bowl and matching tongs in its decorative arts collection. The Yale University Art Gallery owns a shoe buckle, coffeepot, creamer and more spoons. The Milwaukee Art Museum has a single, but stunning Thomas Shields coffeepot, ornately decorated with a traditional pineapple on top. Sotheby's has auctioned many pieces by Thomas Shields; in 2017, a rather simple creamer gaveled in at $7,500.

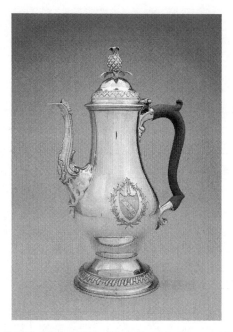

Thomas Shields (Philadelphia, Pennsylvania active ca. 1765-1794)
Coffeepot, 1765-1790, Silver and fruitwood, 13 ½ x 8 7/8 x 5 ¼ in.
Milwaukee Art Museum, Gift of Friends of Art - M1981.5
Photographer credit: Larry Sanders

Indians in Philadelphia

Not more than three miles downriver from Thomas's shop, Province Island was under evacuation orders. There, for the two years preceding 1764, some 140 Natives had been housed at the government's expense. Although of Leni Lenape descent, (more commonly known as Delawares,) these were not tribal people practicing native traditions. These were Christian Indians, converted by the Moravian church, and brought to Philadelphia for their own safety.

The Moravians were formed from a mystical Protestantism in Germany.[9] A wealthy Saxon, Baron Nikolaus Ludwig Count von Zinzendorf, had organized the first order in 1722. As much for freedom from persecution as for the fulfillment of their ordained mission, the sect had sailed to America in 1742 and founded a community in Bethlehem, Pennsylvania, about fifty miles north of Philadelphia. Moravians were passionate, but earnest people. Their intent was to live in self-sustaining harmony and then to save the souls of those who feared no God. Upon settling their first village, they found that their nearest neighbors were ideal candidates for this mission, and they began to engage local Natives in an exchange of cultures. The Moravians might have been idealistic, but they were also pragmatic. They were wise to understand that, in order to convert the great unwashed to a daily tradition of revering their one true God, they must first learn to speak in the Natives' tongue. The Christian concept of an omnipotent, all-seeing deity who had given his only Son to redeem mortal souls for sins men were manifestly born to commit was not something to be explained easily. And

---

[9] Atwood, *Community of the Cross*, pg. 6

certainly not in mime. This was serious education. And the Moravians meant to prove it.

At the juncture of Mahoning Creek and the Lehigh River, they constructed a village of single family huts, which they called Gnadenhütten or "Tents of Grace," to warm, house and feed their new brethren in Christ.[10]

Just as the new town got underway, their chief, Teedyuscung, was murdered. No one knew by whom or for what reason. Then within the month, two more Moravian Indians were murdered. White settlers in the area grew fearful of revenge, assuming (perhaps for good reason) that one or more of their own had been responsible. And as conspiracy stories spiraled, the motives of the white Moravians—openly expressed by their coddling of Native converts—became more and more suspect. Fearing the worst, the Moravians were forced to bring their Native charges to Philadelphia where they would find government protection in abandoned militia barracks on Province Island.

Meanwhile, similar racial conflict was stewing north along the Susquehanna River. Wyalusing Indians there were rounded up and brought to join the refugees in the same barracks. Whereas the German Moravians espoused the idea of educating Natives in the ways of their Christian community, the Scotch-Irish Presbyterians were notorious for ridding their towns of the wholly misunderstood Natives.

In the Indian village of Conestoga outside of Lancaster, Pennsylvania, home to a large family of Delawares, Shawnees, and Senecas, six Natives were murdered, mutilated and scalped. Fleeing for their lives, the rest of the Conestoga Natives found safe-harbor in the courtyard of a Lancaster jail, until, several weeks later, vigilantes of the Scotch-Irish Presbyterian town of Paxton massacred 14 more Natives—men, women and children—none of whom were armed.

The aftermath of the incident was witnessed and documented by one William Henry of Lancaster. A letter he sent to the Moravian leaders included the following horrific details:

"I saw a number of people running down street towards the gaol, which enticed me and other lads to follow them. At about sixty or eighty yards from the gaol, we met from twenty-five to thirty men,

[10] The Morning Call, "Gnadenhütten First Moravian Settlement in Carbon County Keystone Ramblings," https://www.mcall.com/news/mc-xpm-1985-11-24-2497386-story.html

well mounted on horses, and with rifles, tomahawks, and scalping knives, equipped for murder. I ran into the prison yard, and there, O what a horrid sight presented itself to my view! ~ Near the back door of the prison, lay an old Indian and his squaw (wife), particularly well known and esteemed by the people of the town, on account of his placid and friendly conduct. His name was Will Sock; across him and his squaw lay two children, of about the age of three years, whose heads were split with the tomahawk, and their scalps all taken off. Towards the middle of the gaol yard, along the west side of the wall, lay a stout Indian, whom I particularly noticed to have been shot in the breast, his legs were chopped with the tomahawk, his hands cut off, and finally a rifle ball discharged in his mouth; so that his head was blown to atoms, and the brains were splashed against, and yet hanging to the wall, for three or four feet around. This man's hands and feet had also been chopped off with a tomahawk. In this manner lay the whole of them, men, women and children, spread about the prison yard: shot-scalped-hacked-and cut to pieces."[11]

No charges were ever brought against the vigilantes. Despite their doubtless guilt, the Paxton Boys, as they were soon to be called, insisted that not only were the Conestoga Indians to be blamed, but so, too, the Moravian Indians and the Wyalusing. According to white conspiracy theories, all Indian villages harbored a tight network of spies with the means and sole intention of murdering white settlers anywhere; this, despite the very fact that, at least in the last six months, none had.

Yet, the Paxton Boys marched en masse, two hundred strong, into the City of Philadelphia insisting on raiding Province Island, where, by now, hundreds of Natives encamped.

The one man who diffused the situation was Benjamin Franklin. He confronted the posse in Germantown. He allowed that he would publish "notice of their grievances," but only if they dispersed and headed back home. Crisis averted, Franklin saved the day.

---

[11] Engels, "Equipped for Murder": *The Paxton Boys*, pg. 355-81.

Alas, the address of grievances is no longer known, but Franklin did publish "notice" of them. In reporting on the Philadelphia Assembly of June 21, 1764, the *Pennsylvania Gazette* circuitously wrote: "A Petition from the inhabitants of Paxton Township, in the County of Lancaster, and another from the County of Cumberland, were also laid before the House by their respective Members, and severally read; the former praying the House will take into Consideration, and redress, during their present Sitting, the Grievances complained of in a Petition to the Governor some time since presented; the latter such Grievances as are set forth in their Petition of the Twenty-third of March last."

What is painfully clear was how the Native refugees on Province Island fared. Over the course of eighteen months, of the 140 Natives at one time imprisoned there, 47 died of disease or hunger. Furthermore, when the survivors were released, they were forcibly removed to a village much farther north than they had expected, a town that the last of these Moravian Indians called Friedenschutten or "Tents of Peace." Their new village did not last a year.

In a pamphlet he published later in 1764, Franklin wrote about the earlier massacres, extolling his outrage. "But the Wickedness cannot be covered, the Guilt will lie on the whole Land, till Justice is done on the Murderers. THE BLOOD OF THE INNOCENT WILL CRY TO HEAVEN FOR VENGEANCE."

With more measured thought, Franklin argued further: "If an Indian injures me, does it follow that I may revenge that Injury on all Indians? It is well known that Indians are of different Tribes, Nations and Languages, as well as the White People. In Europe, if the French, who are White People, should injure the Dutch, are they to revenge it on the English, because they too are White People? The only Crime of these poor Wretches seems to have been, that they had a reddish brown Skin, and black Hair; and some People of that Sort, it seems, had murdered some of our Relations. If it be right to kill Men for such a Reason, then, should any Man, with a freckled Face and red Hair, kill a Wife or Child of mine, it would be right for me to revenge it, by killing all the freckled red-haired Men, Women and Children, I could afterwards any where meet with."

Yet, despite early public debate, race relations would not improve. Not in central Pennsylvania. Not in the larger province. Not in all of colonial America. If ever they have.

The Science of Surveying

Not unlike an advertisement for a bottle of snake oil, the title of the one most valued instruction manual for surveyors in 18th century America, (first published in 1688,) promised it all:

The Whole Art of Surveying and Measuring of Land Made Easie.
Shewing, by Plain and Practical Rules, How to Survey,
Protract, Cast Up, Reduce or Divide Any Piece of Land Whatsoever;
with New Tables for the Ease of the Surveyor in Reducing the Measures of Land.
Moreover, a More Easie and Sure Way of Surveying by the Chain,
Than Has Hitherto Been Taught.
As Also, How to Lay Out New Lands in America, or Elsewhere;
to Make a Perfect Map of a River's Mouth or Harbour;
with Several Other Things Never Yet Published in Our Language.

John Love's text was reprinted in thirteen editions throughout the century, rarely adding any advancement in technique or science as, in fact, such was rare. Only a few tables published therein were ever amended.

Yet, despite the promising and grand title, surveying western lands in mid-century colonial America was anything but "easie." It was both laborious and extremely dangerous. The work required a crew of at least four men, a pack horse (in addition to other riding horses,) much heavy equipment, including many tools, and, of course, the aforementioned chains.

A surveyor's duty was to accurately measure the distance of single, straight lines mapped onto a representative "plat" which, encompassing a presumptive number of acres, recorded the geographical direction of each

border line according to the compass. The surveyor, with a decent understanding of geometry and trigonometry, could, by this plat, determine the
actual land mass, give or take allowances for particularly rough topography
or seasonal flooding along waterways.

Gunter chains, (so named after British mathematician Edmund Gunter, who in 1620, developed a system of surveying using a standard 100-link
chain,) were made of iron and brass. One link of a Gunter chain was to
measure 7.92 inches and, if forged with any consistency, 100 links equaled
66 feet. Sixty-six feet equaled 4 rods (or "perches"). Forty rods or 10 chain
lengths equaled a furlong. One hundred-sixty square rods (10 chain lengths
by 1 chain length) equaled one acre. (And for the puzzled urban reader, 640
acres equals one square mile.) Yet, the chain Gunter standardized for his
English topography was much too long to use efficiently in the dense forests
of the western frontier. So, almost from its first application on foreign soil,
the Gunter chain in colonial America was shortened by half—to 33 feet.[12]

In effect, colonial surveyors had to work twice as hard.

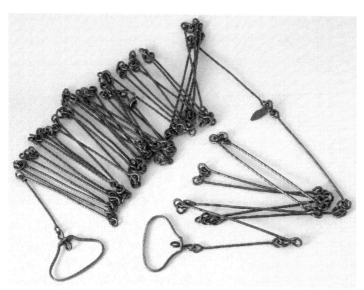

An "American" Gunter chain. Credit: Preston R. Bassett, National Museum of American History,
Smithsonian Institution, Washington, DC.

---

[12] Bailey, "A Surveyor for the King", *CW Journal, https://research.colonialwilliamsburg.org/foundation/
journal/Summer01/Surveyor.cfm*

The critical and most expensive instrument on the surveyor's pack horse was the "circumferentor," a large compass encased in either wood or brass that could be made level once mounted on a tripod. Swiveling around the compass were two vertical arms extending about a foot across, each arm having an eye hole for the surveyor to site a landmark in either direction along the same line. Gunter chains were then drawn out in each direction from the central compass and pulled taut. The ends of each chain were then marked by a large stake, called a "pin," from which, in turn, further Gunter lines would extend until they met the distant mark or claim stake desired. The process would require the use of an axe, as much for clearing brush or small trees, as to chop the head off of a threatening snake. Of course, a gun was always handy, too; dinner might be grazing nearby. Or a wolf pack or bear might interlope. Not to mention Indians who, familiar with the activities of a surveying team, knew what would come to their hunting grounds, figuratively and literally, if the surveyor was successful in completing his task.

A crew of surveyors could not help but be obvious. Consider that each measurement by chain required a crew member to carry out that chain to its full extension (33 feet) and then double back to its point of origin. In laying down a border of, say, one mile—supposing two lengths of chain were employed—the circumferentor would need to be repositioned a minimum of 80 times. Thus, anyone chainman would have to walk almost three miles to prove just one mile. Of course, rivers and streams posed certain challenges; steep foothills their own.

In 1750, Augusta County Deputy Surveyor John Buchanan reported that his party had surveyed eight tracts totaling 17,000 acres in 15 working days. [13] The reference does not identify how many men were in Buchanan's party, but it must have been an army.

However long the weeks or months a surveying team might take in the lush virgin forests of western Virginia or Pennsylvania, the process—from claiming land to legally owning it—could take years. The procedure would begin with the eager settler staking his land by tomahawk; that is, marking significant trees, discoverable to a later visiting county surveyor, by way of hacking a unique symbol high up on that tree's most visible bark. By submitting the claim to the province's land office, the potential owner might

---

[13] Clock, "Surveyor's Chain," Colonial Williamsburg Official History Site, October 5, 2011.

receive a Warrant, an unsigned document that loosely identified the location of the property. A warrant then compelled the County surveyor to go out and measure the actual site. The warrantee would pay the surveyor a modest fee per acre (often just shillings per acre, but to which the surveyor could add extra fees based on the number of men he had to employ or the speed by which the survey was to be completed.) The surveyor then submitted his work to the county or province to approve and record it. (Often, the same surveyor was responsible for approving the very survey he had himself conducted. Of course, he could decide to reject it, requiring him—or an idle associate—to do it all over again.) If all was successful, the once eager settler would be given a Patent for the land he now, ipso facto, "owned." A land patent, recorded in the county land office, was as official as it got.

But the early law did not require any patent holder to settle on the land he so claimed. In the first half of the century, he didn't even have to clear it or improve upon it in anyway. In fact, he could just turn around and sell the property to someone else. Or, to many. Patented land could be vast by original survey—say, hundreds of thousands of acres—and, yet, the patent holder could subdivide his property and sell it (or lease it) in smaller tracts as he saw fit. It was just a matter of what market might be interested.

Thus was born the land speculator. For the cost of exploration and a few shillings per acre tossed to the county surveyor, a minimum investment could yield exponential riches.

A Letter from George

On September 17, 1767, George Washington, otherwise lamenting recent tobacco harvests that were barely profitable,[14] wrote to his good friend and fellow surveyor William Crawford:

"...By this time it may be easy for you to discover, that my Plan is to secure a good deal of Land, You will consequently come in for a very handsome quantity and as you will obtain it without any Costs, or expenc I am in hopes you will be encourag'd to begin this search in time. I woud choose if it were practicable, to get pretty large Tracts together, and it might be desirable to have them as near your Settlement, or Fort Pitt as we coud get them good; but not to neglect others at a greater distance if fine & bodies of it lye in a place.

"...For my own part I shoud have no objection to a Grant of Land upon the Ohio a good way below Pittsburg but woud willingly secure some good Tracts nearer hand first.

"...I woud recommend it to you to keep this whole matter a profound Secret, or Trust it only with those in whom you can confide & who can assist you in bringing it to bear by their discoveries of Land and this advice proceeds from several very good Reasons, and in the first place because I might be censurd for the opinion I have given in respect to the Kings Proclamation & then if the Scheme I am now proposing to you was known it might give the alarm to

---

[14] Stark, *Young Washington*, pg. 411

others & by putting them upon a Plan of the same nature (before we coud lay a proper foundation for success ourselves) set the different Interests a clashing and very probably in the end overturn the whole all which may be avoided by a Silent management & the [Scheme][15] snugly carried on by you under the pretence of hunting other Game which you may I presume effectually do at the same time you are in pursuit of Land which when fully discovered advise me of it & if there appears but a bear possibility of succeeding any time hence I will have the Lands immediately Surveyed to keep others off & leave the rest to time & my own Assiduity to Accomplish.

"If this letter should reach your hands before you set out I should be glad to have your thoughts full expressed on the Plan I have proposed, or as soon afterwards as conveniently may be as I am desirous of knowing in time how you approve of the Scheme. I am Dr Sir
        Yr Very Hble Servt
        Go. Washington"[16]

To be fair, the use of the word "scheme" in British parlance did not connote anything necessarily nefarious or deceptive. The context of this letter, however, suggests something quite contrary. Washington did indeed seek out vast lands for his own personal aggrandizement.

---

[15] Brackets attributed to original transcription at the National Archives.

[16] Letters from George Washington to William Crawford, https://founders.archives.gov

A Treaty at Fort Stanwix

Well before the Moravian Indians were forcibly removed from their Philadelphia refugee camp to their more inhospitable lodgings at Friedenshutten, the disruption of settlers advancing west incited scores of skirmishes and inestimable uprisings between settlers and Natives defending their own lands.

In fact, no sooner had the French laid down their arms to the British than Pontiac's War incited further fear and loathing across the Ohio country. Pontiac, an Odawa warrior, was given credit for inciting the war, but Chief Guyasuta (or Kiashuta) was just as influential. And, so, all of the forts along the Great Lakes, once defended by the French, now commanded by the Crown, were besieged by Pontiac's Ottowas and Ojibways—and Guyasuta's Senecas and Mingos—who, having found themselves newly subject to British justice, rebelled for two intense years. It was a war for independence and it was bloody and ruthless. A Royal Proclamation of 1763 had intended to appease Pontiac by giving back to the Natives all land west of the Alleghenies. But ever-encroaching settlers ignored the proclamation altogether. So, knowing full well that white treaties were only as good as the parchment on which they were written, Pontiac's war parties advanced farther east until, on May 29, 1763, they completely surrounded Fort Pitt. Colonel Henry Bouquet's ensuing march to vanquish the Indians there was first met with resistance on an open meadow just west of Fort Ligonier. The Battle of Bushy Run, in which 400 braves opposed as many militiamen, effectively ended Pontiac's War.

Proof that Pontiac had been right in the first place, the Treaty at Fort Stanwix, signed among the colonies and Six Nations in 1768, rescinded the constricting boundaries for white settlement established just five years earlier. Now, the Ohio country was fair game for expansion. So, too, were lands reaching down to the Tennessee River, including mighty tributaries of the Ohio like the Great and Little Kanawha Rivers. Once again, the Iroquois and its Six Nations sold out hundreds of thousands of square miles for a paltry price. In this case, £10,000.

Just as before, the Shawnees and Delawares had had no say in the matter.

A Delaware Indian.
with his Tomohawk Scalping knife &c.

An illustration published in 1766 in Pierre-François-Xavier de Charlevoix's *A voyage to North-America: undertaken by command of the present King of France*. The image may represent the European's idea of a member of the Leni Lenape (or *Original People*) but commonly called among the new colonies Delawares. Public domain.

The Kanawha Expedition

On October 13, 1770, George Washington met up with William Crawford at his homestead at Stewart's Crossing (now Connellsville, Pennsylvania.) Here was a simple log cabin, mounded gardens, a shed, and some fencing for his horses and livestock. A convenient spring spewed forth nearby. In fact, William had named his homestead Spring Garden. A day's ride distant, Crawford showed Washington several tracts he had loosely surveyed and allowed Washington his pick. Some tracts George would claim for himself, others for his brother and several cousins.

This was land with which Washington had some familiarity. He had passed through this country several times, most significantly on his march with General Braddock along the road to Fort Pitt and, before that, in his failed effort to defend Fort Necessity. For those commands, Washington was now qualified and deserving of land, authorized by the Crown, in compensation for his rank and office in the Virginia militia. The proclamation of 1754, signed by Governor Dinwiddie, allotted him 200,000 acres. Of course, every other officer and soldier under his command was qualified to share in that claim, but it was Washington's own volition—and privileged position—to accommodate himself first, then perhaps his soldiers, to other tracts the colonel would deem available. With the help of Crawford and his aides, Washington would make this real estate "real."

Of course, George already owned more than 3,000 acres on the Potomac, having inherited Mount Vernon in 1762 following the death of his remarried sister-in-law, Anne Fairfax Washington Lee.[17] Earlier acquisitions of 2,682

---

[17] Stark, *Young Washington*, pg. 181

acres in Loudon County, 2,314 acres on Bullskin Run, and three tracts of about 230 acres each in the wilds near Pittsburgh, enriched his portfolio by well more than 8,000 acres.[18] Now Washington could add much larger tracts he had been owed for many years.

For much of the land that Crawford had "run out" before Washington's planned visit and inspection, there was some uncertainty, however, as to which province—Pennsylvania or Virginia—would claim jurisdiction due to the boundary dispute Messrs. Mason and Dixon were only now helping to resolve. Nevertheless, Crawford made certain that his friend and client would get the best. And to pre-qualify Washington's imminent claims, Crawford had already solicited the advice of the Provincial Land Officer who would have to approve his surveys. To Washington, he wrote: "When you come up [from Williamsburg,] you will see the whole of your tract finished. You can have it all patented in one tract. I spoke to Mr. Tilghman [Supervisor of the Land Office in Philadelphia] about it, and told him that you wanted to command some part of the river. He agreed that the surveyor should run it out and you pay all under one, and have a patent for the whole in one."

And now, George had come up. So, too, had his good friend, Dr. James Craik, a surgeon who had survived many of the same battles as he. With but an afternoon's rest and another day's trip to see a nearby cave, they departed Spring Garden for Fort Pitt.

By the Fall of 1770, the towering ramparts at the Forks of the Ohio must have been a comforting site. To Washington, they likely swelled his pride, for here, returning after his fourth visit twelve years earlier, then leading General John Forbes to take back a deserted Fort Duquesne, was the man who had first convinced the Ohio Land Company, under contract to the Crown, that immense resources were to be expended at this strategic location. The site had been the one most important foothold in all of the French and Indians Wars. And, now, it survived as one of only three manned forts held by the British to have stood up against Pontiac's Rebellion just seven years earlier. In 1770, it was a monument—appropriately aged and shabby—to the tenacity of white settlers. Not only had it served its original military purposes, but it now fostered a thriving village outside

---

[18] *The Papers of George Washington*, Retirement Series, vol. 4, pp. 512-527

its gates. Accommodated in log houses erected along straight lines (mostly parallel to the Monongahela side of the triangle) was a population of maybe 200 souls.

Fort Pitt was then under the command of Colonel Charles Edmundsen who welcomed Washington and his small entourage for a tour of the garrisons, as well as for dinner. Joining him there was George Croghan, the legendary Indian trader, and a longtime acquaintance of both Washington and Crawford. Croghan invited his friends to dinner at his own residence the next night and, there, too, he invited Kanaghragait, the Seneca sachem whom the British called "White Mingo."

The evening was something like a class reunion. Washington had first met Kanaghragait on his 1753 expedition to serve Dinwiddie's demands on the French commander at Fort La Boeuf. But times had turned; his people had since allied with the French. Now, the Indian wished that, not unlike old rivals on the varsity team, Washington would forget their former indifferences. Kanaghragait, along with a few tribesmen, presented Washington with a string of wampum, and appealed to his matured view of the world as he knew it. Washington recorded the sentiments of the Native's speech:

> "…they were come to bid me welcome to this Country, and to desire that the People of Virginia woud consider them as friends & Brothers linked together in one chain—that I wd. inform the Governor, that it was their wish to live in peace and harmy. with the white People, & that tho their had been some unhappy differences between them and the People upon our Frontiers, it was all made up, and they hopd forgotten; and concluded with saying, that, their Brothers of Virginia did not come among them and Trade as the Inhabitants of the other Provences did, from whence they were afraid that we did not look upon them with so friendly an Eye as they coud wish.
>
> "To this I answerd (after thanking them for their friendly welcome) that all the Injuries & Affronts that had passd on either side was now totally forgotten, and that I was sure nothing was more wishd and desird by the People of Virginia than to live in the strictest friendship with them. That the Virginians were a People not so much engagd in Trade as the Pensylvanians, &ca., wch. was the

Reason of their not being so frequently among them; but that it was possible they might for the time to come have stricter connections with them, and that I woud acquaint the Govr. with their desires."

Of the thousands of letters archived in Washington's life, none reflect the favor of acquainting any Governor of any Indian's desires. An ersatz statesman, Washington might have demonstrated good intentions, but apparently he made no later mind of Kanaghragait's gesture. Besides, for the present moment, he had more important work to do.

Washington's diary for October 20, 1770, recorded his departure for a long expedition to seek and survey lands descending the banks of the Ohio River. The journey began with this introduction:

> "We Imbarked in a large Canoe with sufficient Stores of Provision & Necessaries, & the following Persons (besides Dr. Craik & myself) to wit—Captn. Crawford[,] Josh Nicholson[,] Robt. Bell– –William Harrison—Chs. Morgan & Danl. Reardon a boy of Captn. Crawfords, & the Indians who went in a Canoe by themselves."

Dorothy Twohig, Editor of the University of Virginia's eight-year project to transcribe Washington's Diaries, in 1976, identified the "Persons" that Washington recorded here. Josh Nicholson was known to be an experienced "Indian trader." Further, in Twohig's own words, "Robert Bell had served with the Virginia Regiment in 1754 and was discharged for injuries in Jan. 1755. In 1775 he was living near present-day McKee's Rocks, near Pittsburgh. William Harrison was William Crawford's son-in-law. He was killed by Indians on the disastrous Sandusky campaign in 1782, which also claimed the life of his father-in-law." Curiously, she noted "Charles Morgan and Daniel Reardon have not been further identified." The two were, after all, just young assistants.[19]

Washington and his flotilla paddled down the Ohio. Maps of the time– –the most recent one published commercially in 1765 by Joshua Fry—show

---

[19] *The Diaries of George Washington*, vol. 2, *14 January 1766-31 December 1770*, pg. 294.

that the Ohio River was also known as the Allegheny River, that which the French otherwise called La Belle Riviere. Who was to say that the Ohio River began at the "point" of Pittsburgh? Apparently, it never occurred to the French or the Natives that it had.

Doubtful that Washington had any maps other than his own, informed as he may have been by Nicholson and their Native guides, they continued onto Logstown, a landmark trading settlement just beyond present-day Ambridge. What is perhaps remarkable was the ready and certain identity of the several tributaries and creeks that fed into the Ohio. Washington wrote:

> "At 11 we came to the Mouth of big Bever Creek, opposite to which is a good Situation for a House, & above it, on the same side (that is the west) there appears to be a body of fine Land. About 5 Miles lower down on the East side comes in Racoon C[ree]k at the Mouth of which, & up it appears to be a body of good Land also. All the Land between this Creek & the Monongahela & for 15 Miles back, is claimd by Colo. Croghan under a purchase from the Indians (and which sale, he says is confirmd by his Majesty). On this Creek where the Branches thereof interlock with the Waters of Shirtees Creek there is, according to Colo. Croghan's Acct. a body of fine Rich level Land. This Tract he wants to sell, & offers it at £5 sterg. pr. hundd. with an exemption of Quitrents for 20 years; after which, to be subject to the payment of 4/2 Sterg. pr. Hundd., provided he can sell it in 10,000 Acre Lots."

Ever the Virginian whose worth would be measured by the flat, open and fertile land he could turn to profit, Washington had his eye on "Shirtees Creek." He had remembered it from his last (perhaps, as well as his first) visit to the Forks, and now his notes attest to some disappointment, if not circumspection, that his friend George Croghan claimed ownership. Washington was keen to have recorded Croghan's pricing; he might have thought that this land was as valuable as £5 per hundred acres, or he might have been thinking that other yet-to-be-seen lands, perhaps more favorable to his eye, could even begin to approach that exorbitant price. In either case, Washington concluded his diary entry with a caution: "Note the unsettled state of this Country renders any purchase dangerous."

On the third day of their expedition, Washington and Crawford arrived at Mingo Town, seventy-three miles from Fort Pitt. Known today as Mingo Junction, Ohio, it was a seasonal village of maybe 150 Natives. Upon arriving there, the party was forewarned that two white traders further down the Ohio had just been murdered.

Undaunted, the party of eight launched again, and the expedition continued another 150 miles down the Ohio, coming ashore often, but notably on October 28 upon the sighting of a camp of Seneca hunters. Here, Washington met up with Chief Guyasuta. At 56 years of age, Guyasuta was now a much respected Seneca elder. He had assisted Washington in his first journey up to Fort Le Boeuf. Since then, however, he led a war party to ambush and kill more than 350 British in General James Grants' attempt to reclaim Fort Duquesne and, then, during Pontiac's Rebellion, he had laid siege to Fort Pitt. He was also defeated at Bushy Run. Now, Guyasuta opened his arms and welcomed Washington.

> "In the Person of Kiashuta I found an old acquaintance. He being one of the Indians that went with me to the French in 1753. He expressd a satisfaction in seeing me and treated us with great kindness, giving us a Quarter of very fine Buffalo. He insisted upon our spending that Night with him, and in order to retard us as little as possible movd his Camp down the River about 3 Miles just below the Mouth of a Creek the name of which I could not learn (it not being large). At this place we all Incampd. After much Councelling the overnight they all came to my fire the next Morning, with great formality; when Kiashuta rehearsing what had passd between me & the Sachems at Colo. Croghan's, thankd me for saying that Peace & friendship was the wish of the People of Virginia (with them) & for recommending it to the Traders to deal with them upon a fair & equitable footing; and then again expressd their desire of having a Trade opend with Virginia, & that the Governor thereof might not only be made acquainted therewith, but of their friendly disposition towards the white People. This I promisd to do."

If he ever did, history makes no note. Washington and company paddled on that morning.

For William Crawford and "his boy's" part, the expedition required that they remember their client's running commentary of certain "bottoms"—a yeoman's term for very fertile, flat and well irrigated river banks—as they made their way down the Ohio. Unlikely that either would have brought out ink and pen to record Washington's interests, they would have had to remember certain bottoms or forest compositions only by proximity to the openings of known tributaries. Their Indian guides might have helped, but certainly the task relied on skills only born woodsmen could boast. Of course, having descended the river, they would return the same way, thereby allowing Washington, and thus Crawford, the perspective of seeing the forest for all the trees they passed.

Imagine, along unmolested river banks, paddling two hundred and fifty miles through virgin forests. Washington's party might well have been among the first 500 white men to float down the Ohio. Here were seen beaver and otter by the hundreds, squirrels by the thousands, and turkey, deer, and bison so numerous even a poor shot could feed a village for weeks. Below them, in water as pure as the snow that fed it, were pike and bass (not to mention, catfish) of prehistoric size. Imagine, too, in the peak of October, witnessing the autumnal palette of brilliant colors displayed for no audience other than the few who dared paddle down unchartered currents.

On All Hallow's Eve, they reached the mouth of the Great Kanawha River. Today, it is the site of Point Pleasant, West Virginia. They paddled up its mouth, but after only fifteen miles, returned back to the Ohio for their return trip. Washington was not greatly impressed.

> "The Land from the Rivers appeard but indifferent, & very broken; whether these ridges might not be those that divide the Waters of the Ohio from the Kanhawa is not certain, but I believe they are. If so the Lands may yet be good. If not, that which lyes of the River bottoms is good for little."

Yet, Washington did remember his deserving soldiers in this expedition.

> "Saturday 3d. We set of[f] down the River on our return homewards, and Incampd at the Mouth; at the Beginning of the Bottom above the Junction of the Rivers, and at the Mouth of a branch on

the Eastside, I markd two Maples, an Elm, & Hoopwood Tree as A Cornr. of the Soldiers L[an]d (if we can get it) intending to take all the bottom from hence to the Rapids in the Great Bent into one Survey. I also markd at the Mouth of another Gut lower down on the West side (at the lower end of the long bottom) an Ash and hoopwood for the Beginning of another of the Soldiers Survey to extend up so as to Include all the Bottom (in a body) on the West side."

Two hundred sixty-six miles from Fort Pitt, their journey upriver would take seven days longer to return. Even though they would be paddling against the current, a good portion of this time was spent marking the trees that would later define Crawford's surveys. Often, the marking process required a young man of some agility to climb limbs with a tomahawk. No doubt, this duty fell to Crawford's boy, Daniel.

Of this journey, Crawford would have eight different plats drawn up (within the next two years) for Washington, his officers, and a few distinguished soldiers. A hand drawn copy of the original map is archived at the Library of Congress. It cites allotments for acres that may—or may not—have been realized, but were submitted to respective land offices for the conveyance of patents to the following:

George Washington	Plat 1	10,990	acres
Dr. James Craik	Plat 2	6,026	"
William Bronaugh[20]	" "	6,000	"
George Muse[21]	" "	100	"
George Washington	Plat 3	3,953	"
George Muse	" "	3,323	"
Dr. James Craik	Plat 4	4,232	"
George Washington	Plat 7	2,950	"

Of this journey, too, came a rather forthright observation of the Native people Washington encountered.

---

[20] Bronaugh was with George Washington at Ft. Necessity, Braddock's March

[21] Muse was also at Ft. Necessity, but "dismissed for cowardice"

"The Indians who are very dexterous (even there women) in the Management of Canoes, have there Hunting Camps & Cabins all along the River for the convenience of Transporting their Skins by Water to Market. In the Fall, so soon as the Hunting Season comes on, they set out with their Familys for this purpose; & in Hunting will move there Camps from place to place till by the spring they get 2 or 300, or more Miles from there Towns; Then Bever catch it in there way up which frequently brings them into the Month of May, when the Women are employd in Plantg.—the Men at Market, & in Idleness, till the Fall again; when they pursue the same course again. During the Summer Months they live a poor & perishing life.

"The Indians who live upon the Ohio (the upper parts of it at least) are composd of Shawnas, Delawares, & some of the Mingos, who getting but little part of the Consideration that was given for the Lands Eastward of the Ohio, view the Settlement of the People upon this River with an uneasy & jealous Eye, & do not scruple to say that they must be compensated for their Right if the People settle thereon, notwithstanding the Cession of the Six Nations thereto."

On November 18, a few days later than planned, the party disembarked at Mingo Town for their treks back home. If not for the promise of patenting land now marked, the expedition was also successful in their safe return. Of the warning they received when first landing at Mingo Town, they were later apprised that only one settler had died, and not at the hands of any savage. He had drowned quite accidentally.

Washington, Craik, Crawford, and their two young aides hiked back to Fort Pitt, and then, the latter four to Spring Garden. However detailed he kept his journals, George Washington may have been mistaken in recording the name of Daniel Reardon. That this boy, never since identified by historians, was someone else is certainly possible. It is also pure conjecture. Yet, by the following spring, William Crawford would return to the very same sites he and Washington had just claimed. With him would be a boy sixteen years his junior.[22] That boy, at 22 years of age, was Daniel *Leet*.

---

[22] *The Papers of George Washington*, Colonial Series, vol. 9, *8 January 1772 – 18 March 1774*, pg. 328-331.

Of Currency and Coins

On October 28, 1767, Thomas Shields married Lydia Morris. Because Thomas had inherited little from his father's estate a few years before, the engagement of Thomas to Lydia suggests that he was doing well in business. It may suggest further that, as a yeoman's son, he found himself in a social status somewhat elevated from his birth. Lydia Morris was the daughter of Thomas Morris and Lydia Lewis of Blockley Township (long since absorbed by the City of Philadelphia) who, upon Mr. Morris's death in 1769, owned 60 acres, two horses and three cattle.[23]

So, when in October of 1771, Thomas Shields opened a new shop, his reputation was evidently well established. Situated now just six doors down from the drawbridge on Front Street, (the major mercantile corridor running along the water*front* of colonial Philadelphia,) "The Golden Cup and Crown" enjoyed a remarkable volume of trade.

Shields's original account books still exist. In one month alone, receipts showed he paid out £12 sterling for a silver platter he shipped to London for engraving, £30 more for five silver watches, and £25, 10s. (shillings,) for a single gold watch. These were items he would resell at some greater profit, but it proves he had cash reserves of significant volume. Compare this to a purchase he made the same year for a new feather bed at a cost of just 6s., 11p. (pence.) (Or that £5 then could buy him 100 acres outside of Philadelphia.)

The bed may have been purchased upon the birth of his third child, James. Just nine months and a few days after their wedding, Lydia and Thomas had welcomed Mary. Thomas Jr. came along eighteen months after

---

[23] Tax records of Blockley Twp. 1769: http://files.usgwarchives.net/pa/philadelphia/taxlist/blockley1769.txt

Mary. The young family of five now lived on Dock Street, a very convenient walk to "The Golden Cup."

*   *   *   *   *

The value of colonial currency any time before the Revolution fluctuated regularly among provinces and the bigger cities. In a fledgling society, there were few standards and regulations. Coins were to be of a certain weight, but the value of that coin—that is, its representative buying power—changed often. That vexing issue was likely the subject of heated discussion as often as coins—or "specie"—were exchanged, particularly in large transactions. Weekly newspapers published prevailing currency values. But, the fact is, local merchants regularly set monetary standards among themselves. As a result, the same gold Guinea (supposedly worth £1 and 1 shilling, or 21 shillings) tendered in Philadelphia might be worth six shillings more in Connecticut, or two shillings less in New York. Retail merchants tried to set standards because, for the most part, they were the only business class operating in specie. While the rural economy traded in standards of tobacco and whiskey, the larger industries like shipping or boatbuilding functioned almost solely on notes of credit and debt. No one, but no one, in colonial America conducted business—personal or otherwise—without a ledger to record every transaction. First, if there was a debt owed, it was essential to make note of it for future collection, and if a tax was paid, it was just as important to have acquired the tax collector's signature—scrawled right on the all-important ledger—to prove the debt was paid.

Portuguese "Half-Joe's" with the hallmark of John Bayley's shop.
Image used by permission of Tom Pilitowski, US Rare Coin Investments, Inc.

Thomas Shields not only transacted his business in currency; he actually crafted it *from* currency. That is, his primary source of metal—be it gold or silver—came from the very coins circulating in the colonies. His craft was a matter of pounding flat the very Guineas, "Half-Joes" (prized Portuguese gold coins named for King Johannes), and silver coins any other tradesman might have taken to the bank. Metal of any kind was rare; rarer still if it was hammered into a stylish sugar bowl, elegant salt cellar or ornate coffee pot. The cost of the transformed item was, of course, the value of the coins employed. And yet so much more. In a very real way, whatever he invested in crafting his wares was truly his own sweat and tears. Also calculated into his revenues was the time spent carving the oak molds, the expense of tools necessary to impress the metal to the mold, and the cost of burning constant fuel. Of course, as one of many silversmiths in Philadelphia, his competitive edge had to evidence creativity, flourish, and, yes, a lot of polish, too.

In truth Thomas Shields minted his own wealth. And, yet, he was known to be scrupulously honest.

Like the story of George Washington confessing to his father that he had indeed chopped down the cherry tree, legend says that Thomas Shields was a man of unusual integrity. As a young apprentice, he was trained to weigh every coin that came into his master's shop. Because some coins weighed more than others (the early methods of minting were hardly precise,) young Thomas would shave down heavier coins to their proper weight and, finding after some labor a decent pile of shavings, determined on his own that, while he could have easily kept the precious flakes for himself, he would sleep better if he offered them up to his boss. Which, so the story goes, he did.

Further to his good character is witness of several ads appearing in the Philadelphia Gazette in the early 1770s. One informs the citizens of Philadelphia of a lost silver watch for which he would pay 25s. reward for its safe return to his client. Another advertises his possession of a Diamond Set Mourning Ring, "in memory of a person deceased, aged 83 years. Whoever has lost the same, by proving their property, and paying the charges, may have it again."

Intriguing is the following notice which appeared on April 6, 1774:

"A PERSON called upon the subscriber to dispose of a piece of SILVER, from the form of which piece, and the appearance of the person, I judge is to be the property of some Goldsmith.—A Gold Button, left with him, which was found some time ago.—A pair of square carved open-work Silver Shoe Buckles was offered for sale, by a suspicious person. The owners of any of the afore described articles, are desired to come, and prove their property, and take them away.   —THOMAS SHIELDS."

Fittingly, Thomas was a devout Baptist. He canvassed and collected tithes, hosted visiting clergy, served on "grievance" committees, and later became a deacon of the First Baptist Church of Philadelphia.[24]

At 19 years of age, Shields had been baptized by the Reverend Morgan Edwards, a powerful preacher, masterful missionary and politically-popular orator. The Welsh-born evangelist was known to have drawn large audiences. A Whig, he also "served time" under house arrest. Although he resigned from his Philadelphia pulpit in 1772, Edwards would go on to found Brown University.

Shields might well have been motivated, too, by Samuel Miles, a political powerhouse and fellow deacon of the First Baptist congregation. Miles, for whom Shields's ledgers show many hundreds of church tithes collected, would later become Mayor of Philadelphia during the aftermath of its British occupation just three years hence.

In 1774, Thomas, his wife, and, now, four children—Mary, Thomas, Jr., James and Robert—moved into a larger house at 27 South Second Street in the Chestnut Ward, five or so blocks north.[25] Thomas thus paid taxes on two houses (keeping his Dock Street address,) and paid rent and taxes for his business to the Luke Morris Estate. Now, too, with business aplenty, Shields bought land outside of the city. Way outside. He purchased three tracts of wilderness 170 miles up the Delaware River in Northampton County.

There, in years otherwise devoted to enjoying his retirement, he will build his own Baptist Church.

But not before bringing into the world two more sons: John in 1778, and, on Wednesday, August 16, 1780, David Morris Shields.

---

[24] Thompson, *Philadelphia's First Baptists*, pg. 14

[25] http://maps.archives.upenn.edu/WestPhila1777/map.php

Kanawha and Ken-Tuk-Kee

Daniel Leet was not a big man. From his brother's own description, he may have topped out at five feet, ten inches in his late teens.[26] Stocky and strong, he was able to lug heavy broadaxes, climb trees, portage canoes, and carry a freshly killed deer miles when returning tired and famished to camp. Few men his age would survive the wilderness without such stamina. He was also endowed with an aptitude for math. Who may have taught him algebra, geometry and the "magnetic mysteries" of the compass, is not truly known, yet likely, just as William Crawford had been indentured to John Vance, Daniel learned from Crawford. Clearly, he was bright, capable, and a valuable asset to his mentor.

Not only did they pack in to the Kanawha the following year, but they explored and surveyed even deeper into Ken-Tuk-Kee.[27] This, of course, was Native territory, but of a different kind. Tribal alliances over the years had set aside rich hunting grounds for that singular purpose. It was understood that no tribe was to settle there, but that these lands were free and open for all to hunt. That was the Indian way; share and share alike. Which made the trespass of any white man, most particularly surveyors, a matter of lethal risk. Natives showed little tolerance for the teams of chain men whose presence could only mean one thing. As a consequence, a young man of Daniel's intelligence would have had to act as both surveyor *and* sentry.

---

[26] Draper Manuscripts, 8NN2

[27] Creigh, *History of Washington County*, pg. 288

It was a job to dread. Sentries might save the lives of those they protected, but only at the peril of their own. To a young Daniel Leet, however, it was a duty he owed his mentor, a fearful task that might earn him a profession.

More and more, as settlers ventured west into dangerous territory, "lookouts" became as necessary as the guns they carried.[28] At any distance, fear was endemic on the frontier. The deeper the trespass, the weaker the defense. It jangled one's nerves as much as any chain dragged out in unchartered woods.

The one antidote to the constancy of danger might have been steely resolve, an absolute commitment to task. Stoicism unspoken. Daniel Leet seemed to possess this in spades. By all accounts, he was a man of few words.

Wherever home was, Daniel was said to have worked "near Crawford and Washington" applying his field notes in the latter's presence. Likely, the "home office" was in Winchester, Virginia. First known as Fredericksburg, Washington visited there often. Not only had the town provided many of the early militia Washington enlisted for his forays up and over Forbes' Road, it served as a staging ground for increasingly large numbers of settlers heading due west over the Blue Mountains or through the Cumberland Gap.

No sooner had Crawford and Leet drawn up the plats which bestowed Washington and Dr. Craik their multiple claims along the Kanawha, these same gentlemen then promoted their lands for lease. First, in September, 1773, Craik advertised his properties in his home town paper, The Maryland Gazette, based in Annapolis, not far from Port Tobacco where he lived. The studied doctor had clearly labored over his expectations through his offer:

> "Whereas the subscriber has obtained patents for near six thousand acres of land, thirteen hundred of which upon the banks of the Ohio, beginning at the second large bottom below the mouth of the little Kanhawa, and four thousand two hundred about two miles above Col. George Washington's ten thousand acre tract upon the banks of the Great Kanhawa; he proposes to divide the same into suitable tenements as may be desired, and lease them upon moderate

---

[28] Draper Manuscripts, 2S4

terms, allowing a refundable number of years rent free provided within the space of two years, from the last of October next; three acres for every fifty contained in each lot, and proportionably for a lesser quantity shall be cleared, fenced, and tilled; and that by or before the commencement of the first rent, five acres for every hundred, and proportionably as above shall be enclosed and laid down in good grass for meadow, and that at least fifty good fruit trees shall be planted on the premises. Any person inclinable to settle - on those lands, may be more fully informed, by applying to the subscriber near Port-Tobacco, and would do well in communicating their intentions before the first of November next, that a sufficient number of lots may be laid off to answer the demand. The land is well watered and very rich, abounding with fine fish and wild fowl of various kinds.

— James Craik"

George Washington advertised an offer nearly identical to Craik's in the Virginia Gazette, the Maryland Gazette and the Williamsburg Gazette. But not to be outdone by his physician friend, he added to the above description more promising "information" which may not have been, as yet, wholly accurate:

"From every Part of these Lands Water Carriage is now had to *Fort Pitt*, by an easy Communication; and from *Fort Pitt*, up the *Monongehela*, to *Redstone*, Vessels of convenient Burthen may, and do pass continually; from whence, by means of *Cheat* River, and other navigable Branches of the *Monongehela*, it is thought the Portage to *Potowmack* may, and will, be reduced within the Compass of a few Miles, for the great Ease and Convenience of the Settlers in transporting the Produce of their Lands to Market."

Doubtful that any portage from the Monongahela to the Potomac might ever have been lauded with words like Ease or Convenience, it is just as doubtful the lands were officially patented. Not in 1773. Not even ten years later. The "unsettled Counsels" to which Washington referred were just as unsettled in 1787.

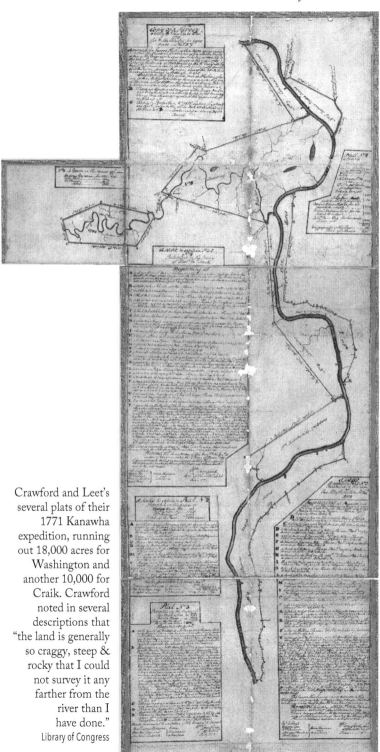

Crawford and Leet's several plats of their 1771 Kanawha expedition, running out 18,000 acres for Washington and another 10,000 for Craik. Crawford noted in several descriptions that "the land is generally so craggy, steep & rocky that I could not survey it any farther from the river than I have done."
Library of Congress

Even as he promoted his Kanawha lands, Washington was actively seeking to buy more. He wrote to Crawford in September of 1773.

Mount Vernon 25th Septr 1773.

"Dear Sir,

"I have heard (the truth of which, if you saw Lord Dunmore in his way to or from Pittsburg, you possibly are better acquainted with than I am) that his Lordship will grant Patents for Lands laying below the Scioto, to the Officers & Soldiers who claim under the Proclamation of October 1763. If so, I think no time should be lost in having them surveyed, lest some new revolution should again happen in our political System...

"By Mr Leet I inform'd you of the unhappy cause, which prevented my coming out this Fall, but I hope nothing will prevent my seeing you in that Country in the Spring..."

Then by December of that same year, Washington wrote to Mrs. Rind, the publisher of one of Williamsburg's several newspapers, wishing her to record the names of the many officers and militiamen who, by taking up the lands Washington had allotted them along the Kanawha, owed him money. Here appeared many more names than were recorded on the plat, suggesting that Washington's expedition two years before was perhaps more altruistic than it first seemed. However, Washington wanted to be made whole, admonishing his debtors with these instructions:

"In making the above allotment of these five tracts of land, it may not be amiss to remark, that those who were deficient of their respective quantities at the last distribution have been considered in the present; and as the issuing of these patents will compleat the grant of 200,000 acres, under the proclamation aforesaid, it is hoped, and expected, that all those who have contributed nothing, or partially towards the completion of it, will *now* (without more delay) think it reasonable and just to pay their several proportions of the expences attending this undertaking into the hands of theirs and your most humble servant,

— George Washington"

Early in 1774, Washington obtained permission to claim 3,000 more acres of bounty land under the same royal proclamation that had already awarded him his portion of the 200,000 acres supposedly now settled. By way of purchasing a warrant from one John Rootes, Washington also claimed rights to three tracts of land on the Little Miami River. The Little Miami descends from present-day Springfield, Ohio, past Dayton, and then down toward Cincinnati, where about 30 miles southeast, it flows through the towns of Williamsburg and Batavia into the Ohio River.

Still land hungry, Washington was hardly finished. A man much favored in the Virginia militia, he had inordinate power in arguing for dutiful compensation. And, so, that same year, settling as he did for lands far distant from any he could reach in less than a month's journey, he played his cards to purchase warrants from other officers who saw no value in the Ohio country. And, by purchase of a warrant for 3,000 acres owed to Captain John Posey, Washington laid claim to 2,813 acres on Miller's Run on *Chartiers* Creek. This was the fertile land he had seen on his first visit to the Forks of the Ohio. This was in part the same land that George Croghan had boasted was his, the land about which Washington seemed circumspect Croghan really owned—the land Croghan had priced at £5 per hundred. It was now claimed by Washington for nothing.

Of the remainder due him under the Posey agreement, he then laid claim to 187 acres at Round Bottom. This was a much prized stretch along the Ohio he had passed with Crawford and Leet in 1771. It sits below Moundsville, West Virginia. Washington would later fight tooth and nail for this one single bottom, as, before he himself could settle it, interlopers of all sorts rested their homesteads on it. And would, happily or not, ever after.

Gnadenhütten Settled

In the Fall of 1771, Moravian leader David Zeisberger introduced to the Indian council at Gekelemukpechunk[29] the divine concept of a pious commune—one purposely disassociated from the failings of society at large—in which its members live together, united as brothers. This Unitas Fratrum, Zeisberger explained, was a devout expression of man's love for each other. As if to prove his point, Zeisberger impressed the Chief, an old sachem known as Pakanke, by speaking to him in his native tongue. Zeisberger's concept of community was not much different from the Indian way, he would profess. Share and share alike. Shelter and be sheltered. No man is an island; no man stands alone.

Zeisberger elaborated on his intentions. This commune of which he spoke also served a higher purpose: to adore their savior, Jesus Christ, who had died for their sins. This man Christ, Zeisberger explained, was the living son of their Great Father, their one true God, to which they owed everything. This God had created the sun and earth and all of its creatures including man—and that included Pakanke and all of the Delaware, Shawnees, and Iroquois. But man had committed many atrocities according to the laws of their God. Jesus had come to live among them to teach his Father's love and to redeem their sins. In fact, this son of their God had died for that very purpose: to forgive each and everyone. (And that, too, included the Delaware.) But for those who truly believed in Him, for those who showed their love for Him—for those, in particular, who asked for His forgiveness—there was a bonus, an extra benefit, a true gift: eternal life. Well,

---

[29] A Delaware village, meaning "Still Water," at present-day Newcomerstown, Ohio.

kind of. Eternal life, Zeisberger had to explain, meant that a man's body might die, but his spirit would live on in heaven. That is, there was an afterlife for which, and because of which, death should not be feared.

Of course, to Zeisberger and his Moravians, heaven was as certain as the love of Jesus. But to the Native, in terms of their spiritual tradition, any promise of an afterlife was as much conditioned on luck as it was an uncertain favor bestowed by the Great Spirit. If anything, it was nothing to be obsessed over. As can only have been interpreted by arrogant white men, the Native's concept of what happens after death had to be something much simpler. Upon death, an Indian's journey is stopped at a river separating him from the other side. If the Native can swim or forge the river, he is home free. If, however, the river sweeps him away, he is gone forever.

Pakanke and his council apparently appreciated Zeisberger's inclusive evangelism. They took to heart some faith that the Moravians' teachings would assure the fallen Native his peace. And, if Jesus Christ, the son of God, could bring him eternal life, what's not to like?

Pakanke granted whatever tracts of land the Moravians should desire. Zeisberger returned to his Native brethren at Friedensstadt (near New Castle, Pennsylvania.) They then mapped out a large tract of land 75 miles west along the banks of the Tuscarawas, with a good spring, a small lake, favorable planting fields, much game, and every other convenience for the support of an Indian colony. There, too, they knew existed the protective remains of three Great Indian Mounds built by ancestral tribes.

Brother Zeisberger gave it the name Schönbrunn or "Beautiful Spring."

Five Moravian families first set out on the 14th of April, 1772, and, arriving on May 3rd, prepared the village. Other Native tribes in the Ohios took notice. According to Moravian lore, "upon news of the arrival of the Brethren, the enemies of the Gospel were so much alarmed that many of them left the place, not being able to bear a doctrine so directly opposite to their heathenish abominations and sinful manner of living. A neighboring Chief even forsook his village, and with all his people moved into a distant country."[30]

By July, 240 more Moravians—Native converts and white brethren alike—prepared their migration, herding 70 oxen and even more horses,

---

[30] Zeisberger, *Moravian Mission Diaries*, pg. 82

loading wagons and whatever conveyances they had built for the journey. It did not go smoothly. Rolling over narrow paths, having to cut wider swaths for wagons to pass, they managed barely five miles a day.

Brother Ettwein stepped "upon a snake with 15 rattles." It scared him so much, he would not move—nor did the caravan—for four days.

Stranger events followed. Wrote Moravian historian George Loskial in 1838, "the most troublesome plague both to man and beast, especially in passing through a tract of country, named 'a place avoided by all men,' was a kind of insect, called by the Indian 'Ponk' or Living Ashes, from their being so small that they are hardly visible, and they bite as painful as the burning of red-hot ashes." As soon as the evening fires were kindled, the cattle, in order to get rid of these insects, "ran furiously toward the fire, crowding into the smoke…" likewise scattering the tired and hungry pilgrims who then had to beat them back.

Somehow, the Moravians managed.

Schönbrunn was soon settled, and by August, efforts were made to make peace and seek assurances from the Shawnees that they would be unmolested, especially in light of their intentions to develop more villages.

"This man [the Sachem of the Shawnees] received the brethren very civilly; and when upon his inquiry into the aim of their visit, Zeisberger answered, that he brought him the words of eternal life…" to which the sachem replied, "…A year ago I became convinced that we are altogether sinful creatures, and that none of our good works will save us; but we did not know what to do to gain eternal salvation." Continued the sachem in words only a pious Moravian might have translated, "…Now you are come, and I verily believe, that God has sent you to make his word known to us."

On October 10, 1772, the village of Gnadenhütten was established 15 miles farther south on the banks of the Tuscarawas. The idea of a second village was led by Josua, a Mohican convert and who, with Zeisberger, assembled other Mohicans and Munsee natives to share in a commune of their own making, albeit under strict obedience to Moravian principles. Discipline in faith to God meant daily worship, conferences, school, attendance at all guest visitations, providing to the sick and poor, and every other requisition for the prosperity of the congregation including that all men and women be separated in worship. Each sex and age group comprised "choirs."

The rules were many, most of which demanded behavior not uncommon to any pious community. Some, however, were very specific to Moravian ideals:

1) No thieves, murderers, drunkards, adulterers, and whoremongers, shall be suffered among us.
2) No one that attendeth dances, sacrifices or heathenish festivals, can live among us.
3) No one using Tschappich (or witchcraft) in hunting, shall be suffered among us.
4) We will renounce all juggles, lies, and deceits of Satan.
5) We will not be idle and lazy—nor tell lies of one another—nor strike each other—we will live peaceably together.
6) We will not permit any rum, or spirituous liquor, to be brought into our towns. If strangers or traders happen to bring any, the helpers (national assistants) are to take it into their possession, and take care not to deliver it to them until they set off again.
7) No man inclining to go to war—which is the shedding of blood, can remain among us.
8) Whosoever purchases goods or articles of warriors, knowing at the time that such have been stolen or plundered, must leave us. We look upon this as giving encouragement to murder and theft.[31]

In their towns, the Gospel was preached often, attracting the curious. One Chief, called Echpalawehund, believed it with such conviction that he renounced his heathenism and wished to live with the Brethren. This so alarmed his tribe that they in turn demanded that the Moravians should be banished for having disturbed their peace. Yet another group of heathens embraced the Gospel, declared their sobriety, rejected any trader who wished to visit their town (as, certainly, he would introduce many new sins among them,) and appointed a council of six braves to keep their new order, without the intercourse of the missionaries. So devout were they to their new way of living, they seized ten casks of rum belonging to a traveling trader

---

[31] Loskiel, *History of the Moravian Missions*, pg. 202

and smashed them in the open street. "But alas, in a short time, these good resolutions proved abortive, and they were as drunk as ever."[32]

Back in Friedensstadt from whence the newcomers had come, the town was besieged by Natives misunderstanding the indifference that the Moravians had had for those who would not convert. They took to drinking long and often, just outside of town. In March of 1773, one Native became so drunk he raided the house of one Brother Rothe while he was convalescing from some severe illness. He was tied and dragged to the street. Within weeks, the Moravian brethren convened and decided to shut down the town. They razed their church, too, because it was believed the Natives would use it as a dance hall. And then they packed up and moved to Schönbrunn and Gnadenhütten.

Eventually, a third town, Salem, sprang forth. All three villages were within twenty miles of each other, all conveniently connected by the Tuscarawas River.

But the Moravian Delawares, in the ensuing years of strife among the Senecas, Wyandots, Shawnees and "the heathen Delawares," were looked upon unfavorably by their tribal relatives, unwilling, as they avowed, to aid in their war against the white man. To the tribal Delawares, the Moravian converts were nothing more than traitorous White Indians. Thus, they were given the name Schwonnaks.[33]

During Lord Dunmore's Wars, when Ohio Natives were most all inclined to serve the interests of the British, they marched incessantly through the peaceful towns of Schönbrunn and Gnadenhütten, cursing the Moravian Delawares who seemed wholly indifferent—if not understandably ignorant—to the common intolerance of the ever encroaching white settlers.

Yet the British, knowing a good thing when they saw it, prohibited their allied tribes from molesting the Moravian towns. "Let sleeping dogs lay," they advised. And so, the Moravian missionaries then enjoyed a long peace. And with that peace came greater prosperity, which the Moravians were kind to share with the tribal Delawares.

Sympathetic to this turn of events was Chief White Eyes; he and old Chief Pakanke laid down an oath to declare the truth of Jesus Christ.[34]

---

[32] Zeisberger, *Moravian Mission Diaries*, pgs. 124-127

[33] Ibid., pg. 235

[34] Loskiel, *History of the Moravian Missions*, pg. 207

"You and I are both old, and know not how long we shall live. Therefore let us do good work before we depart, and leave a testimony to our children and posterity, that we have received the word of God. Let this be our last will and testament."

Schönbrunn grew by hundreds of Native supplicants. Then, the brethren council conceded that other white settlers, devout in their passion for Christ, could join, too. So pious and peaceful became these towns that, according to the Moravians, the Spirit of Christ emanated in ways they could not have hoped or prayed.

One story reveals the effect Moravians had on more heathen Indians. A passing Mohican Brave had asked a sister of the faith, "whether all the people at church had a feeling of this great love of God?" Replied the Moravian woman, "I cannot tell you whether all feel it ...[but] I will introduce a simile. Suppose there was a very delicious meal prepared in this room, and many people attending; those only who eat, can say that the victuals taste well, the other cannot say so. Thus it is with our Saviour. Once those who have tasted of his love can speak of it, ...they never forget it."[35]

But more and more settlers homesteading into the Ohio country then broke the peace, ever threatened as it was by the British in their constant manipulation of Native interests. Hurons and Mingos also descended into the Ohio country. And, so, in the later months of 1776, the security of peaceful relations among white settlements, Moravian communes, British operatives, and fickle tribes like the Shawnees and Wyandots, began to crumble.

---

[35] Ibid., pg. 226

Leet's Claims

In 1774, and for many years still, the land Washington claimed southeast of Cincinnati along the Little Miami was as much Kentucky as it was Ohio country. Just where Crawford and Leet had surveyed that year or the next is vague. Yet, there are some intriguing clues.

Plats or maps of this expedition no longer exist; they were burned in fires at Williamsburg in 1781 or, if not then, at William and Mary College in 1865. Either way, recorded in the surviving letters of George Mason are certain references to his professional engagement of Captain Hancock Lee, William Crawford, and Crawford's assistant, "one Leet," on behalf of the Ohio Land Company. Mason, a wealthy Virginian from birth, was Treasurer of the Ohio Company for more than 40 years. He was also a close neighbor of Washington on whose word he likely relied to hire Crawford.

Mason stated in a letter dated March 12, 1776, "Captain Hancock Lee and one Leet are returned, from surveying the Ohio Company's 200,000 acres of land... They have got it all in one tract, upon a large creek called Licking Creek, which falls into the Ohio river on the southeast side, about 150 miles below the Scioto river."[36] Recorded just three months before this letter in a Fincastle County land book for December 7, 1775, are claims made by Daniel Leet for "400 Acres of Land upon the north fork of Elkhorn Creek 7 or 8 Miles Above the forks Including an Improvement & Cabbin. Also 400 acres joining the above at a Cabin & Improvement. Also 400

---

[36] James, *The Ohio Company, Its Inner History*, pg. 163

Joining the Ohio Co.ys Survey, Beginning at a Hicory & Sug.r Tree the 3 d Corner in the Survey…"

Footnotes to this historic record suggest the land Leet claimed as being in Scott County. It also states that Leet was awarded 1,000 acres on "the north fork" in 1780.[37] But just like the surveys lost to fire, no warrants, patents or deeds exist for Leet's claims.

Promotional material for Scott County, which sits just north of Lexington, Kentucky, says the area "was explored as early as 1774" (meaning, of course, by a white person.)[38] The "large creek called Licking Creek," falling "into the Ohio River about 150 miles below the Scioto River" is today the Licking River and it flows into the Ohio River just south of Cincinnati. (Fincastle County, where Leet's claims were supposedly recorded, was then under Virginia's domain, because, of course, the colony deemed itself to include all land west to the Mississippi.) Elkhorn Creek, however, lies just east of Frankfort, Kentucky, and, as such, runs through Scott County today.

200,000 acres surveyed in 1774 and 1775 by Crawford and Leet would represent 312 square miles. If the survey abutted Elkhorn Creek and followed north along Licking River, it could well include Cincinnati or Batavia, Ohio, just 70 miles north.

Crawford and Leet's erstwhile client, Washington, who seemed not to have concerned himself with this particular venture of the Ohio Company, was nonetheless invested in the very same region.

Whatever may have happened to Leet's own surveys, plats or maps—very likely drawn in his own hand and saved for his personal benefit—would become a subject of much speculation almost a hundred years later.

---

[37] Ibid, pg. 269
[38] https://scottky.gov

Cresswell's Journal

Nicholas Cresswell "tomahawked" his claim on American history when, as a young English gentleman, he sailed to the colonies to find his path in the brave new world. In 1774, at the age of twenty-four, he landed on the banks of the Potomac, after six weeks at sea. He was sick for most of the voyage, yet he would survive worse ailments along his many travels deep into the Ohio country, all while astutely keeping a diary of his every adventure. The Journal of Nicholas Cresswell is a rare, first-person narrative, revealing insights of the customs and traditions of pre-Revolutionary America, not the least of which were his Tory sentiments by which he excoriated the patriots who had turned on his beloved King. For these outbursts, he was suspected of being a spy. Albeit a keen observer of the follies and passions of the times, he was not.

But of the three years he experienced America, one particular month's journey took him down the Ohio to the Kanawha and up the Muskingum River. He visited a village of Christian Indians there and, upon returning, visited William Crawford at his homestead, Spring Garden, where also, month's before, he met Crawford's brother, Valentine.

Sunday, August 27th, 1775.
"Proceeded on our journey and about noon got to an Indian Town called Wale-hack-tap-poke[39], or the Town with a good Spring, on the Banks of the Muskingham and inhabited by Delawarr Indians. Christianized under the Moravian Sect, it is a pretty town consisting of

---

[39] The Indian name for the town called Schönbrunn by the Moravians.

about sixty houses, and is built of logs and covered with Clapboards. It is regularly laid out in three spacious streets which meet in the centre, where there is a large meeting house built of logs sixty foot square covered with Shingles, Glass in the windows and a Bell, a good plank floor with two rows of forms. Adorned with some few pieces of Scripture painting, but very indifferently executed. All about the meeting house is kept very clean.

"In the evening went to the meeting. But never was I more astonished in my life. I expected to have seen nothing but anarchy and confusion, as I have been taught to look upon these beings with contempt. Instead of that, here is the greatest regularity, order, and decorum, I ever saw in any place of Worship, in my life. With the solemnity of behaviour and modest, religious deportment would do honour to the first religious society on earth, and put a bigot or enthusiast out of countenance. The Parson was a Dutchman, but preached in English. He had an Indian interpreter, who explained it to the Indians by sentences. They sung in the Indian language. The men sit on one row of forms and the women on the other with the children in front. Each sex comes-on and goes out of their own life of the house. The old men sit one each side of the parson. Treated with Tea, Coffe, and Boiled Bacon at supper. The Sugar they make themselves out of the sap of a certain tree. Lodged at Whiteman's house, married to an Indian woman."

Saturday, September 2nd, 1775.

"….Crossed the River and got to Newcomers Town. Very sick. Nancy is gone to fetch an old Indian woman to cure me as she says, therefore I must lay by my pen." [Nancy, or "N." is a young Indian squaw he has been "loaned" so as to assist him on this particular leg of his expedition.]

Sunday, September 3rd, 1775.

"Last night, Nancy brought an Indian Squaw which called me her Nilum. i.e. Nephew, as Mr. Anderson [Cresswell's hired Indian guide] told me, and behaved very kindly to me, She put her hand on my head for some time, then took a small brown root out of her pocket and with her knife chopped part of it small, then mixed it with water which she gave me to drink, or rather swallow, being about a spoonful, but this I evaded by keeping it in my mouth till I found an opportunity to spit it out. She then took some in her mouth and chewed it and spit on the top of my head, rubbing my head well at the same time. Then she unbuttoned my shirt collar and spat another mouthful down my back. This was uncomfortable but I bore it with patience. She lent me her Matchcoat and told me to go to sleep. Nancy was ordered not to give me any water till morning, however, I prevailed on the good-natured creature to let me take a vomit [an emetic, like ipecac] that Mr. Anderson had with him as soon as the old woman was gone, which has cured me, tho' the old woman believes that her nostrum did it. Obliged to stay here this day, somebody has stolen one of Mr. A's horses."

Monday, September 4th, 1775.

"Saw an Indian scalp. Heard an Indian play upon a Tin Violin and make tolerable good music. Went to Kanaughtonhead[40] walked all the way, my horse loaded with skins. Camped close by the Town. Nancy's kindness to be remembered."

Tuesday, September 5th, 1775.

"At Kanaughtonhead. Went to the meeting where Divine service was performed in Dutch and English with great solemnity. This Chapel is much neater than that at Wale-hack-tap-poke. Adorned with basket work in various colours all round, with a spinet made by Mr. Smith the parson, and played by an Indian. Drank Tea with Captn. White-Eyes and Captn. Wingenund at an Indian house in Town. This Tea is made of the tops of Ginsing, and I think it very much like Bohea Tea. The leaves are put into a tin canister made water tight and boiled till it is dry, by this means the juices do not evaporate. N. did not choose to go into the town, but employed herself in making me a pair of Mockesons."

---

[40] Cresswell's misspelling of Gnadenhütten.

Wednesday, September 6th, 1775.

"Left Kanaughtonhead. Mr. Anderson bought several cows there which he intends to take to Fort Pitt. Camped within two miles of Wale-hacktappoke."

Thursday, September 7th, 1775.

"Got to Walehacktap-poke to breakfast. N. refused to go into the Town, knowing that the Moravians will not allow anyone to cohabit with Indians in their town. Saw an Indian child baptized, eight Godfathers and four Godmothers, could not understand the ceremony as it was performed in Indian."

Friday, September 8th, 1775.

"At Walehacktappoke. Find my body invaded with an army of small animals which will be a little troublesome to dislodge. Saw an Indian seat house. It is built of logs about eight feet by five and about two feet high, with a small door and covered all over with earth to keep in the steam… The patient creeps into the house wrapped in his Blanket, when his friends put in large stones red hot and a pail of water, then make up the door as close as possible, the patient throws the water upon the hot stones all the house is filled with hot steam and vapor. He continues in this little hell as long as he is able to bear it, when the door is opened and the patient instantly plunged into the River. This method of treating the Smallpox has been destructive too many of them. Bought a blanket made of a Buffalo skin."

Saturday, September 9th, 1775.

"Left the town. Mr. Anderson, N. And I went to the Tuscarora town. Then got lost in the Woods and rambled till dark, when we camped by the side of a little run. Very merry this afternoon with our misfortune."

Sunday, September 10th, 1775.

"Rambled till noon when we found ourselves at Bouquet's old Fort now demolished. Went to an Indian Camp, where Mr. Anderson met with an old wife of his, who would go with him, which he agreed to. We have each of us a Girl. It is an odd way of traveling, but we obliged to submit to it. Met with Mr. Anderson's people in the evening, camped by the side of Tuscarora Creek. Saw the vestige, the Tuscarora town, but now deserted."[41]

Fort Pitt - Thursday, September 14th, 1775.

"Got to Fort Pitt about noon. Left our Girls amongst the Indians that are coming to the Treaty. Great numbers of people in Town come to the Treaty. Terrible news from the Northward, but so confused I hoped there is little truth in it."

Friday, September 15th, 1775.

"Very few of the Indians come in yet, the commissioners have been waiting for them a week. Shall be obliged to stay here some time to see the Treaty."

Saturday, September 16th, 1775.

"Got acquainted with Mr. Ephraim Douglas, an Indian trader. N. finished my Leggings and Mockeysons, very neat ones."

Sunday, September 17th, 1775.

"Here are members of Congress to treat with the Indians, Delegates from the Conventions of Virginia and Pensylvania for the purpose, and Commissioners from the Convention of Virginia to settle the accounts of the last campaign against the Indians. All Coins. [Colonels], Majors, or Captains and very big with their own importance. Confound them altogether. Colonial disputes are very high between Virginia and Pensylvania and if not timely suppressed will end in tragical consequences."

Tuesday, September 26th, 1775.

"This morning N. informed me that the Indians would come to the Council fire. About noon the Shawnees and Dellawars Indians

---

[41] Bouquet's old fort was situated near Bolivar, OH, the later site of Fort Laurens. The *vestige* to which Cresswell refers is a large Indian Mound. It is not as impressive as the one he later sees and describes on October 9th.

with one of the Ottawa Chiefs crossed the River in two Canoes, about thirty in number. They were met at the River side by the Delegates and Garrison under arms, who saluted them with a Volley, which the Indian Warriors returned, then proceeded to the Council house, dancing, beating the drum, and singing the Peace Song, all the way. When they got to the Council house the Dancing ceased and all took their places according to seniority, and a profound silence ensued for the space of ten minutes. One of their old men then got up and spoke a few words to the Delegates, signifying that he hoped they should brighten the chain of Friendship and gave them a small string of white wampum, several others spoke and gave Wampum. Then they lighted a pipe and smoked with everyone in the house out of one pipe. The Delegates had an artfull speech prepared for them and adjourned the business till to-morrow. The Indians seem a little confused."

Wednesday, September 27th, 1775.

"The Treaty renewed to-day when the Ottawa Chief made one of the best speeches I ever heard from any man. Determined to get a copy of it if possible. My Landlady informs me that I am likely to be took up for a Spy by the Delegates."

Thursday, September 28th, 1775.

"My peltry arrived this day, which I sold to Mr. Anderson, but find I shall be a loser upon the whole. Determined to leave the town on Monday."

Friday, September 29th, 1775.

"The Indians seem displeased at something. Meet at the Council house every day."

Saturday, September 30th, 1775.

"Went over the River and bought a Porcupine Skin of an Indian. It is something like our Hedgehog at home, only the quills are longer, the Indians dye them of various colours and work them on their trinkets. Mr. Edward Rice promised me his horse to carry me to V. Crawford's on Monday. Sold my Gun to Mr. James Berwick, who gave me a copy of the Indian speech. Saw the Indians dance in the Council house. N. very uneasy, she weeps plentifully. I am unhappy that this honest creature has taken such a fancy to me."

Sunday, October 1st, 1775.

"Took leave of most of my acquaintants in town. Mr. Douglas gave me an Indian Tobacco pouch made of a Mink Skin adorned with porcupine quills. He is desirous of keeping a correspondence with me, which in all probability will be for the interest of us both. I have conceived a great regard for the Indians and really feel a most sensible regret in parting from them, however contemptible opinion others may entertain of these honest poor creatures. If we take an impartial view of an Indian's general conduct with all the disadvantages they labour under, at the same time divest ourselves of prejudice, I believe every honest man's sentiments would be in favour of them. As soon as an Indian comes into the world he is tied with his back to a board which serves for bed and cradle, and by putting a string through the end of the board next his head is very conveniently conveyed from place to place on his Mother's back. He is kept in this position till half a year old, but often plunged in the water in Summer and rolled in the Snow in Winter. He is then set at liberty to walk as soon as he can. Their Youth is never troubled with severe Pedagogues to whip their senses away, for they are entirely unacquainted with letter or figures. The little knowledge they have of past times is handed to them by hieroglyphics or tradition, subject to numberless errors and misrepresentations. Hunting is their diversion as well as support, and in this they are initiated early in life.

"There is established in each Nation a Species of Government which I cannot just now find a name for. It is neither despotic, Aristocratical, Democratical, but rather a compound of the two last. Their Kings have no more honour or respect paid them than another man, and is obliged to hunt for his living as well as the rest. Except in Council, he has a right to speak first, and if he be an old man in whose ability they can confide, his advice is generally observed. In War he acts as General. When anything of consequence is to be done, the whole nation is convened at the Council house built for that purpose. Everyone has a right to speak, but it is generally left to the old men to debate the matter, as they pay the greatest attention to the voice of wisdom which experience has conferred on the aged. Everything is conducted with the greatest regularity and decorum, silence and deliberation, only one speaks at once, and then the most profound silence and attention is observed.

"Those famed for oratory have an opportunity of displaying their talents to the greatest advantage. They express themselves in a bold figurative style, accompanied with violent gestures, tho' exceedingly natural and well adapted to what they are saying and in general as expressive as their words. Their dress, attitude and firmness of countenance (when speaking) even to a person ignorant of their language, strike his mind with something awful and his ideas with something great and noble... In all their trades with the Europeans they are imposed on in the greatest manner. Their sensibility is quick and their passions ungoverned, I may say ungovernable, and it is not to be wondered at if they make returns in kind whenever it is in their power. It is said they are cruel and barbarous and I believe they exercise some cruelties, the thought of which makes human nature shudder, but this is to be attributed to their national customs. It is a general opinion with White men that their difference in colour, and advantages of education give them a superiority over those poor people which Heaven and Nature never designed. They are beings endowed with reason and common sense and I make not the least doubt but they are as valuable in the eyes of their Maker as we are, our fellow creatures, and in general above our level in many virtues that give real preeminence, however despicably we think of or injuriously we treat them.

"Their persons are tall and remarkably straight, of a copper colour, with long black hair, regular features and fine black eyes. The dress of the men is short, white linen or calico shirts which come a little below their hips without buttons at neck or wrist and in general ruffled and a great number of small silver brooches stuck in it. Silver plates about three inches broad round the wrists of their arms, silver wheels in their ears, which are stretched long enough for the tip of the ear to touch the shoulder, silver rings in their noses, Breechclout and Mockeysons with a matchcoat that serves them for a bed at night. They cut off their hair except a lock on the crown of the head and go bareheaded, pluck out their beards. The women wear the same sort of shirts as the men and a sort of short petticoat that comes no lower than the knee, leggings and Mockeysons, the same as the men. Wear their hair long, curled down the back in silver plates, if they can afford it, if not tied in a club with red gartering. No rings in the nose but plenty in the ears. Both men and women paint with Vermillion and other colours mixed with Bear's Oil and adorn themselves with any tawdry thing they think pretty. Their language is soft, copious and expressive. God in the Delawar is Wale-hak-ma-neta, the Devil, Menta, Bread, Augh-pone. They cannot curse or swear in their own language, are obliged to the Europeans for that vice.

"Religion they have little amongst them and that seems to have something of the Jewish manner in it. They have some particular dances at the full and change of the moon, and sometimes pay a sort of adoration to the Sun. At certain periods the women absent themselves from society for a few days and will not suffer anyone to touch a rag of their clothes or eat with them. Before they join their friends again they wash all their clothes and purify every vessel they have made use of with fire. Marriage is little observed, as they live together no longer than they can agree. The woman keeps all the children. Wives are absolute slaves to their husbands. It is very rare for a couple to live all their life together without changing. Polygamy is not allowed. They pay great respect to the dead, particularly those that have rendered themselves conspicuous in War. Their houses are built of Logs or Bark with the fire in the middle and benches on each side the house which serve for chairs, beds, and tables. In Summer they chiefly live in the woods, in Bark tents, smoke much tobacco mixed with the leaves of Sumack which is very pleasant. Inclined much to Silence, except when in liquor which they are very fond of, and then they are very loquacious committing the greatest outrages on each other. The women always hide all offensive weapons as soon as the men get intoxicated, and it is observed that they never all get drunk together, one of them will keep sober to take care of the rest. There is upwards of thirty different nations nearly similar in customs and manner, none of them very numerous. Since spirituous liquors were introduced amongst them they have depopulated fast. Smallpox has made terrible havoc."

Monday, October 2nd, 1775.

"Am informed that the Delegates intend to examine my papers. I will prevent the scoundrels, if possible. Settled my affairs with Mr. John Anderson, who has behaved more like a Father than a common acquaintance. Made him a compliment of my silver buckles and agreed to keep up a correspondence. Parting with N. was the most affecting thing I have ever experienced since I left home. The poor creature wept most plentifully. However base it may appear to conscientious people, it is absolutely necessary to take a temporary wife if they have to travel amongst the Indians. Left Fort Pitt. Dined at widow Myers. Got to Mr. John De Camp's."

Thursday, October 5th, 1775.

"At V. Crawford's. Performed the part of a Clergyman at the funeral of an infant. At the Grave the parents and friends Wept and drank Whiskey alternately. V. Crawford promised to hire me a horse to carry me over the mountain before I went to Fort Pitt, but I believe he never intends to perform."

Friday, October 6th, 1775.

"Went to Captn. Gist's to see if he could assist me with a horse. He treated me very kindly, but could not furnish me with a horse. Lodged there."

Saturday, October 7th, 1775.

"Returned to V. Crawford's. Find V. wants to take advantage of my necessity. Experience teaches me adversity is the touchstone of friendship."

Sunday, October 8th, 1775.

"At V. Crawford's very uneasy, my clothes wore out and my money almost expended. I have made an unfortunate summer's work of it, but cannot tax myself with extravagance, but with a great deal of imprudence in the choice of my companion Rice."

Monday, October 9th, 1775.

"On my way to Major Crawford's saw the vestiges of an old fortification. It appears to me that this country has been inhabited by a race of people superior in military knowledge to the present Indians. In different parts of the country there are the vestiges of regular fortifications, and it is well known the Indians have not the least knowledge of that art. When, or by whom, these places were built, I leave to more able antiquarians than I am to determine. [42] Fortunately for me Zachariah Connel is going over the Mountain to-morrow and will find me a horse to go along with him. Returned to V. Crawford's."

Allegany Mountain - Tuesday, October 10th, 1775.

"Left V. Crawford's, whom I believe to be a scoundrel. Set out with Mr. Zac. Connel for Winchester.

---

[42] Cresswell is commenting on a Great Indian Mound he has just seen, but says not where.

The Great Indian Mounds

Across the Ohio River from the site of Washington's much beloved tract he called Round Bottom stands a formidable natural monument to the mysteries of the continent's earliest inhabitants. Moundsville, West Virginia, is so named for the man-made earthwork that looms six stories high and 240 feet around. Archeologists have calculated that the volume of dirt exceeds that of three million bushels. The earthwork sits less than a quarter mile up from the river. A spiral flight of steps climbs to its peak. From this height, one can see a vista unimagined from the banks of the Ohio.

In his famous journal written in the years 1774 to 1777, Nicholas Cresswell noted seeing two different Indian mounds, one of which was adjacent to an early fort built by Colonel Henry Bouquet, later employed in Girty's circular charade, the other near Washington's Round Bottom at Moundsville. Cresswell's entry of September 10, 1775, marked the first English sighting of any of the Great Indian Mounds.

In 1839, the great Moundsville earthwork was excavated by the Tomlinson brothers who had settled nearby. They discovered the remains of two bodies in a chamber below ground level. From the top of the mound they later drilled a central shaft and discovered a second tomb higher up. It contained just one body. That higher tomb revealed a copper bracelet and sheets of a similar alloy laid under the skeleton in repose.

In 1880, archeologists from the Smithsonian Institution visited Moundsville to measure and explore the site, but did little excavation. Their scientific mission was then to map out the few other mounds that settlers had identified in the newly emerging Ohio communities. The mounds were apparently more prolific in number than anyone had ever imagined. More than 70 ancient earthworks today have been mapped, measured, studied, and protected either under historic preservation laws or through private owner-ship. Certainly, there were hundreds more that have been lost to erosion or engulfed by natural vegetation. The same archeologists discovered, too, that all across the state, the mounds varied greatly by size, shape, dimension and purpose. The massive earthworks in Moundsville, known today as the Grave Creek Mound, is the largest conical type in North America. The Serpent Mound in Peebles, Ohio, is visited by thousands of tourists each year; many archeologists claim that the curved snake formation aligns with precise ver-nal settings of the sun as well as autumnal phases of the moon. The Fort Hill mound in Hillsboro, Ohio, one of the largest, has a circumference of 1.53 miles, enclosing 35 acres. Not all of the mounds were used for burials. And those that were had curiously few bodies interred.

Archeologists have attributed the development of the great earthworks to two indigenous cultures that preceded then-current tribal Natives by well more than two thousand years. The Adena culture is thought to have started building mounds as early as 400 B.C. A second culture, called the Hopewells, apparently coexisted, yet did not build their mounds until two or three centuries later. Neither culture is known today by any name they might have called themselves; no original language survives.

Fig. 36.—GREAT MOUND AT GRAVE CREEK.

Moundsville, W.Va. Great Mound at Grave Creek., 1848. https://www.loc.gov/item/2004679658

Thomas Worthington, Governor of Ohio from 1814 to 1818, is credited for bestowing the Adena name on the earlier culture. His Chillicothe estate, "Adena," came from a Hebrew word meaning "places remarkable for the delightfulness of their situation." The Hopewell culture was named by another white man, Mordecai Hopewell, who discovered earthworks on his Ohio farm sometime before 1820. A map and interpretation of what was thought to be a tribal defense was included in the first book ever published by the Smithsonian Institution, *Ancient Monuments of the Mississippi Valley*, in 1847. It is still today the best primary source of information about the great and mysterious earthworks of North America.

Leet's License

Daniel Leet earned his surveyor's license from William and Mary College on April 17, 1776. Of course, "earned" may not be the correct term. Like Washington and Crawford before him, neither of whom attended classes at the royal institution, Leet was unceremoniously commissioned as a deputy surveyor for a specific district. In Leet's case, West Augusta, Virginia. Only the college could grant such authority. However, it was really William Crawford who sponsored his candidacy, and, just as certainly, Washington who endorsed Crawford's nomination. Daniel Leet attended no classes at William and Mary College; by virtue of an interview with a requisite dean or provost, Leet was deemed to have the skills necessary to his profession. As a licensed surveyor, he was bestowed certain rights. Most significantly, this official recognition allowed him the privilege to demand compensation for his work. He could demand it from his own clients, and, in cases of dispute or failure to collect, he could demand it from the land office, the courts, or the Governor. Leet was 28.

With his new commission came a definition of the domain in which he would labor. Once the amorphous blob of sprawling forests, winding tributaries and treacherous Indian paths, West Augusta was now terrain with a defined boundary. That is, as passed by an Act of the General Assembly of Virginia (and by which the State adopted its Constitution on June 12, 1776,) the delineations of West Augusta were determined to be as follows:

> "Beginning on the Alleghany Mountains between the heads of Potomack, Cheat and Greenbrier Rivers: thence along the ridge of mountains which divides the waters of Cheat River from those of

Greenbrier, and that branch of the Monongahela River called Tygart's Valley River to the Monongahela River; thence up the said river and the west fork thereof to Bingamon's Creek, on the north west of the said west fork; thence in a direct course to the head of Middle Island Creek, a branch of the Ohio, and thence to the Ohio including all the waters of the aforesaid creek, in the aforesaid district of West Augusta, all that territory lying to the northward of the aforesaid boundary, and to the westward of the states Pennsylvania and Maryland, shall be deemed and is hereby declared to be within the district of West Augusta."

"Aforesaid," the boundaries defined by this Act were no more clear to Leet than to anyone wishing to settle within them. Such was the geography of a yet unborn nation.

To the modern layman, this definition of West Augusta was meant to include West Virginia's present-day panhandle, Greene County, Washington County, and western chunks of Allegheny and Beaver counties. Although the Mason-Dixon line was the agreed separation between Maryland and Pennsylvania, there was still no definition of any border between Virginia and Pennsylvania (witness the above southern boundary of West Augusta) and no western (i.e. longitudinal) border for Pennsylvania. These would not come until 1779.

In fact, for more than three years, the residents of West Augusta, as well as those who "had eyes" on promised bounty lands, argued for the relative benefits of being situated in either Pennsylvania or Virginia. Pennsylvanians were inclined to seek the comfort of loyalist jurisdiction; the Crown, even beyond the Allegheny mountains, had tried-and-true means to resolve disputes that western Virginians would rather (and more expediently) resolve themselves. Land speculators were apprehensive, if not wise, to seek warrants from just one land office, fearing that the eventual decision of a boundary might not go in their favor, effectively making null and void any paperwork submitted to another office. Hedging one's bet by seeking warrants from two different land offices would require two sets of surveys, and, as "scientific" as the practice of surveying might have been in colonial times, any differences in the two would create a headache far more expensive than one misplaced bet.

But land jurisdictions and property disputes were hardly the only issues stirring. To the pioneer carving out a life for his family in the wilds of West Augusta, far more important was his safety and protection from Indian raids. Which is exactly why most local militias were raised. Yet militias needed guns and ammunition and significant funding. And, so, just whose province would provide such "necessaries" when the locals could not themselves? Like so many more issues of governance, it all depended on which side of the surveyor's line one stood.

Whether or not Leet had immediate opportunity to "run out his chains" in the summer of 1776, by late fall, he was marching eastward to meet up with his esteemed client along the Delaware River.

Word was that George Washington was in serious trouble.

PART TWO
(1776-1782)

*In which a young country fights
two bloody wars at the same time
yet promises free land as bounty.*

The Battle of Trenton

Just two months after a different silversmith would react famously to two lamps hung "if by sea," George Washington was made Commander in Chief of the Continental Army. In June of 1775, thus honored, he left Philadelphia and assembled a motley crew of militia in Boston where the British laid siege until the Spring of 1776. That's when Lieutenant-General Sir William Howe, commander of the British forces, evacuated the harbor and sailed to New York.

Washington descended with no more than 7,000 men to fend off the British now focused on Manhattan. The subsequent Battles of Long Island, Fort Washington and Fort Lee were military disasters, complicated as much by his several generals' bickering as by Washington's own indecisions. As many as 2,000 men were captured. Just as many defected. Most, in fact, were committed to serving the Continental Army only until their term of duty would expire on December 31st. Military service was after all just a paid gig.

Washington retreated south through New Jersey and headed toward Philadelphia. Desperate for more recruits, he stopped in Hackensack with his Adjutant-General where they lamented their certain demise. Thus, pondered Washington, "[If] we retreat to the back parts of Pennsylvania, will the Pennsylvanians support us?" Replied his aide, "If the lower counties are subdued and give up, the back counties will do the same." Washington thought for a moment, supposedly massaging his throat, "My neck does not feel as though it was made for a halter. We must retire to Augusta County, Virginia. Numbers will be obliged to repair to us for safety; and we must try what we can do in carrying on a predatory war; and if overpowered we must cross the Alleghany Mountains."[1]

At the time, however, Augusta County, was coming to them.

Although appointed to the lieutenancy of Virginia's Fifth Regiment on February 13 of that year, William Crawford was promoted just two weeks later to Colonel of Virginia's Seventh. As its principal field officer, he was responsible for recruiting militia primarily from West Augusta. Whether he had recruited Daniel Leet to the Fifth or Seventh Regiment, or to follow a militia comprised of West Augustans, matters little; Leet marched east with a brigade of non-uniformed, untrained, and ill-equipped recruits. His only assignment was to meet up with Washington's army somewhere along the Delaware River. First, however, he marched through Bethlehem, Pennsylvania, where his brigade camped at the Moravian village there. Onward, Leet eventually met Washington and his revolutionary forces at McConkey's Ferry.

But not so Crawford. Even before passing over the Alleghenies, he was reassigned—again—to form a new regiment, Virginia's 13th. His orders were to protect the western frontier.

*   *   *   *   *

Leet's participation in the Battle of Trenton was, for him, as well as for the British, a moment of shock and awe. That the weather on Christmas Day was so brutally cold—a sleeting nor'easter pelted them nonstop—was not nearly as surprising as how suddenly events unfolded. Only 600 or so men of the revolutionary forces were able to cross the Delaware on that Christmas night. Both Continental Major Generals Cadwalader and Ewing stationed at different river crossings could not get their troops to cut through the fast-freezing Delaware. Only Washington, commanding his two brigades—one led by John Sullivan, the other by Nathanael Greene—were able to do so. And it took them well until three in the morning to cross and lead their troops marching down two different roads that would eventually merge into Trenton. Even before dawn, they slogged another two hours, hauling howitzers and cannons to the western boundary of the city. Then around eight in the morning enemy pickets fired warning shots, not so much in defense

---

[1] Stryker, William S., *The Battles of Trenton and Princeton*, pg. 5, quoting Rev. William Gordon, D.D. History of the American Revolution, source unknown.

as to awaken their grog-filled comrades asleep in pillaged townhouses on King Street. Without a second thought, Sullivan's team marched to block the southern Assunpink Bridge, while Greene's team, burdened with heavy, yet critical artillery, advanced north to the high point of town, and there positioned cannons to have a clear shot down both King Street and the parallel-descending Queen Street. When the more than 1,000 Hessians stationed in Trenton were roused from their warm blankets, they quickly realized they had nowhere to run, trapped as they quickly discovered between both lines of artillery fire. Likely, Leet commanded one of a swath of second floor windows, across Queen Street, behind which his company was positioned, to fire down on the German mercenaries. A few volleys ensued. Some Hessians did run (to a nearby orchard) but, within the hour, most all of the enemy's arms were surrendered, their valuable artillery, too. The entirety of the conflict, from crossing the Delaware to capturing the enemy, took little more than half a day.

Of course, the Battle of Trenton was significant for many reasons. Foremost was the continental army's decisive victory. It was, by some accounts, their first. After so many defeats since repelling the redcoats from Lexington and Concord, Washington's long-failing forces could, at long last, hold their heads high. For the General himself, he could hold his a little higher. His decision to attack Trenton had been a huge gamble. Had he not attempted some sort of last-minute engagement with the Brits, his reputation would have become as tattered as the men he then commanded. Literally, within days, most every soldier under his command could have walked back home, their commissions fulfilled by the first day of the next year. Washington had placed his bets for incredible success against incredible odds.

More than 900 German mercenaries were either taken prisoner or fled for their lives. 83 were wounded. 22 were killed.

Of Washington's forces, only five were wounded; none killed.

Of the five wounded were two men of some note. Colonel William Washington, a second cousin, was shot in both hands while taking one of the enemy cannons.

Another wounded, doing the very same thing, was James Monroe. He was shot in the shoulder. The disability would not come to affect the 5th President of the United States.

To both Revolutionary and cultural historians, the Battle of Trenton was significant for discovering another rising "star"—the one, the only, Alexander Hamilton. Scrappy and hungry, just like his country, marching the rear, showing no fear, was a righteous soldier Washington held dear. Hamilton, in few months, would become Washington's most favored—and most faithful—aide-de-camp. How and why did Washington ever take notice? Apparently, Hamilton liked to march alongside the cannon to which he was assigned. He would regularly pat it, as if it were a favored horse or excited dog.[2] This amused Washington to no end.

For Daniel Leet, his own participation in the succinct but momentous victory would become a badge of honor preceding him in most every engagement hence.

Scholars cannot agree if Alexander Hamilton was born in 1755 or 1757. As such, this portrait was drawn "from life," on his 18th or 16th birthday, and, in either case, less than four years before the Battle of Trenton. www.loc.gov/item/2010648300/

---

[2] Randall, "Hamilton Takes Command," *Smithsonian Magazine*, January, 2003.

Cause and Bounties

Daniel Leet joined the forces assembled along the Delaware to serve the interests of colonial independence. Of this, there can be no doubt. Yet, he had many other reasons to do so, too. Foremost was the favor he would repay his mentor William Crawford who desperately needed to fill a quota set by *his* client, now Commander in Chief, General George Washington. But then there was the promise of cold, hard cash, too, and the not unrealistic prospect of earning bounty land.

Even before the second Continental Congress met to discuss a draft, the notion of rewarding soldiers with land was a well-established practice. King George II had advanced the idea to recruit his many loyalist Governors and agents. Indeed, Washington had already cashed in his chips for having served in the conflict with the French and Indians. The Proclamation of 1763 had set a minimum promise of 200 acres for each commissioned officer and 50 acres per "Private Man" who served in the "late War." No conditions were set relative to the time served.

In 1775, the Continental Congress was willing to "up the ante," yet, for a commitment of one full year. However, by the end of 1776, the incentive program was not working as well as Congress had first hoped. Indeed, a few young men were signing up, but mostly for reasons of camaraderie and male machismo. Such motivation would last only until a soldier's ego came face to face with real mortal combat. The promise of $10 sterling for a year's service was, at first, welcome incentive—especially in a society otherwise bereft of any steady means to steadier wages. For most young men, trying to carve out a meager existence in a wholly seasonal economy, $10 was a small fortune. Moreover, until that reward was paid, all other expenses were to be covered, too. The promise of rum and other daily rations, not to mention sturdy boots, a warm blanket and a shiny musket were hard to pass up.

But little did these men realize how trying it would be for the continental army to supply such basic needs, and, least of all, how arduous the actual labor of war really was.

By early winter of 1776, Washington's army was demoralized, hopeless, starving and ill-equipped to withstand the wet, frigid cold. While the battlefield death toll for the Trenton victors was officially "none," the fact is, there had been two: both men froze to death on the march into battle.

And, now, there was Daniel Leet, scurrying amidst the chaos of comrades celebrating a surprising victory, sorting out the ranks of captured Hessians, and marching them off to confinement in a warehouse across a frozen river which would take his regiment three times longer to ford than it had the night before, and from whence he would have to march farther still to set up camp, make shelter, and, at long last, slake his thirst, swallow some slop, and, perchance, sleep.

That military discipline should keep soldiers in line, honorable in their duty, and responsive to the least command was an ideal shared only by higher ranking authority. It was doubted by Washington as it was by many in the early congress. Even with the victory at Trenton, and soon to be seen at the Battle of Princeton, the "powers that be" in Philadelphia feared for their lives. If no more recruits could be drawn to support Washington's army, the British forces were just waiting to administer the final blow.

What drove young men like Leet, Hamilton, and Monroe to carry on? Certainly, the instant promise of another $10 sterling was not to be dismissed. That the offer would demand just six months of commitment would help sway some minds. And, further, those considering returning to their labors back home would know that January, February and March could be so cruel.

All too likely, Leet saw little difference in returning to West Augusta. There, he had no wife to comfort and no fields to prepare. But he did have his surveyor's commission. Would he have his county re-engage him as a surveyor dragging chains for any client who wasn't otherwise preoccupied defending the frontier?

For Hamilton and Monroe, each were advancing in their ranks. Both had commanded artillery that had clearly decided the all-too-sudden victory at Trenton. Each were eyed by Washington, respectively, for valor or injury in battle. In fact, within the month, Hamilton was brought to Washington's headquarters in Morristown. There, the Commander directly asked the bright, young patter-of-cannons to serve in his administration. Described by Washington as "boyish, yet handsome," Hamilton was made a Lieutenant Colonel on the spot.

Monroe convalesced. Already a Lieutenant, in two months, he would be promoted to Major.

Daniel Leet apparently considered his options. Whether he had been truly enlisted, "volunteered" for duty or, like many others, had simply marched along with a militia would ultimately mean different things, rewards for each being wholly inequitable, and, ultimately, irreconcilable. Up until 1778, all conscription came from the ranks of county militias, anyhow. There was no continental draft because the Continental Congress had no powers to affect a "national" call to arms. The early congress, could, however, send out recruiters to stir up the masses to fight for the cause. Men like William Crawford had done just that. One of the many "promises" recruiters could offer was bounty lands. By what authority they did so is not totally clear, but only the colonies with far reaching western wilds, like Virginia or Pennsylvania, could ever fulfill such enticing opportunity.

The fact is it cost the Continental recruiter absolutely nothing. It was no skin off *his* nose. Only if and when colonial independence was fully secured could such claims be fulfilled anyhow.

And, so, even if exhausted from the triumph at Trenton, Daniel Leet stuck around. He enlisted and was then promoted to Regimental Quartermaster of the 13th Virginia line. And he was ordered to return home. The command was no respite. Stationed at Fort Pitt, his regiment was desperately in need of arms, horses, and "all the necessaries" an army must have just to consider removing itself from the safety of a garrison. Nine companies strong, Leet would have to manage the acquisition, distribution and logistics of transporting equipment that existed neither in the west nor, now depleted by battle, in the east. These were matters he would need to take up with his new commander, Colonel William Crawford.

The Night Before

The renowned reputation of Lieutenant-General Sir William Howe was that he was methodical, plodding, obstinate and lazy. That he could have made a swift end-run around Washington's beleaguered troops, then slogging through New Jersey, and attacked defenseless militia in Philadelphia was a certainty then not executed by the British. That Washington's forces had no means to rush to Philadelphia's aid was also clear. Instead, Howe and his army hunkered down for the winter. And for much of the following spring, too. As before, they occupied Manhattan, sprawled out, to rest.

Washington encamped in Morristown.

In Philadelphia, merchants, craftsmen and artisans like Thomas Shields both feared and accepted the inevitable. Members of the Continental Congress removed themselves to Baltimore, as did their coterie of clerks and courtesans.

Curious efforts were put into effect to raise Continental dollars, then so necessary to purchase arms for the war. One scheme was a lottery. Four "games" were announced in February of 1777. For just ten dollars, one lucky person could win $10,000. Twenty-thousand other winners could double their "adventure." In the forty dollar game, the luckiest winner won $50,000, but 26,000 others could win a $10 "profit" on their investment.[3]

Philadelphia papers took notice of the divisive politics played out among five classes of citizens. Rank Tories "esteemed no arts too base to injure or betray the friends of America." Moderate Men were those who wished to return to 1763 when the Crown was supreme and uncontested. Timid

---

[3] *The Pennsylvania Packet*, February 11, 1777, pg. 4

Whigs "entertain a false idea of the [true] power and resources of America," while Furious Whigs would have Tories "tomahawked, scalped and roasted alive." Best, the papers assured their readers, were the Staunch Whigs who "have an unshaken faith in divine justice, and they esteem it a mark of equal folly and impiety to believe that Great Britain can ever subdue America."[4]

From Congress came the adoption of a new flag in June. "Resolved, That the FLAG of the United States be THIRTEEN STRIPES alternate red and white; that the Union be THIRTEEN STARS white in a blue field, representing a new constellation."[5]

Yet, seething silently in the security of New York's city was Howe waiting to make his next move.

As if drunk from a long night's celebration of patriotic furor, Philadelphia dreaded how it was going to cope the next day.

---

[4] *Ibid.,* March 18, 1777, pg. 1

[5] *The Maryland Gazette,* September 11, 1777, pg. 1

Back Home

Back in West Augusta, Daniel Leet learned of many changes since his earlier departure to fight at Trenton. First was a new distinction of territories in his district. Now, because of jurisdictional disputes (more or less a natural result of increased population and density issues,) were three new "counties": Youghogania, Monongalia, and, Ohio, meaning west of the Ohio River (which naturally included the Ohio country.) Further, those favoring the idea that they were Pennsylvanians labeled their neck of the woods Westmoreland County. Those living "west of Laurel Hill" identified as West Augustans and, as such, were very much aligned with Virginia.

As hills and dales became more and more populated the need for more local governance became ever more clear. And from this social intercourse connecting once disparate fiefdoms grew something much larger than a village, yet perhaps not quite a town. The community once colloquially known as Catfish Camp became the center of Youghogania County. Here, even before 1776, the "powers that be" (and those powers looked to Virginia for their authority) were granted a "committee of assembly" to have "full power to meet at such times as they shall judge necessary, and in case of any emergency to call the committee to the district together, and shall be vested with the same power and authority as the other standing committee and committees of correspondence [as] are in the other counties within the colony."[6]

Among the 28 men "elected" to this committee—of course, any duly elected committee was likely the organic result of all who showed up—were George Croghan and William Crawford.

---

[6] Crumrine, *History of Washington County, Pennsylvania*, pg. 184

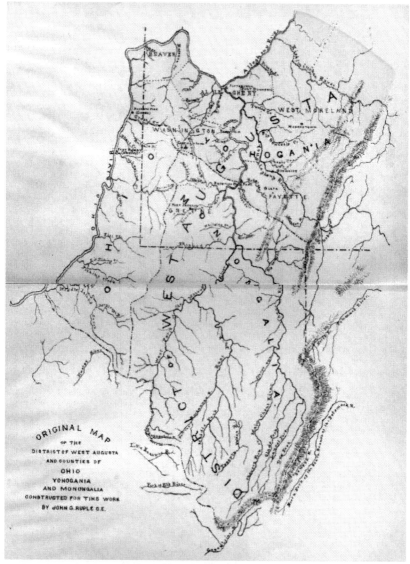

Map credited to the "Semi-Centennial History of West Virginia," by James Morton Callahan, 1913.

Quickly, the committee moved to resolve the following (much abbreviated) measures:

1) that the committee have the "highest sense of spirited behavior" in opposing those who would "invade American rights..;"
2) that the committee shall stockpile gunpowder, lead and flints;
3) that the committee will collect two shillings and sixpence from all who will tithe to defray the expense of the above ammunition; and,

4) that the committee will endeavor to cultivate a friendship with the Indians, and if any person shall be so depraved as to take the life of any Indian that may come to us in a friendly manner, we will, as one man, use our utmost endeavors to bring such offenders to condign punishment..."

Evidently, the men of West Augusta were as fearful of Indian attacks as they were of the dangers marching east to take up arms in the fight for independence. Already one company of militia had been mustered—Daniel Leet among them—barely armed and poorly equipped, yet sent east to meet at Trenton. Now, it appears, the community was able to muster yet another company of men, also poorly armed, but who could stay close to their wives and children. This company became the regiment Colonel William Crawford would command. Even though barracked at Fort Pitt, they were comprised almost wholly of Youghogania County residents and thus, or so, were called the West Augusta Regiment. To the Commander in Chief of the Revolutionary Army, they were directed as Virginia's 13th Regiment.

A member of the same committee who had also enlisted was a gentleman with an unusual name. He, like Crawford and Leet, was a surveyor. In fact, he was a surveyor to George Croghan, and had assisted Croghan in running out the lines of the Chartiers Creek lands that Washington had thought better to purchase, but by twist of fate, became his anyway.

A settler, surveyor, committee member, and true character, that gentleman was Dorsey Pentecost.

Valentine and Hugh

Likely one of few men who could write as well as calculate 'rithmetics, Daniel Leet's job was to record the circulation and depletion of the regiment's equipment—items like cooking kettles, sleeping blankets, and saddles—much in short supply. Leet settled into the barracks of Fort Pitt and enjoyed basic comforts he had not known in well over a year.

But it would not last long. Colonel Crawford received two bits of news. First, he learned that his brother had died.

In January of 1777, Valentine Crawford slipped through a sheet of ice and died. Two days later, his half-brother, Hugh Stephenson died, too. Neither had prepared a will. As their closest and most respected relative, William was obliged to manage their estates. Matters of debt and credit required immediate attention. Wives and children could be laid destitute without a proper balancing of the books, nor could one brother allow siblings to rival for possessions left behind. A family's honor was often at stake, as the debts of a father could befall on anyone: son, sister, cousin, or grandchild.

Then, he received a letter from Washington with "immediate orders." Battles were impending south of Philadelphia. British ships, having sailed around New Jersey, were expected sometime soon to land up the Delaware River. Crawford would have to march right away.

William Crawford begged George Washington for precious time to tend to his affairs.

Washington replied:

"...Peculiarly circumstanced as you are, I shall not object to your taking some reasonable time to settle matters relative to your deceased Brother's Estate, if your Regt comes this way, altho' I can assure you that it goes much against my Inclination to part with a good Officer. Your other Field Officers must attend the Regt.

"I regret exceedingly the loss of your two Brothers, & thank you for your kind offer of serving me in any business I may have west of the Alleganies, but my time is so constantly taken up & ingrossed by public Matters, that I scarce bestow a thought on my private Affairs beyond my Famy at Mount Vernon. I am very sincerely D. Sir

Your obedt Servt"

—Go: Washington"

Washington's marching orders might have excused Crawford, but not his West Augusta Regiment. The fact remained that Crawford's regiment was barely armed. He had complained in a letter, "should they be ordered away before they get blankets and other necessaries, I do not see how they are to be moved.."

But moved they were. Marching out of Fort Pitt on May 22, 1777, the 13th Virginia headed east and into the camp of the First Virginia Brigade under the command of General Peter Muhlenberg, freshly arrived from southern battles, now to join forces with General Nathanael Greene.

Of course, Daniel Leet marched, too, returning full circle to the same brigade he had left just months before.

The Morning After

On September 27, 1777, the British invaded Philadelphia.

With the late summer's defeat of Washington's armies while defending Chad's Ford and the Brandywine crossings, in August and September of 1777, many more fled the hot city. But many stayed, too, welcoming the opportunity of commerce and service to the British forces who, now occupying the city, took over abandoned boarding rooms and vacated houses, as well as most every tavern, alehouse, dram shop and tippling place.

Philadelphia nearly tripled its population within a month and, despite Washington's best efforts to choke off food supplies rolling into enemy commissaries, a new service economy emerged to fulfill the needs of the British soldier. Advertisements in the *Philadelphia Ledger*, the short-lived Tory newspaper of the time, appealed to the vanity of British soldiers in need of shirts, riding boots or traveling "camp-case[s], containing 33 different articles fit for a gentleman officer." Haberdashers offered to clean and polish epaulettes, silver lace, and gold buttons. Barbers seemed much in demand, not just for a soldier's hair but for his horse's mane. Local printers even sold regional maps of the outlying colonies "especially those which are now, or probably may be, the theatre of war." A local apothecary promoted its abundant supply of "Dr. Keyser's pills" for "rheumatism, asthma, dropsy, apoplexy and venereal disorders." One can only assume that a single medication was meant to cure all of these ills.

Patriot merchants who evacuated their shops on Front or Market Streets prior to the occupation came to regret their early decision. Those very shops were soon leased to Tories looking to make a quick buck off their loyalist comrades.

Yet, because the demand for basic goods like flour, sugar, butter and butchered meats arose exponentially, the valuation of any currency dropped in equal measure. At first, inflation was rampant. When, after the first two months of occupation British trading ships finally sailed up the Delaware, the once fragile colonial economy shifted quickly to more profitable opportunities with steadier supplies. And, yet, the British authorities regulated much of what was consumed. Alcohol, for example, was heavily controlled by fees and restricted by its origins. So, too, were food supplies, particularly flour and barreled meats. Even once abundant firewood was now in dire supply. As such, Philadelphians later returning to an evacuated city would find their former residences emptied of floor boards, furniture, and even the wood lathe that held up the plaster of their walls.[7]

The damage to the city was immense. And residents were only able to seek compensation many years later. Thomas Shields filed a claim for £577.10. In 1771, he had purchased a house and stable on South Second Street, at the corner of Black Horse Alley, in the Chestnut Ward of the city.[8] (After the war, the house number would become 27. Today, the Benjamin Franklin Beer Distributor occupies the same lot.) By comparison, Levi Hollingsworth, a close friend and good customer of Shields's in the Northern section of Dock Ward, sought reparations of £1,665.2.[9] In 1779, they paid taxes assessed at £155 and £200, respectively.[10]

Although the British occupation may have been a bonanza for many Philadelphia merchants, Thomas Shields was not among them. One who might have been categorized a "staunch whig," he left town soon after the invasion. As a devoted husband and father, he would have insisted on his family's safety. His prosperity, too, would have allowed him to shut down his shop. His daybook and accounts show no transactions from October, 1777, to September the next year. One entry suggests he may have gone to Baltimore where his younger brother, Caleb Shields, resided. A revolutionary patriot, Thomas Shields pledged his fidelity to the goals of independence, and yet, never took up arms. Rather, as only more wealthy and privileged citizens could afford, he paid for a military surrogate to serve in his place.

---

[7] Mishoff, "Business in Philadelphia during the British Occupation," pg. 165-81

[8] https://maps.archives.upenn.edu/WestPhila1777/view-parcel.php?pid=7972&popup=1

[9] Cuthbert, "Assessment of Damages Done by the British Troops during the Occupation", 1777-1778," *pg.* 323

[10] http://files.usgwarchives.net/pa/philadelphia/taxlist/dockwardnest1779.txt

The original framed certificate of fidelity by which Thomas Shields paid a mercenary to serve in his place during the Revolution. From a private collection.

At Valley Forge

At first, the camp seemed civilized. Washington's surviving force of 11,000 men were instructed to build log huts in rows, nestled among trees too large to fell, spaced apart for reasons of fire safety, yet aligned as straight as was expedient. As a surveyor and deep woodsman, Leet was instrumental in building out the camp's quarters. By January of 1778, the army had constructed nearly 2,000 huts. Each cabin measured 14' x 16' with a height of just 5' per exterior wall, having a vaulted ceiling just high enough for a taller man to stand upright inside. Covered by cloth, the single entryway, however, was only 4' high. There were no windows.

Each cabin would sleep twelve men, cheek to jowl. Inside were no cots, no hammocks, no benches, and no wood floor. A single stone fireplace opened onto one end of the hut. Otherwise, the only source of heat was that which a human body could generate under a woolen blanket, if such a luxury was to be had. Outdoor fires were for cooking food, boiling water, and sharing conversation. In temperatures that dipped well below freezing, radiant heat could do little to warm one's soul, let alone outstretched palms.

At first, there was fresh meat, hunted from surrounding woods and forests.

At first, there was general health, yet, of injuries sustained, there was lockjaw to fear, spirits to mend, and trauma to forget.

At first, there was rain. And a lot of it. Then came the snow.

Weary, yet stoic, Washington had marched his scraggly forces onto the plateau of Valley Forge on December 19, 1777. The site served logistically for its safe distance from Philadelphia on which the General and his scouts could "keep an eye." Also remote from other outlying villages, the camp would not further exasperate their like-suffering.

Even before arriving at Valley Forge, Daniel Leet was promoted to Regimental Paymaster. Already a Quartermaster, he was responsible for hauling the wagons of Virginia's 13th Regiment in their campaign east. Of the regiment's 175 men mustered to Colonel Muhlenberg's Brigade, only 69 were deemed "fit for duty." Which is to say, unlike the other continental soldiers who survived the Battles of Brandywine and Paoli, they might still have owned a coat or shoes.

The men at Valley Forge had many needs. Perhaps secondary to shoes––one third of Washington's forces had none––winter clothing, blankets, even basic hunting shirts, were of the most dire. Washington learned from his Quartermaster General that upon encampment, there were no such items in reserve.

Washington wrote immediately to the President of the Continental Congress, Arthur Laurens, to state his plight:

Valley Forge Decemb. 23d 1777.

"Sir

Full as I was in my representation of matters in the Commissary's department yesterday, fresh and more powerful reasons oblige me to add, that I am now convinced beyond a doubt, that unless some great and capital change suddenly takes place in that line this Army must inevitably be reduced to one or other of these three things. Starve––dissolve––or disperse, in order to obtain subsistence in the best manner they can, rest assured, Sir, this is not an exaggerated picture, and that I have abundant reason to support what I say.

"Since the month of July we have had no assistance from the Quarter Master General, and to want of assistance from this department, the Commissary General charges great part of his deficiency––to this I am to add, that notwithstanding it is a standing order and often repeated, that the Troops shall always have two days provisions by them, that they might be ready at any sudden call, yet no opportunity has scarcely ever offered of taking advantage of the Enemy, that has not been either totally obstructed, or greatly impeded on this account: and this the great & crying evil is not all. Soap––Vinegar and other articles allowed by Congress we see none of, nor have we seen them, I believe, since the battle of Brandywine. The first indeed we have now little occasion for, few men having more than one shirt—many only the moiety of one, and some none at all.

"I can assure those Gentlemen, that it is a much easier and less distressing thing, to draw Remonstrances in a comfortable room by a good fire side, than to occupy a cold, bleak hill, and sleep under frost & snow without Cloaths or Blankets: However, although they seem to have little feeling for the naked and distressed Soldier, I feel superabundantly for them, and from my soul pity those miseries, which it is neither in my power to releive or prevent."

Geo. Washington

Often an honorary title given to more senior officers, the Quartermaster General was responsible as much for maneuvering large bodies of soldiers with their requisite equipment, as for the acquisition of that equipment. Horses, tents, wagons, blankets, clothing, and shoes were essential items, no less important than the food supplies for which the Commissary General was responsible, or the artillery and muskets, for which an Ordinance General took charge. But at Valley Forge, retreating from the most recent defeat at Germantown and White Marsh, Washington's army had depleted or abandoned most everything. Younger Generals like Anthony Wayne and Nathanael Greene were dispatched to buy up as many cattle, sheep, hogs and poultry as they could find from the perimeters of the occupied city twenty miles away. No doubt, the several regimental quartermasters, including Leet, went to neighboring farmers to scour for necessities and provisions, too. Except that regimental quartermasters were only responsible for the logistics of doling out—or, in harder times, rationing—of goods. Their job was not to acquire them. All of that job fell to the Continental Army's Quartermaster General, Thomas Mifflin.

A son of Philadelphia, and graduate of the College of Philadelphia, Mifflin had developed a significant career in the mercantile trade of Philadelphia with his brother, George. At 32 years of age, having staked his intolerance against British taxation, and having railed upon the madness of the King, none were more spirited—nor apparently more eloquent—than Mifflin. He was said to have been the youngest and most radical member of the First

Continental Congress. In May 1775, he was made a Major; in June, he served as General Washington's first aide-de-camp, and, by August, became the first Quartermaster General of the Continental Army. Unfortunately, he hated the job. Twice before Valley Forge, he had actively sought to be released from his Quartermaster title, and twice he had been relinquished of the same.[11] But with no one else to turn to, congress persuaded Mifflin to carry on wearing the same old hat. He was not amused. Nor were his troops.

Thus, it was, under Mifflin's indifference, that Daniel Leet was in charge of supplies for his particular regiment. Newly arrived, he was responsible for its accounts now, too. The role of the paymaster was to manage the books of all supplies and provisions allotted to his regiment and thus expended.

Almost immediately after arriving in Valley Forge, knowledgeable of Mifflin's appalling disregard, Washington published announcements in Lancaster and other sympathetic communities ordering every farming resident to thresh half of their grain for immediate delivery to Valley Forge. Those grains would not come until February.

In his defense, Mifflin's hands had been tied. Favored Philadelphia merchants had closed shop. Many merchants of the city either abandoned their stores to ply their trades in safer communities west of the city, or they closed altogether. And even if they had stayed to serve the "foreign visitors," there was little chance that wagons would be allowed to leave the guarded confines of the British occupation.

Fortunately, there were better men than Mifflin willing and able to help. When one Col. Ephraim Blaine, owner of some of the largest mills in Pennsylvania (and an investor in several closer to Valley Forge,) was promoted to General of the Commissary, his personal wealth and influence delivered the average of five thousand barrels of flour, twenty-five hogshead of rum and 65,000 pounds of beef each month.[12] Much of that flour, in fact, was provided through a competitive network of local millers and regional merchants. In fact, Thomas Shields's client and friend, Levi Hollingsworth, had developed the network. Albeit designed for price protections, the system, however, served no purpose in times like these. Just one of many millers who

---

[11] US Army Quartermaster Foundation,
   https://achive.is/20120907233402/http://www.qmfound.com/MG_Thomas_Mifflin.htm
[12] Blaine, *The Blaine Family*, pg. 28

subscribed to Hollingsworth's network, Ephraim Blaine stepped forward to save the day.

Yet, even if flour became available, bread was not. Soldiers survived mainly on eating fire cakes; just flour and water—no salt, no leavening, no oils or fat—slapped against a burning log, charred black, and eaten as soon as the tongue would dare.

Not until March did new coats or shoes arrive.

In just six months of encampment, as many as 2,500 men died from disease, much of it brought on by hunger and poor nutrition. More than 700 horses expired, too.

Typhus, dysentery and smallpox managed to worm their ways through cabins crowded with louse-infested soldiers. By March, the conditions within the huts had become so toxic that Washington instructed the men to cut out two windows in each hut to provide a draft of fresh, albeit, freezing air.

But if Valley Forge offered any salvation for the Continental Army, it came by way of discipline and training. The former is credited to General Washington himself who, although quartered in a remote stone house with his attending officers, insisted on being among his men, and sharing with them the hardships of military service and debilitating cold. The latter came by way of one Baron Frederich Wilhelm Augustus Von Steuben. His efforts would not be evidenced until the Battle of Monmouth in July of 1778, but Von Steuben very effectively instilled decorum and order to an army that had known no better.

Further, in commendation of the colonial force's success at the Battles of Saratoga the previous fall—and in support of rebuilding its strength at Valley Forge—the French decided to back the Revolutionaries in common defiance with Britain's other foreign enemies. By the Spring of 1778, not only were Washington's men refreshed for battle, but so were their chances of triumph.

Washington and his men marched out of Valley Forge exactly six months to the day on June 19, 1778.

Daniel Leet actually left a month earlier. In May, he and Virginia's 13th Regiment had been directed to return to Fort Pitt. From there, they would construct a new fort far west in the Tuscarawas, deep in Indian country, on land of which Leet was almost solely familiar.

A Treaty at Fort Pitt

Arriving back at Fort Pitt, Daniel Leet rejoined William Crawford who, despite his absence at Valley Forge, was still very much in charge of Virginia's 13th.. Crawford was full of local stories of Indian raids, murders and unforgivable injustices.

Just two months earlier, Alexander Negley discovered that the Indians were actively pillaging his neighbors' cabins in Westmoreland County. A late snow had fallen. To make a quick escape, Negley hitched a horse to a sled on which he bundled his wife and four of his five children. Bidding them due haste to the protection of Fort Ligonier, he stayed behind to scout for the Indians, hoping to ambush them with gunfire before they got sight of the sled tracks in the snow. Sure enough, the Indians followed, two on foot and one mounted. Negley prepared himself, taking aim, waiting to shoot only when the savages were close enough. By perverse fortune, Negley's first shot killed the Indian's horse, leaving his three pursuers on foot which would give him all good hope to get his wife and kids inside the fort safely. Except that his rifle shot had scared his own horse carrying the sleigh, breaking one of its runners which, in Negley's lagging behind, Mrs. Negley had had to repair herself. Just as Alexander was certain his family had made it safely inside the fort, he discovered them only approaching the gates. And now he had to fire to delay his pursuers once more. The story goes he at least wounded one of the Indians.

Mrs. Negley, so frightened by the ordeal, refused to move back to the family homestead in the wilds. While temporarily residing at Fort Pitt, Alexander Negley purchased 300 acres along the Allegheny River. (This land would become the neighborhood of Highland Park.)

Crawford told Leet other tales. Just weeks earlier, Captain Samuel Miller, an officer of Pennsylvania's 8th Regiment, was sent with nine other men to transport grains from the Greensburg area to stockpiles closer to Fort Pitt. Ambushed by a small, but well-armed band of Indians, he and seven of his men were killed, scalped and stripped naked right in the middle of the road on which they were traveling. The two men who had escaped were sent back to bury the remains on the very same spot.

And now, Crawford was informed that the Indians wished to make peace. Word came from Chief White Eyes that the Delawares of the Tuscarawas and Muskingum regions, and specifically the three most revered leaders of the tribe—Killbuck, Captain Pipe, and Wingenund—were assembling a peace party to meet at Fort Pitt to reforge their chains of brotherly affections. A date was set for July 23. But Crawford's superior, General Lachlan McIntosh, a Georgian newly appointed by Washington to construct new western defenses, had not yet committed to his command at Fort Pitt. So the treaty date was reset for September.

Nicholas Cresswell waited in Pittsburgh to witness this very same treaty.

Curiously, no one had informed Congress. On July 25, 1778, Congress resolved "That Brigadier General McIntosh be directed to assemble at Fort Pitt as many continental troops and militia as will amount to fifteen hundred, and proceed, without delay, to destroy such towns of the hostile Indians as he in his discretion shall think will most effectually tend to chastise and terrify the savages, and to check their ravages on the frontiers of these states."[13]

By September 10, McIntosh and Brodhead had arrived and, despite any congressional intervention, the meeting with the Delawares began two days later. Colonel Crawford and his Adjutant, Daniel Leet, attended the meeting. It ended on the 17th of September, 1778, with a signed document.[14]

McIntosh's intention going into the pow-wow was that he would negotiate a clear and protected path to Detroit where, upon erecting certain forts, he could rid the British of their reliance on the Wyandots of that region. The Delaware council gave no resistance, nor does it seem they asked for much in the way of arms, blankets or other essential goods. In fact, the Delawares, hoping to rekindle "warm fires of friendship," pledged corn, meat

---

[13] Thompson, *Broadside from the Continental Congress, July 25th, 1778*, Library of Congress

[14] Sipe, *History of Fort Ligonier and its Times*, p.446

and a party of sixty warriors (including Killbuck) to assist McIntosh's expedition. In kind, McIntosh promised to build a fort for the protection of those elderly Natives who would be deserving of the "comforts" of such a crude and stationary edifice (one of course he was charged to build anyway.) Further, the two parties agreed to measures of fair trade and blind justice, that either party would serve in the defense of the other, "as brothers do."

But there was one other issue that the Delawares hoped to promote. It had been Chief White Eye's idea all along and, no doubt, the notion that had inspired his effort to seek a treaty in the first place. White Eyes had envisioned that the Delaware Nation—distinct as it was from the Shawnees and any tribe of the Six Nations—should become the 14th State of the American Union. McIntosh agreed. But he added a caveat. And it applied to all other provisions of the treaty, too. The parties each jointly and separately agreed the treaty would be ratified "provided nothing contained in this article be considered as conclusive until it meets the approbation of congress."

The treaty, of course, was never presented to congress and, in fact, relations between Killbuck and his appointed counterpart, Colonel George Morgan (who was not even present for the signing) quickly crumbled. It seems there had never been any intention to entertain a new treaty or to work toward some lasting peace.

It may have been for this reason that McIntosh delayed his long march on Detroit. It might also have been due to his vanity. Almost immediately he set forth to build Fort McIntosh.

Fort McIntosh

Set curiously—and laboriously—high on a bluff overlooking the mouth of Big Beaver Creek on the Ohio, the fort would serve as a defense for... well, it could only then be reasoned—Fort Pitt. Defensively, the new fort's location just thirty miles west on the Ohio would only stop enemy forces if they were to paddle up the great river. The British were never likely to do that—not even in the swiftest of canoes. If the new fort was situated for the purposes of giving quick shelter to surrounding pioneers, it would have only served those pioneers settled nearby. Few had. The fact is, most every pioneer village had not one but several outlying stockades to run to if and when attacked. Surely, the presence of 150 armed soldiers garrisoned nearby might make a marauding pack of Indians think twice about venturing so close to Ohio River settlements, but Natives—whether on foot, horse, or by canoe—never raided settlers in such large numbers as that for which a military chain-of-command would be needed.

Colonel Brodhead had thought it silly that this newly appointed General of the Western Division should not only build a fort so close to Fort Pitt, but, indeed, to have named it for himself. (Actually a French engineer, Lt. Col. Louis Jean Baptiste Cambray-Digny, had named it in his honor. Needless to add, McIntosh did not refuse.)

Lieutenant William Crawford was given the task of building the new fort. Originally, it was built as a stockade, fifty yards square with four bastions at each corner. The fort sat 130 feet above the Ohio River on jagged rock with difficult access to the water below. Originally, it was armed with two cannons, one in each of the river-facing bastions. Later there would be as many as six pieces of artillery.[15] None were ever fired in battle.

It was McIntosh's idea from the outset that Fort Pitt should give up its men to garrison in the new fort. No doubt, after nearly twenty years of use, the conditions at the old fort were poor, grimy and decrepit. But strategically, there was very little purpose in positioning troops thirty miles from the established settlement of Pittsburgh where commerce and community abounded. Ill-positioned and hardly practical in defending settlements far west, Fort McIntosh was, at best, an idea that looked good on paper, if not particularly on a map.

Nevertheless, Daniel Leet, appointed Adjutant by his mentor, employer and ranking officer, Lieutenant Crawford, ran out the lines and laid down the timber that became Fort McIntosh. Little did he know then that he would return several years later to make it into a "modern" American city.

But first, Leet would move on to build another fort by year's end.

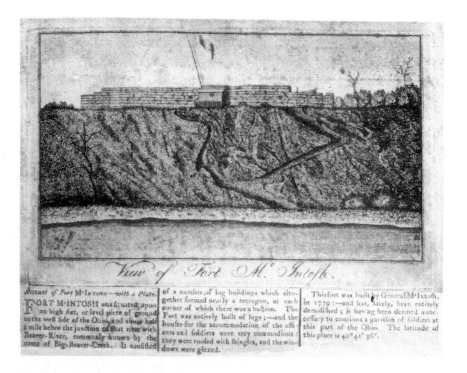

View of Fort Mc Intosh.

Account of Fort McIntosh—with a Plate.

FORT McINTOSH was situated upon an high flat, or level piece of ground on the west side of the Ohio, and about half a mile below the junction of that river with Beaver-River, commonly known by the name of Big-Beaver-Creek. It consisted of a number of log buildings which altogether formed nearly a tetragon, at each corner of which there was a bastion. The Fort was entirely built of logs;—and the houses for the accommodation of the officers and soldiers were very commodious; they were roofed with shingles, and the windows were glazed. This fort was built by General McIntosh, in 1779:—and has, lately, been entirely demolished; it having been deemed unnecessary to continue a garrison of soldiers at this part of the Ohio. The latitude of this place is 40°41′36″.

---

15 http://www.fortwiki.com/Fort_McIntosh_(3)

Fort Laurens

By October of 1778, General Lachlan McIntosh and his brigade of 1,300 men marched northwest from Beaver toward Detroit. They did not get far. With sufficient cattle to sustain his forces for the impending expedition, salt needed to butcher the meat still had not arrived. But winter approached. So they drove the livestock through dense woodlands. As such, their first seventy-five miles took more than two weeks. The further they marched, however, the longer they would have to wait for the salt to find them. Several days later, they stopped at the Tuscarawas River.

There were three compelling reasons to construct Fort Laurens in the Ohio country. The first was to defend the colonies' western pioneers from the British and Wyandot alliances gathered at Detroit. The second reason was to establish alliances of their own, particularly with the Delawares that had settled along the Tuscarawas. The third reason was to mitigate any eastward advance to Fort Pitt or into Pennsylvania.

The deployment to the Ohio country was approved by Congress, but it really came at the discretion of McIntosh, promoted by Washington to command the Western Division. McIntosh was a Georgian, having arrived there from Scotland when he was eight years old. As a teen, his father was captured and imprisoned by the Spanish. An orphan, young McIntosh was enlisted as a regimental recruit at Fort Frederica on St. Simon's Island, and from there mustered out to find a career in Charleston, South Carolina.

Before marrying in 1756, he landed a job in the employment of one Henry Laurens, a merchant of Charleston and a gentleman of some political clout. The two would partner in many endeavors, the most lucrative of which were rice fields in Georgia.

Laurens owned and sailed more than five ships, trading in indigo, rum, rice, and slaves. Through several successive partnerships, he amassed a significant fortune and acquired as many as six different plantations in both Georgia and South Carolina. When his first wife, who had given him thirteen children, died in 1770, Laurens sailed with his eldest sons to enroll them in schools in Switzerland. And while in Europe he was asked to submit the colony's grievances to King George. He returned to Charleston in 1774 and was elected to represent South Carolina in the Continental Congress the next year. In 1777, he became the second President of the Continental Congress following John Hancock.

By early November, Daniel Leet and his crew had barely begun construction on Fort Laurens. It stood on level land. However, some hundred yards distant, and in clear view, was a Great Indian Mound. The site had actually served an earlier stockade defense of Colonel Bouquet's advances during Pontiac's Rebellion. Like Fort McIntosh, it was a square stockade with four corner bastions. Yet it also featured a long stockaded entry way and a perimeter of trenches. Several log huts served as the regiment's garrison, while others stored munitions and winter provisions. The fort was completed in just under two months. (Ironically, seventeen days after construction had begun, Henry Laurens resigned as President of the Continental Congress.)

And so, Fort Laurens came to be the only American fort built in the Ohio country. It would not stand for more than a year.

From the outset, McIntosh's decision to build the fort was both rushed and rash. Undermanned, ill-equipped and still awaiting the damn salt with which to march his meat-hungry men to battle, he decided not to advance any closer to Detroit. (Fort Laurens stood near Bolivar, Ohio, just five miles south of present-day Canton, still a good two hundred miles from Detroit.) The stockade defense would hardly serve as an expedient retreat if they were to advance just another twenty miles westward. Rather, McIntosh, a southern boy, blamed the November cold; they would move on to Detroit early the following spring.

At the least, Fort Laurens would check one of his boxes. It would serve in some proximity to the Christian Delawares living in Schönbrunn (New Philadelphia, Ohio) just ten miles south, as well as Gnadenhütten, another five miles down the Tuscarawas. These were the Natives McIntosh ignorantly believed would be instrumental in supporting his efforts to defeat the

British. Except that, as Christian Indians, they had no interest in war; in fact, by oath to their Moravian leaders, they had denounced any such violence.

Of what benefit these pacifist Natives could have been to a militia bent on attacking Wyandots further north one can only ponder. If McIntosh could not have understood their indifference, Daniel Leet surely did. He had passed through Bethlehem on more than a few occasions and had witnessed the kindness and brotherhood of a true Moravian community.

In fact, Fort Lauren's proximity to the Moravian villages may have been its undoing. News spread quickly that the Americans had constructed a "defense" very nearby. The Shawnees took notice, the Senecas took umbrage, and the Muncees and Mingos took up arms. Perhaps, more significantly, the Wyandots and their British allies soon saw the beginning advance of the July Resolution of Congress.

But McIntosh took no alarm. Facing an impossibly cold and long winter, he placed Colonel John Gibson in charge and returned to his eponymous fort back in Beaver, leaving a scant 150 men—and much fewer cattle—to hunker down in their new little fort.

Lucky for those who, like Leet, departed, too, the Wyandots laid siege outside Fort Laurens. And so did belligerent Delawares, now scorned by the inertia of the treaty they had just signed. Along came Simon Girty, too, the infamous white trader who had turned-coat on his American brothers. Too many failed treaties, too many heinous acts of cowardice and dishonest trades with the Indians (on whose good relations he depended,) allied him in defense of the British at Fort Detroit. He and more than one hundred Natives surrounded Fort Laurens in the deep freeze of January.

Inside, Colonel Gibson's militia could do little.

First, their paltry store of meat spoiled, then their flour went bad; within the month, they were starving. The men nearly mutinied Gibson whose efforts to draw reinforcements from Fort Pitt fell on deaf and frostbitten ears. By March, they resorted to boiling their moccasins for whatever nutrients the leather might offer.

Although by all accounts Gibson's men were well armed, they had little confidence in their chances. The sad truth is Gibson had miscounted the enemy forces outside. He thought his men were outnumbered two-to-one, when in fact there might not have been as many as one hundred all told.

Simon Girty was a wily fox and liked to play games of deception. To make his numbers seem larger than even plausible, Girty and his men devised a scheme to drill regularly, parading in a circle around the nearby ancient Indian mound. They fooled the American militia into thinking their numbers were twice as great as they were. The trick was done by seemingly marching "in single time" circling the front of the mound, but, when disappearing behind it, running in triple time to reappear quickly on the other side in single step again. In effect, the number of enemy that might be marching behind the mound, (presumably as many as those visibly marching in front) didn't really exist.

But the late winter of 1779 played no favorites. By the first thaw of April, Simon Girty and his allied braves were also starving. Low on ammunition, with what few of their horses were healthy or useful, they negotiated to relinquish their siege in exchange for a safe retreat.

Also, by March of that unproductive year, General Lachlan McIntosh begged his commander in chief to accept his resignation for a miserably failed commission. Washington did so immediately.

Colonel Daniel Brodhead once again took Western command, deployed the militia at Fort McIntosh to return to Fort Pitt, and never spoke another word about Fort Laurens. By the Fall of 1779, the fort was emptied and left to rot.

In recent years the Friends of Fort Laurens, a nonprofit organization devoted to interpreting the history of Ohio's only Revolutionary fort, has held a fundraiser. It is a grand barbecue of freshly-butchered meats, presumably seasoned with all the salt one should like. The event is famously billed as the annual "Moccasin Roast."

Washington County

Patriotic pride is made of stories from Lexington and Concord, from the Delaware River on a freezing Christmas Day, from the long-suffering camps at Valley Forge, from the Battle of Brandywine and the capture of Cornwallis. By the Fall of 1781, Washington would lay siege at Yorktown. Yet, he was not convinced the revolution was won. Worrisome battalions of Brits still fought for control of the Carolinas and they still occupied much of New York. Only by the Treaty of Paris did the conflict with Britain come to closure. The war for the west, however, would last one hundred years more.

McIntosh's squandered mission into the Ohio country did nothing to quell Native ire over ever-populating settlements. Constant were the raids and ransackings; both sides exacting revenge, regularly. Incursions of Shawnees and Delawares on unsuspecting homesteaders were reviled for their savagery, while vengeful posses of pioneers returned the outrages with horrific, unpardonable results.

Returning first to Fort McIntosh and then garrisoned at Fort Pitt, Daniel Leet was now a Brigade Major, serving in the capacity of whatever militia was then assembled for whichever mission his commander, Colonel William Crawford, deemed compelling. Leet would serve in this capacity until the end of the war. Pension records, however, show he retired as an officer of the Continental Army in 1778. It is plausible, however, that for his services in laying out the two forts he had built, he was paid as a surveyor of Virginia, rather than as a soldier of its 13th Regiment. The timing makes sense and the compensation would certainly have been better. Thus, a free agent, he made new plans.

Along Chartiers Creek, just up from Catfish Camp, Daniel Leet settled his parents in a log cabin on land he claimed without much authority and for which—or, perhaps, because of which—he named, "Leet's Fancy." The cabin was modest by even pioneer standards: few windows, one door, and a single, short chimney. Photographs exist of Leet's Fancy, captured for a state survey of historic places. Remarkably, the cabin remained standing, just as Daniel and his father had first built it, until 1900.

Long known in the region as Crawford's deputy, Leet was a "regular" in the area, some say, as early as 1773. Likely, his family were residents, too. The earliest records prove that brother William was an unmarried resident in 1781, and that Daniel, his brother Isaac, Jr. and father, Isaac, were exonerated from a 1783 assessment—"by reason of the repeated incursions and depredations of the savage Enemy"—for sufficient taxes already paid. The same list of exhonorees suggests that Jonathan, the youngest brother, may have lived with Daniel.[16]

A year before his return from Fort Laurens, Augusta Town—renamed from the original Catfish Camp (or variably West Augusta Town)—became the civic hub of Youghogania County. Monongalia, Westmoreland, and Ohio Counties had been created, too. Of course, territories further west were still called the Ohio country, yet it was territory long since claimed by and for Virginia. As early as 1779, Pennsylvania had recognized Bedford County as its own. Residents of Westmoreland County identified themselves as Pennsylvanians, too. Those living in Youghogania, however, were most decidedly Virginians.

In July of 1779, commissioners from both Virginia and Pennsylvania slogged through the picayune issues that would allow the Mason-Dixon line to extend west on its same latitude until reaching the Commonwealth's current western boundary, separating it from, really, the Ohio country, but all of that which Virginia still claimed. The problem with what became known as the Baltimore Agreement of 1779 was that land hitherto warranted and patented under Virginia law would now be subject to—and perhaps re-surveyed under—Pennsylvania law. This likelihood did not sit well with current landowners, especially those whose tracts might have straddled both states. The acrimony between Virginians and Pennsylvanians only got worse.

---

[16] Pennsylvania, U.S., Tax and Exoneration Records, Strabane Township, 1768-1801

As a result, in November of 1780, President Reed of the Pennsylvania Assembly, promising to bring the issue to some resolution, addressed the following to his electors:

"The final settlement of the contested boundaries of this State and Virginia induces us to lay before you the propriety and policy of setting off one or more counties so as to introduce law, order, and good government, where they have been long and much wanted. We think it would also conduce much to the defense of the frontiers and safety of the interior country, as the strength of those parts might then be organized & systematically drawn forth in case of necessity."

The Baltimore Agreement did necessitate new and more local government. In that context, Westmoreland County was subdivided, giving the residents of Augusta Town a new county for which it would need to nominate local citizens to serve in both judicial and military capacities.

On March 28, 1781, "all that part of the State of Pennsylvania west of the Monongahela river, and south of the Ohio [river] ... to the line run by Mason and Dixon [and a longitudinal line 5 degrees west of the Delaware River]" would be known as Washington County.

Although the Commander in Chief had not as yet cornered Cornwallis, and the Brits still occupied the Bronx, Washington "had firmly fixed himself in the hearts of the American people, soon to give them the avails of victory."[17] Win or lose, in 1781, two years before the eastern Revolutionary conflicts would end, Washington was decidedly a hero.

And now, Washington was a county, too.

On that same day, Daniel Leet was commissioned to survey and purchase land for a courthouse. A week later, County Lieutenant James Marshel appointed him to serve as one of two Sub-Lieutenants. By August, Daniel Leet also served as a Justice of the Peace of the Court of Common Pleas.[18] He was then 33.

---

[17] *Ibid.*, pg. 223
[18] Creigh, *History of Washington County*, pg. 58

Speculation

Back in Philadelphia, merchants everywhere looked to improve markets in times of uncertainty, fear and frustration. As had been the norm, the rarity of species and credit only superseded demand. Yet some tradesmen, otherwise reluctant to invest in low-margin inventory or ineffective marketing, looked to other creative income streams. Artisans like Thomas Shields and wholesalers like Levi Hollingsworth had the means and the curiosity to invest in other ventures. And now, since the war had ended, many believed there could be nothing more patriotic than owning a part of their hard-fought country, leveraging the value of its deep woods or propelling the dreams of pioneers seeking subsistence in new and more promising days.

Shields and Hollingsworth, in fact, teamed up to purchase western lands, partnering in their shared optimism for Pennsylvania and its people.

Land speculation became a romantic notion in large part, because there was no competitive system governing its opportunities. Each state eagerly offered its best assets in simple trade for cash or securities. And, yet, each state went about their business differently. Few states had any centralized process whereby speculators had to wait their turn, had to prove their wealth or had to submit plans beneficial to the state's intentions.[19] Speculators could win big, not just because they priced the market right or marketed their offerings well, or because they purchased land strategically to meet the interests of one buyer as opposed to another, but because—and only because—fortune shone upon them. It was all just a game of chance played with very few rules.

---

[19] Doerflinger, *A Vigorous Spirit of Enterprise*, pg. 314

Dorsey Pentecost

As one of the first officers of the new county, Leet would take on responsibilities few pioneers had ever assumed. One such task was laying out a town to serve as the county seat, one in which the new courthouse would serve as its civic center. In fact, David Hoge, the original patentee of the highest elevated property near Catfish Camp, took on the actual drawing of the plan. Laid out in 1781 were more than 270 lots, comprising some sixteen "city" blocks. Monongahela Street ran at their center north and south; Ohio Street ran east and west. Both major thoroughfares were staked to a 66-foot breadth. The courthouse, when built, would sit on Lot A at their intersection. Notes on the original plan, archived at the Washington County Historical Society, seem to suggest that the town was intended to be known as Basset, an apparent predilection of Hoge. Just when that name was scrapped is not known. Clearly those in charge of laying out the town wished to hitch their wagon to the President and not a hound.

Lest it seem that Leet was a lone, rising star at the birth of the new jurisdiction, there were many who took similar offices. Of note, John Canon served as the other Sub-Lieutenant of Washington County. He had come to own land in the region as early as 1774, had served as a justice for Youghogania County that then governed his property, and by dint of his Virginia affiliations, had also acquired more than 1,200 acres in the region. He was said to have owned all of Abington, Mt. Airy, and Canon Hill. The first two properties make up the city of Canonsburg today.

Thomas Scott was appointed Prothonotary to the new county, having served as a Justice in Westmoreland County and therefore loyal to Pennsylvania's interests. As such, he was later elected to represent the county at the state convention that would ratify the country's new constitution, and so became the first Representative of Washington County in the U.S. Congress. He would serve three terms.

William Crawford had for some months already served as a Justice for Bedford County. When Westmoreland was recognized as a county early in 1773, he served on its court. With the formation of the three counties of Monongalia, Youghogania, and Ohio, Crawford was made a Justice of Youghogania, too. His successive duties parallel those of Canon and Scott, all of whom were evidently well respected.

And then there was Dorsey Pentecost. A surveyor by profession, he had come to the region to map, among other tracts, the 150,000 or so acres George Croghan first claimed along Chartiers Creek. Apparently, Pentecost had moved onto property in Westmoreland County not long after, acquired other tracts in the area, and then moved onto lands in Youghogania, homesteading thousands of acres he was likely given by Croghan as compensation for his earlier services. This, of course, was common practice. But Croghan, as Pentecost also likely knew, did not have clear title to the lands he gave Pentecost. When Pennsylvania President Reed signed the Baltimore Agreement, Pentecost wisely feared his properties would be subject to scrutiny, and, at the very least, would need to be re-surveyed for Pennsylvania. A hardline Virginian, he was not happy.

He let President Reed know where he stood in several letters addressed in the Spring of 1781. Pentecost argued that since the Mason-Dixon line had not yet been "run out," (even though there was no misunderstanding of the latitude at which it would be,) there could be no assertion of Pennsylvania's authority on assembling new counties, new courts, or even new militia. (As such, of course, there could be no arm of the law.) Apparently, Pentecost approached John Canon, a loyal Virginian himself, and argued the same point. Canon may have expressed some sympathies, but he also added fuel to Pentecost's ire.

Indicative of the early politics of Washington County, James Marshel wrote about his frustrations to President Reed.

> "Sir— Since my arrival in this County, I have been making what progress I Can in organizing a Militia, altho as yet, Deprived of the Assistance of the Sub-Lieutenants by the Indefatigable Opposition

of a Certain Mr. Penticost and a few of his adherents,... they have resolved to go on with the jurisdiction of Virginia, both Civil and Military until the line is Actually run. Whereupon the said Penticost swore into an Old Commission of County Lieutenant that he pretended to have by him for a long time, and thereupon assumed the Command of the Militia. Mr. Canon (a Civil Officer under the government of Virginia,) one of our Sub-Lieutenants, publickly declares that government have Infringed upon the Rights of the people in appointing officers for them before they were represented, and instead of assisting me in Organizing the Militia, is using all his Influence to prevent it. Mr. Lite [Leet] the other Sub-Lieutenant refuses doing anything until the artists [surveyors] arrive on the spot, which leaves me without assistance, and must Consequently delay the formation of the Militia. ...For altho the people at large are well affected to this government, the junto aforesaid are Indefatigable, and a failure on the part of the artists would afford them great Opportunity of doeing Mischief; in a word Mr. Penticost and Mr. Cannon are ringleaders of Sedition, and are doeing everything in their power to revive the jurisdiction of Virginia,.. Two or three words of an Order from your Excellency would put the affairs of this Country into a better situation, and at the same time oblige a whole County."

Marshel whined on further.

"The Indians have not done any damage on the frontiers of this County for some time past, altho they never had a better Opportunity, ...let me hope then, that as soon as there may be a Necessity, you will Enable us to Call out a number of our Militia for the defense of the Frontiers, and that we may be supplied with ammunition as soon as possible.

"I have the Honor to be with Very great Respect and Esteem your Excellency's Most Obedient and very Humble servant."[20]

The singular issue Marshel hoped to resolve was the establishment of a capable militia. The fact is, Dorsey Pentecost had been appointed Captain

---

of the Youghougania Militia some years before (although it is uncertain how long or how actively he served in that capacity.) He had also been appointed the official Clerk of Courts of that county in 1777. But it seems he was absent for several critical sessions, and a Mr. James Innis served as his surrogate. When Mr. Innis failed to preside at court, a Mr. Isaac Cox entered into bond and took his seat. And minutes before Cox was to be sworn into the Clerkship, Pentecost surprised his fellow Justices by appearing before them to beg forgiveness. Witnessed William Crawford, then one of the Justices: "He, the said Pentecost, Convinced this Court that it was out of his power to attend, he being at that Time confined in the Small Pox..." Pentecost was excused, and Cox, forced to resign his bond, stood aside.

In the parlance of the time, Dorsey Pentecost seemed to be "a regular rascal." He would prove this soon enough again.

Natives and Militia

There was never just one incident that called out the militia. As often as a settler or his family might have been killed or kidnapped, news of another incident might have come to town. Fear caused everyday worry about what atrocity the savages might commit next, especially if no militia went out to avenge them, (which, if done, would surely precipitate revenge.) The stories of bloodshed never ceased, the tales of savagery grew more horrid, and the outrage of senseless murders got louder and louder.

In new Washington County, the promise of a new militia seemed remote. Those able, armed and willing to fight feared more what might befall their families at home. If all the men were to mount their horses in an expedition of war, none could stay behind to protect his wife and children. A typical settler might own but one horse and a gun, maybe two. Separating these necessities from the family homestead was an invitation for disaster. Further, there was little reward for exacting justice. God-fearing Presbyterians, Baptists, and Methodists knew that murder and revenge were immoral. Compensation by means of bounty or duty-pay just compounded the sin. Yet there was no alternative. Kill or get killed. Scalp or get scalped. Stand up or get slaughtered.

The unspoken truth was that even the three hundred men attached to Colonel Brodhead at Fort Pitt were starving.[21] Staples like salt, blankets, and munitions were not sent for dire need by Continental soldiers back east. Local foods were unstable, subject to the season, and edible only if mills were operating well in the spring, or if the rivers had not bottomed out in the

---

[21] Sipe, *Fort Ligonier and Its Times*, pgs. 499 and 507

droughts of summer. Woodland rangers and the settlers they protected may have been better off; nomadic foragers, hunting in closer forests, they had venison and turkeys aplenty from which to subsist.

At the mouth of Reardon Run on Raccoon Creek, five men and six children of the Whittaker, Turner, and Foulkes families went out to tap sugar trees on March 12, 1780. They were ambushed by Wyandots. The men were all killed and scalped. The children—George Foulkes, 11, Elizabeth Foulkes, 9, Samuel Whittaker, 11, and Betsy, Polly and William Turner (ages unknown)—were captured and taken to a British post near Detroit. William did not survive the journey. Betsy and Polly were ransomed. The fate of the other children is not known.[22]

In her husband's absence, a mother and baby homesteading near Jefferysville in Youghogania County were captured by Delaware. Rushed from their cabin, the baby cried. Fearing the father might track the kidnappers by his child's screams, they killed the baby. The mother refused to leave it behind. She carried her dead child in her apron.

A father and his children at Redstone on the Monongahela ventured from their cabin down a long dirt path to tend to their cattle. The youngest boy of four children was meant to stay behind with his mother, but followed anyhow. When tattled on by the older children, the father, some distance ahead, turned to find the boy had vanished. Weeks of searching uncovered no trace, until months later a passing Indian trader told the father he had seen a young white boy at an Indian village he recently visited. No such boy could be found, but some fifteen years later, a young, white Brave visited his mother, only to tell her he had met a young squaw he intended to marry. He was never seen again.[23]

Her husband John in town, Martha VanMetre, her daughters Mary and Hanna, and three younger boys, Isaac, 12, Abraham, 10, and Johnny, 6, did their daily chores along Stott's Run, a tributary of Buffalo Creek. While washing clothes near their cabin, Mary and Hanna were attacked by Wyandots brandishing tomahawks. They were both scalped. Mary died instantly, but Hanna, left for dead, crawled behind a fallen log. The six Indians then approached the cabin, opened the door and shot Martha while rushing for her sons at the threshold. The two oldest boys jumped through the opposing

---

[22] *Ibid.,* pg. 500
[23] Draper MSS, 8NN59

cabin window and fled for their lives. The youngest boy, Johnny, too small to reach the window, was captured and carried away. Hanna, later discovered by neighbors, was able only to tell her tale, before dying in her father's arms.[24]

Such were all-too-typical the stories that settlers suffered and shared, fomenting unfathomable fear and outrage. But also typical to the white man's history of these times was the unsettling silence and abject horror of like-stories relating righteous revenge. Missing from the pages of these early days were the devious exploits of the white man's wrath. Seemingly only those events of military might have made it into the books of men whose bravery belied absolute bigotry.

---

[24] Eckert, *That Dark and Bloody River*, pg. 253

The Art of Scalping

Silent, too, are the origins of scalping. Hammurabi's Code of ancient times laid down the law Jesus later reviled. "An eye for an eye; a tooth for a tooth" spoke to a sense of justice that all men could understand. Popular, too, was the belief that the 12th century Crusades were waged with such brutality that claiming severed body parts became trophy for religious sport. But, while "a head for a head" might have served some logical explanation, the facts are incontrovertible; the Native American practice of scalping, first witnessed by French explorers, was a curious ritual they had never heard or seen before.

Jacques Cartier, having sailed up and down the St. Lawrence in 1535 (his second mission,) noted seeing five scalps of red skin and hair "stretched on hoops like parchment." The victims were tribal foes of the Stadaconans whose village Cartier visited on his river voyage to Hochelaga (now Montreal.)[25]

In 1564, on the St. Johns River in Florida, another French explorer, Jacques LeMoyne, witnessed the Timucuan tribe:

> "In their skirmishes, any who fall are instantly dragged off by persons detailed for the purpose; who, with slips of reeds sharper than any steel blade, cut the skin of the head to the bone, from front to back, all the way round, and pull it off with the hair, more than a foot and a half long, still adhering, done up in a knot on the crown... Then, if they have time, they dig a hole in the ground, and make

---

[25] Axtell, *American Heritage Magazine*, Vol. 28, Is. 3

a fire ... and then dry these scalps to a state as hard as parchment."[26]

Linguists studying the various Iroquois cultures of the Mohawks, Oneidas, Onondagas, Algonquins and Delawares noted that each tribe had words
unique to their own tongue describing the practice of scalping. If the ritual
was born from European origins, it would stand to reason that a more common expression would have been adopted. Conversely, linguists note that
the English word "scalp" was then only an active verb: to scoop, to scrape,
and to carve. The noun "scalp," meaning the skin on one's head, did not
come into common use in Europe until after American colonists spoke of
the Indian atrocities.[27]

Further to note, archeologists who have studied the human remains
found in hundreds of Aden and Hopewellian earthworks—the mysterious
Great Indian Mounds of America—documented evidence of linear circum-
ferential cuts on skulls.[28] The ritual of scalping could well predate the earliest European crusades by 1,200 years.

In his "Military Journal during the American Revolutionary War: 1775-
1783," Dr. James Thacher described a treatment he learned to restore the
scalp of a one Captain Gregg who had been ambushed by tomahawk-wield-
ing "savages" while stationed at Fort Stanwix on the Mohawk River in 1777.
The procedure he described is barbaric and repulsive, but no less so is the
explanation he offers his colleagues of how one is scalped.

"With a knife they make a circular cut from the forehead, quite round,
just above the ears, then taking hold of the skin with their teeth, they tear
off the whole hairy scalp in an instant, with wonderful dexterity. This they
carefully dry and preserve as a trophy, showing the number of their victims,
and they have a method of painting on the dried scalp, different figures, and
colors, to designate the sex and age of the victim, and also the manner and
circumstances of the murder."

Because of the practice of painting a scalp—most often, it would seem,
red—colonialists who saw these scalps hanging in native villages called them
"red skins." It was from this term that the derogatory moniker came.

---

[26] LeMoyne de Morgues, *Narrative of Le Moyne: An Artist who Accompanied the French Expedition*, pg. 49

[27] Axtell, *American Heritage Magazine*, Vol. 28, Is. 3

[28] *Ibid.*

But to suggest that native tribes alone scalped their victims is false. During the earliest conflicts between the Europeans and Natives, the white man, too, scalped his rival. "An eye for an eye, a scalp for a scalp" embodied a very practical equation for bounty. As early as the Susquehannock Wars of 1645, the British throne authorized reimbursement for the capture of Indians, but also rewarded the earliest settlers for retrieving their scalps. Willem Keift, governor of the Dutch colony of New Amsterdam, awarded such bounties to frontiersmen until he could no longer afford his offer.

And now, again, in 1780, in contest with British bounties offered for white men's scalps brought to them by their Native allies, President Reed of the Pennsylvania Executive Council, wrote to a Colonel Samuel Hunter:

> "The council would and do for this purpose authorize you to offer the following premiums for every male prisoner whether white or Indian, if the former is acting with the latter, Fifteen Hundred Dollars, and One Thousand Dollars for every Indian scalp."[29]

This offer would stand for only two years. Just how many scalps were ever tendered for bounty or how much was ever paid out by Pennsylvania has been lost—or destroyed.

---

[29] Sipe, *Fort Ligonier and Its Times*, pg. 508

Lenape v. Baptist

It is both impolitic and impossible to give true expression to the religious beliefs of the Leni Lenape, the self-proclaimed "Original People," during the colonial times of America. All that we know today has been filtered and processed through a Judeo-Christian mindset. We may properly hold true the tenet that Indians did not "own" land because, from the white man's interpretation of Indian lore, Natives believed they were "*of* the land." The Lenape creation story goes something like this: from a primordial world of water rose the back of a great turtle. From that shell grew a tree and, from the roots of that tree, came man. When the tree bent its branches to the ground came woman. And all else came forth from a Great Spirit and flourished.

In the Native's version of Genesis, man was not born to rule dominion over all beasts, nor was he challenged to do good or renounce evil, but to live in harmony with all things animate and inanimate. There was no preordained hierarchy of spirits who naturally embodied a stream, a deer, or a rock. He had no sense that his participation in the grand mix of things was deemed anything greater or lesser than any other, anything more deserving or less entitled than any other, anything wiser or subservient to that which was organically whole, mysterious and real. And the land—the soil, the mountain, the plains—was no more his than the stream, the deer, or the rock.

Until the white man came to clear land only for himself, Native Americans had not seen such self-centered arrogance. Until the white man came, the Native had little sense of wealth or of power, of class or caste, or of religious paths to personal salvation laid out in words printed for all to interpret in ways that would forever stoke division or discord.

Until the white man came, the fear of burning in hell for all eternity was so foreign to indigenous ideology, the Native had to ask, "What are these white men thinking? Where do they even come up with this stuff. And why?'

The cynical answer is one charting the power of societal domination. The more acute answer, of course, is one that addresses organized religion's discernment of the "afterlife." What happens to us when we die is a question that is considered by all cultures. And there are as many "discernments" as there are sects among all religious orders.

As in Europe, the Great Awakening befell colonial America much like a satchel of heavy books dumped on an old desk. Pages fluttered, dust flew, and spines cracked open to once-ancient notions and novel ruminations of man's lot on earth.

One such book that revealed a new "truth" of salvation fell on the pulpit of Pastor Elhanan Winchester, a somewhat itinerant preacher, first known in Newton, Massachusetts, then popular among the slaves of South Carolina, and, penultimately, swarmed by congregants in Philadelphia of 1781.

At the First Baptist Church of that city, he laid down the idea of Universal Restoration. He had come to this new "revelation" through thoughtful dialogue with many pastors he visited on his travels, one of whom first shared with him the book, *The Everlasting Gospel.* The "Doctrine of Universal Restoration," as defended by Elhanan Winchester in his own book of "Dialogues," argues that the Lord will redeem even those who are damned to eternal hell.[30]

This was heresy to colonial Baptists. Disciples of that faith, later famous for their sermons "of fire and brimstone," believed that only the threat of eternal damnation could impede sin and wickedness on earth. If, of course, in the last hours of life, one "saw the light," then Christ the Savior would most assuredly redeem one's soul. But a sinful, wicked life cast into the shadow of death will—for all eternity—"swim in a lake of fire." The message was: Be good, repent now, or you're doomed to eternal hell.

Unfortunately for his sake, Winchester did not stop there. The pastor also believed that God was so good—so loving—that even "the devil and other fallen angels" could be restored. If, indeed, there was any chance of salvation for a soul lost to Satan's way, declared Winchester, it didn't mean

---

[30] Elhanan, *The Universal Restoration*, pg. 28

that the Lord God gave up on even the most licentious of these sinners. No, even *after* death, there was hope. And, always, there was love.

Winchester even dared to parse the words of the Gospel. He examined each instance of phrases like "forever and ever" and argued that if forever means forever, than why add an "and ever?" If so necessary, he posed, then *forever* must have some limitation. *Endless damnation*, as interpreted by modern scripture, was never an absolute; rather, according to Winchester, God's infinite mercy promised *endless happiness*. Further, Winchester challenged the crux of Baptist hypocrisy. By damning the "estate of wicked men, their aversion to good, their love of vice, their hardness of heart, and opposition to every method taken to reclaim them," the Baptist betrays his faith in God's grace. Just by positing the "infinity of sin" impugns the almighty love of Christ. "Nothing is too hard for God," Winchester declared, "Christ being far more infinite to save, than sin can be to destroy."

"Apostasy!," screamed the outraged Baptists. If licentiousness could be forgiven *after* death, why, pray tell, should anyone heed the very commandments Moses brought down from the mountain top? Why even behave?

In the course of three months of preaching in Philadelphia that year, Elhanan Winchester so confounded the Baptists' core doctrine that he was censured and run out of town.

Among the righteous members of the First Baptist Church of Philadelphia, Thomas Shields was one of the first congregants to sign a petition of censure. So outraged was he by the heresy, he had his wife sign, too.[31]

Of the lore of the Leni Lenape, the "afterlife" was met upon crossing a Great River. Swim across or float away; to whence one journeyed, who could say?

To the white man, the mortal sensitivities of Natives may have seemed as simple as that. Of course, they were not. But to the Native, the white man's fear of death and of "the dark beyond" was so palpable, so peculiar, it must have come from some innate guilt. From whence came this fear of doom, of banishment or of imprisonment? Somehow this must all relate to his obsession for justice. If true, no wonder the white man called it his "judgement day."

---

[31] Spencer, *Early Baptists of Philadelphia*, pg. 130

Williamson's Militia

The late winter of 1782 had been a warm one in and around Washington County. Sneaky savages had raided a number of pioneer homes when they were otherwise expected to keep to their villages in colder months.

On February 10, Robert Wallace, a sometime private of the local militia, had business in Washington town, visiting there from his homestead on Cross Creek.[32] [33] Upon his return, he found his cabin upended, his few cattle all shot dead, and his wife and three children missing. He feared the worst and went to the nearest fort to muster a search party.

At the court house there, he alerted James Marshel who, by honor of being chief judge was also the County's Lieutenant. At long last, he had organized a militia for Washington County. But Marshel was unable to draw men together quickly; any search party that went out was gathered by Wallace himself. They may not have found tracks to follow, and if they had, those tracks led to no immediate discovery as nightfall darkened their efforts.

The next day, farther south near Wheeling, two other militia privates were guarding a sugar camp, preparing to tap maples for the spring run. They were attacked by two Wyandots. Richard Davis escaped, but Hugh Cameron was shot in the hand. Apparently the ambush so traumatized Cameron, he did not run. With his woolen cap ripped from his head, he was tomahawked, scalped, and left in a puddle of blood.[34]

---

[32] Reader, *Some Pioneers of Washington County, PA.*, pg. 40

[33] Dodds, *Vance's Fort*, http://historysbackpages.blogspot.com/2011/07/shelter-from-storm.html

[34] Eckert, *That Dark and Bloody River*, pg. 312

On February 16, John Carpenter, working his land near Buffalo Creek, was captured by a party of six Delawares. He was taken, with two of his horses, across the Ohio, and led some good distance up the Muskingum along which he witnessed many more parties of Indians descending from the Tuscarawas Creek. That night, he escaped with his horses. He fled to Fort Laurens and then to Fort Pitt, alerting anyone along the way to the dangers of an imminent raid. When asked where he thought the Delawares were leading him, he said with some certainty that two spoke "good Dutch" and, so, claimed they were Moravian Delawares.[35] Surely, he averred, they were leading him to a Moravian village, of which there were three well situated on the Tuscarawas.

Carpenter's witness of the several war parties descending from the Muskingum was sufficient proof that something awful was about to happen. Families were alerted, forts were put to the ready with food stocks and extra ammunition, and the town councils were pressed to assemble their militias. Of course, the greater defense would have to come from Fort Pitt, but its commander, General William Irvine (who had only recently replaced Brodhead,) was in Carlisle getting his "house in order" before returning to his new command at Fort Pitt. Next in charge was Colonel John Gibson, he who had survived the siege of Fort Laurens. Gibson ordered his next in command, Lt. Colonel David Williamson of the Washington County militia, to muster his men and proceed up to the Moravian villages.

David Williamson was a "hot head" with an intemperate past. He was thought to have been a member of the Paxton Boys, one of the many vigilantes whose antipathy to the Conestoga Indians had led them to murder fourteen defenseless souls sequestered in a local jail. (Yet while the prejudices of his Scotch-Irish upbringing may have influenced his indifference to Native Americans, he was too young to have participated in the Lancaster massacre.) Born in Carlisle, Pennsylvania, in 1752, he had come west as early as 1774, perhaps resettling his parents on Buffalo Creek where they owned as much as 900 acres.[36] Land records show that Williamson himself owned 800

---

[35] *Ibid.*, pg. 313

[36] Williston, *The 1782 Volunteer Militia from Washington County, Pa,*
http://freepages.rootsweb.com/~gwilli824/genealogy/moravian.html

acres in 1781. At the age of 30, he was a fortunate man, however it was he may have claimed his stake.

A resident of Donegal Township at that time, he was also a militia officer for Westmoreland County. So, when James Marshel formed his militia in Washington County, he seated Williamson as his second in command, and created the Fourth Battalion of Washington County. Relevant to this assignment was the allegiance each held to Pennsylvania. That issue of state loyalty was ever present.

Militia in colonial America operated on local democratic principles. An expedition leader was not appointed by merit of his military rank alone, but, rather, by the vote of the men who were to follow him. Williamson was nominated and duly elected to lead. Among the first militia men who fell into the ranks were Robert Wallace, Richard Davis, and John Carpenter. Wallace and Davis were already privates—Carpenter was a lieutenant—but each would have joined instantly for the enmity they shared from recent events.

Sources vary in quantifying the number of men that actually assembled for Williamson's Moravian expedition. General Irvine, who was nowhere nearby, wrote within the year that 300 men had assembled. Another source suggests more. Yet based on records held in the Pennsylvania Archives (albeit discovered more than 100 years after the event) the number was more likely 160. The Pennsylvania Archives reflect the names of those who were paid for militia service between March 1 to March 8, 1782.[37] It does not state the activities for which they were engaged that infamous week.

Of those who assembled in Washington town or who would rendezvous the next day in Wheeling were 196 men, not all of whom (can it be stated with any certainty) marched to the Muskingum River and then up the Tuscarawas. Among those who did *not* march are Dorsey Pentecost, John Canon, James Marshel or William Crawford. Each of these men well exceeded the average age of hearty, active militia men, typically in their mid-twenties. At 34, however, Daniel Leet, Sub-Lieutenant of Washington County, qualified for service. He saddled up.

---

[37] Ibid.

Gnadenhütten, 1782

On March 5, 1782, 150 Moravian Delawares left their winter village at Captive's Town on the Sandusky River and headed southeast in groups of about fifty each to the three abandoned villages of Schönbrunn, Salem and Gnadenhütten. Hungry from the long winter, they headed down to scour the fields of last fall's crops to carry back to Captive's Town much needed sustenance. They had no reason to stay any longer than the time it would take to scavenge what they could find.

Once arrived at Gnadenhütten, the fifty or so Delawares there were visited by Wyandot warriors who were seeking food themselves. The Wyandots traded with the Delawares for corn. Among the items they apparently traded were warm clothing and other items for personal comfort. They did not trade guns or ammunition because the Moravian Indians were strict pacifists. Although they carried knives and tomahawks out of necessity, they had no need for other weapons. Satisfied with their business, the Wyandots departed.

The next day, Colonel Williamson and his militia arrived in Gnadenhütten. They may have been surprised to see so many women and children, and hardly the number of men they would have thought necessary to defend Gnadenhütten. But the Moravians were there only out of certain hunger. Williamson, learning their plight, offered to take them all to Fort Pitt where they would be properly fed and sheltered for the remaining weeks of winter. When informed that a similar party of Moravian Indians were scavenging the remains of crops in Salem, Williamson sent a small team of his men to bring them to Gnadenhütten. The next day, forty or more Moravian Delawares arrived. As promised, he invited them also to enjoy the hospitality of Fort Pitt. Apparently, they seemed altogether amenable because, at Williamson's request, they then gave up their knives and tomahawks to be carried in satchels to the fort.

This seems both a telling request and an odd submission. Murkier still is what incited sudden terror.

According to some, Robert Wallace saw that one of the women was wearing his wife's dress, the very one she had been wearing the day his entire family vanished.[38] According to others, Richard Davis recognized the woolen cap his buddy Hugh Cameron had on the day he was shot. Either way, the white men stoked their own suspicions.

Or, just as likely, Williamson acted upon intentions he had had all along. He separated the now unarmed men from the women and children, and had them all tied and bound in separate locked houses.

No definitive narrative relates what happened next. Moravian history suggests there were many hours of prayer, introspection and debate on both sides. Whether or not the Natives were informed that they would all be murdered the next morning, or whether or not Williamson first sought a democratic vote from his militia, cannot be certain. There were few voices willing to speak about what actually happened.

What is certain is that 96 Moravian Indians were massacred at the hands of Williamson's men.

John Heckewelder, a Moravian leader who had been teaching the Natives in Salem, gathered and compiled the few journals he encountered in the years following. From those original journals, now all lost, he described the scene in his own thoughtful way.

> "Finding that all entreaties to save their lives was to no purpose—
> —and that some [of the militia], more blood thirsty than their comrades, were anxious to begin upon them, they united in begging a short delay, that they might prepare themselves for death—which request at length was granted them. Then asking pardon of whatever offense they had given, or grief they had occasioned to each other, they kneeled down; offering fervent prayers to God their Saviour—and kissing one another, under a flood of tears fully resigned to his will, they sang praises unto him, in the joyful hope, that they

---

[38] Sipe, *Fort Ligonier and Its Times*, pg. 540

would soon be relieved from all pains, and join their redeemer in everlasting bliss."[39]

Heckewelder also noted the reticence of some of Williamson's men.

"During the time of their [captives'] devotion, the murderers were consulting on the manner, in which they would put them to death. Some were for setting fire to the houses they were in, and burning them alive. Others wanted to take their scalps home with them, as a signal of victory; while others remonstrated against either of these plans, declaring, that they never would be guilty of murdering a people, whose innocence was so satisfactorily evinced, and these proposed to set them at liberty… that they [wished to be] innocent of the blood of these harmless Christian Indians, they withdrew to some distance from the scene of slaughter."[40]

Of the narratives shared in the months following that morning of March 8, 1782, the first deaths were inflicted by the use of a cooper's mallet. Fourteen victims fell to it instantly. That the mallet may have been wielded by Charles Bilderback, a large man of some earlier "history" with the Delawares, is befitting of his known temper, but is wholly unsubstantiated.[41] Who in fact wielded the first blow, if indeed a cooper's mallet was ever used, cannot be known. The house in which the Native men were murdered, however, was the home of the village cooper.

The majority of the captive Moravians were shot or killed by tomahawk. It is wholly presumed that most were scalped, as there was then a rich bounty in Pennsylvania.

In his collective narrative, Heckewelder noted all but four of the 96 Christian Indians "were killed in the slaughter houses. Those four included young Shabosh, who was killed several miles and many more hours before the militia reached the town, Jacob who had been shot paddling a canoe, and two young brethren, Paul and Anthony, who, perceiving the murderers intentions, were shot along the bank of the river, while attempting to escape.

---

[39] Heckewelder, *A Narrative of the Mission,* pg. 318

[40] Ibid., pg. 319

[41] Eckert, *That Dark and Bloody River,* pg. 319

Of the above number, 62 were grown persons, one-third of whom were women; the remaining 34 were children."[42]

One child did escape. Scalped and left for dead among the sixty bodies lying in the second house, he managed to crawl under a recess in the floor, and waited.

When both houses were set on fire and left to burn, the boy climbed out from under the bloody floor and fled. It was from this one boy's eye-witness account that others recorded the heinous events. The calcified remains of 92 Moravian bodies were many months later collected in a large burial mound which still stands at Gnadenhütten today.

Were it not for the one child who escaped, and yet whose name is un-known to this day, the events of March 8, 1782, would likely not have been shared in any narrative ever. Yet, no first-person account exists.

Of particular interest to Heckewelder is the murder of the young Native men that preceded the massacre. That they were killed before Mrs. Wallace's dress was seen, or Cameron's cap was spotted, is testimony of intent. These first deaths are sound evidence that Williamson's plan was always to wipe out the entire village, although it is quite certain he and his fellow militia were in no way united in that intent; they could have had no expectation of the number of Moravian Delawares they would encounter that day. Yet, no matter the number, all would be killed. And all were.

After then burning down the deserted village of Schönbrunn, Williamson's white warriors walked home.

---

[42] Heckewelder, *A Narrative of the Mission*, pg. 318

The Aftermath

Of course, Williamson's expedition had the opposite effect it intended. Outraged by the senseless massacre, Delawares, Wyandots, Mingos and Shawnees alike convened with the British at Detroit, solidifying a once tenuous alliance to rid the Ohios of all white families. Meeting just west of the Sandusky Plains, they assembled warriors from far and wide, determined to seek absolute revenge.

Back in Washington County, news of the massacre, as well as impending retaliation for the same, created an apoplexy of recrimination, shame, and sorrow. Williamson's men scrambled back to their homesteads and went on tending to spring chores, as if nothing had happened.

Daniel Leet, however, resigned from his county office as Sub-Lieutenant. On March 22, 1782, he stepped down.[43] Minutes of the meeting bear no explanation. A Mr. James Alison was nominated in his place.[44]

From Fort Pitt, newly returned, General Irvine wrote to his wife in Carlisle:

"My Dearest Love: —

"I received your two letters by Captain [Major Isaac] Craig and Mr. Hughes; I am therefore in arrears in a letter way; but the fault is not in me, being extremely anxious to inform you of my arrival here, but I have not had a single opportunity...

"Things were in a strange state when I arrived. A number of the country people had just returned from the Moravian towns, about

---

[43] Crumrine, *The History of Washington County*, pg. 472
[44] *Colonial Records of Pennsylvania*, pg. 240

one hundred miles distant, where, it is said, they did not spare either age or sex. What was more extraordinary, they did it in cool blood, having deliberated three days, during which time they were industrious in collecting all hands into their churches (they had embraced Christianity), when they fell on them while they were singing hymns and killed the whole. Many children were killed in their wretched mothers' arms. Whether this was right or wrong, I do not pretend to determine...

"People who have had fathers, mothers, brothers or children, butchered, tortured, scalped, by the savages, reason very differently on the subject of killing the Moravians, to what people who live in the interior part of the country in perfect safety do. Their feelings are very different. Whatever your private opinion of these matters may be, I conjure you by all the ties of affection and as you value my reputation, that you will keep your mind to yourself, and that you will not express any sentiment for or against these deeds;—as it may be alleged, the sentiments you express may come from me or be mine. No man knows whether I approve or disapprove of killing the Moravians..."

Once news reached the Supreme Executive Council in Philadelphia— whether or not heard before Daniel Leet had resigned, or, in all likelihood, contemporaneous to his resignation—an order was put forth to investigate the matter. Appointed to that task were General Irvine and Dorsey Pentecost. Irvine, of course, was in charge of the Western Division; any "conduct unbecoming an officer" would fall under his authority to punish. Pentecost, as Washington County's representative to the Council, would undertake the actual investigation.

Of the few surviving letters that circulated between Pentecost and the Council, one addressed by Pentecost concluded with this explanation:

"It is said here, and I believe with truth, that sundry articles were found amongst the Indians that were taken from the inhabitants of Washington County, and that the Indians confessed themselves... an investigation may produce serious effects, and at least leave us as ignorant as when we began, and instead of rendering a service may produce confusion and ill-will amongst the people."[45]

Pentecost wished to justify the massacre at Gnadenhütten based on the "sundry articles" found—Wallace's wife's dress and Cameron's cap—as if two misappropriated articles of clothing were proof of treacherous deceit and willful murder. To this he added, "the Indians had confessed..!" Apparently, nothing less could justify the massacre of 96 unarmed Christian souls, 55 of whom were women and children.

Irvine and Pentecost effectively dropped their investigation. Irvine was wholly conflicted as to which side to take, fearing disloyalty from his own men. Because his post had been so brief before the massacre, he had no confidence in his ability to command troops he knew not well.[46] But Irvine might have been hiding something else. He feared that those who outranked him back east suspected he did not even hold weight in his own family. His wife was a wealthy Philadelphia heiress.

Pentecost, however, predicted even worse consequences in pursuing the matter. A political chameleon, duplicitous in his role as representative to Pennsylvania's highest authority, and yet Virginian to his core, he made little effort. He was also a significant landowner, at least as shown by patents he might not have had proof to defend. Again, as an early surveyor to George Croghan, he continued in some capacity to serve as an agent to sell that land back east. Partners of his, like Levi Hollingsworth, need not know that Pentecost would actually defend such barbarous behavior. Pentecost knew, as did many, that the moral values of citizens living safely in Philadelphia were at extreme odds with those of terrorized—and, quite evidently, terroristic—settlers on the western frontier.

If there was one person who had acted on ethical grounds, it was Daniel Leet. He was the only one to resign his public office.[47] Yet, not once, it has been said, did he ever speak—or speak out—about the massacre.[48]

Perhaps he had intended to, but was threatened by "certain others" to remain quiet "or else." Logically, there would have been only three such

[45] Creigh, *History of Washington County*, pg. 287

[46] Barr, *A Colony Sprung from Hell*, pg. 248

[47] Supreme Executive Counsel Minute Books, (Roll 691), 1781-1782

[48] Draper MSS, D124

"others." Williamson, his superior officer, could not have cared much less and General Irvine could ill afford to take sides. Pentecost, however—the only other person of authority—had issues with Leet. Both were competing surveyors, one of whom was far more respected than the other. If, indeed, the horror that compelled Leet to resign was evinced as much by Williamson's leadership as by the deceit of his campaign, his testimony would require all three men to face a court of criminal law. And a trial, whether in Washington or Philadelphia, would never bring back the innocent.

Had Daniel Leet stood to protest, his voice would have been lost to the wind.

Crawford's Will

Of course no one faced any kind of judgement, political, civil or otherwise. Unlike Irvine or Pentecost whose extant letters relate personal fears of betrayal and public scandal, Leet stayed silent. If he was tormented by shame or anger for the events of March 8, he let no one know.

That is, until news of a second and larger expedition was to assemble the following month.

Daniel Leet insisted on meeting with his mentor William Crawford. He knew that local fears were no more allayed now than when Williamson's expedition first marched to the Moravian villages. But he had to have questioned if further aggression would solve anything. Only Crawford would know what to do. And yet, far removed from Fort Pitt where preparations were underway for the second expedition, Crawford already knew something was up. The days were thick with fear.

For no other reason apparent, Crawford decided to get his legal affairs in order. The chore was something that had weighed on him since the sudden death of his younger brother and step-brother five years earlier. At 60, he drew up his first will and testament. To his wife, Hannah, he gave all of Spring Garden, as well as the furniture, cattle and swine. Drawing from patented lands he had surveyed and earned by commission from George Washington, he left his son John 500 acres on the Ohio, and to John's two sons, Richard and Moses, he left an additional 400 acres each. His granddaughter, Ann McCormick, also received 400 acres from the same plat.

But he had other people to remember in his will. And from this bequest comes proof of certain marital indiscretions. Nicholas Cresswell had alluded to them in his diary. Having visited Crawford on several occasions, he suspected that William was having an unseemly affair with his niece, Ann Connell, who lived on a farm very near Spring Garden.[49] Ann was the daughter of Hanna's sister Elizabeth Vance whose husband James Connell had died when the Crawford's still lived on Cattail Run. In his new will, Crawford bequeathed to her the farm on which she lived, as well as the livestock and all equipment. The Connell's had been childless at James's death. Yet, Crawford also bequeathed 500 acres each to Ann's two sons, William and James, "upon their age of majority," and 600 more acres to her two daughters, Nancy and Polly.[50] One can conjecture whatever one likes, but not all of Ann's children may have been Crawford's. And yet, while one can value land by many criteria, the "Connell children" received more acres than Crawford's "own."

---

[49] Cresswell, *The Journal of Nicholas Cresswell*, pg. 120

[50] Crawford's Last Will & Testament, Westmoreland County, PA Probate Court, Will Book No.1, 6.

Preparations

Ever concerned about public opinion, General William Irvine listened to David Williamson and James Marshel express their convictions that all the forces now organized at Sandusky were headed their way. They argued that Irvine must mount a counter-offensive immediately. Irvine was adamant, however, that whatever should happen next could not be jeopardized by the slightest indecision. It seems Williamson might have admitted to Irvine that some of his men at Gnadenhütten had disobeyed his command, that some had had second thoughts. Williamson might even have excused the massacre on the frenzy of a few. That happens, especially with militias, Williamson might have added. Irvine knew that only a true military operation could ensure loyalty of command; the misgivings of the massacre, in Irvine's circular thinking, were now only the result of a soft leader allowing his men a voice in their actions. Going forward, no such "militia mentality" would stand.

Irvine committed to raising an expedition of at least 300 men, but not before sending out a small party to gather intelligence at Sandusky. That reconnaissance team did not get far before one of the Native scouts admitted he hoped to betray the mission and lead the party into an ambush. For this admission, the scout was executed at Fort Pitt.[51] By such action, Irvine proved he was committed to an imminent attack.

Irvine informed Commander in Chief Washington about his efforts and about the execution. He also included notice of an apparent effort by westerners, outraged by the still unsettled line drawn between Pennsylvania and Virginia, to create yet a new state in the Ohios. Wrote Irvine: "Should these

---

[51] Washington-Irvine Letters, April 20, 1782

people actually emigrate they must be either entirely cut off or immediately take protection from the British—which I fear is the real design of some of the party tho I think a great majority have no other views than to acquire lands..."

Irvine reached out to Crawford to get his advice. His intentions were coy, however, because he knew well that Williamson intended to lead the new mission. Fearing a repeat of another Gnadenhütten, Irvine wanted someone who could command respect by way of his military experience—one who would dole out punishments for insubordination, treason or cowardice—a qualification lacking of the younger militia leader. Perhaps for this reason, Irvine sought to enlist volunteers as Continental soldiers. Indeed, for this same reason, he offered Crawford the promised assistance of Irvine's own aide-de-camp, Lieutenant Major John Rose.

If not by evidence of having completed his will, or by being entrusted with Irvine's right-hand man, Crawford knew this would be a major command for which he would be forever judged. He thus assembled his able offspring to join him.

And he solicited Daniel Leet, who had resigned his military office, to march with him, yet again. Ever loyal, Leet actually re-enlisted to serve. As always, his younger brothers stood with him.

By mid-May, just a little more than two months after the horrors of Gnadenhütten, Colonel William Crawford, Lt. Colonel David Williamson, Major John Rose, Major Daniel Leet, Crawford's son John, his nephew John Stephenson, his son-in-law William Harrison, and as many as 460 mounted men—well more than Irvine's expectations—assembled at Mingo Bottom. There they would sort out their duties and elect a commander.

Informing Washington again, on May 21, Irvine wrote:

"...They are Accordingly assembling this day at the Kings [Mingo] Bottom, all on Horseback with thirty days provision— They have Asked of me Only a few Flints and a small supply of Powder.

"As they will Elect their Officers, I have taken some pains to get Colonel Crawford appointed to Command, & hope he will be, he lift [left] me yesterday on his way down to the place of Rendezvous, he does not wish to go with a smaller number than four hundred, whether this number will assemble I can not say, he pressed me for some Officers, I have sent with him Lieutenant Rose my Aid De Camp, A very Vigilant Active Brave young Gentleman well Acquainted with service, and A Surgeon, these two [Crawford and Rose] are all I could venture to spare—several were solicitous for my going, but I did not think my self at liberty consistent with the Spirit of Your Excellencys Instructions..."

At Mingo Bottom, the men assembled and called for a vote. Williamson seemed to be the favored candidate. Before any votes were cast, however, Major Rose recorded that Daniel Leet stood his ground and exclaimed that if Williamson were to be elected, he would not continue on. It was inferred, too, that Crawford said as much, as had Major Rose. But it was recorded by Leet's brother William, who was also present, that the election went down somewhat differently.

In a face-to-face interview conducted by Lyman C. Draper with William Leet many years later, the latter affirmed there had been a first vote; Williamson was elected to lead. But the younger Leet also averred that his brother Daniel had affected, by his protests, a second vote.[52] That vote was recorded by John Rose as 230 for Williamson and 235 for Crawford. By such a narrow margin, it might have been assumed by Williamson that he had earned his role as second in command, which Crawford was said to have accepted. However, Daniel Leet was then made Brigade Major, a title often bestowed upon that position. The appointment of a Brigade Major was an absolute necessity because 460 men would have to be divided into eighteen companies. As such, whichever military responsibilities were decided, Leet's authority could be superseded only by Crawford. In following military law, thus, Leet's orders would outrank Williamson's; Crawford's army, very much now on the payroll of the Continental Congress, would abide by strict military law.

The role of Major John Rose, however, was not made clear. A longtime assistant to Irvine, Rose was actually a Russian of some nobility. His real name was Baron Gustav Heinrich de Rosenthal who had prepared for a diplomatic career through formal education in Germany. He spoke fluent

---

[52] Draper MSS, 2S4a

English, and, indeed, was trained as a surgeon. He had met Irvine early on at Fort Ticonderoga, served as a surgeon at Valley Forge and then joined the Continental Navy during which duty his ship was captured by the British. Exchanged as a prisoner just one year earlier, Rose had returned to Irvine's command—and trust—at Fort Pitt. For these reasons, Irvine had expressly asked Rose to record the expedition in a journal which would serve Irvine, in his absence, in future expeditions on the western frontier. It is likely, too, that Irvine, suspicious of the success Crawford had had in raising such a large body of men, wanted to know if they held true interest in creating a new Ohio state.

Rose was one to have his nose in the air, but not to sniff out any ulterior motives. He was appalled by the condition of Crawford's men. He wrote about how poorly they groomed and fed their horses, how unkempt they dressed, and how ill-trained they seemed for military duty. Likewise, he took great care in writing several pages describing remedies he proposed for lightening the horses' burdens, for securing them when in battle, for preparing three-day's provisions before battle, for choreographing swifter passage through narrow paths, for securing the attention of sentries, and so on and so on. He laments that none of his advice was accepted, yet Rose deemed it all worthy to record for Irvine.

Rose also made somewhat cryptic notes about the expeditions' leaders. Of Crawford, he wrote, "C. is a man of Sixty and upwards. Blessed with a constitution that may be called robust for his age. Inured to fatigue from his childhood, and by repeated campaigns against the Indians acquainted with their manner of engaging—In his private Life, kind and exceedingly affectionate; in his military character, personally Brave, and patient of hardships…—As a Commanding Officer, cool in danger, but not systematical."

Of Williamson, Rose noted, "W. is brave as Caesar and active; but divested of conduct. Fond of thrusting himself into danger, he leaves everything else to chance… His Oratory is suited to the taste of the people[,] his countrymen, and their Bigoted notions stand him in lieu of arguments. It is a pity but he had military opportunities of instruction, as his natural talents are not despicable, and his toughly heat might prove the bane of the Country."

Daniel Leet figured into his commentary. "L. is too easy and neglectful for his post, though the only man, any ways acquainted with duty. He is allowed to have behaved with much Bravery; yet, I believe, unnecessarily so."

The Advance

On May 25, 1782, Colonel William Crawford, having ordered his men ready to mount by eight in the morning, was still assembling them after ten.[53] Like most armies newly-mustered, the men were slow to advance. The plan was to ride in formation "four across" with two scouts leading a nimble advance team. Even with four columns, the army extended 120 horses long. Yet, when trails were not sufficiently wide enough, or when passages over steep terrain had narrow opportunity, the columns were otherwise reduced to two columns or, worse, one. When reaching fast streams or riverbeds, the men scrambled helter-skelter to cross as best they could. At times, the expedition stretched nearly a mile long. Without a wide advance, the army was more vulnerable to ambush which might split the lines of defense like a severed snake. Not only were common paths narrow, but the steep hilly topography provided few grasslands from which the horses could feed. Resting the first night after only ten miles, many of the horses wandered off to feed themselves, which, by necessitating the men to go find them, had delayed any early departure that first morning. As Brigade Major, this was just one of Leet's many headaches and is what likely gave rise to Rose's many admonitions which he addressed so smugly to Irvine.

The fact is the expedition needed to move some 25 miles a day. Two critical challenges they had to meet were a swift surprise on the enemy and

---

[53] The following account of Crawford's expedition is derived from several historians--Butterfield, Eckert and Thompson--each of whom relied principally on oral histories collected by Hugh Henry Brackenridge and Lyman C. Draper. As such, I have not cited claims common to all three authors, but I have footnoted sources that provide information seemingly different from one or the others.

sufficient rations to get them there. A slower advance risked extra time being spotted by Indian scouts and a greater depletion of the foods they carried. There were no wagons; every man carried his own "victuals," not to mention, heavy ammunition. Indeed, their horses were overladen, and with little grass to graze, the army dragged on.

By nightfall three days later, Crawford's expedition came within eight miles of Gnadenhütten. From there the western Ohio plains opened up to flatter terrain and more plentiful grasslands. The decision posed to Crawford and Leet was to make up lost time by advancing due west on this more for-giving ground, yet which, by doing so, especially near the Moravian villages, would likely expose them to the very Natives who despised them most. The alternative route was to head north through hillier, "hidden" terrain. Craw-ford made two mistakes that night. First, he allowed his officers to weigh in on the decision and, secondly, he abided their council.

The following morning, approaching Gnadenhütten, Major Rose, Colonel Williamson and Brigade Major Daniel Leet went on foot "to rec-onnoitre the town, whether we could discover any indian Warriors at it…" The three men poked through scattered debris and fire pits to find evidence of any recent visits. They even checked the stream bed of the Tuscarawas to see if pots or other implements had been submerged for later good use. Rose's journal states, "the town was burnt some time last winter and the ruins of the lowest house in town were mixed with the calcine bones of the burnt bodies of the Indians."[54]

How or why Rose would have said "some time last winter" is curious. Studying the scene along with Williamson and Leet, he would have known the bodies were burned just two months earlier. (Yet, by "winter," he may have meant before the current spring.)

That evening, having proceeded well past Gnadenhütten on the open plain, Crawford's advance men were spotted by enemy Natives. They com-menced a short volley of fire, yet neither party was hit. Now, however, "the ghost was up." Within the next two days, still plenty of miles from the Sanduskys, the expedition, again, was sighted. Once more, Crawford rea-soned a strategy with his elite council. With fewer than ten days of ration for each man remaining, with the two recent exposures to enemy scouts, and yet

---

[54] Stone, "Journal of a Volunteer Expedition to Sandusky," pg. 141

with still two days more to reach their objective, he proposed they should either turn back or avenge a different "savage stronghold" thought to be just ten miles north. At the least, he argued, they could affect one small victory before returning home.

Again, Crawford allowed his council to overrule his better instincts.

On June 3, they reached the open plains. There was no turning back now.

The Sanduskys were something few white men had ever seen, although often heard described. Here were hundreds of square miles of thick, coarse grass which, even in early spring, grew well more than three feet tall. It was a virtual sea of undulating sage-green under which lived its own ecosystem of prairie fowl, tortoises, rodents, and poisonous snakes. The plains extended as far as the eye could see. And while there were several elevated groves of trees from which to look down on the wet savannah, any trespass by man or horse created evidence visible for miles. There were a few Indian routes crossing the plains, but none that would permit an army of four hundred men to pass undetected.

It mattered not. Crawford and his army had been tracked long since by warriors who were now well-prepared for battle.

Day One

The worst thing a rifleman could do, other than letting his musket sit out in the rain, was to load it incorrectly.

Contemporary to Crawford's expedition, a soldier would have prepared paper cartridges, each containing gunpowder and a lead ball. One would bite off the powder end of the cartridge, pour a bit into the flash pan, and then load the remaining cartridge into the barrel, powder first, then ramrod the ball and paper to the deepest recess of the barrel. Often in extended battle, however, a soldier would run out of cartridges. In this case, he would use his powder horn, and load the lead ball without use of paper. If, in the heat of battle, he sunk the ball before loading the powder, he had a problem. The process of removing the ball under this condition was called "briching," no doubt a vernacular form of breech.[55]

Another vexing issue was the build-up of burnt powder in the flash pan, requiring the owner to scrape debris down to the metal plate against which the flint sparked. "Picking the flint" got everything working again.[56]

But muskets had many other inherent inefficiencies. If the musket was a "Brown Bess," it likely carried a bayonet projecting from the open barrel. If so, the bayonet served as a sighting line. But the common musket had no rear sight.[57] Thus, only the most experienced rifleman could shoot with any accuracy. To all others, it was a crap shoot. Furthermore, the range of a musket required real bravery. To think that one might actually hit an enemy

---

[55] Dyke, "The Pennsylvania Rifle," 1974, in a letter to Parker Brown, "The Battle of Sandusky," pg. 129
[56] Draper, MSS 11 BB, pg. 20-21
[57] Barbieri, *Journal of the American Revolution*, Aug. 2013

combatant meant firing the weapon somewhere within a range closer than 200 yards. Even then, one had to aim high. At a velocity of only 1,000 feet per second, a musket ball, weighing about an ounce, will drop 18 inches from "dead reckoning" due to sheer gravity. For this reason, during the war for independence, more soldiers died from the bayonet than from a bullet.[58]

Wet weather, however, made everything worse. And, as Crawford's men awoke on the edge of the Sandusky Plains, they discovered their muskets, left leaning upright overnight, were covered in dew. A formidable morning fog bode they would see a very hot, humid day.[59]

No sooner had the men attempted to test-fire their slick guns than they heard the loud retort of artillery to the northwest. Without the least knowledge of the size or might of the enemy ahead, Crawford engaged two dozen volunteers, led by William Leet's light guard, to lead a reconnaissance on the Upper Sandusky village several miles across the plain. There they would find Captive's Town, the village from which the Moravian Indians had returned to Gnadenhütten two months before.

They rode through dense fog enshrouding their advance. The suspect village was not so far that, despite the cloak of fog, anyone inside might not hear them. They advanced quietly, expecting to hear the least evidence of women preparing for the day, children laughing, or warriors chattering impatiently for food. This would be sufficient news to return to Crawford. Yet, there was not even the smell of smoke. As they approached the gates of the village, the silence was ominous. Several men dismounted and slowly swung open the doors. The first thing they saw was a dog darting behind a fallen shelter. William Leet may have first scratched his head and turned to his men, bewildered by the quiet. The village was deserted, completely. They found no warm fires, no abandoned pots, no blankets or stools. In fact, the village was so dismantled, it seemed the residents might have departed weeks before. Leet and his men were spooked.

Riding back to the main forces, William Leet relayed his fears; any element of surprise had long since expired. Clearly, decidedly, the Indians were well informed of Crawford's expedition. They had removed their women and children to safety, and the warriors, if soon to be encountered, would be "hot and ready."

---

[58] Harrington, *Journal of the American Revolution*, July 2013
[59] Thompson, *Disaster on the Sandusky*, pg. 196

Once again, Crawford assembled a small counsel of his officers. The majority opinion was to call off the expedition. But the dissenting voice of Col. David Williamson spoke to the shame they would bear if not a single shot was fired. John Slover, one of Crawford's scouts who had for ten years lived among the Wyandots, knew there was another village ten miles beyond. To Slover, that seemed to be the distance from which the early morning cannon fire was heard. There, he was certain, assembled the warriors they had come to subdue. Thus, with evidence the enemy was not far, Williamson turned on Crawford, taunting his apparent cowardice, and convinced the Colonel to proceed.

Crawford directed Major John Rose to select fifty men and lead an advance company along a distant path, marked by a visible ravine lined with trees. This road would take them north amidst the other several towering groves that projected up from the grassy plains. These the men called "islands," floating, as they seemed, among the billowing sea of green.

Before proceeding very far, in fact, Rose directed his mounted men to lighten their loads in the nearest island grove, elevated as it was, and, as such, dry and cool from the shade. If needed, the island would serve as a decent retreat and, no matter how far they might have to ride, easily identifiable upon their safe return. Rose, ever concerned with military decorum and the efficiencies of swift travel, was propitious in this directive.

He led his men along the northward path, advancing perhaps three miles toward the next village, when for no reason since remembered, he called a halt. All at once, several warriors jumped up from the grassy ravine, which gave Rose reason for a full charge. Just as suddenly, an entire wing of warriors fanned out from the rear of the ravine, firing and whooping, tomahawks raised, circling to envelope Rose's smaller company. Fortunately, the militia, because it had charged, was well ahead of the warrior circle. Volleys ensued, gunfire exploded on both sides; a cacophony of muskets gave rise to clouds of black smoke perhaps seen by Crawford's lagging forces. Rose dodged a tomahawk to his face, later crediting his expert horsemanship. He then commanded his forces back to the island. Its cover of trees and odd elevation would serve in their defense. Crawford's larger army made a beeline to the same advantage point.

Firing a musket on horseback is mostly futile. To give any pause to the advancing enemy meant dismounting, loading, firing, then remounting and, again, retreating. Many volleys required many iterations of this fearful effort. Rose's retreat took well more than an hour. The warriors charged, some managing to flank the eastern end of the "island." Others attempted to circle to the rear, trapping Crawford's adjoining forces into a tangle of trees and underbrush. But Crawford's men, more capable than Rose might have thought, cleared the rear and staked their positions behind wide tree trunks and the tall prairie grass. Some of the better riflemen climbed up onto tree limbs to great advantage.

Four hundred and fifty men firing muskets under the canopy of a wooded copse created a density of smoke that choked one and all. With the morning's fog burned off, the day's heat and humidity intensified the thick smoke of booming gunfire, raining ashes of saltpeter and sulfur on sweating cheeks and parched throats. Three hours into steady battle, the men were calling for water. None was to be had. At least, not from any known source nearby. John Sherrard volunteered to grab as many canteens and snake off under cover. He found no spring or stream, but he did discover a trough of water trapped in a fallen trunk. He carried many canteens back to the men. When again they were parched, he returned to find the well now dried up, and went to find another like reserve. Again, he brought back water. Doubtless in desperation, he had not stopped to think how stagnant water might render the thirsty.

Despite the constant terror of attack while exposed and, yet, entrapped on what, by sundown, they would call "Battle Island," Crawford's men held up well. Dr. Knight, the staff surgeon, attended to nineteen men smashed by lead balls, some sailing clear through ribs, a few snapping leg bones impossible to reset. One man lost the full side of his mouth to a flying tomahawk. Just five men, by nightfall, were spared their pain by death. Knight, however, was certain more would die by sunrise. Crawford's forces stood exhausted, yet ready to escape. To stave off any midnight attack, Crawford ordered campfires set at a wider perimeter than would serve his clustered army. Already, the superior Native count put his chances of retreat at slim odds. And then, the enemy fell back and built larger bonfires safely distant from Crawford's, ensuring good visibility if the white men attempted to move out of darkness. For now, however, the convention of sleep would embrace all men, foreign or domestic, white or red.

But few men slept. If not for the rampant fear of surprise, the men huddled in fours; two standing sentry while two tried sleeping. The warriors had a habit of screeching ear-piercing whoops at all hours of the night, awakening the few that might have dozed off. Horses constantly rustled, straining for grass beyond the covered island.

Even still, by sunrise, fifteen men managed to escape. Crawford might have been amused. Had he known that additional enemy forces were then arriving from the north, he should have been irate.

Day Two

By the first light of dawn, the Indians had already fired several volleys into the island. Dr. Knight noted four more men had died. Those who had drunk Sherrard's putrid water were writhing in pain or listless from dehydration. Crawford accounted for the poor reserves of food and ammunition; the situation was dire. He called for another council meeting to discuss a retreat; by all accounts, he intended on escape.

Once again, Williamson berated Crawford's defeatist attitude. He argued for an immediate attack on the savages situated closest to them. But as he spoke, his sentries saw another 150 Shawnees circling into positions as back-up to the very warriors Williamson proposed they attack. Despite occasional volleys, they waited in stand-off.

Little did the men know—least of all Crawford, Williamson, Rose, or Leet—that a larger body of Delawares, Wyandots, Shawnees, and British Rangers were now positioned, armed and ready to charge Battle Island from the north. Crawford's son John spotted the distinct green uniforms of the Rangers. He may have also witnessed the formation of the front lines of the attack. Under distant orders, with guns raised skywards, the enemy line fired off a rolling volley of musket fire, a wave of thunder that might have lasted several minutes. This was something the French called a "Feu de Joie," which, wholly designed to terrorize, was anything but a fire of joy. The show let Crawford's men hear the full complement of their power.

Yet, before the enemy advanced, a lone man approached on foot, waving the universally respected white flag, demanding to speak to Crawford.

To the many who knew him, they recognized Simon Girty instantly. He was the most famous white ally of the Natives. A onetime acquaintance of

George Washington, a longtime friend of Crawford, an early frontier trader and a respected scout for the Revolutionary Army defending the wild west, Girty had turned coat. He stood for the Natives, their lands, and their honor. And, yet, knowing the white man's way, he offered immediate peace if Crawford would lay down his arms.

Whether or not Crawford thought, perhaps for good reason, Girty was up to some dastardly trick, he did not answer.

Girty walked the length of the island's perimeter calling for Crawford's response. None came. And so he walked back to his British and Native allies.

In the heat of the day, few men could move fast enough to affect any lasting offense—or defense. The afternoon was lost to scavenging for food, tending to the weak and injured, scraping together ammunition and preparing for the worst. Perhaps, Girty saw this. Perhaps he knew that any afternoon attack would result in a mass slaughter far greater than Gnadenhütten. Perhaps he knew that the safest move on his part would be to allow Crawford and his sad forces a last chance to escape. And, perhaps, not.[60]

Under a rising moon, Crawford again held counsel. He ordered Leet to assemble a retreat in columns of four. The other officers disagreed. There was no one direction they could take without immediate attack and, even if united by consensus, they could muster no speed to outrun the enemy forces presumed ready and waiting. Crawford may have suggested using the southeast route by which they found Battle Island. Brigadier Major Daniel Leet recommended a path due west, which, despite leading farther into Indian territory, seemed the least guarded by the outlying forces. Rose may have noted that that route was heavy with marshes, as he had seen cranberry bogs before his attack at the southwestern ravine. Major James Brinton, fifth in command, likely supported Leet's strategy. Col. John McClelland, already directed to lead the rear companies, knew that whichever direction they would take, he and his men would be hit the hardest. Crawford ruled; the route would be south, across familiar terrain, four men abreast.

He directed his men to bury the dead and light a fire above their graves, discouraging the savages from exhuming their bodies for scalps. The injured

---

[60] Of the many accounts of Girty waving his white flag at Battle Island, all agree that Girty was distinguishable by the red scarf hat he wore while riding his signature white horse. Authors Butterfield, Eckert, and Thompson record his presence. Only Girty denies it. In several letters, he avows he was never a part of the fight on the plains of Sandusky. But, of course, he would appear soon enough later.

and ill, he directed, should be laid on make-shift litters, dragged by horses in the center columns. Dr. Knight triaged who could survive, who would not, and who, for the sake of all others, should be left to their own devices.

There were, in fact, injured men for whom the prospect of a retreat was more frightening than abandonment. One of Daniel Leet's captains, evidently in a catatonic state, professed he would not, could not, ride. Leet ordered him to mount. The man, in deep shock, stood between his commanding officer and God, insisting he would only ride if he could confess his sins to the Almighty. He wished only to say the Lord's Prayer. The injured captain recited the first line, "Our Father, which art in heaven, hallowed be…." and stumbled, his tongue parched, unable to get the words out. He tried again. "Our Father, in heaven, hallowed by thy name; thy kingdom…will be done." Leet ordered the man to mount, but, sobbing, he refused until he was safe in the love of his savior. He tried yet again. And again he could not get the words right. The men were anxious to ride. The poor captain tried one last time. But Leet would have no more of it. He grabbed the captain by his collar, hoisted him with one arm, and flung him to the mount of a fellow rider. Now was no time for God.[61]

Before Crawford could give the command to retreat, a full company under Captain John Hardin, suddenly broke ranks and fled to the southeast. Outraged, Crawford called for sufficient men to follow him to restrain Hardin and his defecting posse. He handed his official command to Daniel Leet. Within minutes, the warriors chased Hardin's men and fired. Crawford tried to take up the Indian pursuit from the rear. And he, too, fired. Thinking the warriors were in full attack now, Leet's companies, not all of whom were yet mounted, started fleeing. And as they dashed off, the assembled columns scattered, galloping in their own senseless directions. The mass exodus of mounted riders crashed in the confusion, aimless, their horses rearing to follow the fleet. Others steered clear, riding defenseless, alone, into the black sea of swirling grass.

McClelland may have been the first casualty. In offering up his horse to a lame soldier, he was crushed in the stampede.

Crawford, realizing his impulse to follow Hardin had been a fool's errand, returned to restore order. Too late, he called for Major Rose and John

---

[61] Draper, MSS 2S4

Slover. Dr. Knight, still tending to the wounded, helped some men mount in desperate hope of escape. And, while the imminent assault had not advanced onto Battle Island, he told others remaining to flee for their lives. But of the sentries, strictly prohibited from leaving their posts, Crawford gave no command. He knew not where his son or son-in-law had gone, and protective of them, searched wildly in the darkness of the plains.

Meanwhile, Leet and Brinton now headed southwest, steering well away from the stampede Hardin had incited. As Leet had proposed, the marshes due south might provide passage if they could steer clear to the west. Yet other companies saw them in the rising moon light, and seeing Leet's more organized drive, they followed at a quickening pace. Reaching the road at which Rose had been nearly ambushed, they were charged once again by waiting Shawnees, and so dashed into the denser grasses heading to the marsh. Major Brinton was hit. Leet assured him he would get them both to safety. Yet, some horses could not ply the tall weeds, slowing down dangerously in their dodge. Others charged straight into the bogs, sinking their horses into a mire so deep the riders could do nothing more than abandon their mounts and swim to safety.

John Slover had done just this. Leaving his horse to fend for his life, he splashed through the dark bog, seeking an edge from which to crawl out. But several warriors heard him, and only by using his wet musket as a club did Slover manage to fend them off. He was not the only one wet and terrified. He came upon six other exhausted men nearly drowned in the mire. They teamed up to walk due east all night long.

Major Rose had affected his own company's escape, heading due west, until, noticing the moon's odd position, he realized his error. Reversing course, he managed to get a full company to ride south before heading east, as he had first intended.

Of the 400 or more men who had fled Battle Island hours before, Leet may have led the largest companies. Williamson, however, led the most men. Proving Crawford had been right, Williamson's success may have been the daunting breadth of his riders, even moving at a pace that accommodated the injured on litters. Despite untold casualties afflicted by gunshot, tomahawk, exhaustion, dehydration or sheer terror, they reached the abandoned village that had spooked them just three day before. There, they rested, filled canteens and proceeded east toward Schönbrunn. Along the way, riding evidently at a faster gait, Major Rose met up with Williamson and joined forces.

Rose however was not comfortable at the speed Williamson's men were driving, fearing the Delawares or Shawnees would soon catch up. In fact, the British Rangers were faster and, indeed, they found Williamson's companies at a spot called Olentangy. The Shawnees soon arrived. Dismounted in battle for a full hour, Williamson's men managed to repel the enemy forces in what may have been the one victory of the entire expedition. He and his men were able to retreat to the protection of the wooded hills east of the Muskingum, and there find what they needed most: deep, restful sleep.

For Crawford and Knight, this would not come for days.

At the Stake

The tribes of the Six Nations, as well as of the Delawares, Shawnees, and Hurons, had many rules of war. Of these, one was inviolate: an enemy captured by one tribe belonged to that tribe. If white, the captive could not be traded, bartered or ransomed between, or among, other tribes. If white *and* lucky, he could be ransomed to the British, French or Americans, but not to another tribe. A captive's fate could only be decided by the people who had "won" him in battle.

A second custom was that of face painting. Tribes had their own distinctive war paints and each colorful grease mark had its own meaning. Some were meant to frighten the enemy in battle, others to honor the spirit of their ancestors. At other times, certain face painting gave recognition to the bravery of a young warrior, the wisdom of an elder chief, or the fate of a captured enemy. When a man was condemned to death, his face was painted black.

Not long after meeting up with five exhausted men skulking on knees through the dense Sandusky Plains to seek safety across the Muskingum, Colonel Crawford and Dr. Knight were captured by four Delaware warriors scouting for stragglers or scalps. The Natives knew instantly whom they had caught. The reward for Crawford's scalp alone would be so much greater than the value of all others. Brought back alive, he would be worth even more. The Delawares tied their captives to separate horses and made them each march the entirety of the long trek back to the Delawares' village northwest. None was in any condition to resist—or to walk.

At Captive's Town, Crawford was greeted by each of the two most respected sachem of the Delawares: Hopocan, (sometimes called Pimoacan,) but known to the white man as Captain Pipe, and Wingenund. Each knew Crawford well. Captain Pipe had met with him at Fort Pitt. And Wingenund, a close friend of Simon Girty, had once visited Crawford at his own Spring Garden homestead.[62] Ever since their respective first meetings, they had heard much about his exploits and of his political clout to the east. Yet, they were not pleased to see him.

Word among the villagers spread quickly. The "Big Chief" of the avenging white man had been brought into town. The other captives had been bound and tied, waiting to learn their fates. They witnessed returning warriors showing off scalps retrieved from the bloody grasses of the Sandusky. In Hopocan's village, not ten miles beyond, the village was preparing for trial. There the two chiefs would decide what to do with Colonel Crawford and Dr. Knight. Less concerned were they about the lower ranked captives, whose ransoms were no more valuable to them than the scalp bounties the British might pay. Captain Pipe and Wingenund allowed for their immediate disposal. The women and children of the small village descended on the lesser captives with clubs and burning torches and did away with the helpless souls. But not before, of course, claiming their scalps.

With his only witnesses executed without ceremony, Crawford must have known he would be next. If he had but one chance of survival, he might have hoped that Simon Girty would intervene. Crawford asked expressly to meet with Girty. And, surprisingly, Captain Pipe allowed it. Except that Girty was in a different town, and not the one in which he and Knight were "condemned" to stand trial. Separated from Dr. Knight, Crawford was bound and marched off to the homestead of one Alex McCormick, a British trader, where Simon Girty was staying. By nightfall, Crawford was dumped at Girty's feet.

Their conversation had to have been pathetic. Crawford's defense had to have been dire, his pleas for forgiveness tearful, and his bribes of inordinate wealth laughable. Girty knew the score. He informed Crawford that the Natives wanted only one thing: revenge for the massacre at Gnadenhütten. Crawford had had nothing to do with that, he argued. But Girty would point out that Colonel Williamson had just fought with Crawford, and that Crawford, by allowing Williamson to join in his failed efforts, was guilty of

---

[62] Creigh, *History of Washington County*, pg. 288

condoning those sins. Crawford protested. He argued that the very reason he was put in charge of the expedition to the Sandusky was to make certain nothing like Gnadenhütten would happen again. Further, Crawford might have argued, his defense at Battle Island was honorable. Girty perhaps countered that an honorable commander would have met with his enemy baring the white flag of peace. Crawford no doubt pleaded for Girty's help, again offering him his horse, or untold quantities of arms, or silver and gold that he might or might not have owned. In return, Girty offered him just one thing. If Crawford were able, he could escape. Girty, however, would not help. And with that suggestion, Crawford was taken away to Hopocan's Town under the tightest bonds, escorted by a full complement of warriors each of whom could outrun the sixty-year old Colonel, even if their tomahawks could not.

Had Girty turned his back, Crawford should have been so lucky.

*   *   *   *   *

American children used to play a cruel schoolyard game. Two teams of children lined up shoulder-to-shoulder in columns facing each other. One child, decided by a random count, or, worse, by bullies amongst them, must scramble between the two phalanxes, crouched "on all fours" while the standing kids get to smack his butt. An agile child would feel no pain. A clumsy or chubby child would. The slower the child, the greater the injury. Feeding off the frenzy, subsequent rounds would inflict the worst on the weakest.

At Captain Pipe's village on June 11, 1782, Crawford was made to "run the gauntlet." He was stripped of shirt and boots. The "teams" through which he was forced to scramble were women and children, all of whom were allowed to use clubs, sharp sticks, or burning branches to slow Crawford's crawl.

On the Native's playground, running the gauntlet allowed the youngest warriors to test their might. Of course, Crawford had nothing to prove. Stabbed, singed and sore, he survived the ordeal and was given rest while the tribal council stood trial.

It is often recorded that native Chiefs were fond of addressing their people in long, thoughtful, and often eloquent expressions of honor and unity. The voice of authority came from the strongest and wisest men. But the truth is that Chiefs always consulted first with their wives and matriarchs. It was the Clan Mothers who had immense latitude to decide critical issues of survival and safety.[63] It was they who worked the hardest (just as Washington had noted.) It was they who ensured that the tribe was fed, was clothed and protected, was strong and sustainable. It was they who held Crawford's fate in their hands. It was they who painted his face black.

Dr. Knight was brought out from some other holding place. The Delaware interpreter John Slover, since captured, was presented, too. They were seated on the ground in front of a large audience of elders, women, children, and braves, all focused on a large fire pit, actively ablaze despite the afternoon's heat. A tall stake had been driven into the ground just to the rear of the fire. Crawford was brought out, stripped naked, and tied to the stake, both arms bound and tethered to a loop high on the pole. His hands, also bound, were tethered to its base. As witness, Dr. Knight would later note that Crawford's short leeway allowed him only to run around the stake but once or twice in either rotation.

Either Wingenund or Captain Pipe issued the trial's verdict. Simon Girty arrived just in time to hear what he knew would come to pass. William Crawford would be burned at the stake. Yet, first things first, he would be tortured to appease the grief and anger that so many of those in attendance could not abide. To his misinformed jury, Crawford had murdered 96 innocent Delawares in cold blood, wholly defenseless, held in locked huts, their bodies then burned to ash. Whether or not Wingenund or Captain Pipe knew that Colonel David Williamson had been the evil perpetrator or that Colonel William Crawford had not even served in that horrific commission was immaterial to the justice these villagers so desperately desired. In fact, by exacting the revenge they demanded, their righteous intent was actually far kinder than Hammurabi's code. The death of one man would weigh in balance to the murder of so many more. Of course, any torture leading up to Crawford's death would be irrelevant to that summation.

Tied to the stake, fevered by exhaustion and sweltering from the flames lapping just inches from his bare skin, Crawford was said to have turned to Simon Girty, asking him if the Indians intended to burn him alive. Girty either nodded "yes" or, more cruelly, replied, "Not yet."

---

[63] Haudenosaunee Confederacy, About Us, https://www.haudenosauneeconfederacy.com/who-we-are/

As many as seventy warriors approached Crawford with their guns loaded only with powder. One by one, or just several at time, they fired at Crawford, shooting white-hot sulfur into his sweating pores, burning his skin to a sickening gray.

It is believed by some that the first round of torture so alarmed Simon Girty he interceded with offers of ransom to Chief Pipe, Wingenund, or whomever would listen. Some said that Girty offered £300 in gold. Others aver that Chief Pipe responded to Girty, saying that if he so valued this murderer, then Girty himself should take the man's place.[64] Just as likely, Simon Girty remained silent throughout.

Chief Pipe approached Crawford and cut off his ears.

Then, younger braves picked up hickory poles whose tips were glowing in the fire. They poked Crawford all over, singeing his nipples, armpits and other body parts not so private to the whooping audience.

The women, too, stood up and, with wooden paddles, scooped burning embers and tossed them at Crawford's feet. The embers were spread to cover any and all ground upon which Crawford could stand. Witnesses like Knight and Slover said that Crawford only moaned. No doubt, too exhausted to scream, he was able only to mumble prayers for his immediate death. Yet, witnesses say, too, the torture went on for another hour, perhaps longer.

Once contorted and charred to bare bones, his black face slumped on a steaming chest, Crawford, at last dead, was scalped.

---

[64] Eckert, *That Dark and Bloody River*, pg. 388

The Consequences

Daniel Leet would not learn of Crawford's torture until nearly a month later. Dr. Knight, petrified by the trauma he and Slover witnessed firsthand, had been ordered to another village. Along this trek, frail and starving, he was able to convince his lone captor that he would not flee and, yet, once unrestrained to eat with his hands, managed to strike his captor with a tree limb and run. Slover, too, was taken to a different village. Facing certain death, naked and bound to a tree in the darkest hours of his capture, he was able to loosen leather straps, tiptoe to a corral of horses and escape. Although pursued for miles, his woodland skills won his freedom.

By July 4th, Dr. Knight would appear exhausted and emaciated, having walked some two hundred miles back to Fort Pitt. Among the details he and Slover shared of the entire expedition was news that both Crawford's nephew and son-in-law had been scalped and murdered. Crawford's son John, however, made it home safely to his mother Hannah, although he knew not then where his father had gone. Colonel David Williamson also returned home, celebrating his triumph in fleeing Battle Island as well as repelling the British Rangers at Olentangy. Of his several letters to Irvine, boasting of his bravery, he never showed any remorse for the disastrous decisions he had coerced Crawford's council to accept, nor did he—or would he have thought to—accept dishonor for having left Crawford to die for his own outrageous sins. Thus greeted as a hero back in Washington, Williamson was elected a County Lieutenant, and then Sheriff. Years later, however, he ventured into many successive business opportunities, all of which failed. He died in 1814, an alcoholic in absolute poverty.

As for Daniel Leet and his wounded comrade Major John Brinton, both returned also to Washington town. Daniel took Brinton to rest in his lone cabin, seeking medical aid likely from Dr. Absalom Baird. Together the two men convalesced, healing wounds, feeding failed egos, accepting their own frail mortalities.

Just days after returning from their own personal nightmares, news of the raid on Hanna's Town, just fifty miles east, haunted their waking dreams.

Washington County, Pennsylvania – 1782

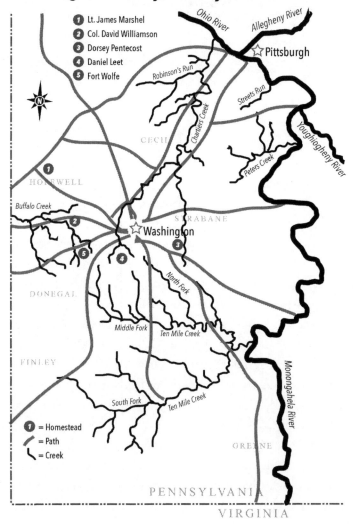

Fort Wolfe

Of course, Leet, too, had been hailed a hero upon returning to Washington. Apparently, victory was not a prerequisite to earning that honor; only survival was. But Leet was credited for having commanded the swift, albeit chaotic, retreat from Battle Island, and he was further credited by Major Brinton for having saved his life, and that of his own company, leading them to escape by a route others had not considered, or, if considered, discredited. Besides the Shawnees ambush that threatened those who followed Leet, his large companies escaped unscathed, yet, wholly traumatized.

Legend says that Daniel Leet never spoke about Crawford's Defeat, never shared a single story about the long, arduous advance, the bloody and parched conditions of battle, nor the harried retreat to safety. Testimony from his brothers proves that Leet experienced it all, but from Daniel's own lips, none could recall a single word.[65] The miserable events happened, and that was all. Daniel Leet wished it would be forgotten.

But there were others who wanted to know everything. Eagerly greeting the survivors in Mingo Bottom was Dorsey Pentecost. His report to Pennsylvania's President Moore on that date, explained the horrific odds Crawford had met on the plains of what he spelled "St. Duskie." In part, it read:

> "As the people were much confused when I met them, I could not get the information requisite… I am told that the Indians were much superior to our people, and that in the engagement they suffered greatly, and also that Col. Crawford strongly recommended to

---

[65] Draper MSS 2S4

return before they got to the town, alleging that our people were too weak, as the Indians had early intelligence of their coming, but he was overruled by the rest of the officers."[66]

The truth of the events leading to—and escaping from—Battle Island were embellished from the start. By July, the real story was what had happened to Colonel Crawford. Only three white men, Knight and Slover, and Simon Girty, were able to say for sure. But the news so piqued local interests that a young lawyer, newly arrived from Maryland, sat at Knight's bedside to take down his oral history. He would soon publish a book relating Knight's and Slover's tales, edited, of course, for narrative continuity, and shaped—why not?—for dramatic purpose.

Hugh Henry Brackenridge was an outspoken racist who vilified every contribution any Native had offered in the name of peace, slandering any white survivor who faulted himself for the misfortunes or wounds brought on by his vicious enemy, vindicating all who had marched to the Sandusky, a clearly bothersome campaign necessitated only because of the warrantless terrorism threatened by the wicked savages.

After retelling the Sandusky survivors' accounts, he addended an essay, arguing with his own "sound" Christian principles for the wholesale eradication of the American Indian.

> "The whole of this earth was given to man, and all descendants of Adam have a right to share it equally. There is no right of the primogeniture in the laws of nature and of nations…
>
> "What use do these ring streaked, spotted and speckled cattle make of the soil? Do they till it? Revelation said to man, "Thou shalt till the ground." This alone is human life. It is favorable to population, to science, to the information of a human mind in the worship of a God…
>
> "If we could have any faith in the savages, I would suffer them to live, provided they would no longer make war amongst themselves, or against others by lurking privately on the path ways of the wood, and putting unarmed and defenceless inhabitants to death, or

---

[66] Creigh, *History of Washington County*, pg. 290

attacking women and children in the frontier families, and on their ceasing in the mean to exercise torture..."

"I do not know but I ought to recall my word and say, that even reforming from these practices, they ought not to live: These nations are so degenerate from the life of man, so devoid of every sentiment of generosity, so prone to every vicious excess of passion, so faithless, and so incapable of all civilization, that it is dangerous to the good order of the world that they should exist in it."[67]

Brackenridge was not without his fans, literary or otherwise. His racial sentiments were shared by many, particularly on the western frontier. Without benefit of extant letters from Daniel Leet—or any of the men Leet had led to safety—it is not known how he justified his own participation in the effort to rid the Sandusky Natives so soon after the massacre at Gnadenhütten, whether or not he had participated in any part of the earlier atrocity.

It is known, however, from Dorsey Pentecost, that plans were discussed immediately to mount a third campaign. Daniel Leet took no part in that. Yet his brother William took command of Vance's Fort (near Burgettstown, Pennsylvania) to prepare for an Indian retaliation. Fort Vance, a simple blockade with only a few cabins in which to shelter local families, was the fort where Robert Wallace had hoped to muster a search party for his missing wife and children.

In fact, hundreds of similar forts were built all around the western frontier. Neither funded by the Continental Congress nor local counties, they were built mostly by residents for their own protection. Some were just simple stockade enclosures protecting a lone homestead. Others were blockhouses stocked with ammunition and dried foods. They served the local community in times of Indian raids or fear of the same.

Closest to Daniel Leet's homestead was Fort Wolfe. Built in 1780 by Jacob Wolfe for his family's own safety, it enclosed both his cabin and a blockhouse. It was here, after a singularly unselfish act of bravery few men would ever come to believe, Daniel Leet met his wife.

---

[67] Brackenridge, *Narratives of a Late Expedition*, pg. 42

PART THREE
(1782-1799)

*In which cheap land becomes
prohibitively expensive to those
whose greed has no boundaries.*

Philadelphia's Health

As in any densely populated society, Philadelphians were subject to many infectious diseases. Scarlet fever, diphtheria, measles, small pox, and tuberculosis all had their rounds. Children were particularly susceptible to bacteria and viruses contacted through poor hygiene and contaminated water sources for which the city had no process of purification as yet. In 1783, and again in 1784, scarlet fever affected many, both young and old, but it was the young to which the disease was most dangerous.

Scarlet fever was something like strep throat, engorging the victim's "fauces" and tonsils with a raw and acrid inflammation. The disease also caused a child to break out in a red rash across the chest and arms. A fever often ensued for days, sometimes weeks, debilitating the child who would be quarantined to bedrest, and left immobile, sometimes for months on end.

Dr. William Buchan's *Treatise on Domestic Medicine* offered the following care for symptoms of the disease: "There is seldom any occasion for medicine in this disease. The patient ought, however, to keep within doors, to abstain from flesh, strong liquors, and cordials, and to take plenty of cool diluting drink. If the fever runs high, the belly must be kept gently open by emollient clysters, or small doses of nitre and rhubarb. A scruple of the former, with five grains of the latter, may be taken thrice a-day, or oftener if necessary."[1]

Not until 1924 was scarlet fever first abated with antitoxins; only in 1940, with the introduction of penicillin, was there a proven cure.

---

[1] Buchan, *Domestic Medicine*, pg. 246

Thomas Shields' young family did not escape the ravages of childhood disease. Although blessed with seven children between 1768 and 1783—Mary, Thomas Jr., James, Robert, John, David, Lydia, and William—Thomas and Lydia lost their second daughter, Lydia, born at noon on Tuesday, September 21, 1781. She died just eleven months and four days later.

Pediatric studies of the decade suggest that nearly half of all children did not survive their fifth birthday.[2] Whether that percentage was greater or less for children raised in more rural settings is not certain. Yet, privileged by wealth and community, Thomas Shields had access to the best healthcare Philadelphia could then offer. It came knocking at his front door in the name of Dr. Benjamin Rush.

An early signer of the Declaration of Independence, Dr. Rush was one of the more socially minded physicians in Philadelphia. He was a regular essayist who published his many inquiries into, and observations of, disease and issues of public health.

Recorded in Thomas Shields' day journal of June 7, 1782, was the doctor's handwritten inscription: "Received of Mr. Thomas Shields the full value of my account Including for medicines and attendance to his family to this day. B. Rush."

Baby Lydia died on August 22, 1782. The Shields family Bible does not record the cause of death.

---

[2] https://www.statista.com/statistics/1041693/united-states-all-time-child-mortality-rate/

The Tale

Three hundred miles to the west, that same year, 1782, the people of Washington, Pennsylvania, were once again alarmed by marauding Indians. Defending their small homestead along Buffalo Creek, William and Willamina Carson kept their cabin barricaded for fear of attack. They could see the night fires of menacing Indians encamped outside. They would not go away. Days and nights passed. When William heard the gobble of a wild turkey just outside his door, he dared to bag it for supper. William was ambushed, murdered, and scalped. Willamina immediately fled to Fort Wolfe.

Returning home just a few days later, mourning her husband, dressed and veiled in customary black, she again learned that the Indians were seen nearby. Again she retreated to Fort Wolfe. Without her late husband to protect her, she had no choice but to wait out the threat, grieving her husband's death in the company of strangers. Indeed, the Indians did return. They laid siege on Fort Wolfe, intending to starve out the inhabitants just as they had done to the Carson homestead. Nearly a week passed. No word could be sent for help. Certain death waited outside the stockade walls. Fearing the worst, now hungry and sleep ridden, the lone community knew they had to do something. That night, under the cloak of darkness, still wearing her black dress and veil, Willamina Carson saddled up a black mare, and charged out of the fort to ride like hell for help. She steered her horse between the widest distances of the Indians' campfires, and succeeded, after twenty miles, in reaching a blockhouse in Connellsville. There she rallied a militia sufficient to scare off the Indians that had camped outside Fort Wolfe for so many days. Daring, brave, fleet and wily, Willamina Carson became an American hero.

The story was shared far and wide. It travelled by oral tradition in ways that naturally confused her name and her heritage, suiting the interests of the storyteller or the audience. But the tale added organically to early American culture a refreshing depiction of bravery. It embodied, too, an empathy for loss and a brilliance of decisive action, perfect in its timing, and resolute in execution. The story spoke to the welcome contribution of women's pluck and fortitude in ways that Betsy Ross and Molly Pitcher had not. Here was a woman who had not just sewn a flag or carried water to thirsty soldiers; here was a powerhouse of bravery, horsemanship and cunning. Further, the story did not obsess on racism—the outlying enemy could have been any— it spoke of valor. It perversely begged obvious questions of sexism without having to answer them. Where were the "brave" men who were also captive in the fort? Why would they shamelessly allow a widow to risk her own life? Had she alone decided to mount the dark horse?

The Midnight Ride of Willamina (nee Balla) Carson became legend. So, too, did the Midnight Ride of Margarita Bella whose Italian husband had been stationed at Fort Pitt. Also famous was the Midnight Ride of Wilhelmine Ballou, a French Huguenot, who fled to Fort McIntosh. So did Williamina Bally Corson who saved Fort Harmar, as did Willamine Balla save Little Washington. Like any great legend, the truth is not found in the details, but rather in its cultural relevance. For well more than a hundred years, the story gave hope to the western frontier. It promised that "the least" among us could champion the most dire of circumstances: hunger, terror, isolation, depravity—even certain death.

Indeed, there was actual truth to the story, too. The last will and testament of a one William Carson, written in 1781, was executed in 1783:

> "In the name of God Amen, I William Carson of Washington County, state of Pennsylvania, being weak of body but of sound & perfect mind & memory [,] blessed be almighty God for the same [,] do make and publish this my last will and testament in manner following (that is to say) First I give & bequaith unto my beloved wife Willamina[3] Carson all my moveable affects in my dwelling house on buffalo Creek except my weaving. Apparel also, I give and

---

[3] The spelling as it appears in William Carson's will, whether written by Carson or an acquaintance of his, would forever appear later as Wilhelmina.

bequaith unto said Willamina my black mare and woman's riding saddle, likewise her choise of aney one of my Cows likewise three sheep her the said Willamina to have her choice."

Whether or not William Carson died in an Indian ambush, he *did* reside on Buffalo Creek near Fort Wolfe, he *was* listed in local tax records of the area, and he *did* own a black horse and a women's riding saddle. Furthermore, his probate was recorded on March 18 of 1783.

Wilhelmina Balla was said to have been born on December 28, 1748, in or near Valley Forge, Pennsylvania. She would have been 35 at her husband's demise. As such, she would have been fit and able to ride a horse, especially a familiar black mare on her own riding saddle.

These dates lend even further truth to all of this. Within two months of her husband's death, Wilhelmina Carson married Daniel Leet. So smitten by her bravery and beauty, goes the legend, Daniel asked for her hand in marriage and she agreed without hesitation. There is no record of that date, nor of the ceremony or its location, but, on February 27, 1784, nine months after their indeterminate nuptials, Eliza Marie Leet was born.

Leet's Brinton

With the birth of Eliza, Daniel and Wilhelmina nestled in their cabin on Chartiers Creek. Long after settling his parents in Leet's Fancy, and well before falling for his heroic wife, Daniel Leet had claimed his own homestead by benefit of a Virginia certificate, allowing him up to 400 acres. A tax exoneration record of 1783, however, states that his assets were 600 acres, 3 horses, and 2 cows.[4] While it would have been likely the certificate he earned was bounty for his service in the Revolution, the fact is the certificate was issued as a matter of state house-cleaning. The Virginia Land Office Act of 1779 awarded those who had settled on unclaimed land prior to 1778 a "preemption" certificate. The Act exclusively addressed the issue of settlers in four districts, once collectively known as West Augusta, fully intending to clean up the state's records because, for the five years prior, in light of more important concerns, the land office had simply been closed.

Leet had laid claim to property three miles away from his parents' homestead to build his own. At some point soon thereafter, he purchased—or possibly just "improved upon"—another 200 acres. In September of 1784, Leet officially surveyed his 600 acres on Chartiers Creek. He would later prove his warrant in March of 1785; evidence of a functional cabin was more than sufficient. On October 12, 1785, the Honorable Charles Biddle, President of the Pennsylvania Supreme Council, signed the patent. For the record, Leet paid three pounds, six shillings and eight pence for all or part of the property he then named "Brinton."[5]

---

[4] Pennsylvania, US Tax and Exoneration, Straban Township, 1768-1801

[5] The document however spells it "Brenton."

That patent, a sheet of original parchment approximately 15" x 12" with wax remnants of the state's seal still intact, was discovered in the attic of a home in California in July, 2020.

The document was gifted to the Washington County Historical Society where it resides with another patent, issued in 1787, assigned to Daniel Leet, on behalf of his sister, Elizabeth. Not until 1790 were women allowed to own property in their own name.

Both documents predate the US Constitution.

Well after this book was already half-written, the original deed for "Brinton" was discovered, quite serendipitously, in an attic in California. Courtesy of the Sewickley Valley Historical Society and the Washington County Historical Society where it is archived.

Peace Ratified

On April 15, 1783, the Continental Congress ratified a preliminary peace treaty with the British, effectively ending the Revolutionary War. Following Cornwallis's capture at Yorktown, the French took the opportunity to coerce the Americans into peace talks in Paris. John Jay, John Adams, and Benjamin Franklin took up the charge. Henry Laurens, once president of the Continental Congress, was then a naval prisoner of the Brits; it was his exchange that returned Cornwallis to London. Spain and the Netherlands also joined into the discussion, each having been at war with Great Britain, too. The peace talks did not conclude until September 3 when the Americans, French and Spaniards all signed separate treaties. In particular, the British treaty ceded back the land that France had claimed—that which was lost to the Brits in the French & Indian War—known as the Northwest Territory. It was what the American frontiersman had been calling for decades the Ohio country. Of course, it was so much more.

To modern Americans, the territory included all of present-day Ohio, Michigan, Indiana, Illinois, Wisconsin, and a large chunk of Minnesota, too.

The promise of united American states claiming their manifest opportunity to expand farther west was now at hand. Those who had speculated that the country's wealth could only be earned through such opportunity now went to work. And, like others, Dorsey Pentecost, a mere County Councilor to the State Assembly took to his soapbox to speak publicly of a land scheme in the Ohio country, destined to become the next state.

In June of 1783, he wrote to James Wilson, a federal lawyer and Pennsylvania representative, but more presciently, a close associate of Robert Morris who, in designing the Bank of North America, served as his chief legal counsel. Whether or not Pentecost knew then that Wilson was as hungry to profit from a new land scheme as he himself was, his letter addressed more altruistic opportunities for federal interests to defray the national debt.

Dated June 26, 1783, from Washington County, PA:

> "Dear Sir,
>
> "On my return from your City to this County the Last Spring I was inform'd by Sundry persons that many partie's of People in this Country ware prepairing to go into what is called the Indean Country to improve Lands, and soon after I was applied to by Some Gentlemen for my Opinion of Such a Measure, after receiving every mark of my disapprobation, and all argument that I was Capable to advance against a measure in my Opinion so Destructive to good Order, and in its self Impolitic and unjust, I was shewn ... some resolutions that Congress had made relaiting to the Lands of the back Country in General..."

Here, Pentecost alludes to a Resolution of Congress to subdivide lands, yet, allowing current settlers immediate rights to that which had been settled.

> "In Consequence of their great faith on those Resolutions, and the natural propensity in mankind to Engroce property, many People have Crosed the river Ohio and made improvements without Number. Large Parties are now actually in the Country (Some for the avowed purpose of taking Possession at the Mouth of Muskingum) and more are prepairing to go, their, to the Sciota [River] and other places. I have been in and Seen People from almost every part of this Country Since my return home, and find a disposition in many from Every Quarter to go into this business, and its no wonder for I am assured that the Improvers have Sold their Claims to great advantage, Some upwards of a £100 a Tract..."

And now Pentecost lays down his grand idea.

> "First then I would advise that Congress Should Settle with the Indians, either by placing Strong Garrisa[ns] at Niagary and Detroit, or else by a Treaty... Secondly and immediately Lay out the

Lands North of the Ohio up to Lake Erie, West of the Western
bounds of this State to include the rivers Muskingum and Sciota
into a New State for the Sole Purpose of accommodating, and ful-
filing our engagements to our Patriotic Army to whome we owe our
Existance as a people...

"Then Sir I would lay out the rest of the Country into Compact
and Convenient States, Set a Very Moderate price on the Lands (I
mean the whole Except what is already in Occupence under Title,
and the Lands laid out for the Army) let it be so Very moderate that
the Price and the Soil would Invite people from all parts of the world
to Come and Settle them... I Know it may be said and with great
reason that we are indebted and our faith Plighted to our worthy
alleys, our army and our friends, and that the Easiest Eligable, most
Certain, and Speedy way to pay those debts will be by the Sale of
those Lands Ceded to us, and that we have got as much from Bre-
tain as will pay the Expense of the War...

"If you Sell the Lands to any that please to purchase, Large
Tracts will fall into the hands of Individuals, which is alwaye injurious to a Commonwealth perticuliar in its Infancy, and when a
Country is well peopled, there can be no want of publick money
when the Inhabitants are Industrious..."

Pentecost's letter hardly ends with this warning. His admonitions are as
speculative as his spelling is self-taught. But he prattled on for several para-
graphs more before attempting to conclude his letter to James Wilson.

"... I Know a Question will arise, what is to be done with the
Indians on your plan Especially as you prefer a Treaty. I answer Lay
out as much Lands for them as will Support them by Cultivation,
withhold from them Arms, and ammunition (which may be effected
by proper regulations) and reduce them to Labour for their Living
as we do, If it should be said their Trade would be advantagious to
the Community, I answer not so much as their peace, and that their
Trade is much declined, and if the Peltry business is still Valuable
let our own people be Imployed in it and receive the Benefit.

"When I set down to write I intended only to give you a Narative of the Land Jobing business now carrying on amongst us, but that seemed so materially Connected with the rest that I was led to say something on the Scale of Politicks, and although it comes from an obscure man, Seclused from the Bustle on the Bank of Ohio, yet permit me to assure you that its from the heart of an honest friend to his contry, I Shall therefore conclude with assuring you that I am with perfect Esteem,

Yr Very obd* Hmb Serv*

Dorsey Pentecost

"P. S. Permit me to Suggest a nother reason for my opinion in Seling our back Lands Cheap & to none but setlers. If Congress can bring the States into the Measure to a Tax upon Imported Articles (which is Certainly the most Just Tax upon Earth, and no plan can posibly be Devised Equal to it, for Ease and Quikness) I Say Sr that if the States will adopt the Plan our National Debt will be Easily paid and our Lands peopled, and in that Case there can be no Necessity for a heavy price on the Lands.   Yrs&c. DP."

By 1789, Wilson would become an Associate Justice of the Supreme Court. Sooner than that, however, Pentecost would find himself in serious debt, owing to his partnership with Levi Hollingsworth with whom he invested in the Ohio Trading Company. Currency matters did not improve. And land values, as a result of poor sales, got no better. In 1786, he was defrocked from his public office by the debtor's courts of Pennsylvania.

By then, of course, the federal union had engaged the Ohio Indians in a series of treaties to rid them of their lands. Native tribes of the Ohio country included the Shawnees, Delawares, Miamis, and Wyandots. So, naturally, in October, 1784, Americans signed the Treaty of Fort Stanwix with the Iroquois. The treaty ceded all of the Ohio country to the free colonists.[6] Except that, the Iroquois had no rights to cede it. If any tribes did, they would have been the Shawnees, Delawares, Miamis or Wyandots.

---

[6] Text of Treaty: https://ohiohistorycentral.org/w/Treaty_of_Fort_Stanwix_(1784)_(Transcript)

Yet Another Treaty

It was a simple document. The Treaty of Fort Stanwix contained just four articles. In addition to a prisoner exchange and assuring the Tuscaroras and Oneida tribes sovereignty over lands already occupied (and hardly contested) in northern New York, the treaty attempted to outline boundaries beyond which the Iroquois would have no rights. The description relies on the names of Indian creeks and trading posts no longer familiar, and asserts boundaries of Pennsylvania and north-south longitudes hardly scientific. Essentially the treaty defined not the Ohio country, but the western and southern limit to the Iroquois homelands. It also did not clarify Pennsylvania's sovereign rights to the "Erie triangle" until a subsequent treaty, agreed at Fort McIntosh in 1785, then formalized later at Fort Harmar, did that trick.

So, with the United States of America now in possession of the Northwest Territory—despite any objections Natives might have held and, yet, over which the Americans could now govern—and the "signing" of the Treaties of Fort Stanwix and Fort McIntosh, Pennsylvania became the geographic "Commonwealth" it is today. And, as a public Commonwealth, the state now had the sovereign power to sell land for the common good.

If the Northwest Territory was ever intended to become a "land grab," Pennsylvania surely would now. Or so its commissioners hoped. Clearly, they wished to upstage any interest in the Ohio lands. And yet, perhaps, Dorsey Pentecost had had a good idea.

The first item of Pennsylvania's strategy was to sell western lands under the promise of the Continental Army's offer of bounties to its victorious soldiers and officers. To satisfy that same offer Daniel Leet and others had considered while staying with their regiments after the victory at Trenton,

Congress owed land bounties even to the lowliest Continental fifer. The terms and values, of course, were undecided then, and the promise was good only as long as victory was had. The offer was realized in the form of certificates valued at the current market rate for gold or silver. However, by the time the Treaty of Paris was effectuated, the value of gold and silver had plummeted drastically.

A Pennsylvania Act of December 18th, 1780, attempted to adjust for the depreciation then experienced and proposed to "make good" on any future depreciation of the certificates. The gambit was based on selling property, mostly in the east, forfeited by Tories who had committed treason in their loyalty to the throne. An earlier act of 1778 had allowed Congress to confiscate estates and reclaim land owned by "traitors and seditious persons." Unfortunately, as it would turn out, the value of these estates seemed to have evaporated when their owners sailed back to England. As such, the trade of state-issued certificates for continental assets—or even the other way around—did not really equate.

Still, the sum of all the certificates represented a massive debt owed by Pennsylvania. If, after the war, the Federal debt was $25 million, Pennsylvania's debt was then at least one-tenth of that.

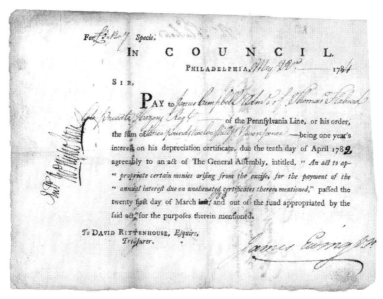

One of thousands of Depreciation Certificates, this one was issued in the amount of £3, 12 s., 7 p., but was re-purchased by Nicholson for far less than value.

Of course, the prevailing value of one certificate to a then-supposed value of gold became any economist's guess. One historian has suggested that what might have been an original rate of three-to-one in 1777, had weakened to a rate of forty-to-one by 1780. By the end of 1782, the depreciation was well more than seventy-five-to-one.[7]

To "correct" depreciated certificates, Pennsylvania's Supreme Executive Council appointed a body of commissioners to buy out one-third of the depreciation certificates—many destitute veterans were willing to sell them for next to nothing—and then grant new certificates for the prevailing value. Two gentlemen were appointed to lead that commission, James Stevenson and John Nicholson. Stevenson was William Crawford's half-brother. Nicholson, from Philadelphia, had been a clerk for the Continental Congress, serving mostly in that capacity as a deputy treasurer. An outspoken Antifederalist, he glommed onto his commission with a certain enthusiasm soon to be revealed. And reviled.

---

[7] Agnew, *History of the region of Pennsylvania*, pg. 21

The Depreciation Lands

In March, 1783, Pennsylvania's Supreme Executive Council also acted to create bounty lands. Offering a section of western Pennsylvania to war veterans not only absolved its debt to them, but it was a good idea for a wholly different reason. If settled, the veterans might be very helpful in defending Pennsylvania from the very Natives whose Ohio lands had just been threatened. Placing military might on the very frontier of danger would serve to help civilize the rest of the commonwealth.

The plan was simple. Two areas near the Ohio border, each greater than three million acres, would be run out, one north and one south of a line drawn east and west between the Ohio River and a tributary to the Allegheny River. The section north of that line would be deemed "Donation Lands" and the section south, "Depreciation Lands."

With fewer waterways and no significant river, the Donation Lands were set aside for soldiers who had enlisted after 1780. The Depreciation Lands, however, settled along the Ohio River, were available to any soldier or officer who, at auction, could secure his purchase—within twenty days—by gold, silver or the very depreciation certificates he had long owned.

Evidently more valuable, the Depreciation Lands would be surveyed first. The southern boundary was defined as a point on Pennsylvania's western border where the Ohio River crossed it, then east along the north banks of the Ohio River and farther north-east along the continuous bank of the Allegheny River, until its confluence with Mahoning Creek (then preposterously called Mogulbughtiton Creek,) and, from there, then due west to the Ohio border, and then south along the border to the starting point. This body of land was then subdivided into five vertical rectangles of somewhat equal proportion along north and south divisions. The Council intended to hire five surveyors.

No doubt, scores of deputy surveyors, some local and others as far away as Philadelphia, lobbied the Surveyor-General, John Lukens, for the lucrative assignments. At the age of 35, lately married with a newborn child, Daniel Leet forwarded his name, too.

General William Irvine was still commander of Fort Pitt. Because his post was responsible to Philadelphia for the safety of western homesteaders, he was charged to protect the efforts of surveying teams who would descend upon his territory. He may have helped Leet get commissioned in the new land development. Although otherwise engaged as the district's representative to Council, Dorsey Pentecost might have been considered, too—of course, it was *his* idea, after all—but the fact is, Irvine trusted Leet. It would be of extreme importance to the efforts of the Supreme Executive Council that, if any effort to survey the designated lands was exasperated by *injun incursions*, the news could be kept "hush-hush." Pentecost was anything but discreet. Western Pennsylvania was now to be known as a land of promise and not the place of constant Indian raids it certainly was. Irvine knew that Leet was not just a modest man, but he was very capable of managing military affairs in the face of public outrage.

Daniel Leet was assigned to District Two. He was instructed to survey adjoining lots of not more than 350 acres, and not less than 200. Each lot was to be described accurately for its quality vis a vis ground water or evident creeks, extant mining, population density (i.e., Native villages or occupied forts) and tree species (which indicated soil conditions.) This description would be provided to the Surveyor-General and other State commissioners, but not detailed to the public. Perhaps, the disclosure of certain assets of one lot versus the limitations of another, might feed a bidding frenzy for some tracts while conversely tarnishing others. (Better to have many lots sold at a similar value, than just a few prized ones at greater value.) In any case, the lots were to be drawn onto a plat showing their contiguous borders and indicating any water flowing from one to the next. Surely, the riverfront lots would sell first.

District One, closest to the western Ohio border, was run out by Alexander McLean, a deputy surveyor. He was chosen because of his experience—shared with John Lukens—defining Pennsylvania's western border.

District Three was assigned to Nathaniel Breading (pronounced "brading" and thus sometimes recorded as Braden,) but which was actually subdivided and surveyed by four more surveyors: William Alexander, Samuel Nicholson, Captain Douglas and Samuel Jones. James Cunningham surveyed District Four, and both Joshua Elder and John Morris surveyed District Five.

District Two was notable for certain landmarks. First, there was Big Beaver Creek flowing south into the most northern bend of the Ohio River. Just west of that mouth was old Fort McIntosh. Several miles east was Logstown, long inhabited by Delawares, Wyandots, Shawnees and Mingos. It had been a trading post well-known during the French & Indian War and, by the end of the Revolutionary War, still populated by Natives seeking peace and fortune with western settlers. A large sandbar was evident in the north center of the Ohio River just southeast of Logstown. The seasonal rise of the river would prohibit the bar from any year-round use, but even then it may have been seen by Leet to have been populated. (Later archeological digs would prove that the site had been used by indigenous cultures as far back as 1250 B.C. Evidence of clay firing and nut processing was discovered there in 2010.)[8] In like context, Leet, too, identified an abrogation in the terrain close to Little Sewickley Creek along the north bank of the Ohio. Situated perhaps a mile from the most eastern border of his assignment was a Great Indian Mound. Not nearly as large as those which he might have seen on his first voyage down the Ohio with George Washington, this mound (and lesser ones discovered later) would prove to be the most eastern location of any of the Great Indian Mounds. It was a mystery to Leet then as it would be to contemporary Natives and white pioneers for years to come.

Certainly Leet studied the Ohio shoreline of the entire boundary of the Depreciation Lands. District Two offered the most riverfront exposure of any of the five districts. Owing to the deep northern "indent" of the Beaver river, and natural to its flow, District Two was also distinct in one other respect: it offered long, wide and fertile "bottoms." Big and Little Sewickley Creeks crossed a particularly large, flat expanse. As George Washington had recognized, "well watered" bottoms promised exceptionally fertile soil.

---

[8] Anderson, *Phase III Archaeological Investigations at the Leetsdale Site*, US Army Corps of Engineers, pg. 214

Before Leet could run his first lines, however, certain chicanery reared its head. General William Irvine, protective of "his" new and promising land development, wrote to Council President, John Dickinson, on June 3, 1783:

> "I am informed that companies are formed & plans laid, in Phila'd & other places, for purchasing at their own terms, large tracts of the prime lands which are appropriated by law for the redemption of officers holding certificates. From everything I can learn it will require great vigilance & a decisive line of conduct in the Executive authority to prevent harmful effects, particularly as I have reason to believe those Companies intend connecting themselves with the Surveyors: and I am certain the Military will keep a watchful eye over the whole of this transaction. If therefore the surveyors should by any finesse, mistake or otherwise, break over the bounds prescribed by law, troublesome turbulencies may ensue."

Dickinson's response was a letter grateful for the information. He advised the Surveyor-General to pay attention.

Irvine's fears may have been two-fold. The first was that fat, wealthy Philadelphians, and not lean, orderly officers of the Continental Army, would scarf up the best lands. As a prideful General, Irvine might have relished the power and respect he would earn from this new community of patriotic veterans. Were hoity-toity Philadelphia landgrabbers to enter into his development, Irvine could muster little respect or authority. The second fear was more forgivable; less-practiced surveyors, eager to please their clients with quick patent applications, often miscalculated and, sometimes, purposefully so. An extra chain length here or a mistaken landmark there could add dozens of "free" acres to a claim. A mis-marked tree on one claim could innocently beget errors on three contiguous tracts. And, any land development offering hundreds of adjacent lots, once laid out, could wind up so off-kilter as to beg forgiveness rather than a much costlier "do-over."

How or where Irvine may have heard that certain companies and land schemes were brewing in the east is not certain. That Dorsey Pentecost had been snubbed from a lucrative opportunity, or that he was in regular correspondence with his Philadelphia client, Levi Hollingsworth, are reasonable conjectures of mistrust. Only someone who was known to be loose-lipped, however, may have conveyed such possibilities to authorities. Of course, even the avarice of prominent citizens like George Washington was known to his contemporaries. Primarily for this reason, the Supreme Council had intended to engage just five surveyors. In fact, Daniel Leet was the sole commissioned surveyor for his assigned district. Indeed, he employed a full crew of brawny chain men and spry assistants to commence work. His brothers William and Jonathan assisted him, too.

District Two comprised approximately 540 square miles or 32,400 acres most of which Leet would have to parcel out in lots less than the dictated 350 acres.[9] From the start, he was instructed to leave a reserve of 3,000 acres around Fort McIntosh at Beaver. Although mostly uninhabited, the tall banks of the Ohio there promised some advantage against flooding if a town were to be laid out. (Another 3,000 acres were reserved, too, in District Five, just opposite Pittsburgh.) For having laid out Fort McIntosh in the first place, Daniel Leet had recommended its "prominence" to the Supreme Council.

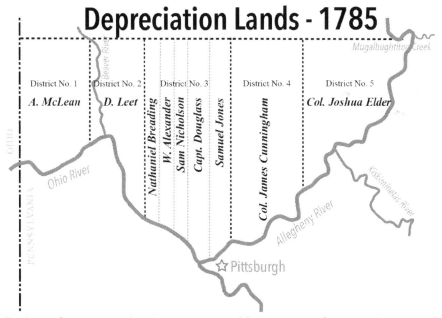

Bordering Ohio on the left and reaching east to Mogulbughtiton Creek, the Depreciation Lands were divided into five districts of which Daniel Leet surveyed District 2, second from left, encompassing the most northern bend of the Ohio River, thirty miles from Pittsburgh.

---

[9] Winner, "The Depreciation and Donation Lands," pg. 4

As to tackling the rest of his commission, Leet's greater challenge (other than having to manage chain crews for months on end) was divvying up lots judiciously. Although District Two was rectangular at top, the Ohio River created many issues, some beneficial, others restrictive, below. The Big Beaver Creek also dissected its northwest corner. Naturally, tracts laid out along the river or larger creeks would provide access in equal measure. Lots distant from the rivers, however, would have to offer some advantages by way of streams or springs, if not extra acreage. Balancing these apportionments with those of steeper terrain or less favorable soil conditions, Leet had many decisions to make.

Except, the Supreme Council delayed the surveying schedule again. In early April, the Council received intelligence that Indian raids were imminent. (One might have asked, when were they not?) And there was still consternation over the sovereignty of the Erie triangle to the north, which, if not secured, would affect the Donation Lands. The Treaty at Fort Harmar would attempt to solve that. So, not until April of 1785, did Leet and other surveyors actually hire their teams to drag Gunter chains into the woods.

For each tract surveyed, Leet would earn £3, 8 shillings or about $.50 in Continental currency.[10, 11] He would earn this money directly from the Commonwealth, even if any tract was not later patented. Thus, his commission assured him a compensation of more than £700.[12] By modern calculation that would equal something like $135,000 today.[13] Of course, he wouldn't get paid anytime soon and the rate was less than his customary fees, but as it represented solid work for more than six months, it was welcome income. Further, it represented an altogether new opportunity to streamline the process of land acquisition.

Now, there was no warrant to prove, no first tomahawk to respect; no anxious client to impress. Now, there was just a survey to run out and patents to issue. Essentially, Leet was employed to cut up a birthday cake. Of course, the cake was irregularly shaped and Leet knew not whom the birthday guests were. For this more officious celebration, in fact, there was no birthday boy for whom he might reserve the best piece of cake. He would cut the cake so

---

[10] *Aurora General Advertiser*, Sept. 13, 1791, pg. 2

[11] Colonial Records. United States, State, 1853

[12] Resolution of the Minutes of the Supreme Council, Vol. 16, Sept 9, 1790, pg. 448

[13] https://www.historicalstatistics.org/Currencyconverter.html

everyone had an equal piece. Except that, because he himself cut the cake, only Daniel Leet knew which pieces were truly the best.

And yet, as a duly commissioned surveyor, he was prohibited by professional ethics from claiming any tracts for himself. Tempting as it may have been, he claimed nothing.

As it would turn out, however, the best tracts of his survey—seven in all that straddled both the Big and Little Sewickley Creeks along rich, well-watered bottoms—would be claimed by "friends."

An Auction

By the end of summer, Leet and his chain men had filed with the Pennsylvania Land Office well more than 100 surveys of individual tracts in District Two. Unlike any of the other plats which may have been assembled for Districts One, Three, Four or Five, Leet's map showed exceptional care in his land apportionments. Leet divvied up riverfront tracts angled specifically to equalize shoreline access. As such, lots behind those were sometimes proportioned in triangles or trapezoids. Without exception, all the other Districts were divided into grids of rigid rectangles, running due north and south. Whether for this reason, or for the sheer speed by which Leet had filed more surveys than any other deputy, District Two lots were offered first.

On the 20th of September, 1785, an ad appeared on the bottom left cover of the Pennsylvania Gazette in Philadelphia:

> "Notice is hereby given, that by virtue of an act of assembly, passed the 18th day of December, 1780, entituled an act to settle and adjust the accounts of the troops of this state in the service of the United States, and for other purposes therein mentioned, and divers other acts of the ligislature; and also pursuant to directions given the subscribers by the supreme executive council of the state of Pennsylvania, on the 21st day of November next, at 10 o'clock in the Forenoon, at the Pennsylvania Coffee House, in Philadelphia, will begin the Sale of One Hundred LOTS of LAND, part of the tract of land appropriated for the redemption of the Depreciation Certificates, and to continue from day to day until the whole shall be sold.

"These lands are situate in the district of Daniel Leet, No. 2, beginning about 9 miles below Fort Pitt, on the west side of the river Ohio, and extending down the said river near to the mouth of the Big Beaver creek, in the vicinity of Fort McIntosh, distant about 30 miles from Fort Pitt, and running up the said creek about 7 miles, including several of its branches, the several mouths of Big and little Sewickley, Log's town run, Crow's town run and its branches, and Dutchman's run. In general these lands are extremely fertile, and well calculated for mills, iron works, grazing, & other farms. For a more particular description whereof, the public are referred to a map now fixed up in the Coffee House, made out by the said Daniel Leet; to which is annexed his description of said lands.

"The patents to be made in either gold or silver, or in the certificates aforesaid; one half of the consideration to be paid in five days from the sale, the other half in fifteen days more, or the sale to be void. The surveyor's fees (and other office fees, agreeable to law) to be discharged at the same time the purchase money shall be paid."

JOHN LUKENS, Surv. Gen.
DAVID KENNEDY, Sec. L. O.
FRANCIS JOHNSTON, R. G.

Northampton County

Yet, the Depreciation Lands of western Pennsylvania were not the only lands ready and available for sale. To impose a new and necessary property tax following the war, the Land Office in Philadelphia attempted to define all of the other unsettled lands in the Commonwealth. To do this meant identifying properties that *were* settled. The state decreed that, to be fair to those who had been paying their share of taxes all along, current land holdings and occupied estates theretofore registered would be exempt from the proposed new tax. Perhaps unintentionally, that declaration created an immediate market for settled lands that were now exempt.

In July of 1784, the Land Office informed its many county surveyors that unimproved land east of the Allegheny Range would be sold for $26.66 per hundred acres.[14] That price, however, excluded taxes, surveyor or warrant fees, and it required buyers to purchase contiguous lots of no less than 400 acres. Thus a single purchase, including taxes and fees, might be something close to $30 per hundred acres.

That same month, Thomas Shields engaged George Palmer, deputy surveyor for the northeast Pennsylvania county of Northampton (since subdivided into four counties including Monroe, Wayne, and Pike) to survey a tract of land with a run of five miles along the northern Delaware River.[15] The land was not wholly unseated. Yet, it was mostly exempt from the new land tax. The property belonged to the Penn family, descendants of William, the original "Proprietor" of Pennsylvania. As such, the land was exempt from

---

[14] Munger, *Pennsylvania Land Records*, pg. 150

[15] Thomas Shields's Day Book

any tax by dint of his original charter. The property Shields purchased was known as Damascus Manor and encompassed some 30,000 to 40,000 acres. No records show what he paid for the estate, but he would not have purchased it for anything near $30 per hundred acre.

Also that summer, Shields purchased more than 23,000 acres in Washington County. He did so in collaboration with his good friend and customer Levi Hollingsworth.[16] The land was entirely unimproved. And, because it was west of the Alleghenies, the Land Office set an alluring price of just $9.33 per hundred acres. Intersecting southwestern Washington County with a northern span of Greene County, the property, (which comprised what would later become West Finley Township,) was purchased for less than $.10 per acre.

Even earlier, Shields managed to buy several unimproved tracts in Turtle Creek. Dorsey Pentecost had parlayed them as surveyor and land agent to Levi Hollingsworth, who then offered them to Shields. Even at less than $.50 per acre, the investment was a more promising "scheme" than any Philadelphia bank could offer an enterprising young silversmith.

That Thomas Shields was in a financial position following the economic depression of the war to invest in land is not surprising. That he had an interest in real estate is neither; by 1783, Shields owned quite a few properties in and around Philadelphia. In addition to his house in Chestnut Ward, he now owned two properties in Dock Ward and was in the process of building a house in Passayunk. Receipts for nails, plaster and lime are plentiful in his daybook. So, too, are tax receipts. In 1780 alone, Shields paid well more than £1,300 on property taxes—some local, some to the county, a lesser tax for the "poor"—but all of it "acceptable and necessary" for the benefit of a more civilized society.

That Thomas Shields would purchase 23,000 acres in Washington County or 40,000 acres in Northampton County in 1784 is as much evidence of his wealth as it was his appetite to venture into new and unchartered waters. A man who had always parlayed his success in currency, who had shaped opportunity out of a steady acquisition of specie, who could save fine grains of precious metal if just to prove his own good character, now turned to seek advancement from the sale of land. It would seem an odd strategy

---

[16] Crumrine, *History of Washington County*, pg. 982

for an urban artisan. But Shields had good reasons to diversify his "portfolio." First, even if there was robust trade in finely crafted silver goods, there were few reliable means by which to earn interest on his savings. Fellow compatriots like Levi Hollingsworth, all coping with depressed returns on food commodities, knew well that settlers were fleeing their markets, heading west, and purchasing land from the state or other such entrepreneurs who had earlier purchased tracts at even better prices. Further, everywhere on the eastern seaboard gentrified businessmen realized that their path to recovery was going to be a long, slow slog. The constant grind of daily journal entries, deliveries, distribution, accounting and bill collections—all of which would have to be expensed against a return of fewer pennies on a weaker dollar—was hardly appealing.

Land speculation, on the other hand, was alluring. It promised great wealth for far less work. And, like a siren beckoning from rocky shoals, the idea of realizing more immediate wealth was now something less remote— both figuratively and literally. One need only visit the Land Office in Philadelphia, scan a few maps of western Pennsylvania, and purchase warrants for what pleased the eye. The minimum price per hundred acre was now regulated by the Commonwealth and, so, could only go up. Indeed, for the next decade land prices did increase, but not because of demand. Speculators who dreamt of instant sales to foreign buyers found themselves paying taxes on the same property year after year, its value having increased by the sole evidence that someone was willing to pay taxes on it. However painful it was to sustain that dream, the speculator who hoped for massive sales to European investors found, rather like the daily grind of paperwork he eschewed, the petty gnawing away of two hundred acres here and three hundred there by singular settlers imploring to purchase a single homestead. The fact was, despite some early successes by "land jobbers," (a term then meaning middle men who wholesaled large tracts of land they themselves did not own,) the market at hand was conducive only to the interests of settlers, not investors. After all, settlers were always the end-users.

If Hollingsworth had not realized that then, Shields did have some inkling. In Northampton County, a neighbor, Henry Drinker, had purchased thousands of acres before the war had ended. He knew every acre of the property he had for sale, he personally knew it to be fertile, and he knew that to attract the interests of settlers considering his lands he would need to build community infrastructure first.[17] He was a hands-on speculator. In 1780, that meant constructing a sawmill and grist mill. The likelihood that any other land speculator at the time would have even visited the property he owned, would have known anything of its agricultural value, or might have thought to construct a community resource was laughable. Yet, to Shields, it was clear the market was all about the end-user. An artisan whose inventory was worthless when still sitting in his shop, Shields knew that the value of his investment in frontier land was an investment in the toil and sweat of the American pioneer. Only he had use for it. Only he could make his land valuable. Only he had the energy, persistence and tenacity to make it worth something more than dirt and rocks.

But, did Thomas Shields know these people? They were not really his peers. They who placed their value in loam and lumber, whose hopes could be realized only in the soil and streams of distant lands, were not the same folk he greeted in his shop or knelt with in church. Yet these were the children whose coming-of-age would yield America's future. Thomas Shields wagered great wealth on their success.

In fact, he staked everything he owned on it.

---

[17] Doerflinger, *A Vigorous Spirit of Enterprise*, pg. 322-323

Washington in Western Pennsylvania

Since taking command of the Continental Army, Washington, in fact, had paid little attention to the lands he had acquired either by British bounty, Virginia certificates or by speculative investment. The same year that Thomas Shields settled up on his purchase in Northampton County, George Washington decided to tour the vast lands he owned in Western Pennsylvania, Western Virginia and the Ohio country.

Once again, he called on his good friend Dr. Craik to join him on a journey of hundreds of miles, assuring him in his invitation, "I am not going to explore the country, nor am I in search of fresh lands."[18] Yet, as he stated later in his diary, he was interested in examining the potential "communication" of roads, aqueducts and waterways, connecting those by which canals might bring greater commerce to the west. (His earlier advertisements, offering his Chartiers Creek lands for sale, had spoken about the ease and convenience of portaging from the Youghiogheny to the Potomac, which might have been a good idea, but was nothing near the truth.) It is clear, however, that, by whatever means or improvements could be made practicable, Washington was now focused on western expansion.[19] He knew the miserable conditions of the federal coffers; more homesteaders settling in the west would only help the young country. And, yet, he personally had much to gain in making his more western lands available to willing buyers.

Washington owned staggering swaths of raw, unsettled acreage. On the Great Kanawha River he owned 23,000 acres. On and around the Little

---

[18] Washington, *Washington and the West*, pg. 21

[19] Achenbach, *The Grand Idea*, pg. 264

Kanawha, including his prized Round Bottoms at Moundsville, he owned almost 10,000 acres. In the Ohio country, along the Little Miami River, he had 3,000 acres. In Kentucky, he claimed 5,000 acres. And, in Western Pennsylvania, in the year 1784, he had patents on nearly 1,200 acres at the present-day site of Perryopolis, 234 acres at Great Meadows (just outside Fort Necessity where he had had to surrender so many years earlier,) and 3,000 acres along his beloved "Shurtees Creek."

But he also owned one big problem there, too. Squatters who were members of a strict sect of Scotch-Irish Presbyterians had settled on his property for some twelve years. William Crawford, years earlier, had tried to chase them off. But they believed that Washington no more owned the land than had George Croghan. The fact is, the Presbyterians had made significant improvements on the property. Of course, William Crawford had erected an earlier first structure, but the sect had managed to build their cabins abutting it, blocking any access or use of that original cabin.

As would become the argument of western courts for decades, the once accepted practice of seeking a patent could be superseded only by those who could claim—and prove—they had made improvements to the property.

For the present issue, fought over the course of three days in September, George Washington, the country's heroic Commander in Chief, argued his claim in a trial held at his grist mill in Venice (present-day Cecil Township, Pennsylvania) and, only many months later, successfully rid his property of the squatters.

Washington's later records suggest, by its absence, that he must have sold his Venice property, but, of course, no other records prove that he ever first owned it.

Hollingsworth & Shields

Assembling for the auction at the Pennsylvania Coffee House (sometimes called the London or Old Coffee House) on November 21, 1785, were many of the more wealthy merchants, tradesmen, and industrialists of Philadelphia. Among the swarm of spectators and speculators looking over the plat drawn up by Daniel Leet (and now hanging on a wall at the corner of Front and High Streets) were gentlemen who, in their lives, had ventured no farther west than Lebanon and, perhaps, no farther north than New York City.

The public house also bustled with more common businessmen of whom many had served in the Revolution and, so, were likely holding Depreciation Certificates. Because of the day's auction, they could be worth no more elsewhere than if applied to the purchase of land. Merchants like John Mills, Jacob Beery, and Caleb Way nervously awaited the proceedings.

Perhaps distinguished in finer clothes, two other gentlemen were particularly eager to make opening bids on the unseen, unseated and, now, newly unleashed property along the Ohio River. Neither had ever enlisted in the war for independence and, as such, neither would have earned Depreciation Certificates for their service to the effort, yet both may well have had plenty of the paper in their pockets that promising day.

The truth is any fine Philadelphian or ordinary officer could bid on any lot he so chose. And tendering Depreciation Certificates was not a precondition of purchase. In fact, the Supreme Executive Council, fearing that certificate-wielding veterans would not show up, decided just days before the auction that bidders could purchase Leet's carefully apportioned lands by the acreage and not by tract.

And so, on Monday, November 21, 1785, "A. St. Clair & Co. Auctioneers" gaveled the first auction of Depreciation Lands at the popular Coffee House. No narrative exists as to how the auction was conducted, nor in what order or priority the land was sold.

Levi Hollingsworth and Thomas Shields positioned themselves for recognition by the auctioneer. Did they stand side-by-side, or, for cunning reason, did they separate?

Bidding high, Hollingsworth won the very first tract—or, at least, Tract One. Two hundred-fifty lush acres nestled along the wild banks of the Ohio River formed a triangle commanding the longest riverfront property of all the tracts in Leet's District Two. The land is, today, the very center of Sewickley, Pennsylvania, its eastern border now known as Division Street. The only street that crosses the village diagonally, it defined the separation of Leet's District Two surveys from Nathaniel Breading's District Three.

Caleb Way won Tract Two. With two hundred acres, its southeastern border today marks Academy Avenue which defines the beginning of Edgeworth just west of Sewickley.

Thomas Shields bid on and won Tract Three. He also won Tracts Five and Six, ascending northwest along the river. And Hollingsworth also bid again, winning Tracts Eight and Nine.

Only Tracts Four and Seven intervened in the apparent effort by Hollingsworth and Shields to own the very best bottoms of Leet's Depreciation lands. Jacob Beery won the former and John Mills the latter. Beery, however, never paid up. By terms the auction originally set forth, he failed to pay for his winning bid within the twenty days allotted.

Yet, of all the prime tracts so enumerated, only Caleb Way ultimately took possession as patentee of the land on which he bid.

Within days of the auction, Hollingsworth and Shields sold their winning bids to a third man, an apparent confidant, Mark Wilcox.

Mark Wilcox was proprietor of the Ivy Mills of Delaware County. The company made paper, much of it originally purchased by Benjamin Franklin for his print shop, but much more was bought by Robert Morris for the Treasury and on which was printed Continental currency. When money became "not worth a Continental," Wilcox's paper was used to print the even more valuable Depreciation Certificates which, as everyone attending the auction that day knew, was the coin of the realm. For good reason, Wilcox did not attend the auction.

Of the highest bids of the day, it seems Hollingsworth and Shields had had no intention to settle their lands for themselves, nor even to patent them for their own investment portfolios.

Every one of these tracts was purchased, ultimately, by Daniel Leet. 1,446 acres of prime, well-watered bottoms became his. There was, of course, no regulation prohibiting the immediate re-sale of tracts won.

The original patent for Tract Five, signed by Charles Biddle, President of the Supreme Executive Council of Pennsylvania, cites the property name as "Newington." Mark Wilcox's payment of three hundred and sixty-five pounds to the Receiver-General's Office of "this Commonwealth" for two hundred acres was recorded on January 19, 1786. The certificate takes some pains to clarify that the "described Tract is marked in the Survey and Plan of the said District, [as] No. 5 and was sold to *the said Thomas Shields* at Public Auction, he being the highest Bidder *who released the same to the said Mark Wilcox.*

For all the excitement the auction had generated, for all the paperwork necessary to record the winning bids—for all the signatures required by Philadelphia's Land Office to authorize the official documents—no one would know that Daniel Leet acquired the very best properties he had surveyed.

Except, of course, Wilcox, Hollingsworth, and Shields.

Was this proof of the conspiracy of land speculators that General Irvine had feared and first shared with his superiors? That "Companies were formed & plans laid for purchasing large tracts..?" Were Hollingsworth and Shields in cahoots with a surveyor whose foreknowledge of the property at auction would benefit only him? Had Daniel Leet set up the scheme? Or was it Mark Wilcox? If neither, did Thomas Shields know Daniel Leet? Or should that question be asked the other way around?

Whatever truly transpired, Daniel Leet now had his piece of the cake.

Clearly, the auction went well. In fact, the bidding must have been so protracted because the auction required a second day, set just two days later.

All 142 tracts prepared by Daniel Leet were sold. More than 32,200 acres brought in £13,987 and 14 shillings, averaging eight shillings five pence or $1.12 per acre. Some bids were tendered as high as 50 shillings per acre.[20] Marc Wilcox purchased Tract Five from Thomas Shields for 36 shillings per acre. And yet, the fair market value, presupposed by the land office in 1784, was just six shillings or $.80 per acre.[21] As such, the commissioners were pleased. In fact, they were so pleased they directed that surveyed lands in Breading's District 3 should be prepared for auction on the 28th and 30th the following week.

That might have been a mistake.

[20] Annual Report of the Sec'y of Internal Affairs of the Commonwealth of PA, year ending 1892 Part 1

[21] Bausman, *The History of Beaver County*, Vol. III pg. 1228

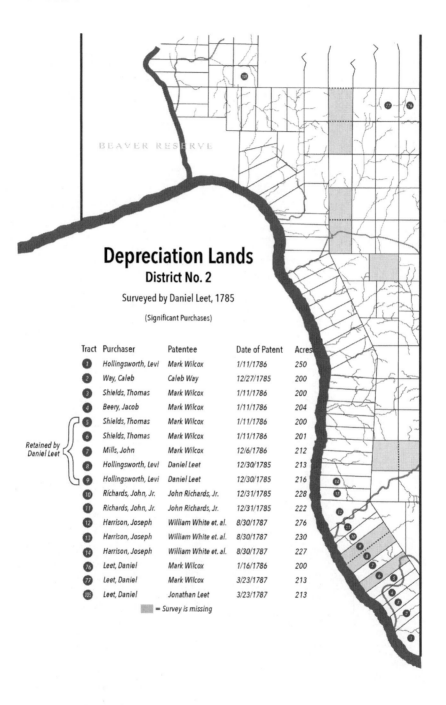

Depreciation Lands
District No. 2

Surveyed by Daniel Leet, 1785

(Significant Purchases)

Tract	Purchaser	Patentee	Date of Patent	Acres
1	Hollingsworth, Levi	Mark Wilcox	1/11/1786	250
2	Way, Caleb	Caleb Way	12/27/1785	200
3	Shields, Thomas	Mark Wilcox	1/11/1786	200
4	Beery, Jacob	Mark Wilcox	1/11/1786	204
5	Shields, Thomas	Mark Wilcox	1/11/1786	200
6	Shields, Thomas	Mark Wilcox	1/11/1786	201
7	Mills, John	Mark Wilcox	12/6/1786	212
8	Hollingsworth, Levi	Daniel Leet	12/30/1785	213
9	Hollingsworth, Levi	Daniel Leet	12/30/1785	216
10	Richards, John, Jr.	John Richards, Jr.	12/31/1785	228
11	Richards, John, Jr.	John Richards, Jr.	12/31/1785	222
12	Harrison, Joseph	William White et. al.	8/30/1787	276
13	Harrison, Joseph	William White et. al.	8/30/1787	230
14	Harrison, Joseph	William White et. al.	8/30/1787	227
76	Leet, Daniel	Mark Wilcox	1/16/1786	200
77	Leet, Daniel	Mark Wilcox	3/23/1787	213
105	Leet, Daniel	Jonathan Leet	3/23/1787	213

Retained by Daniel Leet {7, 8, 9}

= Survey is missing

A Second Auction

One week later, the coffee house again became abuzz with a swarm of speculators inspecting the wall plats of Nathaniel Breading's District Three. Another one hundred plus tracts, just several miles closer to Pittsburgh, were now available to the highest bidders, many of whom would be the same people who had been at the last auction. But this time, Levi Hollingsworth was not to be seen. And, yet, Mark Wilcox was. So, too, were men like William Finley, Henry Pratt and Thomas McKean. Thomas Shields was there, too.

The auction, however, turned out to be nothing like the frenzy the first had been. The bidding was lackluster, hesitant, and lethargic. The hunger for property so far removed from Philadelphia had lost its appeal. Once again, the audience was not made up of war veterans looking to start a new life out west, but rather of wizened and wealthy gentlemen playing a competitive round of whist. In terms of the state's expectations, the costs of preparing the surveys combined with the expense of producing the auction, begged a scenario in which bidders would drive up revenues to some magic margin higher than $.80 per acre.

William Finley amassed 6,711 acres made up from more than 20 tracts. An immigrant to Westmoreland County, he would soon serve on the Supreme Executive Council for Pennsylvania and rise to serve four terms as a U.S. Representative. He sold two tracts to Thomas Shields, the only Depreciation land that Shields actually held for more than a decade. Finley also sold six tracts to Thomas KcKean who had himself, at auction, purchased 624 acres on two lots. He also patented two lots purchased by the elusive Jacob Beery. He had an appetite to acquire much more, however. Thomas McKean was then a Chief Justice of the Commonwealth. In 1799, he would begin serving two terms as Pennsylvania's second Governor. And, Henry Pratt purchased more than 1,800 acres, all of which he patented unto himself. A shipping tycoon and land speculator much like his friend Robert Morris, he eventually bought Morris's Schuykill Estate in 1799. Pratt was in fact related to McKean, whose grandson would bear the name, Henry Pratt McKean. Despite the reality that Philadelphia's social circle was quite small, its pool of wealth seemed almost incestuous.

Once again, Pennsylvania's intent to resolve its debt to veterans had completely missed the mark.

When Breading's 126 tracts were put on the auction block, the average sale came in at just $.33 per acre. Combined with Leet's auction, the average fell below the presumed $.80.

The commissioners were stumped. So, too, was the Supreme Council. Whatever explanation or excuses were debated in chambers, no more auctions would be scheduled until March of the following year.

During all the period that the Depreciation Lands were exposed to sale, a total of 316,935 acres were sold for the equivalent of $87,805.33, or an average price of just $.28 cents per acre.[22]

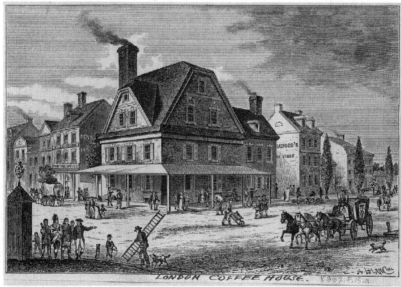

Situated at the corner of Front and High Streets on Philadelphia's waterfront, the Old Coffee House served as a public meeting place for all trade including the auction of slaves and real estate until it closed in 1791. Library Company of Philadelphia.

---

[22] Annual Report of the Sec'y of Internal Affairs of the Commonwealth of PA, year ending 1892 Part 1

A Steamboat Design

On January 26, 1786, an announcement appeared in The Pennsylvania Packet of Philadelphia, promoting an experiment of some intrigue.

To the Encouragers of Useful Arts.

"The subscriber humbly begs leave to inform the Public, that he has proposed a Machine for the improvement of Navigation, with other useful Arts—That it has been honored with the Approbation of many men of the first characters for philosophical and mechanical knowledge…"

The announcement sought subscribers to purchase a map of the Northwestern parts of the United States, "one half of the money [will be] contributed, in constructing and bringing to perfection, a Machine that promises to be of infinite advantage to the United States."

The announcement was signed by John Fitch.

In that Mr. Fitch was likely unknown to many readers, he added an endorsement of his solicitation, signed by gentlemen the public would know.

"UPON considering the extent of the principles on which Mr. Fitch proposes to construct his Steam-Boat, and the quantity of motion that may be produced by the elastic force of steam, we are of opinion, that, if the execution could by any means be made to answer the theory when reduced to practice, it might be beneficial to the public, and it seems to be deserving of a fair experiment, which alone can justify the expectations of success."[23]

Among five gentlemen, including the names Ebenezer Cowel, Samuel Wetherill, William Poyntell, and Thomas Bradford, the announcement was endorsed by—and subscriptions could be tendered to—Thomas Shields. The absence of any information about where Shields resided or how any of these other men might be reached purports that such was not necessary.

American history books credit the launch of the first steamboat to Robert Fulton who, on August 17, 1807, piloted the *Clermont* up the Hudson River from New York to Albany. The truth is Fitch designed the first steamboat, the *Perseverance*, which navigated the Delaware River on August 27, 1787, a full twenty years earlier.

The *Perseverance* was an odd-looking duck because it operated much like one. Fitch's idea, in addition to employing steam power, was to affix a series of oars along each side of his 45 foot vessel. The mechanics of the boat operated alternating arms, powering the paddles to propel the boat like the webbed feet of a duck. The *Perseverance* moved at a speed of six miles per hour. The boat operated successfully for several years, transporting people and goods between Philadelphia and Burlington, New Jersey. Fitch, however, never wholly managed—nor documented—the expense of his craft or its operation. Some called it Fitch's Folly.

Why Thomas Shields might have had any interest in a steam powered water craft is worth pondering. As a silversmith and merchant trading with the gentry of Philadelphia, he would have had no use for local water transportation. On the other hand, if a steam vessel could ply the farthest rivers of America's frontier, well then, a steamboat might make his journey to Damascus Manor a comparative breeze.

In what might be the most uncanny connection, Fitch, too, was a silversmith—and a surveyor—and an agent purveying specialty goods during the Revolutionary War. Not only was he a professional acquaintance of Thomas Shields, Fitch regularly provided rum, tobacco and beer to the regimental quartermasters at Valley Forge.

---

[23] *The Pennsylvania Packet,* January 26, 1786, pg. 4

A Society to Abolish Slavery

More than 400 Black Philadelphians attended the funeral of Anthony Benezet on May 8, 1784.[24] A Quaker, educator, author, and organizer of the first secondary school for girls in the city, Benezet, in 1775, had founded The Society for the Relief of Free Negroes Unlawfully Held in Bondage. It was the first such organization in America to promote the abolition of slavery, and it was sanctioned and populated by Quakers to raise funds necessary to educate black students.

Within two years of Benezet's death, the twelve-year-old organization reformed and became known as the Pennsylvania Society for Promoting the Abolition of Slavery. The elections of its board were apparently so important that the by-laws of the Society were published in all of the city's four newspapers: *The Pennsylvania Packet, The Freeman's Journal, The Independent Gazette* and the *Pennsylvania Gazette*. Serving as President was Benjamin Franklin.[25] Dr. Benjamin Rush was elected one of two secretaries. And of the six members appointed by Franklin and Rush to the Acting Committee responsible for the actual work of the board—doing "such business as shall occur in the recess of the society"—was Thomas Shields.[26]

At 43 years of age, Shields had become a man of great esteem, alone indicated by his standings as a deacon of the First Baptist Church, yet collectively supported by his participation in a number of other civic and political committees, none perhaps more prestigious than this. In other news

---

[24] https://www.history.com/this-day-in-history/first-american-abolition-society-founded-in-philadelphia

[25] To be sure, despite his presidency, Franklin had been a slaveowner for more than fifty years.

[26] *The Pennsylvania Packet* (and others), May 23, 1787

items of his time, Shields was found to serve his Dock Street neighborhood in collecting donations for victims of a recent fire. Another item associated him with Mark Wilcox in auditing the estate of a man recently brought to court for an undisclosed matter. Shields was also seen in the papers for his participation in organizing a school for orphans.

Personal accounts of the gentleman suggest he liked to talk. And not just a little. "His mind was stored with anecdotes," said one. "These he found pleasure in imparting, and his friends ever found their beauty and point more than compensate for [his] incidental prolixity."[27]

Miniature portrait of Thomas Shields, Silversmith, Philadelphia.
Artist unknown. From a private collection.

President Washington

It came as no surprise to anyone when, in April of 1789, the votes of the electoral college were officially counted, unanimously calling for George Washington to serve as the first President of the United States. Ten states had by then ratified the Constitution. New York State was the only one not to have organized its electors in time. Little did it matter. All 69 eligible electors chose Washington. In the run-up, 34 chose John Adams to serve as Vice President.

The votes had been cast in February. Yet, it took more than two months for a quorum of Congress to convene and certify the election.

Washington, who had retired in 1783, was enjoying his many agricultural pursuits at Mount Vernon when he learned the news. Duty bound, he left for New York City within two days to accept the job.

Of the countless accomplishments he would claim in his first 150 days, including adopting the Bill of Rights, establishing the Federal Judiciary (seating a six-member Supreme Court, as well as an Attorney General,) nominating two of his first four cabinet members (long-serving friends and Trenton veterans Alexander Hamilton and Henry Knox,) imposing a 5% tariff on all imported goods, and convening the first joint session of Congress (actually on the 153rd day of his presidency,) Washington also assembled a picture of the new nation's debt.

It was not pretty.

This he learned on his 47th day in office: the Federal domestic debt was $27,000,000, the Foreign debt was $10,000,000, and the total of all the states' debts was $21,500,000.[28] Of course, one of the many purposes behind ratifying the Constitution was to consolidate a national economy. Each state had its own tax schedules, its own currencies, its own property valuations, its own debt-structuring strategies; in short, each had its own financial headaches. Hamilton had a plan to acquire state debts and free up capital to foster economic growth. Indeed, with the independence of the states, albeit united under a federal republic, came the necessity to manufacture and trade goods of its own. No longer was it prudent or profitable to import shoes or paper or glassware. America would have to make good on its independence. And that meant raising its own federal revenues.

One of Hamilton's earliest schemes was imposing a federal excise tax on distilled spirits. Whereas rum was largely imported from the Caribbean, whiskey was almost entirely homemade. It served as its own currency, just as tobacco once had, and was easily distilled, traded, shipped, and, of course, consumed. To the western settler who could grow plentiful wheat or rye, loading a wagon full of whiskey barrels was a sight more profitable than loading an equivalent 20 wagons of raw grain.

In Western Pennsylvania, the much preferred distillate was made from rye. "Old Mon" was the drink of choice. "Mon" was a truncation of Monongahela. And, of course, the longer it aged—the *older* it sat—the sweeter it tasted. As a promising revenue source to cut the federal debt, it was thought to be much sweeter.

---

[28] https://www.mountvernon.org/george-washington/the-first-president/washingtons-first-100-days/#-

Hollingsworth & Pentecost

Never shy to impose his intellectual brilliance on men more powerful than he, Dorsey Pentecost wrote the President of the United States in July of 1789:

> "Sir —
>
> A few days ago I received the unwelcome News of the Death of Mr Thomas Hutchins Geographer to the United States, by which Accident the Publick has lost a Worthy faithful and Capable Servant, and that Office becomes Vacant.
>
> "Permit me Sir in the most respectful manner to solicit your Excellencys indulgence in appointing me to succeed the said deceased Mr Hutchins as Geographer to the united States of America.
>
> "I am well apprised Sir of the Importance of the Office, as well as the Presumption of this Application, and must confess that it needs an Apology but Sir Providence has been pleased to place you in a Situation that subjects you to numberless applications of this kind, which I know must be irksom, perplexing & sometimes vexatious… this reflection especially at a time when there is an inundation of Applicants makes this address exceeding disagreable to me, but the Necessity of doing it now or never I hope in some measure will plead my excuse. and I asshore you Sir if I am rejected I shall not be dissatisfied or even disappointed but on the other hand if I should be so fortunate as to meet with your Excellencys approbation I shall receive it as a favour Never to be forgotten, and hope that my deportment will Justify the Indulgence, at least it shall be my endeavour to deserve it."

Pentecost's ambitious letter, which rambled on two pages longer, threw out names of personal references and other political connections, including the same deceased Thomas Hutchins who Pentecost apparently had met in Pittsburgh some years earlier and, who, surprisingly then, had said to Pentecost that he "was very desirous that I Should be his Sucessor that he knew of no person whose Situation and Knowledge of the Country it would suit as well as myself (especally as I had told him at our last interview that I proposed to remove back to the western Country) and farther that I was his choice because he was acquainted with my principles, and abilities... that it was a respectable office and worth the Acceptance of any Gentleman, that he was desirous, and wished to Serve me, that he knew the publick could not be better Served then in the appointment of myself, that if I pleased he would resign in my favour and use all his Interest & Influence for me..."

The notion that Pentecost had once become the endeared acquaintance of Hutchins at some earlier date is as likely as the dead man's ringing endorsement of him. Thomas Hutchins, at the direction of George Washington, had surveyed much of the Florida and Louisiana Territories, had been named the official engineer of the southern continental armies, had mapped out much of the Northwest Territory, and was in the process of surveying the Seven Ranges of eastern Ohio when he died. He was the first and only man to hold the title of Geographer of the United States. There is little evidence that Pentecost ever surveyed lands in the southern territories or the Ohio country, or that Hutchins would have ever witnessed his principles or abilities. It is true that Hutchins was in Pittsburgh. He was buried at the First Presbyterian Church there in May of 1789.

Humility found no hope in Dorsey Pentecost. In fact, at the time he wrote to George Washington, Pentecost was drowning in debt. And all because of the braggadocio with which he conducted his business. It would seem that as land agent and surveyor to the partnership of Levi Hollingsworth and Thomas Shields, Pentecost not only overstepped his bounds, but wholly misrepresented the Power of Attorney that Hollingsworth had, in one instance only, conferred on him. Yet, in one case after another—in courts from Indiana to Maryland—Hollingsworth found himself a defendant against claims he knew nothing about.

Archives in Philadelphia hold handwritten copies of the many letters Hollingsworth wrote to Pentecost. They allude to issues of law and ethics that need no further elucidation beyond the angst Hollingsworth expressed.

March 17, 1787

"Mr. Dorsey Pentecost

Sir

I wrote you the 23 Feby. & sundry letters about that date, which I suppose had got to your hand, but from your not complying with my request therein expressed of coming immediately to this City. In these letters I mentioned that Wynkoop had obtained judgement against you, that Willing had obtained Judgement against Clark; & that I expected by this time you would have obtained a full and certain account of the Quantity of the lands bought of him …

You say you have property enough in the State to pay all his debt & I shall not lose, but what has your Property to do with my Paying the Money. Am I then to look to your property over the Mountains when I am first ruined? Come forward to take your share of these Burdens, I pray you, or I shall lose that Esteem I once bore you. You well know that if judgement goes against us, the Cash must be paid or my Estate seized & sold or my Person imprisoned as being on the Spot, either of which would ruin us for ever & with it my family.

"I hope your lady is recovered by this date & to see you as soon as possible

"Mr. Shields complains heavily of your Conduct, come & answer for yourself."

October 3, 1787

"Dorsey Pentecost

Dear Sir

I have paid Wm. Wynkoop half his Sum & shall pay the balance when due—Also & Smith £12 as ordered in your letter of the 25th. Your resolution respecting Thruston Estate gives me some hope of your determinations to extricate yourself from this ruinous bargain & I hope it may be effected… I am this day called upon by the holders of your Bill drawn by Joseph Titbull for £100 which I have refused payment of. For God sake and your own attend to this business now under your journey & let nothing swerve you from the Adjustments of the several objects you had in view when you left me.

December 16, 1787

"Dorsey Pentecost

I have received no advice from you since your letter dated at Baltimore in which you promise to write by every opportunity and as the Members of Assembly and Convention from Washington and Westmoreland have both been down you may judge of my disappointment in receiving no letters especially as you gave me every assurance and reason to expect large remittances from you when at Washington. General Neville informs me today that he understands you are yet either in Washington or Westmoreland County, how can you reconcile this delay I know not. When you know that by early exertions on your art depends our future wildfire and you must also know that the only probable prospect of your raising money is from the sale of the Kaskaskie Estate… if you have no intention of attending to these several weighty concerns you should in candour tell me so. I wish you well and hope this letter will rouse you from a lethargy which I fear is grinding upon you.

March 12 , 1788

"Mr. Dorsey Pentecost

"…the fault lays in your delaying it so long. I wish you may accomplish it in March or April & that the lands may please him. Your delay in going down the Ohio & settling your business at Kaskaskie is reprehensible… I should have been better prepared for the disappointment that must arise from it. The Salt Rock on Sandy is truly Visionary unless you can accomplish the other Business under your Care because these lands with all others must be sacrificed with out Money can be had to support our engagements. "He that grasps at too much looses all" is an old Maxim and is certainly true.

"I am sorry for the fall and hurt you received but as you are better hope no time will be lost in carrying that plan into execution which you undertook to accomplish before you left this City. You then gave me assurances that I should have remittances from you as soon as you arrived in Washington. I have seen Mr. O' Harra he said he had no Instruction..."

Hollingsworth demanded from Pentecost full restitution of every debt and mortgage never paid. It would seem Pentecost relinquished only several deeds, one including his own family's homestead in Indiana, to Hollingsworth.

Early in 1795, Mrs. Dorsey Pentecost received a deed of trust on land her husband had sold on account of his debt to Levi Hollingsworth. 700 acres on Chartiers Creek were to be shared in perpetuity by Catherine Pentecost or her seven children. The deed stated, "Doctor Absalom Baird... permits Catherine Pentecost, wife of Dorsey Pentecost, now or late of Washington County aforesaid yeoman...a life interest in this acreage and then on Catherine's demise each of her seven children is to receive his or her portion." [29]

Sometime before then, Dorsey Pentecost had left the region to travel to Kentucky. Whether he had gone to survey property or proffer other services to a client is unknown. No word, true or false, was ever again heard from the rascal.

If Levi Hollingsworth had once thought the business of land speculation could not have been nearly as bothersome as the daily grind of keeping mercantile accounts in order, he knew better now. Sprinkled throughout Hollingsworth's papers, however, is correspondence admitting to his partnerships with those whose lands he had jointly acquired.

August 17, 1787

"Mr. Wm Kimble On his Journey to Washington County
Dear Sir,

"I herewith send by you a Mortgage from Dorsey Pentecost to me for to get recorded in washington County and town of the same name, please leave the mortgage as you go up and when recorded bring it back with you—I will pay the cost.

---

[29] Diener, *The Honorable Dorsey Pentecost, Esquire*, pg. 88

"You also have a letter for Daniel Leet, esq., who will show you the lands or send a person for that purpose, on the west side of the Ohio, which he surveyed and was held in company with Mark Wilcox, B. Wynkoop, Thomas Shields, Mr. Leet and myself, but now divided. the Lotts I hold are No. 27, 28 and 86 in the General Draught, of which you have a copy.

"When in Washington County, Enquire for In. Goble who will also shew you some Lands I hold in Company with him & Thomas Shields—but now divided, when your Business is done in that Country, if you return by Washington, please call and bring the Mortgage back, be sure to have it recorded.

"Wishing you a safe journey and hoping the Lands may please, I am with great Regard, Yours & C. Levi Hollingsworth

August 17, 1787

"Daniel Leet, esq.
Washington County
Dear Sir
I am to request the favor of you to shew the bearer Mr. Wm. Kimble the lands I held in Company with Mark Wilcox, Thomas Shields, Benjamin Wynkoop and yourself, being No. 27, 28 & 86 in the general Draft agreeable to our division which Mr. Wilcox hath conveyed to me. Should it not be in your power to go with Mr. Kimble yourself please send some Person - Say one of the chain Carriers or some other suitable Person if to be had and I will gladly pay you the expense. Mr. Kimble hath thoughts of becoming a Purchaser if he likes the Lands and will probably take with him several reputable Families.

Your friendship in this business will much oblige,
Your humble Svt,   Levi Hollingsworth"

No records exist as to the disposition of the tracts he had hoped Mr. Kimble would purchase.

Lydia Morris Shields

On March 10, 1791, Lydia Morris Shields, Thomas's wife of 24 years and mother to eight children (two deceased,) died of unknown cause. She was 47 years old. Life expectancy in 18th century America then averaged 53 years. Philadelphia, even in 1790, had yet to offer a sewer system. Cases of typhoid and cholera were regularly announced in local papers. Ships arriving from foreign harbors imported all sorts of rare and infectious disease. But at 47, Lydia, the third born of four, already survived her three siblings. Each of them had died forty years earlier, likely from a common disease or an horrific accident.

Lydia Morris Shields was not related to Robert Morris nor to any of the other prominent Philadelphia Morrisses. From a private collection.

*   *   *   *   *

The following year, in May, 1792, the Shields's third-born, James, died, too. He was just 21.

Living in such close proximity as his family did to the waterfront of Philadelphia, visiting as often as he must have his father's shop on Front Street, exposed regularly to Philadelphia's loading docks and warehouses and sailors, who was to say what "ill-vapors" wafted about the streets?

John Nicholson

Not unlike Virginia's early Council President Thomas Lee, who, with Washington's elder brothers created the Ohio Company to capitalize on the colonists' western expansion, John Nicholson devised his own scheme.

In his role as commissioner to settle Revolutionary War veterans into the Depreciation Lands, Nicholson travelled throughout the state (although mostly in its eastern counties) to certify and distribute depreciation certificates. In this capacity, he often purchased the certificates back from those entitled to receive them. He did so for his own personal gain. By offering the veterans just pennies on the dollar, he amassed a small fortune in paper certificates.

Now, as the commissioner foremost responsible for the fiduciary health of Pennsylvania's Land Office, and, in 1790, also appointed Comptroller General for all of Pennsylvania, Nicholson saw an opportunity for a private company to assist the Commonwealth in selling its other frontier lands. Since the last auction at the Old Coffee House proved there was little appetite for land in the wilds west of Pittsburgh, and likely because he felt powerless to affect the market in any other way, he created the Pennsylvania Population Company.

It was a clever name. It bode of mass migration, progressive civilization, public access, and pride in the Commonwealth. It spoke directly to the mission to which Nicholson had first been assigned and it seemingly pledged to open doors that had remained closed for much too long. Here was a plan to franchise the state's greatest resource: land.

All that was required for Nicholson to succeed was a bundle of depreciation certificates and a few wealthy, "cash" investors.

There was no property then claimed, there were no warrants, patents or buyers awaiting settlement; there was, in fact, no immediate business at hand. But there was a singular opportunity: the Act of April 3, 1792. No doubt influenced by Nicholson himself, the Act was designed to open up the Erie Triangle lands that had been secured through the treaty at Fort Harmar. Here were flat, fertile lands situated at the shore of Lake Erie, yet otherwise loosely defined by that which was west of the Connewango Creek (a seventy-mile tributary to the Allegheny River,) and north of the Ohio River.

It did not hurt Nicholson in the least that John Lukens, Pennsylvania's first Surveyor-General, had died just two years earlier. Colonel Daniel Brodhead had now taken Lukens' seat. Arguably competent in military affairs, Brodhead was inept at the business of managing surveyors, recording certificates and processing paperwork. (Knowing that his wife was sister-in-law to the Governor might have explained a lot.)[30]

The treaty at Fort Harmar (Marietta, Ohio) had been a nebulous affair. Henry Knox, now Washington's Secretary of War, had insisted that the newly appointed Governor of the all-new Northwest Territory, Arthur St. Clair, stop the incessant Indian unrest. The Wyandots, Delawares, Chippewas, and Shawnees convened with him to explain quite succinctly that the preceding Treaty of Fort McIntosh had not been signed by them and they owed no allegiance to the agreement settled with the Iroquois at Fort Stanwix.[31, 32] St. Clair nonetheless threatened to run the lot of them out of the Northwest Territory unless they agreed to the prior treaty. Begrudgingly, they accepted a bundle of peace offerings to forget about it.

Of course, this did nothing to settle affairs in the Erie Triangle where the Iroquois, Shawnees, Delawares and Wyandots continued to run settlers off of their still illegitimate encroachments.

The Act of April 3, 1792, however, was seriously flawed. It allowed settlers dual, yet conflicting paths to ownership. The first route had always been the original course to land acquisition: tomahawk (or stake) a claim, file the claim for a warrant, have the county surveyor run out the lines, make improvements on the land (either by way of fencing-in a portion of it, building a cabin, or both,) and then, with proof of improvement, apply for the patent.

---

[30] Munger, *Pennsylvania Land Records*, pg. 189

[31] It had been signed, actually, but by other, younger braves who may have been induced by spirituous liquors.

[32] https://ohiohistorycentral.org/w/Treaty_of_Fort_Harmar_(1789)

The alternative route now was to purchase a prepared warrant from the land office (or soon, the Pennsylvania Population Company,) have it surveyed and patented, and then promise, *within two years*, to make improvements on that land. The Act imposed a minimum purchase of 400 acres, (give or take six percent for public rights of way.) Further, the new law protected any once-settled homesteader, even if as yet not warranted, from being ejected in his claim by those who sought a warrant directly from the land office. That seemed fair.

But what the Act of 1792 also included was a proviso that eventually protected outright speculation.

> "Provided always nevertheless, that if any such actual settler, or any warrantee in any such original or succeeding warrant, shall by force of arms of the *enemies of the United States*, be prevented from making such actual settlement, or be driven therefrom, and shall persist in his endeavors to make such actual settlement as aforesaid, then, in either case, he and his heirs shall be entitled to have and to hold the said lands, in the same manner as if the actual settlement had been made and continued."

The "enemies of the United States," of course, meant Native Americans, the Indians—savages.

The Act of 1792 provided for what were called prevention certificates. The two-year "promise to improve" window could now be extended to four years or five. Or six. In the western wilds of the Commonwealth, Native skirmishes were no less frequent, no less violent and certainly no less injurious to any settlers' prospect of finding his own little piece of heaven. One day's raid alone was worth a full year's claim of having been "prevented to settle." Now land speculators, guided by Nicholson, could "own" significant chunks of Pennsylvania at rock-bottom prices and wait out the market or the intemperate patience of the Natives. The excuse that speculators were "prevented" from improving their lands saved them the expense of any improvement. To "prove prevention" was simply a matter of getting a certificate stating as much.

Perhaps more egregious was what the Act did not say. The Act did not state what might happen if a warranted owner never made improvements.

Would the warrant eventually become void? And when? What rights might an interloping settler have if, after making improvements, he sought a legal patent? In the long run, the absence of forethought created a legal havoc which fed the offices of local lawyers for decades to come.

Nicholson's Pennsylvania Population Company was founded just eleven days after the passage of the Act. He did so with the cooperation and investment of the principal agent of the Holland Land Company, Theophilus Cazenove. The Holland Land Company was invested mostly in New York State lands which, for similar reasons, were not selling well. Other early investors in the Population Company included attorney Aaron Burr, Supreme Court Justice James Wilson, and Robert Morris, the latter of whom, already well invested in southwestern Pennsylvania, could not get enough of the promise Nicholson held out for him. Morris was Nicholson's largest investor, and a much trusted confidante.

Immediately, Nicholson negotiated a huge deal with both the state and federal powers-that-be. He claimed, on the basis of personal credit, more than 200,000 acres of the Erie Triangle and then applied for 390 warrants on the same. For each warrant, he used a different and fictitious name (a practice at the time wholly, yet surprisingly, condoned by the courts and land office.) And then, without so much as flashing a single coin, Nicholson transferred all of these "land rights" to his new company and took shares as President.

For his Board of Managers, Nicholson seated Cazenove, his complicit competitor, William Irvine, commander at Fort Pitt, George Mead, a prominent Philadelphia merchant, Walter Stewart, revenue agent for the Port of Philadelphia, and two deputy surveyors, John Hoge and Daniel Leet.

Neither was hired to survey. Hoge, like Leet, lived in Washington County; he knew the land, the opportunity, and, perhaps, something of the risk, too. Alone, his endorsement of the Pennsylvania Population Company was a valuable asset.

Unlike Hoge, however, Daniel Leet knew it all. While Hoge was familiar with southwestern Pennsylvania, Leet could describe most all of the Ohio country, West Augusta, Monongalia, Kentucky, and other lands few settlers, least of all speculators, had ever studied. He owned a broad context of land valuation from whom men like Thomas Shields, Levi Hollingsworth and Marc Wilcox sought recommendations. To any Philadelphian curious about western land, Daniel Leet was the go-to guy. In fact, he had become something of a celebrity. Anyone who had survived Crawford's Defeat, who had married one of the most legendary women of the frontier, and who now stood amongst influential men like Nicholson, Justice Wilson, and Robert Morris, was someone to esteem. What's more, in the Fall of 1791, he was elected a State Representative for Washington County. Ironically, he would serve two one-year terms under the woefully indifferent Quartermaster General of Valley Forge, Thomas Mifflin, now Governor of the Commonwealth. For this, he had to travel regularly to Philadelphia. There, in addition to attending sessions of the General Assembly, Leet convened with Nicholson and his investors. As a celebrated surveyor, Leet was vital to the company's prospects for success.

Yet, Leet had much more on his plate. By an Act in September of 1791, the state authorized the development of a new town to be situated at the site of Fort McIntosh. One year later, Daniel Leet would lay out the town of Beaver.

The Yellow Fever

From The Pennsylvania Gazette, Monday, September 15, 1793:

"Dr. Rush regrets, that he is unable to comply with all the calls of his Fellow Citizens, who are indisposed, with the prevailing fever. He begs leave to recommend to such of them as cannot have the benefit of medical aid, to take mercurial purges, which may now be had with suitable directions, at most of the Apothecaries, and to lose ten or twelve ounces of blood, as soon as is convenient, after taking the purges, if the head-ach and fever continue. Where the purges cannot be obtained, or do not operate speedily, bleeding may now be used before they are taken. The almost universal success with which it hath pleased God, to bless the remedies of strong mercurial purges, and bleeding in the disorder, enables Dr. Rush to assure his Fellow Citizens, that there is no more danger to be apprehended from it, when those remedies are used in its early stage, than there is, from the meazles, or the influenza."

The first public case of Yellow Fever appeared on the 23rd of August. Philadelphia Mayor Matthew Clarkson attended to it personally. The victim died eight days later. The mayor himself was stricken by the fever two days later, but survived his first round of symptoms.

Yellow Fever struck Philadelphia with such ferocity as had never been witnessed before. The ports had been bustling with news of fanciful and strange imports—items like Chinese Ribbons, Queen's-ware, or Kentings–

–yet silent about what new "germs" had come ashore.[33] People in the streets literally collapsed from high fever or sudden vomiting. Others were left to die in attic dormers or their own backyard privies. Yellow Fever was thought to be so "highly contagious" that house maids and neighbors refused to serve as "blood-letters." Apothecaries sought immediate help by hiring "morally sound" interns to deliver mercurial powders, laudanum, and other aids.[34] Doctors, like the famous Benjamin Rush, raced about town to prescribe therapies and medications of various efficacies, some seemingly more barbaric than the next. To the modern physician, none should have worked. And few did. More than 5,000 citizens of Philadelphia died over the course of just three months. Not until the chill of autumn set in, did the "germ" die off.

(And not for another hundred years would Walter Reed and Jesse Lazear, studying the Yellow Fever epidemic of the Panama Canal, prove that mosquitoes—not germs—were the culprits.)

Widower Thomas Shields and his five remaining children escaped the scourge by fleeing to the countryside. It is no more likely they headed west to see Shields's new tracts of Depreciation lands than north to shelter at Damascus Manor. Neither offered any lodgings nor would traveling for weeks with five teenagers have been probable. Indeed, the family fled to higher, cooler grounds outside of the city. Evidence suggests Chestnut Hill was their safe haven.

Within the year, Thomas would have a new bride. His family Bible makes note that he married Hannah Cox on November 7, 1793. The wedding ceremony, however, was not held at the First Baptist Church of Philadelphia for which records are well intact. Little is known about Hannah. A likely genealogy suggests that the name Cox may have been her widowed name and that her maiden name was Jones. Another identifies one Hannah Cox as a regular attendee at Quaker Friends meetings. Although it seems dubious a devout Baptist would marry a Quaker, it is certain, for reasons later discovered, Hannah Cox was not a Baptist. Whatever her affinity to Thomas, she was said to have been about 40 at the time of their marriage. He was 50.

---

[33] *Aurora General Advertiser*, 9/16/1793 --Chinese ribbons referred to brightly dyed silks, Queensware was a glossy, cream colored porcelain, named for Queen Charlotte; Kentings might have referred to a fabric woven with gold thread from Ghana.

[34] Rush, *An Account of the Bilious remitting Yellow Fever*, pg. 203

Beaver Town

Although Fort McIntosh had survived as the first and largest fort built west of the Ohio River, the purpose for it was long obsolete. Not one cannon had been fired in its eight years of defending the wild west. The square hewn logs erected to accommodate some 1,500 soldiers never saw more than 400 at any one time.[35] By 1790, many of the same logs were pilfered and put to better use by homesteaders far removed from the Beaver Creek bluff over-looking the Ohio River.

The name Beaver, of course, came from the indigenous rodent (*castor canadensis*) that so populated the Ohio tributary the French had named it Riviere au Castor. No doubt, a local sachem of the indigenous Delawares, Tamaqua, known to early settlers as King Beaver, was inspiration, too. Either way, the name was adopted and any honor due Lachlan McIntosh was willingly forgotten.

Daniel Leet started surveying Beaver town in 1792.

Most major colonial cities like Boston had been carved out by foot traffic, and then horse paths. Only New Haven, Connecticut, and America's largest city, Philadelphia, had adopted civic plans.[36] (New Haven's town commons was laid out as a square; its civic leaders thus insisted that all future development around the commons would adhere to the strict geometry.) With a population of about 18,000 in 1750, the streets of Philadelphia were made parallel and perpendicular. Each was given a distinct name, with a

---

[35] Perhaps as many as 1,500 men helped construct the fort, but never as many actually garrisoned there. *Beaver Town 2002, a Place in History—Then …and Now.* pg. 24.

[36] Bushman, *The Refinement of America*, pg. 142

directional prefix for north or south, even if house numbers would not appear until 1790.

On the western frontier, however, the evolution of common roadways everywhere was secondary to situating residences next to well-watered, level fields. At Beaver, above the Ohio River, just several miles long and fewer wide, was a densely wooded plateau, abutting two significant waterways. By benefit of its elevation, however, it was not subject to annual flooding. Whatever the plateau may have lacked in terms of military defenses, it made up in commanding vistas. Leet knew all of this. He had studied the topography when constructing its fort.

Now was an opportunity for Leet to think outside of the proverbial box. Which is to say he adopted a new vision... of many boxes.

Daniel Leet's idea was that 200 acres should be laid out in "residential" blocks—known as "in-lots"—and another 1,000 acres would provide "out-lots." The two hundred acre town would also provide open, green commons by allotting the four most central blocks and the four corner blocks exclusively to public use. Leet was charged with laying out streets and avenues, too. These he decided would have widths of "two perches and six," respectively; that is, streets would be roughly 30 feet wide and avenues an unprecedented 100 feet wide. That the typical wagon was little more than four feet wide suggests Leet had grand expectations for the town.

The lots he devised were rectangular, 120 feet wide by 300 deep. As single-owner tracts, each could accommodate a residence with plenty of room for gardens and livestock. This, of course, was wholly atypical in the western wilds; nowhere else was a man's homestead similar in any way to another's. Here, each was standard and equal. And all were meant to foster community. Sharing public space whether at the center of town or on its outskirts was unlike anything American settlers had practiced before. Not even in Philadelphia.

Already, Beaver represented something very new to America: a planned urban community.

The civic design of Beaver portended a different economy. Leet's vision was something greater than building a center for commerce surrounding a courthouse and churches. Here was the opportunity for the western citizen to ply a living not dependent on property, but on community. If tanners made poor cobblers, if millwrights were lousy bakers, and hog drivers knew not how to make soap or to butcher bacon, then Beaver might weave together an economy few pioneer settlements ever had. Indeed, the town soon boomed; the butcher, a baker and candlestick-makers generated a village commerce on a scale befitting the needs of a tightly-knit community. Leet's notion was remarkable for his time.

A visit to Beaver today proves it.

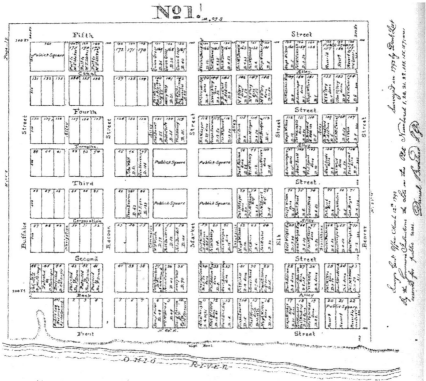

Leet's planned city of Beaver, as submitted to the Department of Internal Affairs of Pennsylvania, showing the "inner lots" of which Leet owned at one time: 4, 10, 14, 44, 49, 50, 66, 67, and 68. The copy above was recreated in 1904. Beaver County Historical Society.

Nearby, Logstown

By the Fall of 1792, not only was Secretary Knox fed up with the savage skirmishes of the Northwest Territory, but now President Washington was, too. By then, he had amassed a considerable investment in lands near present-day Cincinnati: 3,000 acres or more scattered along the Little Miami River in Southwest Ohio. He wanted some protection. But the homesteaders feeding almost daily into the Ohio Valley needed much more. Washington ordered General Anthony Wayne—he they called "Mad" for his rash commands in battle—to come out of retirement and train a spectacular force to rid the Ohio Country of the Natives that Arthur St. Clair and, his successor, Josiah Harmar, had so miserably failed to do.

Daniel Leet knew Wayne from Valley Forge. (It seems everyone had been there.) And, now, in November of 1792, while Leet surveyed the town of Beaver, General Wayne appeared just a stone's throw upriver. With him were about 1,500 men who had first convened to build a new fort in Pittsburgh. (Fort Fayette stood at the present day site of 9th Street and Penn Avenue.) But Wayne thought the town was too promiscuous and, demanding absolute discipline and decorum, marched his men down the banks of the Ohio.

Informed of the poor conditions at Fort McIntosh, General Wayne decided to encamp at Logstown. Here he assembled a fearless "legion" of men trained for battle against the wily Indians. Wayne transformed Logstown into a training facility called Legionville, building barracks, commissaries, store houses and rifle ranges. There were no stockades, no bastions; in fact, it was not a fort, but an open field. Wayne's army trained in rifle fire and bayonet practice. His simple strategy against the Natives was to create a very swift and deadly fleet, one that could attack without hesitation. He abhorred armies that had to waste time preparing for battle. So he devised two solutions to problems earlier encountered. First, he got rid of heavy artillery that slowed down troops; he equipped special teams with smaller howitzers that could be saddled on horseback. Secondly, he designed colorful uniforms that not only bedazzled the enemy, but helped disguise the ranks of his officers. No more flashy metals or distinctive headwear. Troop leaders were to blend in with their subordinates. Natives had always known to attack officers first.

Legionville served eight months of basic training. In fact, it was the very first basic training camp of the new US Army. In its service, General "Mad" Anthony Wayne further widened Beaver Road. This was only the second time the original Indian path had been improved since Col. Henry Bouquet first marched on it in 1764.

In August of 1794, Wayne's expedition to Maumee, Ohio, a once forested town devastated by a tornado, ended in the Battle of Fallen Timbers. Wayne's well-trained scouts and cavalry proved so effective, the battle lasted hardly more than an hour. Blue Jacket's Shawnees, expecting to charge the American forces, were awed by Wayne's military precision and chose to flee to Fort Miamis rather than suffer great loss. Not only did the dragoons chase the Natives down, the British inside the fort refused to give them safe harbor. Still, less than fifty warriors were killed. But their abandonment in the heat of crisis left them to know there was little hope of holding onto lands their ancestors had shared for centuries. Millennia, really.

Once more and forever still, the Natives were forced farther westward.

Although no one knew it then, the Battle of Fallen Timbers would be the last major Indian conflict of the century, opening up most of the Ohio country to white settlement without inordinate fear. Not until Tippecanoe in 1811 would the righteous and greedy again silence Native anger.

A Letter to George

By 1791, the federal excise tax on homemade whiskey became a real problem. Larger distillers who were in the business of selling their spirits—that is, retailing it in significant volume—had to pay six cents on every gallon to a local tax collector. Homestead distillers, however—those for whom a few gallons of moonshine were sufficient compensation to a neighbor for, say, erecting a new fence or painting the barn—were charged nine cents a gallon.[37] That hardly seemed fair.

Especially in Western Pennsylvania, where whiskey was widely traded, the collection of the excise tax became something of a joke. Tax collectors were harassed by locals when they rode into villages seeking intelligence on homesteaders from whom they should collect. Famously, in September of that year, revenue agent Robert Johnson found himself suddenly surrounded by eleven angry men all dressed in women's clothing. They had only wished to intimidate Johnson, but he knew who two of the "disguised" men actually were. That blew their cover, so the "women" tarred and feathered the federal agent. Later that year, another "revenuer" was tied to a tree.

For three years, settlers along the Monongahela, up the Youghiogheny, and down Chartiers Creek fumed about the tax, yet they were angrier still about the regulations of compliance. Hamilton's scheme to raise direct revenue for the Federal government required that distillers pay the tax in cash. That just didn't exist. Whatever cash may have circulated in the Commonwealth was little seen in the western wilds. Half the reason homesteaders made whisky was to use it *as* currency. A keg of Ol' Mon was as good for a

---

[37] https://www.history.com/topics/early-us/whiskey-rebellion

load of hay as a half-dollar might have been—if only one might possess a half-dollar.[38] If excise agents could have collected the tax in whisky barrels, there would never have been an issue. Well, likely not.

Outspoken federalists like Hugh Henry Brackenridge tried to cool things down, but only made them worse. Stories he wrote in the *Pittsburgh Gazette* helped radicalize locals into frenzied mobs. One such confrontation broke out when John Neville, a wealthy landowner just outside of Washington town, assisted federal marshal David Lenox in serving writs on more than sixty local excise-dodging residents. For his patriotic service, he found his house on Bower Hill surrounded by an angry mob. Gunfire ensued and one rebel died. This further enraged the mob who returned a day later with more than seven hundred men. That then brought out the local militia to defend Neville's home which, even after a long cooling-off, burned to the ground. So was born the Whiskey Rebellion.

Within the week, President Washington was notified that now 7,000 rebels had assembled, ready to march through Pittsburgh to do more harm. Washington quickly scrambled in Philadelphia to muster the support he needed to assemble federal marshals to march westward. Of the blessings he needed was that of Supreme Court Chief Justice James Wilson.[39] Because it was his original idea to enforce a federal tax on whiskey, Alexander Hamilton, too, joined the federal militia. Indeed, Washington led some 12,000 men from Philadelphia westward, pausing only at Bedford, PA, when he received word that the mob seemed to have dispersed. Washington turned back, but sent sufficient forces into Pittsburgh to make arrests and bring several rebels back to justice. Within the year, to all who had been brought to trial, Washington issued pardons. Others fearing arrest, however, had just fled the scene, many of whom were never to be seen again.

For the many wives with children, abandoned and now destitute, the situation became quite dire.

Daniel Leet penned a letter to his friend, President Washington, dated December 3, 1795. Although a former State Representative, Leet did so with no particular authority, other than that granted by his age and esteem

---

[38] Barr, *A Colony Sprung from Hell*. Pg. 260

[39] An early and significant investor in the Pennsylvania Population Company, he owned land in western Pennsylvania where the Whiskey Rebellion threatened to test the Federal courts.

in the Washington community, an area from which many of the rebels had apparently fled.

"Sir, The Subject to Which we Would Call your Attention for A few Minutes, is the late unhappy Insurrection in this part of the Country—We are of those who felt themselves in danger during that frenzy—We have seen it totally subside, peace happily Restored, and the Laws in full and free execution—With peculiar pleasure we have Observed the Lenity with which *your Conduct* Sir on this trying Occation was Marked, Operating this Happy effect, even More powerfully than the force employed: But Sir, there are Still A Wretched few to Whom your Clemencey has not been extended, and Whose Miserable families are Still Amongst us exciting Such emotions, as *no doubt,* you Sir will partake of on Reading this, Whilst the Husbands and fathers are, no One knows Where. Now Sir the Question we Would Submit to your Consideration is, Whether it Would be Consistant with public peace and Safety to extend your pardon to all, and thereby Render the Miserable happy, and Relieve us from the painfull feelings Occationed by their presence and Circumstances. We will not presume *Sir* to Urge Arguements to you on this Subject, your Own Mind is Much More Capable of Suggesting the proper—We are Aware that this may be thought an early day to Come forward with this Application: The Condition of the unofending Women and Children is all we Can reply, and are With Great respect Sir your Very humble servant"[40]

The letter, signed by Leet (as well as thirty-six other sympathetic citizens,) was his last correspondence addressed to Washington.

Not until spring did Daniel receive this reply:

"To Daniel Leet and others petitioners in behalf of certain fugitives from justice
        Philadelphia 24th april 1796.
        Gentlemen

---

[40] *Founders Online,* National Archives, https://founders.archives.gov/documents/Washington/05-19-02-0158.

"I have received and considered your petition bearing date the third day of last december for a general pardon of all those concerned in the late western insurrection who having fled from the public justice have not been comprehended in any act of Amnesty. While citizens accused of crimes or misdemeanors are endeavouring to elude a fair trial by the laws of the land, absconding or otherwise keeping themselves from the power of the court to which most properly they are amenable they seem not entitled to the clemency of government; and more especially when that clemency is not solicited by the offenders themselves. Under these circumstances they, in whose behalf you have been led by motives of compassion to intercede, are not deemed now to deserve the forgiveness of their country. I am with great respect gentlemen your most obedient servant."[41]

I DO ⬛ promife, ⬛ to fubmit to the Laws of the United States; that I will ⬛ directly nor indirectly oppofe the execution of the Acts for raifing a Revenue on Diftilled Spirits and Stills, and that I will fupport as far as the Laws require the civil authority in affording the protection due to all officers and other Citizens.

September 11, 1794.

The signature of Daniel Leet, and that of his brother Isaac, Jr. appear on an affidavit obeying Federal law. Courtesy of the Sewickley Valley Historical Society.

---

[41] *Ibid.*, https://founders.archives. gov/documents/Washington/99-01-02-00468.

Cash's Creek

As if the scourge of yellow fever in Philadelphia were akin to the pestilence of the savages elsewhere, both abated by 1795. At long last, the country seemed to be safe. Those who saw great promise in the untapped resources of the wilds, those who might have realized commerce more fluent than in years past, those that would praise God and country for success never once promised, all rose to new occasions.

At 15 years of age, David Shields accompanied his father and two older brothers up the Delaware River from Philadelphia. They would hire a flat boat and oarsmen to transport horses, tools, building supplies and provisions sufficient to make camp. The journey would take a minimum of five days with another full day to haul off all the hardware to a clearing on which they could construct shelter. Their destination was Damascus Manor. Across the river was a former Native village, Coshecton. Two white traders might have camped there then, but meals and lodgings could not be had. The three Shields boys and their father would have to make do.

In 1795, Damascus Manor was barely settled. No grand house was situated anywhere nearby. That the land was called a Manor was only English parlance beckoning sentiments of more feudal times. Damascus Manor had been the property of Pennsylvania's earliest proprietor, since handed down to his heirs John and Richard Penn. Under William Penn's own laws, the land was not taxable. Thomas Shields had purchased 40,000 acres from the Penn brothers on February 6, the same year. This purchase was in addition to another 30,000 to 40,000 acres he had owned in the area since 1784. From Dyeberry Creek to the banks of the Delaware, in townships then named Lebanon, Oregon and Berlin, Thomas Shields held patents on nearly

100,000 acres in the most northeastern section of the Commonwealth. This was then Northampton County.

In 1798, the region became Wayne County in honor of the Mad General who had brought peace to the wild west.

Unlike his other properties in western Pennsylvania, on tracts of 300 acres or more in the Depreciation Lands near Pittsburgh, Shields went to work. Sons John and David helped construct a saw and gristmill on Cash's Creek.[42] On this precipitous tributary to the Delaware, Shields Mill powered the beginnings of the town of Damascus. By 1797, a one Moses Calkins had dragged up and across the frozen Delaware River the town's first burrstones.[43] By then, the Shields boys completed a first homestead. Other buildings came along, too. And the senior Shields, at first in partnership with the men across the river, built a center of commerce for the building trades now plying the region. A bridge would soon be necessary. Roads, too.

In service to their new town, David Shields and his brother John started a regular trade route to Philadelphia, selling hardware, dry goods and "necessaries" on their journeys back and forth. Customary kindness would suggest they delivered local mail, too.

Of course, David and John were in step with the times. By the last decade of the century, peddling had become something of a cultural phenomenon. As American manufacturing increased, the opportunity to serve needy customers in distant settings inspired peddlers to pack up wares to sell one farmhouse to the next. Saddle-bagged items like needles, ribbons, lace and scissors appealed to mothers and daughters learning refined skills to become refined ladies. Heavier wares like buckets, nails, brushes—even shelf clocks––transported by small wagon, appealed to the men of the house. Books about heroic figures like Henry Bouquet, General Wayne and George Washington became something far more entertaining than reading Protestant theology or classical Greek history. In fact, the number of books published in the six years after Washington took office was four times greater than the six years leading up to the Revolution.[44] Clearly, a new generation of Americans hungered for material goods and a cultural identity that suited a new vision of freedom. Whereas storeowners before might have promoted the latest and

---

[42] *The Honesdale Citizen*, Thursday, April 20, 1882

[43] Mathews, *History of Wayne, Pike and Monroe Counties, Pennsylvania*, pg. 458

[44] Jaffee, "Peddlers of Progress and the Transformation of the Rural North," pg. 518

greatest tastes of the genteel gentry, peddlers reached a wider, more humble audience and instructed them in elevating their lives with conveniences and curios never before seen in the wilds.

Yet there was so much land to cover.

While David and John may have peddled goods along the road, they also purveyed, imported and shipped much larger goods—bathing tubs or tin stoves, for example—itinerant pioneers chose not to haul. The Shields brothers had purposeful destinations along a singular route. Thanks to a wealthy father, they also had capital.

Thomas Shields established early commerce in Damascus Manor, Northampton County, with an early mill, roads and a bridge to cross the Delaware River at Coshecton. By 1800, he invited locals to attend the Baptist church he built on his property. From a private collection.

A Daily Schedule

Like so many towns in early Pennsylvania, Bethlehem was founded by religious separatists. The roots of its prosperity were nurtured by a pious community seeking physical isolation from a depraved world of social intolerance. The town was established by a noble German who, despite great popularity in his motherland, sailed to America to establish an early town in which his followers could enjoy the sanctity of religious expression. William Penn had first chartered his "woods" to accept and protect religious freedom. And so, in 1741, Nikolaus Ludwig Count von Zinzendorf, accepted Penn's invitation to plant the seeds of a Moravian mission at the confluence of the Monacacy Creek and Lehigh River.

For its first forty years, Zinzendorf's Moravian community at Bethlehem was closed to all outsiders. The volumes of liturgical papers, prayers and hymns created in those years have been the subject of arduous research and scholarly interpretation. And for good reason. Among other peculiar interests, Zinzendorf and his acolytes were fascinated by the blood and wounds of the crucified Christ. Their litany echoes images of Christ's "death-streaked eyes," His "spit-dripped mouth," and His "fire-baptized corpse." Descriptions of red and purple wounds, of bloody nails and succulent bruises punctuate many hymns. Much is made of the stigmata of Christ's crucifixion, specifically the gash in Christ's ribs from his tormentors' spears. But their adoration of Jesus's pain and suffering on the cross was not intended to compel followers by its inherent sorrow, but by its sensational absolution. According to Zinzendorf, Jesus's blood "flowed out of his body and cascaded like a [once] damned stream which flooded over and blessed the entire world in an instant." The Bethlehem leader believed "in his heart" that Christ's oozing wounds had redeemed all men, even if such sinners did not know or revere Him. Man was saved once and for all. No matter who. Or what sin.

To a devout Baptist like Thomas Shields, Zinzendorf's doctrine would have bordered on the apocryphal, not unlike the dogma of Universal Restoration. Yet to the great unwashed—to those whose only intellectual stimulation might have come by way of deciphering a Sunday's sermon—the Moravian fascination with blood and gore was riveting.

Surprisingly, of all the early separatist movements that found nurture in the soil and streams of a new country, this one Pennsylvania settlement has prospered for more than four hundred years. In fact, the Moravian Book Shop in Bethlehem, Pennsylvania, calls itself the oldest continuously operating bookstore in the world.[45] Few can doubt it.

Moreover, the town can also boast having endowed one of the first schools for girls in the new colonies. Zinzendorf founded the Bethlehem Seminary for Girls in 1742. It is today Moravian College.

Its curriculum as well as its social instruction for young women of the late eighteenth century was both exceptional and—despite "daily lessons in needlework, lace, and fine embroidery of ribbons"—progressive. Beyond the three Rs, students were taught composition and rhetoric, "foreign" language, (meaning, of course, German and Latin,) and the subjects of science: botany, geography, and astronomy. The latter subjects were sometimes combined as "instructions in the globes;" fanciful orbs, made of papier maché, were painted with the continents of the earth on one, and the constellations of the sky on the other. Two "tutoresses" were responsible for up to fifteen students, grouped by age, and led in "choirs." Although not necessarily instructed in choral singing, students were introduced to music in many ways.[46]

The daily schedule dictated that the young girls rise by 5:30 a.m.

A "starting hymn" served as a blessing before breakfast. Once fed, the students returned to their dormitory, made their beds, and prepared for the day's instructions. Then, decorum demanded "they repair quietly to their classes, take their allotted seats, and rather than indulge in noise and idle

---

[45] https://www.moravian.edu/bookshop/about

[46] Smith, *The Moravian Young Ladies' Seminary,* pg.

talk, silently implore God's blessing and aid, so that they may engage with pleasure and profit in the duties before them."

In 1795, as many as sixty young women between the ages of 8 and 15 attended the Moravian Seminary for Girls in Bethlehem. The boarding school was founded nearly thirty years earlier, but not until 1785 did it admit students whose parents were not associated with the church. A similar school for boys opened the same year. It was placed quite purposefully ten miles away in Nazareth, Pennsylvania. Both were popular, each highly respected and, at £20 per academic year, very expensive. Tuition did not include supplies for "tambour-work or drawing," or lessons on the piano-forte or guitar, or the "rent" (at 15 shillings per student) for the personal use of candles, fuel or school books. In addition, students were to arrive at the beginning of the school year with their own beds, linens, and other essentials like eating utensils, tea caddies and sugar.

Meals were included. As such, the girls were advised, "It is unbecoming in young misses at boarding school to murmur at the food that is set before them, and to treat the gifts of God with disrespect. Whatever is not agreeable, let it remain untouched, without expression of dissatisfaction."

The school was sought out by what "nobility" the cities of Boston, Philadelphia, and New York esteemed by wealth. Even George Washington applied to the seminary on behalf of his grand-niece, Maria Washington, admitted in 1797. It is uncertain, then, that she might have come to know one of the senior students. Eliza Marie Leet attended the Moravian Seminary for two full years, "graduating" with thirty-one other girls in her Class of 1797. She was just thirteen at the time.

The irony can be excused only by time, ignorance or, perhaps, indifference. That a man who was present at the massacre of the Moravian mission at Gnadenhütten should enroll his daughter in the school of the very community he so offended is remarkable, if not astounding.

It cannot be known then that Daniel Leet had atoned for any complicity in the event. His earlier resignation from political service suggests that he knew shame. And maybe, just maybe, he had grieved.

Of course, the mass murder had occurred fifteen years earlier. Few men actually knew who all had brazenly ridden to Gnadenhütten, including, certainly, the Moravians responsible for running the Bethlehem school. Perhaps, they knew nothing about it. The murderous posse, upon their return, had said very little, and those responsible for investigating the matter had swept the horrific details under the rug. Surely, the Moravian community in Ohio never exploited the injustice, accepting that their Savior would lead them on a path to forgiveness.

As to his daughter's matriculation, he may have known this one school was his child's best educational opportunity, privileged as he was to have paid a tuition few others could afford.

It can be certain that Eliza, so young and innocent then, knew nothing of her father's presence at the massacre in Ohio. Less certain is that Daniel Leet, or his wife Wilhelmina, believed in the principles of the Moravian church, even if they ever attended any such house of worship themselves. Yet, clearly, Eliza enjoyed her days in Bethlehem.

A poem handwritten to her on a school souvenir evidences a long and lasting friendship:

A Little Wish

That you, my lov'd Eliza, Day by Day
May trace the sweetest Roses in Your Way,
That <u>real</u> Happiness Your Steps attend
And mark those of Your <u>nearest</u>, <u>dearest</u>, friend!

Yea, that our Saviour on Your every Hour,
The choicest Blessings, He has purchas'd, show'rs.

This is the cordial Wish …of A.K.K.

Beth'm March 28, 1804

An Advertisement

1798 brought another summer of sorrow to Philadelphia. Again, Yellow Fever ravaged the city. More than 1,200 citizens died, many discovered convulsing on the streets. The infestation cooled down by autumn.

In November, David Shields announced that he had returned from Chestnut Hill and was now ready for business at his store at 22 Chestnut Street in Philadelphia. His offerings included "Coarse and fine white, red and green Baizes in half pieces," as well as "Coarse and fine white Flannells from 2 shillings 3 pence to 6 shillings a yard." Further, he expected new arrivals from Scotland, Ireland and England any day soon.

David, at eighteen years of age, was now in the business of importing fabrics. (Baizes were then what modern customers would know as felt. Flannel, of course, was something thinner and softer. Both were made from finely napped wool.) Yet, he did not restrict his trade to textiles alone. Evidence of other wares he sold at 22 Chestnut Street suggested he offered household goods—door hinges and candle lanterns—and kitchen wares, like Dutch ovens and wrought iron utensils. "Necessaries" such as these he might have sold on his first trading route from Philadelphia up to Northampton County.

In the same newspaper and on the same date—*The Philadelphia Daily Advertiser*, November 16, 1798—his older brother, John, advertised his services, too, now also "returned from Chestnut Hill," and doing business at 22 Chestnut Street, "Where he holds himself ready to execute…in every branch of his profession, trusting that from a residence in this city of 35 years he has it in his power to render… Lotts, Lands, Houses, Vessels, Certificates of every description and Bills of Exchange, bought and sold, the dockets carefully examined and clear titles made upon the shortest notice…"

John now seems to be either a realtor, a notary, a solicitor or all of the above. Interesting to note is his stated credentials for offering these services is his residency of 35 years. Of course, it would not have been clear to his prospective customers that the house in which he was conducting his business was 35 years old, and not his "residency" therein. Married four years earlier (to a Miss Coombe of Chestnut Hill,)[47] John was just twenty years old, two more than David.

John may have offered his many services to the public in the guise of a professional agent. That is, in journeying to distant villages, he could represent the interests of many merchants and tradesmen by offering their goods or property to a much wider audience than their own work commitments would permit. Acting in a capacity more resourceful than that which a peddler-by-wagon might, John—and soon David, too—could solicit far-distant customers, taking orders for more specific goods, perhaps of greater quantity or size, and then promise delivery, by way of "Bills of Exchange, bought or sold" to greater markets than any one craftsman might reach. If land was for sale, they could represent that as well, necessitating "clear titles made upon the shortest notice." Now, too, John and David would build a network of purveyors and manufacturing resources for all manner of industry and trades, connecting buyers with sellers from diverse regions to which few others might travel. Indeed, well before the close of the century, David would branch out to find new markets, new opportunities and new channels in which to serve as an agent.

---

[47] *The Pennsylvania Gazette*, November 26, 1794, pg. 3

A Scheme

John Nicholson, smart, ambitious, and savvy as a hedge fund operator, earned positions within the Commonwealth that allowed him unfettered access to power more pernicious than profitable. Given extraordinary responsibilities beyond those of the Comptroller General, Nicholson now served as the state's Tax Collector—as well as Escheator General—putting him in charge of liquidating the estates of loyalist-traitors who had long since departed the country. In 1792, Nicholson personally redeemed $60,000 in Pennsylvania debt certificates under a newly re-opened Federal loan program. The certificates were those he bought directly from hapless folk who knew no better. Like the Depreciation certificates he acquired from veterans who much preferred the "few dollars now, than distant acres later," he purchased the debt notes for far less than face value. Of course, his professional duty was to repurchase them for the benefit of the commonwealth. No matter; he bought them himself. But, he then tendered the notes in exchange for federal securities. By doing so, and in the quantities by which he did, the present value of the federal securities rose quite handsomely. (Further, Nicholson obfuscated the responsibility of Pennsylvania to clear its own debt, leaving the collateral for the Feds to untangle.)

The scheme was first discovered by a state clerk examining the books of Robert Morris who was then having issues paying his own debts.[48]

Members of the State Assembly met with the Ways and Means Committee to investigate Nicholson's scheme. Not including interminable court

---

[48] Hogan, "The Pennsylvania State Trials," Pennsylvania General Assembly, 1793-1794. Senate, pg. 68

proceedings, the meetings went on for three years, until, impeached—yet, ultimately acquitted—Nicholson resigned every one of his state offices.

Which meant that, while the fox may have removed himself from the hen house, he was now free to roam the entire farm.

Nicholson's appetite for land became gluttonous. He again partnered with Robert Morris. Between them, they purchased nearly 2 million acres of Pennsylvania land for about $500,000. On the promise of a quick sale to French investors, they discovered too late that the terms once agreed upon ran far afoul of their investors' actual means. Thus holding the property, they leased it outright and capitalized a new company they oddly named the Asylum Company.

They also partnered to create the North American Land Company, a completely separate entity but which might well have held land assets in common with other speculators. Their intent was to sell wide swaths of forested lands to buyers overseas. Morris explained the business model in a prospectus he created for foreign investors, writing, "The proprietor of back lands gives himself no other trouble about them than to pay taxes, which are inconsiderable. As nature left them, so they lie till circumstances give them value. The proprietor is then sought out by the settler who has chanced to pitch upon them, or who has made any improvement thereon, and receives from him a price which fully repays his original advance with interest."[49]

Morris's explanation was both deceptive and self-deceiving. First, he gave no mention to the hardships of accessing or defending western lands in the new America. He said nothing about how his investor might qualify his purchase; he spoke nothing of the role of a surveyor. He offered no suggestion that such lands would necessitate a community to share in the cost of roads, a church or school. Further, he made no recommendations as to whom or how the investor might market his new property. The settler who "chanced to pitch upon" them would not know how to seek out the new owner. Nor did he have cash or credit anyhow. In fact, he would barely have the means—or the growing seasons—by which to trade goods for the species needed to pay the taxes. That Morris had boasted how "inconsiderable" those taxes were became the Achilles heel by which Morris and Nicholson's plans would run aground.

---

[49] Sakolski, *The Great American Land Bubble*, pg. 47

And yet, in another scheme, on swamplands in Northern Virginia, they would draw up plans for a new and improved "national city," principally by which to sell to the Federal government land it could have claimed for itself.

And they acquired enormous stakes in other land companies in Virginia, North Carolina, South Carolina, Georgia, and Kentucky. Separate from any partnerships above, Nicholson also created entities he called the Territorial Land Company, and, independent of the Pennsylvania Population Company, the Pennsylvania Land Company, too.

It might have been a slight overreach.

Insurmountable Debt

Before the Revolution and until the railroads came, among the few people who made any money from the rabid, frenzied land grab of colonial America were the humble surveyors. Even at just shillings per acre, it was money in the bank. Indeed, he had chain men to pay, and horses to feed, and expensive equipment manufactured to calculate exact measurements—instruments made from brass fittings not available in the states. But none of that was insurmountable risk if lost (or if not otherwise pre-expensed by fees any surveyor might pass on.) Professionally licensed and responsible only to his county land office, he had it made. Were it not for the indignity of defending himself from Indians or carnivorous predators, or slogging endless weeks through dense, cold forests, the early surveyor of America's frontier might have elevated his profession to something more respected than it was.

Of course, only he knew how much money he really made.

Pity thus the early American land speculator. That a wealthy gentleman from Philadelphia, Boston, New York, or Baltimore would purchase slips of paper referencing coordinates of western land he might never see, and then try to sell that paper for more than his purchase price, was a fool's game. It was a business model fraught with egregious expectation and devastating delusion. Yet, to those who could afford to dabble, it was the alchemy of its time. In the absence of specie or hard currency, what surely drove the "land-grabber" to speculate was the accumulation of wealth created from little work. Wealth was not determined by money in the bank, but by material possession: horses, cattle, and, as had oft been measured by British royalty and Virginia gentlemen alike, acres and acres of fertile soil. In fact, the premise of the First Bank of the United States was to serve as a land bank. Robert

Morris had been a principal in that endeavor, but when Alexander Hamilton formalized the institution, he argued that only specie—gold or silver currency—could serve to back its holdings. Hamilton abhorred speculation. [50]

Men like Morris, Nicholson, Justice Wilson, Hollingsworth, Wilcox, Cazenove, Craik and Washington played the very first game of Monopoly, acquiring as much property on the board as chance would allow them. Indeed, from "Go," their intentions were to lease their properties. But when no other players came to the board, the costs of improvement (if made) and mounting tax payments (if not made,) threw their cash reserves for a loop. They found few opportunities to win. One everlasting option was to sell it all. Preferably at a great profit. The only other option, in the absence of a sale or lease, was spreading the risk. Land companies created by elite partners became investment havens for the many. Letters of credit were drawn on the collateral of shares, not on specific land. Worse yet, when partners—say, just two among dozens—traded "insider" credit to sell or purchase one or the other's assets, there was no centralized accounting system with which to record the deal. And there were many such deals to record. Thousands of duped shareholders, effectively speculating on speculators, traded on credit in land companies absolutely saddled with debt.

No one collected $200. And many would go straight to jail.

---

[50] Sakolski, *The Great American Land Bubble*, pg. 33

Bankruptcy

In January of 1795, Robert Morris announced his resignation from the Senate. Having nearly completed a six-year term, he was preoccupied with his business interests, and none of it was in good stead. His debts amounted in the hundreds of thousands, and his investments in the North American Land Company, the Asylum Company and the Pennsylvania Population Company had produced nothing but paperwork and plentiful account ledgers of which he could make little sense. He sold his investment in the Population and Asylum companies to Nicholson for a little more than half a million dollars. But he did so, of course, on credit.[51] Meanwhile, he indefensibly promoted the sale of more shares in the North American Land Company, the only value to which could be attributed the collateral of certificates bearing his good name.

Of course, there were many who knew otherwise, unable to collect even the smallest debts Morris owed. Wrote the famed financier to one creditor, "Heavy disappointments repeated one after another has brought me behind my Engagements and I am day by day laboring for the means of facing them." To another, "With ample wealth, I find it next to impossible to get the possession of Ready money at this season."[52]

His shipping business was in limbo, confounded by the war in Europe. And, quite famously, his mansion on Chestnut Street, already two years under construction, was nowhere near completion. Commanding an entire city block, Morris's Folly, as it would soon be called, still stood roofless. Massive marble pillars, towering brick walls, and oversized glass windows all clashed

---

[51] Smith, *Robert Morris's Folly*, pg. 111
[52] Robert Morris Papers, R.M. to Samuel Ogden, Jan 8, 1796

for the attention of passersby who, perhaps for the first time, learned the meaning of ostentation.

While the mansion may not have fallen yet, his house of cards did. In 1798, Robert Morris, shipping tycoon, Senator, statesman, benefactor of the American Revolution and one of only two founding fathers to have signed each of the Declaration of Independence, the Articles of Confederation, and the Constitution, was thrown in debtors prison. He resided there, a stone-cold, two-story jail on Prune Street, for more than three years.

He was not alone. Downstairs in more squalid quarters, were dozens of poor, defenseless artisans, tradesmen and merchants who, too, were affected by the war between France and England, unable to secure once promised goods on which their credit depended.

George Washington, a "friend to the end," visited Morris in his cell in late November of 1798. The retired President had been invited to Philadelphia to discuss matters of national security.[53] He could not forsake his old pal, Robert Morris. But, there was little Washington could do. Before 1800, there was no such thing as bankruptcy laws.

In short time, Morris would be joined by John Nicholson. Unable to divest himself of any significant portion of his holdings, chased by debtors and tax collectors from Georgia to New York, threatened to defend 125 different law suits, owing well more than $12 million, and now completely destitute, he was jailed at Prune Street in August 1799.[54] Enjoying a friendship thicker than thieves, he and Morris barely had time to plan their defense. Within a year, Nicholson was dead, leaving behind a widow and eight hapless children. They—as well as Pennsylvania's Land Office—would have to deal with the legal embroilments for more than forty years.

---

[53] Fearing that France or England would cause certain harm to America, President Adams had asked Washington to lead the Armed Forces in the unlikely event of an invasion. Washington had left Mount Vernon to stand ready.

[54] https://paheritage.wpengine.com/article/john-nicholson-land-lure-infant-nation-1790-1800/

Washington's Portfolio

Not surprisingly, the ides of December were wet and miserably cold. "Morning Snowing & abt. 3 Inches deep. Wind at No. Et. & Mer. at 30." Washington, never complaining of weather, walked his plantation and, that day, marked certain trees he wished to have cut.[55] Always looking for ways to improve the view of his 800-acre estate overlooking the Potomac River, Washington, with well more than 300 slaves working his fields, had made plans to divest himself of this property—both his land *and* his labor—upon his death.

That night, he came down with a feverish cold and an inflamed throat. He had trouble breathing by midnight. Early the next morning, his old friend Dr. Craik came to administer aid which, apropos to the time, meant little more than feeding him purgatives and bloodletting.[56]

Only earlier in July had Washington revisited his will. It accounted for nearly every acre he then owned. In Virginia, excluding Mount Vernon, he owned outright 7,486 acres, which he valued at $104,880. In addition, he listed his interests in many other Virginia land ventures—either city lots leased and managed in Alexandria, Bath, and Winchester, or shares owned in private partnerships—totaling $50,578.

Along the Ohio River, he owned 9,744 acres, valuing them at $10 per acre. This property included his much cherished, but never propagated, Round Bottom (Moundsville, West Virginia) as well as riverfront property at the mouth of the Little Kanawha and extending sixteen miles downstream.

---

[55] George Washington's Diary, December 13, 1799
[56] Achenbach, *The Grand Idea*, pg. 210

Along the Great Kanawha, he owned 23,341 acres, the majority share being that which he claimed, along with Dr. Craik, in his first voyage down the Ohio with William Crawford and his young assistant, Daniel Leet.

In Maryland, Washington owned 600 acres in Charles County, and 519 acres in Montgomery County.

In Pennsylvania, his only remaining property after selling his Perryopolis tracts and much of what he may (or may not have) owned along Chartiers Creek was the Great Meadows, comprising 234 acres near Fort Necessity.

In Kentucky, he owned 5,000 acres. In New York, 1,000 acres. And in western Ohio, along the Little Miami River, he owned 3,051 acres. He valued his Kentucky acres at $2 each and the Ohio acres at $5. Both properties were still arduously remote to settlers seeking their fortunes in the western wilds. The valuation is some indication that closer western Pennsylvania lands might have fetched more than $6 per acre, a significant increase from the $.80 minimum just a decade earlier.

In his Schedule of Property, dated July 9, 1799, George Washington asserted assets of well more than $500,000.[57]

He took none of it with him. Washington died on December 14, 1799.

---

[57] George Washington's Last Will & Testament, , July 9, 1799, Enclosure: Schedule of Property

PART FOUR
(1800-1819)

In which a people settle down
to apply industry for the common good
but discover the evils they hath wrought.

A Mill on Little Sewickley Creek

In 2018, Little Sewickley Creek, winding some 26 stream-miles from Sewickley Hills down to Leetsdale, was rated one of the finest watersheds in Pennsylvania.[1] Factors such as water quality, aquatic life, and the impact of straight "stream reaches" supported a case for conservation that the local watershed association promoted to area landowners whose property abutted the creek. In 2018, the number of owners was 129.

Two hundred and twenty years earlier, there were just five. Of these, Daniel Leet and two of his brothers, Jonathan and William, attended to his Sewickley Bottom tracts. So far away were the other landowners—beneficiaries each of the Philadelphia auction—they had never seen their properties.

William Leet, in fact, not Daniel, is credited for settling Leetsdale in 1796. By settlement, it was meant that he erected an early cabin and cleared some land. Of course that land was Daniel's, but it was William who gave his name to the quiet "dale." Daniel, with his wife Wilhelmina, remained in Washington some forty miles away. Eliza, their daughter, attended the Moravian Seminary for Women. Of course, Daniel had the financial means to employ his brother to clear and cultivate other fields along the bottoms. Early on, there were many grain crops growing in the area. The virgin soil would have provided bountiful harvests.

For this reason, the first non-residential edifice was a mill, built by William, yet no doubt assisted by Jonathan, along the Little Sewickley Creek. Precisely where their first mill was built is lost to ruin, but a reasonable

---

[1] Little Sewickley Creek Watershed Association, Assess Summary, 2018

conjecture would suggest that it sat along the Beaver Road where the Little Sewickley leveled out toward the Ohio River. As such, the mill might have sat on Leet's tract number Seven named Locust Bottom. The present day Nichols Fields is thought to have once served as its reservoir or race. The mill allowed William to harvest crops and to saw timber, later, to store an abundance of flour. Unlike more remote settlers, the Leet brothers enjoyed the proximity of Pittsburgh where they could purchase the materials needed to equip a mill of moderate output. Grindstones were the hardest to obtain; milled wood for gears the easiest. Leet's mill was said to have been operating well before 1800, but there would have been little purpose for its construction much before then. Christopher Gist operated the largest grist mill in the region, but, because it was across the Ohio along Chartiers Creek, the challenges of loading a flatboat begged the construction of Leet's more northern mill.

Indeed, an abundance of flour might have been superfluous to the region unless there was a greater population to feed. In fact, by 1800 there was. The one road west from Pittsburgh was flooded daily with a congestion of transients and tradesmen. Historic estimates of pioneers traveling westward vary dramatically, but train upon train of Conestoga wagons rolled into, and out of, the new state of Ohio with ever-astounding numbers.

Their route took them along the road to Beaver. And on that road, the Leet brothers built a tavern. Sections of the structure show joists that were hand-hewn before any sawmill might have assisted in its framing.[2]

Their stone inn would become a welcome oasis for cattle "drovers" and the many teamsters whose cows, swine, and fowl were not welcome (nor likely safe) in Pittsburgh.[3] Leet's venture was the first commercial enterprise between Pittsburgh and—equidistant to the west—Beaver. Within a few years, in fact, the property became known as the Halfway House. Outside, it provided pens for livestock, corrals for oxen, and troughs for water, feed, and fodder. Inside, a large stone fireplace, warm grub, and spirituous liquors lulled "wagoners" into a good night's sleep, albeit on the wooden floors of its large dining room.

Halfway House—also known as Leet's Tavern and, later, Larks Inn—still stands today as a private residence.

---

[2] Asserted by a resident of the current building.

[3] Teamsters herded turkeys, uncaged, as they were hardly capable of extended flight.

Isaac and Rebecca Leet

Rebecca Leet, Daniel's mother, died on April 29, 1802.

A little more than two weeks later, his father Isaac, died, too. He had served as captain of a West Augusta militia, sat as a Justice of the Peace, and, then as a Magistrate, adjudicating in the Court of Oyer and Terminer, an early criminal division of the local justice system. In 1778, he had assisted William Crawford in a survey that defined Washington County from what was then Ohio County.[4] Later, he was commissioned as a Woods Ranger; that is, he was hired to search for missing or stolen horses whether reported or not. For each horse he found, he received two shillings and six pence. The job also awarded bounties for wolves killed.

Despite what might have seemed a spartan life, Isaac Leet held bonds on many loans he had offered neighbors and acquaintances.[5] Upon his death on May 14, he was owed, with interest accrued to him that date, £1,282, an equivalent of $5,748 today. He was not by any standards then poor. Nor, however, would anyone bow to his wealth.

Ever the yeoman, he provided well for his ten children. Unusual for the time, none preceded him in death, and, at his demise, all of his daughters were married.

Leet's Fancy, the homestead he staked in 1778, was officially patented by a survey returned to the deceased on January 6, 1807.

---

[4] Crumrine, *History of Washington County,* pg. 219

[5] Private documents in collection at Leetsdale.

"Leet's Fancy" as it still stood in 1900, photographed for Charles Stotz's *The Architecture of Western Pennsylvania*, 1931. Courtesy of Carnegie Library of Pittsburgh.

Morris's Monument

Largely because of Robert Morris's plight, Congress in 1800 created a first iteration of bankruptcy laws. Men like Justice James Wilson and dozens of other politically aligned gentlemen who had found near ruin in the Panic of 1796, and so, had turned to speculation in vain hope of recovery, were thus able to stave off their creditors and reorganize a financial footing from which to pay their debts in stepped, yet torturous measure. Morris, however, chose not to file for bankruptcy. Not right away. He devised to sell his assets at painful loss so as to earn back a modicum of social respect and integrity. But when he learned that one property he valued at $100,000 had sold for $800, the pain was too great to bear. He rushed to create a schedule of all of his assets—as only he could account for them—and petitioned the courts to seek the legal protections the new law might afford. He was granted release from the Prune Street Jail, and moved into a rental house at 8th Street and Chestnut. By then, walking the streets of Philadelphia, he could see nothing of his former mansion; the massive, palatial folly had been razed to rubble the year before.

In court, Morris tendered his defense with a statement that ran seventy-four pages long. His confessed debts amounted to a figure far less than what his 86 different creditors sought—a total, submitted by the bankruptcy court, of $2,948,711.11. A trickle of rents from uncontested property in New York helped little. Socially scorned and demoralized, Morris nevertheless tried his hand at several ventures—growing cotton in Florida, importing

Portuguese wine, creating a new commercial bank—but none came to any fruition.[6] He died on May 8, 1806.

Robert Morris's statue, sculpted by Paul Wayland Bartlett in 1925, was placed directly in front of the Second Bank of North America in Philadelphia. Today, it stands starkly alone.

The campus of Robert Morris University, established as an accounting school in downtown Pittsburgh in 1921, is in Moon Township, Pennsylvania. The property was the former estate of Oliver Kaufmann, an executive of the eponymous Pittsburgh department store. That Moon Township was once part of Washington County or that Robert Morris owned nearly 30,000 acres in the county, the bulk of it contiguous to the southern "bottoms" of the Ohio River campus above present-day Coraopolis, is apparently coincidental to the university's southwestern Pennsylvania origins.

An UNFINISHED HOUSE, in Chesnut Street PHILADELPHIA.

Robert Morris's unfinished house on Chestnut Street was razed for his debts. Library of Congress.

---

[6] Smith, *Robert Morris's Folly*, pg. 208

A New Century

Even as Daniel Leet and his brothers created new commerce along Beaver Road, business flourished everywhere in the region. In fact, since the turn of the century, Washington fared as well as Pittsburgh in offering the services, manufactories and provisions that any growing population would need in its time.

By the year 1800, Washington had more tailors, distillers, potters and gunsmiths than Pittsburgh could boast, and each town was served in like quantity by other trades, such as silversmiths, breech-makers, chandlers, and weavers. Only in the manufacture of barrels, horse shoes, saddles and cart wheels did Pittsburgh exceed Washington. An examination of the number of dry goods merchants and food purveyors in each town suggests that the competition was proportionate to the populations they served.

Washington had at least ten different inns, taverns and public houses during the first decade, a figure more representative of the people traveling through Washington than of its own settled population. The White Goose was the oldest whose name under new management in 1806 became The Golden Swan. The Cross-Keys tavern sat just opposite. The largest at the time was The Globe Inn. Other taverns included The Buck, The Spread Eagle, Indian Queen, Green Tree, and Fulton House.[7]

Dr. John Julius LeMoyne was licensed to operate a tavern in 1798 at the location of his log cabin on North Main Street. There he also served as an early physician to the community. Even in the first decade of the nineteenth century, there were three other physicians practicing in Washington. When

---

[7] Crumrine, *History of Washington County*, pg. 494

Dr. Absalom Baird died, LeMoyne's practice surged, allowing him the privilege in 1812 of building the current LeMoyne House, more famously associated with his son Francis Julius. Also a physician, he was an early abolitionist, suffragist and benefactor of the town's first library.[8]

Of the services necessary to the survival of any newly settled community, none could be more appreciated than that of a local physician.

[8] Kilgore, "Looking Back at John Julius LeMoyne," *Washington Observer-Reporter*, July 17, 2017

David in Washington

David Shields came up from Philadelphia, west towards Pittsburgh and crossed the Monongahela River to the banks of Chartiers Creek where, arriving in the busy town of Washington, he took up temporary residence at one of the many inns there. Shortly after arriving in July of 1803, he wrote his father. David was then 23.

> "Dear Father,
>
> I wrote you by Mr. E. Taylor from Phil. about the 16th Ult. informing you of my purposed return to the western country, and since by letter to my brother John Shields, I have requested him to inform you of my arrival at Washington Where I spent about ten days in having been down upon your Wheelen lands and have attended to your business, as it respects taxes, collecting, the best manner in my power, I arrived at this place yesterday and received the balance of my Coffee adventure..."

From whence such beans might have arrived, or, if Coffee was otherwise the name of an investor, why he would have ridden so far west for either is unknown. There were, however, more certain and more important reasons for his visit, and all were seemingly at the behest of his father.[9]

In addition to visiting the Shields property in Turtle Creek, he met with a Mr. Sampson to receive payment on his bond. In "Wheelen" (Wheeling, West Virginia) he also met with a Mr. Swearingen—perhaps, a son of

---

[9] Letter from David Shields to his father, postmarked Pittsburgh, July 10th, 1803, to Damascus Mills.

Andrew Swearingen, one of the town's earliest pioneers—to pick up requisite papers his father might need. Wrote David, "Swearingen's bond, though not collected, is Safe."

Yet, there was one greater purpose for this journey of more than two hundred miles.

> "The principal object of my journey has, with my own approbation, been deferred, until I shall be nearer to a more permanent settlement, as at present I have no home, and am obliged to live, in some measure, a too wandering kind of life, this settlement it is hoped, from your arrangement of business, to take place this fall."

If his intentions had been to settle down in a promising town, one seeking greater commerce with larger cities east, he could not have done much better than Washington, Pennsylvania. That he had a letter of introduction from his father, or knew to call on any particular family for references they might offer, is conjecture supported only by social custom of the time. The young Shields would have needed some sponsorship for any local credit he sought and, yet, any trade or "agency" he brought with him would have deposed his good character to those with whom he engaged in business. A lone gentleman, newly arrived from Philadelphia—with or without a wagon full of goods—would have brought him the attention any stranger might attract, but it is also fair to suggest that the young Shields presented himself with manners begot from a more privileged upbringing no mere stranger would have exhibited or possessed.

Yet, not all of the business his father might have arranged was strictly commercial. Thomas had sent his son to meet certain acquaintances.

When David Shields then met Daniel Leet, it was not a chance occasion. There could have been no coincidence that the young Shields found himself in the presence of the man whose well-watered Ohio River properties had been purchased by *his* father and not have been directed to make an introduction. If, indeed, on that very same occasion, Daniel had just happened to introduce the young man to his daughter Eliza, that opportunity, too, could not have been by chance. To say that it was an "arrangement of business" might have been honest, if not a truth too cold. Certainly, at just nineteen years of age, formally educated at the Moravian Seminary, Eliza would have been a young lady of some keen interest to the young man. And so, with his "own approbation," David took measures to settle down, albeit later in the fall.

That their marriage might have been arranged was hardly unusual. Courtships or less formal rituals of dating were unknown at the turn of the century. And any negotiation of a dowery between fathers—only ever considered among families of wealth and power—did not preclude the approval of the groom. Of course, not so the bride. Marriage arrangements, at the least, allayed the fear of public embarrassment; speculative engagements only incited lasting gossip.

Alas, we know nothing of the wedding ceremony, of who attended, in what church or house it was blessed, nor in whose barn or tavern the happy guests toasted the young bride and groom. But we do know David Morris Shields signed a marriage bond—also customary among the privileged class—committing his intentions to marry Eliza Marie Leet. That bond was signed on November 10, 1803, and the bondsman was Eliza's uncle, Hugh Wilson.[10]

Not quite ten months later, Maria Leet Shields was born to the proud couple on September 21, 1804.

---

[10] Early Marriage Bonds of Washington County, PA, www.chartiers.com/pages-new/articles/paula-marriage.html

Zelienople I

Joannes George Rapp was said to have a soft, cherubic face with cold, steely eyes. Although a man of no great physical stature, he was considered both imposing and charming, traits particularly handy for a man who believed himself to be a prophet. In 1804, like Count von Zinzendorf's Moravian movement before him, Rapp led one of the most successful separatist revolts of the new century, cajoling hundreds of reformed protestants to leave the town of Wurttemburg, Germany, and sail to America.

Rapp arrived first to seek suitable land. In Baltimore, he met the renowned Phillip William Otterbein, the titular head of the Church of the United Brethren, a newly popularized sect of the historic Moravian Church. Among other suggestions, Otterbein recommended that Rapp head to Ohio where two gentlemen owned thousands of acres along the Tuscarawas, in fact, on land earlier settled by Moravians. Rapp went west but was not pleased with what he found.[11] Fortunately, Otterbein had also suggested Rapp seek out one Baron Dettmar William Frederic Basse.[12] A recent immigrant, Basse, who also went by the name of D.B. Mueller, owned ten thousand acres near the more populous port of Pittsburgh.

Baron Basse had been a German envoy to France. An only child privileged with significant wealth, Basse, hoping to escape the certain economic ruin of Napoleon's wars, was intrigued to learn of vast tracts of inexpensive land in western Pennsylvania. Pamphlets sent to Paris by representatives of the Pennsylvania Population Company—or through Robert Morris's own desperate agents—promised an easy life, untrammeled by political

---

[11] Arndt, *Harmony on the Connoquenessing*, pg. 52

[12] Wetsel, *Frontier Musicians on the Connoquenessing* . pg. 8

oppression or religious persecution.[13] In fact, Morris owned nearly 80,000 acres within the Butler area, albeit under 311 different warrants assigned to 311 assumed names.[14]

Basse arrived in Pittsburgh in 1801 to sniff out his best opportunities and purchased 10,000 acres on the Connoquenessing River. Just twenty miles northwest of the city, Basse built a castle—or something like a castle, made of stone, but mostly wood—featuring a crenelated roof. Yet, widowed since living in France, he needed domestic help. His scheme was to entice his only daughter, Zelie, from the motherland. And so he laid out a new town he cleverly named Zelienople. There, sometime in the not too distant future, with his newly arrived daughter and her soon-to-be husband Philippe Passavant, he would establish one of the first and most prosperous German communities in the new United States. Or so he hoped. After all, he owned plenty of land and he had the money to develop it.

In 1804, George Rapp purchased 4,060 acres from Baron Basse. Rapp reported back to his congregants that "God has prepared a little place for us" where "they want you to think and believe what you wish."[15]

By the following year, as many as 100 families attended to building and cultivating Rapp's visionary community which they named Harmony. There, in the newly founded County of Butler would grow a society united in devotion to a sustainable economy and spiritual evolution. Rapp promised that Christ would come to judge them before the Great Millennium, Christ's promised thousand-year reign of peace and love for all who truly believed.

One early admirer of the sect was David Shields. Sometimes a Baptist, yet sympathetic to Moravian sentiment, Shields came up from Washington to inquire about the Society's most earnest needs. Far distant from access to the materials and necessities any emerging settlement would require, Rapp forged a bond of trust with the young agent, seeking his assistance in purchasing supplies while, at the same time, creating markets for his people's produce and wares. From the beginning their relationship was more than that of just buyer and seller—the young Shields even offered Rapp early credit—each committing to a symbiotic relationship by which, if the Harmonists could profit and grow, so, too, would David Shields's fortunes.

---

[13] Passavant, "Romantic Story of Baron Basse", pg. 13

[14] Ryall, "Man After Whom Butler was Named Slain by Indians", *Pittsburgh Press*, January 21, 1934

[15] https://explorepahistory.com/story.php?storyId=1-9-5&chapter=3

Credit

David travelled often. It was the single greatest expense of his profession. It required a fleet of livery stationed at homesteads friendly and hungry for his trade. It required long absences from his small family. And it necessitated a discipline of planning months in advance.

No early American entrepreneur could possibly succeed in business by mere correspondence. (None, perhaps, other than land speculators.) Mail was slow, expensive and unreliable. For David to succeed, it meant shaking hands and "interviewing" his clients—a term he liked to use often—that he "might have as close an understanding as possible as to what may be expected from him."[16] To purchase goods on behalf of his clients required personal inspection. Of course, haggling was important, too. How could one possibly get the best price for wool, flaxseed oil or flour if quality was purely subjective? Furthermore, the issue of credit or debt required a signature. Banks offered no such thing as a checking account. Notes drawn on one bank or another were issued only upon that institution's certainty that funds were first available and, for their service in issuing that note, they demanded prepaid interest on its value. (Two percent was common, but in times of economic fear, the fee could be six percent or higher.) The depositor who maintained a good relationship with his banker could earn significant favor. And that, too, required travel and a lot of firm hand shakes.

---

[16] Letter from David Shields to Frederick. Rapp, 1817

Newborns

Not quite two years after Maria, Wilhelmina Shields was born on July 8, 1806. The baby girl, however, would die on Christmas Day, just six months later.

*   *   *   *   *

Ten months later, on October 19, 1807, Daniel Leet Shields was born. He would forever be called by his middle name and enjoy all the attention any first-born son commands.

In fact, by British tradition, he might have become heir to all of his father's estate. But, not Leet.

Indeed, the traditions of inheritance had changed since the colonists had struggled to develop even the most tenuous of economies. First-born sons were no more important than any other capable son; the more, the better. Daughters, accordingly, were as necessary in the house as they were the barn or the field. A family's success required both strength and stamina proven in large number by plentiful offspring to meet the challenges of survival. As proud as any true American might have been to have eked out a living, he was equally relieved not to have carried with it a title. All men—that is, all white males—were now created equal.

But, not Leet.

His condition, perhaps unknown at birth, would become evident within the year.

Zelienople II

To manage the secular affairs of his growing community, Father Rapp entrusted a young postulant of extraordinary ability. Frederick Reichert, at thirty years of age, had led the second wave of Rapp's congregants, sailing from Amsterdam to Philadelphia, aboard the ship *Atlantic*. He was said to have been accomplished in every discipline of accounting and management, a commendation proven in letters between Fredrick and David Shields that extend nearly twenty-five years. So close were Rapp and Reichert that the former adopted the latter as his own son. Between them, they vested all the powers of the Society, governing the spiritual and secular affairs of each and every member.

By 1807, the village of Harmony peaceably accommodated a population of five hundred "Rappites." More than one hundred families now enjoyed their own log cabins, each measuring eighteen by twenty-four feet, a size of some modest grandeur. The town had its own grist mill for which a "river race" of three-quarters mile had been trenched. Adjacent to the mill stood a barn with a capacity for some 4,000 bushels of grain, grown on hundreds of acres since cleared and irrigated. Harmony also featured a tannery, a dye shop, and a distillery. Evidently, the people had raised sufficient cattle, sheep and rye to make such facilities sustainable. For the curious visitor, the town also offered an inn, laboriously built from stone. David Shields slept there often.

Neighbor Baron Basse then introduced the Harmonists to two Merino sheep he brought back from Germany while fetching his newly-wed daughter and son-in-law.

The fortunes of the Harmonists grew and by the end of the decade, as many as 150 industrious families tended to every aspect of their Christian society. Basse, on the other hand, was relegated to managing his own dwindling fortune. The castle he built overlooking the Connoquenessing cost him dearly. His daughter not only showed little interest in managing her father's affairs, but she refused to live in the cold, creaky castle. She and her husband built their own house in town. Basse then decided to marry again, taking the hand of a widow, a one Mrs. Israel he met and courted in Butler, a burgeoning village nearby. Mrs. Israel, however, was a Washingtonian by birth and so it was there that the marriage of Baron Dettmar William Frederic Basse to the widow Israel was celebrated. Eliza and David Shields hosted the reception.[17] The event was the talk of the town. The marriage, however, lasted little more than a year. The new Mrs. Basse, like the first Mrs. Basse, died of a sudden fever brought on by consumption.

Stoically German, Basse turned his attention to more practical matters. He decided to renew his fortunes by building an iron furnace. Sadly, had he tended to propagating the Merino sheep he first brought to the Harmonists, his wealth would have been more than assured.

---

[17] Jennings, *Some Account of Dettmar Basse and the Passavant Family,* pg. 11

A Letter to Father

July 16, 1808 [Philadelphia]

"Dear Father,

"After leaving you on Thursday 5th Instant I overtook my brother John Shields at Carmichaels beyond Beaverbrook, who accompanied me to Doylestown, from whence he took the road to Robert Young's, from which last mentioned place I received a letter from him this day, dated 13th Instant…

"The city appears to be healthy and improving although there is lately a rumor of the Yellow Fever but which appears groundless. ~ The embargo still continues, and is likely to continue so. It is said that neither France nor England exhibit disposition to relax of their orders and decrees, so highly injurious of our commerce and national prosperity, but wish to embroil these United States into their warfares.

"I yesterday completed my purchases of merchandize and loaded two wagons for Washington and expect to leave this city on Monday - noon, detaining myself one day, in the expectation of getting my title deeds for the property I live on, now in the hands of the scrivener to be completed on Monday 10 O'clock. I shall call on my brother John, on my road, who it is expected and intended will accompany me to Washington of which I shall write you on my return home ~ I would wish you to have the Deed for Rapp executed, and if the weight does not exceed 2 oz., send it by mail, the postage from Philad. to Wash. is 20 cents an Oz., otherwise send it to S. Shewell, for him to forward by a private conveyance which is uncertain.

~

"My best respects to all my friends, while I remain with Sincere wishes for your welfare and happiness, I remain with sentiments of respect

    Your Son affectionately
    David Shields"

By this letter comes some evidence of the economic hardships and opportunities prevailing on the industry of David's efforts back home. Although the country's "national prosperity" might have been in jeopardy, the demand for goods from Philadelphia were worth a full two wagons. Thomas Shields was then occupied with Damascus Manor, building a grand homestead remote from the troubles of America's largest city. In service to his Harmonist clients, David had offered up Thomas's patents on two tracts of Depreciation lands just south of Zelienople which, as later records would prove, eventually sold to other individuals. Apparently, David now played the role of purchasing agent *and* realtor.

Back in Washington

By the first decade's end, city "revenuers" claimed taxes from more and more local trades and professions, and among these were the newer merchants conducting daily business on the streets of Washington. 1809 dockets show that there were as many as twenty shop proprietors. David Shields was among them, but records do not indicate from what address he conducted his business.

The next year, Shields became the town's first clerk.[18] His responsibilities were just part-time, devoted primarily to recording the minutes of Town Council meetings and handling requisite correspondence among, and for, the council members. The job required certain skills—chiefly, writing and arithmetic—not all council members may have possessed.

As part of its original charter, the Bank of Philadelphia authorized a state-wide franchise of eight satellite banks, and, in 1809, The Bank of Philadelphia opened Washington's first chartered bank. David Shields and eleven other businessmen were appointed to its board. The franchise, known locally as the Discount and Deposit Bank, was capitalized by the subscription of shares purchased principally by its board. The bank however ran afoul of the original Philadelphia charter, and it fell victim to economic politics. Despite his youth—he was just 29—David Shields managed to keep the institution afloat. It took up much of his time for which he received little, if any, compensation.

The solvency of banks in Washington, Pittsburgh and Philadelphia, in fact, became everywhere critical. The issue was not a consequence of local

---

[18] Crumrine, *History of Washington County*, pg. 499

wealth or regional trade, but of wholly international concern. Since 1803, before the commencement of Thomas Jefferson's second term, when France and Britain engaged in yet another tariff war, American exports had grown steadily. But then Napoleon cut off all trade with England, and, in retaliation for America stepping in to trade with France, England cut off all trade with America. In hopes of affecting some neutrality in all of this, Jefferson imposed the Embargo Act of 1807, prohibiting America's own merchants from trading with either France or Britain. Jefferson's naive gambit was that patriotic sacrifice would help break the stalemate.

It was not his first political blunder nor his last.

Christian Communism

If the Moravians espoused pious humility, the Harmonists embodied it. Even today, the Moravian mission to share in Jesus's promise of love and redemption, is found in an active brotherhood of 1,500 congregations worldwide, primarily in the Caribbean and Africa, but also in long-established communities in seventeen US states, Canada, and, of course, Germany.

The Harmonists, on the other hand, no longer exist. So pious were the teachings of the sect that, in 1807, Father Rapp called for his congregants to practice celibacy.

The reasons were many. Carnal lust was not so much a human failing as it was an earthly distraction.[19] Like the Shakers who had come before them, the practice of celibacy ensured that followers would devote their undivided attention to the second coming of Christ. Harmonists worked ten hours every day except Sunday; as such, time devoted to raising small children was evidently counterproductive. Besides, for Rapp, the immediacy of a Kingdom that was sure to judge his followers did not need any *more* followers, especially errant youth.

Yet, the strange fact is, unlike the Shakers, Rapp believed that Adam, before his fall, was asexual, the proof of which was abundantly clear: God had never intended to create Eve.

Genesis 2:18-20; "And the LORD God said, It is not good that the man should be alone; I will make him an help meet for him. And out of the ground the LORD God formed every beast of the field, and every fowl of

---

[19] Versluis, "Western Esotericism and the Harmony Society," Michigan State U. http://esoteric.msu.edu/Versluis.html

the air; and brought them unto Adam to see what he would call them: and whatsoever Adam called every living creature, that was the name thereof. And Adam gave names to all cattle, and to the fowl of the air, and to every beast of the field; but for Adam there was not found an help meet for him."[20]

Sexual reproduction, thus, according to Rapp, was not a part of God's human plan.[21] And, so, preparing for what he deemed the Golden Age, only those pure of heart—and, thus, necessarily celibate—could be worthy of greeting Jesus in his thousand-year reign, so very soon to commence.

There was one slight wrinkle in Rapp's plan; the second coming never came.

Still, aside from celibacy, what truly set the Harmonists apart from other spiritual communes was their insistence on disavowing personal financial freedom. Harmonists pooled all of their earnings for the common good. Families invested their savings in the society when joining the sect. Even if the society had not insisted on celibacy, children born from or brought into the sect were disallowed any and all inheritance.

The Rapps and their followers abided by a simple pact, originally signed in 1805. The first of six items in the Articles of Agreement stated that members had to renounce all claims to personal property. The second item pledged that they would obey all rules and laws of the congregation. The third stated that, if any member desired to leave the group, he could make no demands of the society for himself or his family. Items four and five gave any follower the right to attend all meetings, religious services or classroom instructions, and promised them all the necessities of life: food, shelter, and clothing. The final item laid out that, if a family *were* to withdraw from the sect, the congregation *would* restore their original investment, yet, without interest, and only in measured installments of two or three years. Indeed, the pact offered a "backdoor," but there were no back wages and, once departed, no "looking back." Separation was final.

Many other religious and secular movements, too, sought socialist utopias that only remote communities of the new American wilderness might permit. By 1750, as many as 135 separate experiments in communal living had settled in America. Even in the early 1800s, social idealists like the Owenites, "new age" Mormons and the progressive Amana "Inspirationists"

---

[20] King James Bible

[21] Wetsel, *Frontier Musicians on the Connoquenessing*, pg. 9

created distinct communities devoted to sharing wealth for the common good.[22] Not surprisingly, most were led by dynamic personalities. All, however, adapted their missions to changing times, learning by economic, if not political, necessity that cooperative communities were best served by like-minded individuals who were free to tithe.

Still, Rapp's Harmony Society had a remarkable history of success. Industrious, profitable, and progressive in many ways, they sustained their community for nearly 60 years, founding three consecutive communes, the first in Zelienople, Pennsylvania.

As it turned out, Rapp's experiment in Christian communism provided a lifestyle few other Americans would experience in their generation or the next. Harmonists were well-fed, well-clothed, well-educated and, as was evident in their time, well-respected.

---

[22] Pitzer, "How the Harmonists Suffered Disharmony," Hamilton College Digital Commons, 2011.

America Embargoed

Within a year of Jefferson's self-imposed embargo, U.S. exports plummeted from $108 million down to just $22 million. American ships sat idle, unemployment grew exponentially, and agricultural commodities lost most of their margins. Banks everywhere suffered.

When, in a few years, Americans started sneaking goods across the French Canadian border, the War of 1812 brought on the wrath of the Brits. Crippled by naval blockades in U.S. harbors, prominent merchants like Levi Hollingsworth screamed about the senseless stalemate. To an associate, he wrote, "Canada, if conquered, will not be worth the expense, & the Floridas [will] be a source of contest for years to come. We, however, seem determined to 'loose the horse or win the saddle'."[23] A few victorious U.S. battles on Lakes Champlain and Erie ensued—for which the Brits retaliated by burning the White House—but all was forgiven in 1814 with the Treaty of Ghent.

In the meantime, despite then-current conditions, another institution, the Bank of Washington (Pennsylvania) was capitalized in 1813 by the subscription of fifteen board members ponying up $75,000, or about fifteen percent of its assets. This bank, too, would not succeed. Five years after its incorporation it failed to produce revenue exceeding the minimum requirements of its charter. One of its original board members was Daniel Leet, whose investment might have been as much as $5,000. To settle the bank's affairs and shutter its doors, the court appointed David Shields to serve as one of five receivers.[24]

---

[23] Hollingsworth, *Levi Hollingsworth Papers*, William L. Clements Library, The University of Michigan

[24] Crumrine, *History of Washington County*, pg. 526

Like his efforts to save the Discount and Deposit Bank, little is known. Yet, what is obvious now is the esteem with which the young Shields was held in his role as an early, trusted leader of Washington. It may have served him well to have married into Daniel Leet's small family, but David Shields's many contributions to Washington prove his long dedication to the prosperity of the greater community.

Zelienople III

In large part due to visitors curious to learn about the Harmonists' experiment on the Connoquenessing Creek, word of their success spread far and wide. One such narrative, *Travels in the United States of America*, was published in 1815 by John Melish, a Scottish mapmaker. With his companion, Dr. Isaac Cleaver of Philadelphia, he ventured across the Allegheny mountains and, arriving in Pittsburgh just twenty-five miles from the famed town of Harmony, quickly learned how astonishingly productive the Society in Harmony had become. Reported Melish in 1811:

> "The produce of this year was 6,000 bushels of Indian corn, 4,500 bushels of wheat; 4,500 bushels of rye; 5,000 bushels of oats; 10,000 bushels of potatoes; 4,000 lbs. of flax and hemp; 100 bushels of barley brewed into beer; and 50 gallons of sweet oil, made from the seeds of the white poppy, and equal to the imported olive oil. Of this produce they sold 3,000 bushels of corn, 1,000 bushels of potatoes, 1,000 bushels of wheat, and they distilled 1,600 bushels of rye."

For the Harmonists, David Shields sold their produce as well as their many manufactured goods, necessities like shoes and saddles, iron nails and barreled wines. Shields employed dozens of wagons, scores of drivers, and fleets of horses to get them all to market. As he had since first selling goods along the road to Damascus, he was ever engaged in land logistics, deciding efficient routes to deliver goods to neighboring communities while also receiving seeds and oils and lumber to ship back to the society. The

Harmonists depended on Shields as much as he on them. His trading empire included points as far east as Philadelphia, west into Ohio, and south to Baltimore. Never venturing far from their farms on the Connoquenessing, the Harmonists were happy not to haggle over the value of their goods nor were they much inclined to build commercial relationships outside of their safe and always productive mills.

Melish related something of the character of the Harmonists, applauding their academic demeanor as well as their affability:

> "On our arrival at the inn, we learned that the inn-keeper was one of the Society, and had been appointed to that station because he could speak the English language fluently. He told us that we could get every information that we could desire. My fellow-traveller inquired whether they had a doctor; and on being answered in the affirmative, he was sent for; and as he could also talk the English language, and was moreover very agreeable in his manners, and an excellent botanist, we were happy in the proffer of his services. We had next a visit from Mr. Rapp, his son, and several other members of the Society. The old man's face beamed with intelligence, and he appeared to have a consciousness of having performed a good work: but he could not speak English; and as we could only communicate our sentiments by an interpreter, we had but little conversation with him."

Apparently, Baron Basse's introduction of a few Merino sheep had seeded a significant industry:

> "On arriving at the sheep-pens, we found the flock to consist of about 1,000, and they were separated into three divisions. The first were all of the Merino breed, the most of them full-blooded. The second, about half Merinos and half common ; and the third were all common, with some Merino rams amongst them. They were under the charge of three shepherds, who sleep beside them all night in moveable tents ; and a watchman from the town attends them during the night. We were informed the Society intended to

increase the flock as fast as possible to 3,000, and to increase the manufacture of woollen cloth, which they found very lucrative...

"After break-fast we visited the different branches of manufacture. In the wool-loft eight or ten women were employed in teasing and sorting the wool for the carding machine, which is at a distance on the Creek. From hence the roves are brought to the spinning-house in the town, where we found two roving billies and six spinning jennies at work. They were principally wrought by young girls, and they appeared perfectly happy, singing church-music most melodiously. In the weaving-house 16 looms were at work..."

Harmony's economy—often spelled in its time as "oeconomy"—was a marvel to those in America who struggled to produce any sustainable profit from their many labors:

"In our way through the town we observed shoemakers, tailors, and saddlers at work; and we passed on to view the smith-work, which was very extensive. They have four or five forges for ordinary work, and one for nails, at which we were diverted by observing a dog turning a wheel for blowing the bellows...

"We afterwards went to the doctor's house, where he showed us an elegant collection of plants all natives of Harmony, which he had carefully arranged according to the Linnaean system."

Melish and Cleaver also attended the spiritual communion of the society.

"In the evening the Society assembled to divine service; and we attended, accompanied by our innkeeper, who conducted us to a seat appropriated for strangers. The church was quite full, the number of persons being not less than 500. The women sat all in one end, the men in the other. They were singing a hymn, in which they all joined with one accord; and so simply, yet so sweetly did they sing..."

As in most every society of the new country, wine and spirituous liquors were an important commodity, not just to take the slack off of hard work, but for valuable trade. The Harmonists at Zelienople not only distilled rye whisky, but, as Germans would wont, beer, too. Melish describes how the people grew hops in most every garden, even with vines clinging to the brewery itself. Just as remarkable, he describes the terraces the Harmonists created to grow their grapes.

> "Aug. 22. This day, accompanied by the Society's doctor, we went to see the mills and machinery. In our way we passed through one of the vineyards, which is situated on the face of a steep hill on the north side of the Creek, and is converted into a number of terraces supported by walls of stone, in the manner that they cultivate the hills in China. We ascended by a regular flight of 137 steps, and from the top we had a fine view of the whole settlement, and of the country around…"

Also remarkable was how strange the German food seemed to them.

> "On entering the house we found the family at dinner, and we were invited to partake of it. We did not much like the appearance of the dish, which was called Noodles; but on tasting it we found it to be very palatable; and on it, and some eggs with bread and milk, we made a very excellent dinner. Noodles is made in this way—A quantity of flour is kneaded into a paste, and is cut into small slices: these are mixed with small pieces of beef or mutton, and they are boiled together, with or without seasoning, as the taste of the cook may determine."

Of course there were many issues that George and Frederick Rapp had to address. Their labors to grow sustainable grape varieties were a particular headache, no doubt due to western Pennsylvania's climate, but also to complications of the region's clay soil.

Foremost, as time would tell, was the prohibitive expense of commercial transportation. So distant was the village of Harmony from any navigable river, they decided in 1814 to pick up everything and move to new land in Indiana. There, just a few miles from the mouth of the Wabash River, they purchased 25,000 acres.

To make that move possible, Frederick Rapp approached David Shields to consider a commission to sell Harmony. David was more than apprehensive, when he wrote:

> Washington 1st July, 1815
> "Mr. Frederick Rapp,
> "Dr. Sir,
>
> "I have thought maturely on the subject of the sale of Harmony, spoken of at our last interview, and am afraid to venture on so large a purchase, and hope that you may be enabled to make a sale, agreeable to your views and expectations, but if you should not, I will confer with you again on the subject of a purchase ~ Should a sale not be affected, I would have no objection to become your agent for sales or collections, and could make you an advance if requisite of up to 10,000 dollars, to bear interest untill the age could be reproduced from sales. Should I be led by any business N. West of the Allegheny river will call on you ~ In the meantime should be glad to hear from you ~ Requesting a remembrance to our friends, I remain yours
>
> David Shields"

The following year, a Mennonite, Abraham Ziegler, purchased the entirety of the Harmonists' 9,400 acres. Included in the purchase was all of the 130 buildings, barns, manufactories and residences, for $100,000. That is to say, Ziegler at least made a commitment to purchase it all. The results of that sale were never fully realized. David Shields would sort out the matter for many years more. He had now become the commissioned agent he was first so reluctant to play.

The Legacy

In little more than five years, Eliza Shields gave birth to three more children. In addition to Maria (born in 1804,) Wilhelmina (born and deceased in 1806,) and Leet (born 1807,) David and Eliza brought into the world Thomas Leet Shields (April 30, 1809,) John Leet Shields (May 22, 1812,) and Eliza Leet Shields (August 8, 1814.)

The joy of motherhood, however, was then mirrored by the sorrow of Wilhelmina Balla Leet's death. The specific date is nowhere recorded. It can only be assumed she died after baby Eliza's birth, otherwise Wilhelmina's honor would have been memorialized in the girl's middle name. Custom did not dictate it, but Christian sentiment would have.

Wilhelmina's legacy however carried on for years. More than a century later, in 1933, the Daughters of the American Revolution put forward her nomination at the annual Pennsylvania Conference hosted at the George Washington Hotel in Washington, Pennsylvania. Their object was to memorialize her heroism in archives administered by the DAR's national historian, an honor reserved only for women who, like Molly Pitcher, engaged in actual combat. Five years later, in 1938, local historians and journalists advocated for her memorialization outside the historic Blockhouse at Pittsburgh's point. The campaign coincided with plans then to create a national park in Pittsburgh. The idea was to erect a statue of her, "the savior of Fort Pitt and the greatest historical woman in western Pennsylvania."[25]

By 1954, however, less than 20 years later, when Leetsdale planned to celebrate its Golden Jubilee, the local postmaster and the designated

---

[25] Shoemaker, *Altoona Tribune*, January 6, 1938

historian for the celebration admitted he was "befuddled" as to where Wilhelmina Leet—or Wilamine Balla Leet or Margarita Bella Corson or...—went on her midnight ride. Whether to Fort Wolfe, Fort McIntosh, or Fort Harmar, he could be no more certain than how to spell her name.

NOVEMBER 11, 1951   PAGE 7

Roving Reporter

Old Romance Gives Leetsdale Its Name

By WILLIAM A. WHITE
Press Staff Writer

A young widow's daring midnight ride and a romance of the Indian wars of Pennsylvania combined to give Leetsdale it's name.

Margarita Bellah, widow of a sergeant who was killed by Indians while on a scouting expedition, was the heroine of the ride.

It took her from the Sewickley Valley through the lines of Chief Guyasuta and his hostile tribes to Beaver with a plea for help. Thus she saved settlers from possible annihilation by the Redmen.

Mr. White

The Indians under Guyasuta had moved in close to the Sewickley Valley settlement and it was apparent that an attack was contemplated. Major David Leet, in command of the Sewickley forces knew the salvation of the settlement depended upon getting word to General Harmar, in command of a strong force of frontiersmen at Beaver.

Commended In Orders

Major Leet commended Margarita Bellah in the orders of the day and she has been characterized by Henry W. Shoemaker, president of the Pennsylvania Folklore Society, as the State's greatest military heroine. Her midnight ride on the major's black horse had undoubtedly saved the Sewickley Valley settlement from destruction.

Sometime afterwards, when Margarita Bellah had occasion to visit Major Leet's quarters, he asked her to become his wife.

They were married by a frontier pastor—Rev. Doddridge, according to tradition—and lived long and happily afterwards. They were the ancestors, historians say, of the founders of what is today Leetsdale.

Even in 1951, Wilhelmina Leet's story appeared as entertaining fill in local papers. Of course the details all changed—and the heroine's deeds reflect a more subservient role—but the power of myth made her famous well beyond her years. Pittsburgh Press, November 11, 1951.

Caleb, John & Abishai Way

An original and winning bidder on Leet's lots in District Two of the Depreciation Lands, Caleb Way was thought to have been a close friend of Daniel Leet—as several later accounts have inferred—for having shared the brutal experiences of Valley Forge together. But Way's name appears nowhere on the muster rolls of the 13th Virginia regiment nor of any other regiment during the Revolution. And for good reason; Caleb Way was a Quaker. He would not have served in any regiment. It is therefore as likely that Way was brought to show his interest in Leet's lands by someone other: Levi Hollingsworth. In fact, Caleb Way had already purchased forty acres from Hollingsworth's brother Nathaniel in Cain Township of Chester County at Philadelphia.[26] Like Hollingsworth, Way, too, was a prosperous merchant.

Nevertheless, whether Daniel Leet or Levi Hollingsworth introduced Caleb Way to the prime bottoms he purchased, it is doubtful he ever visited the tract named "Way's Desire." No efforts were expended to improve upon it until 1797 when Caleb deeded his 200 acres to his third son John. With his wife Mary Clark, John Way built a log cabin on the river. The next year he built a barn. Thus resided the first white family along Big Sewickley creek.[27]

In 1803, Pennsylvania Governor Thomas McKean, who then owned well more than 30 separate tracts (or about 7,500 acres) of the Depreciation Lands, appointed John Way to serve as one of Allegheny County's first Justices of the Peace. Not necessarily educated as a lawyer, he was cordially—

---

[26] Pennsylvania, U.S., Wills and Probate Records, 1683-1993, Probate March 28, 1812, Chester, PAR

[27] Semple, *Sewickley Cemetery*, pg. 20-21

and colloquially—called "Squire" Way. A Quaker, too, his affiliation with that Brotherhood lent its name to what would be known as Quaker Valley. When he died in 1825, his estate, which included 340 acres and the first brick house in the "valley," was inherited by two sons, Abishai and Nicholas. Abishai, the older son, had settled in Pittsburgh to open a dry goods store. Nicholas converted his father's house into a tavern. That original structure, since remodeled into a larger and fanciful house, still stands today.

Just when Abishai opened his Pittsburgh store is unclear. However, as early as October, 1815, Abishai Way was noticed in the Pittsburgh Weekly Gazette as the proprietor of a shop on Market Street. He was 26 at the time.

*   *   *   *   *

When in 1814, the Harmonists departed for Indiana, David Shields faced many challenges. As a principal agent to Frederick Rapp, he now had to see clear the sale of Harmony, calling on a network of merchants who were in debt to the Society, or to whom the Harmonists owed goods on trade. In the Spring of 1815, Frederick Rapp sent David Shields a Power of Attorney to affect those transactions. By then, too, the Society had erected a warehouse at Beaver, now a viable port with its own boat-building trade. Shields was called on to deplete the warehouse and create much needed revenues from it. One customer was Abishai Way. He consigned to sell many woolen goods for the Harmonists from his own shop. Now, however, with the Harmonists moving to Indiana, that supply would vanish.

A Burgess in Washington

In Washington, Eliza and a single domestic helper cared for five young children on a homestead along Buffalo Creek just several miles due west from David's shop at the center of Washington. Despite necessary and regular trips to Pittsburgh, Zelienople, Beaver, and Wheeling, David Shields stayed closer to home than he had in years past. Three boys and two girls, all under the age of 12, created a household that was busy from dawn until dusk. Although nestled in a house that was something greater than a three-room cabin, the family had to have managed in tight quarters. Dairy stock, chickens, and more than several pack horses had to be "seen to" regularly, while dozens of acres demanded the attention of farmhands and other labor to reap corn, wheat or rye in the harvest months. David played an early role as gentleman farmer, his financial interests hardly dependent on his own land, but rather on the hundreds of thousands of acres his clients managed, by which he earned a growing fortune.

Owing to his trade, the Shields household benefited from innovations few other homes could boast. Free-standing dough boxes, sperm oil lamps or machine-loomed floor coverings were the newest "conveniences." His kitchen had to have had utensils, pots and dinnerware in greater variety and quantity than even larger families might share. The Shields children apparently enjoyed such extravagances as illustrated books in which they could learn to draw, novel items that Frederick Rapp had seen himself and hoped David might purchase for the Harmonist children.[28]

---

[28] Arndt, *A Documentary History of the Indiana Decade of the Harmonists Society*, pg. 133

In 1815, Shields accepted two nominations: the first as Trustee for the newly-erected First Baptist Church of Washington and the second to serve as town Burgess.[29] Much esteemed now for his civic and commercial interests, Shields also earned the honor of being called Esquire. No longer a lowly clerk—a position he held for just two years—Shields served a year in this new commission. Early Washington governance however mandated the election of two Burgesses. John Wilson, an early resident, cabinet-maker, and one of the town's first two Burgesses, served alongside him.

Burgesses, like the boroughs they governed, are terms derivative of Scotch ancestry, but they intended to mean something more pastoral than political; it was best to have two shepherds available lest one be far afield. The duty of the burgess was to convene the town council and decide upon which proposals the council would vote. Records from the early years of the borough are mostly missing, but early newspapers report that meetings were conducted to decide such important issues as the width of pedestrian pavers set alongside muddy streets or to impose fines on any insolent rider daring to gallop within the town limits.[30]

Of course, there were more progressive issues that David Shields and John Wilson faced during their brief tenure together (although Wilson would serve many times more as a town Burgess.) Foremost was the construction of a new public market for Washington. When the town was first laid out on land owned by David Hoge, he planned for a central corridor and four town squares, one of which by then seated the county courthouse. Shops, offices, and a fire house shared one of the other three properties. It was time now to build a large, brick market house, and one that was two stories tall.

At that time, however, David Shields leased his commercial property directly from the borough. From an indeterminate building set aside at Main and Cherry Streets, he retailed goods that might otherwise sell better in a brand-spanking new market house. As such, he was posed with the dilemma of ruling to create competition for his own venue. The issue might have been more contentious if, in fact, Shields was *not* a Burgess. He had, in fact, just signed a 25-year lease.

---

[29] Crumrine, *History of Washington County*, pg. 497

[30] Ibid., pg. 497

A Plan for Newington

Very near the original mill on Little Sewickley Creek and across the Beaver Road from their tavern, the Leet brothers—Daniel, William and Jonathan--started construction of a brick kiln and forge. Logic begs the brick oven was built first. Evidently, the clay soil that the Harmonists had had to deal with was everywhere abundant; this was dredged and mixed with river sand to dry under a long, hot summer sun. With a sufficiency of bricks, the brothers erected a domed oven and ramped up the firing process. From especially dense bricks was born a furnace and the means to hammer out horseshoes or hardware. Stables, a barn and a carpenter's shed would follow.

How early Daniel Leet may have had thoughts of building a "country house" on his finest Depreciation land is not known, nor is the origin of its name, "Newington." The tract, purchased originally by Thomas Shields, was adjacent to those named "Newbury" and "Norwich," but other than the alliteration of old English parishes, there seems no particular affinity by Shields, Leet, or even Mark Wilcox to British soil.

Despite owning the property for nearly twenty-five years, Leet may have never thought to develop the site. Morally conflicted for having claimed property he himself had surveyed, Daniel did not wish to make obvious any impropriety of character. Rather, he resigned to build a commercial mill, tavern, and forge while remaining safely distant in his declared homestead in Washington. Yet, now, upon the recent death of his wife, Daniel might have thought differently. Surely, his investment in Halfway House yielded some profits, but were they sufficient to further invest in a proper dwelling so distant from Washington? Would Daniel ever realize a return on this investment? After all, he was now 66 years of age. Perhaps David was willing to contribute to the project. That his son-in-law would build a country home along the Sewickley Bottoms was fine. After all, the land only came to Leet's possession through Shields' father.

Whether or not David and Eliza themselves ever intended to live in the country home is not a certainty. Jonathan Leet was the "man about town," living in a cabin less than a mile west of Little Sewickley Creek. Jonathan was then about 47, married fourteen years to Mary Moore, and expecting his fifth child and a namesake, Jonathan.

William Leet and his wife Susannah Laycock had moved out of Leetsdale a year after their marriage. Now with three children (of which one was a son also named Jonathan,) they lived in Beaver, which made his assistance at Newington an easy commute. (Susannah's father was an early mayor of the town.)

In fact, the farm house would be built with the sole intention of renting it for the income. Few houses, requiring an investment of such time and labor, were ever built for just one family's tenure. But David, now 34, might have had his eyes on the future.

If so, the strategic benefits David would realize by moving to a new homestead so far from Washington were three: location, location, location. Equidistant between Pittsburgh and the Harmonists' warehouse in Beaver, the site made sense in terms of shipping logistics. A full day's journey north to Zelienople would be shortened by twenty miles. Living so close to the well-trafficked Beaver Road would give him easier access to the circuit of towns and villages he regularly visited. And, above all, to have open, unrestricted access to the Ohio River on which, now more frequently, commercial boats plied both east and west allowed him opportunities neither Buffalo Creek nor Chartiers Creek would ever offer. The notion of boarding a steamboat from one's private dock was an idea newly imagined.

Further, the value of Newington could only be enhanced by building a house—and a "modern" one, at that. Finally and forever, the reality of the opportunity to build a new house—no matter the scheme or succession of occupant families—was that the property would be inherited by Daniel Leet's only heir, Eliza. And to that end, her husband of eleven years proved his devotion.

If, in fact, David and Eliza ever then considered moving from Washington, his business interests would keep him back home.

The Power of Steam

A young Pittsburgh tinkerer, Oliver Evans first used steam power to manufacture the wire teeth assembled in a wool carding machine. Evans had thought his labor-saving contraption would produce 500 teeth per minute, but in fact, it made three times as many.[31] Wool carding is one of the most laborious steps in creating yarn. Once sheared, washed and dried, the fluffy tangles of wool needed to be combed—or "carded"—in order to straighten and separate the fibers. The teeth of the card had to be firm and evenly set. The more teeth, the larger the card; the larger the card, the greater the output of prepared wool. Thus refined, the wool was then spun into single strands which when twisted with a second strand (and more) became yarn.

The irony of Evans's steam-powered invention is that he applied his large cards to mill wheels powered *by water*. Sure, steam engines had been employed in America since 1750—first to pump water from coal mines, then to lift cargo from ships, and ultimately to power the ship itself—but the idea of running an entire mill with steam seemed to challenge even the brightest entrepreneurs. That literal transfer of power took nearly fifty years.[32]

When the industrial revolution exploded in America, few businesses could do better than to apply steam to power their operations. But many struggled with the economics of obtaining fuel to make that steam. As yet, there were only two choices: wood or coal. Both were cheap, but expensive to transport. Western Pennsylvania had it all. Not only was there wood and

---

[31] Lienhard, *Engines of Our Ingenuity*, No. 285, https://www.uh.edu/engines/epi285.htm

[32] Not that hundreds of engineers did not try harder. The fact was that early steam engines had limitations in meeting torque strengths necessary to power larger industrial applications.

coal in sure supply, the rivers made shipping a cinch. Moreover, the area had productive iron foundries of immense capability and diversity *because* of the region's coal. Fabricating a steam engine west of the Alleghenies was economically more advantageous than hauling one over the mountains or, as was only a recent option, floating one across the Erie Canal to land at the Port of Pittsburgh.

By merit of inspiration alone, many hopeful entrepreneurs rushed to adapt steam power to new and promising ventures.

And so it was that in January, 1814, David Shields organized the Washington Steam Mill and Manufacturing Company.

A Farmhouse

The residential design for which David Shields is given sole credit was a two-story rectangle, having three bays on either side and a center hall entrance. "Its style, if it could be said to have any," wrote architectural historian James D. Van Trump in 1968, "was of the simplest sort, reflecting dimly the Georgian of the eastern seaboard."[33]

Essentially, the design created four rooms; two on the first floor and two on the second, accessed by a single hall running along a windowed wall. A single, slim staircase climbed to the second floor hall between two upstairs sleeping quarters. At the exterior of the southern, short end of the house a large brick fireplace and chimney was centered to the single gable. Two interior hearths, one upstairs and down, served as the only heat source. Unique to its construction, however, the chimney also provided for a larger hearth outdoors where, in favorable weather, the home cooking would take place. In fact, for food storage in warmer months, a spring house was excavated outdoors. Just ten feet from the eastern exterior of the house, a windowless room, sunken some six feet below ground, provided a channel for running water, fed by natural spring water through a wooden pipe. Shelved inside, perishable goods like fruits, milk and butter stayed cool.

However simplistic, Newington portended something better than frontier living. Of course, to a more gentrified Philadelphian, the little farmhouse was as crude as a backyard cookhouse.

---

[33] Van Trump, *Antiques Magazine*, May 1968, pg. 656

Hopes and Expectations

Compared to a typical order for muslin, candles, tea, and sugar—say, the weekly needs of a common neighbor—a requisition for twenty tin stoves, eight barrels of "salt pork," or twelve "faggots of blistered iron" was the kind of profitable commerce David Shields sorely missed. Before the Harmonists left for Indiana, not only had they ordered significant quantities of food stock and industrial materials, they had paid in cash.

Now, due to years of trade imbalance, cash, credit and bank notes were nowhere to be had. Wrote John Heckewelder to Frederick Rapp in November of 1814: "Even here in lower Pennsylvania, no notes are accepted anymore except those that are produced in Philadelphia. No one accepts Maryland and Virginia notes and the best Philadelphia notes are exchanged for silver and gold at a loss of 14%."[34]

Since moving to Indiana in 1815, when they first cleared their new lands along the Wabash and settled two hundred families into newly hewn cabins and framed houses, the industrious energy of George Rapp's society—the very trade upon which David's income had so relied—dissipated to a slow shuffle of legal work in the courts of Butler County. Dutiful to the younger Rapp's assignments, David Shields had worked diligently to settle the Harmonists' affairs in western Pennsylvania. But long gone were the constant wagons loaded with heavy machinery to improve the efficiencies of their manufactories or, rued in equal measure, the anticipation of hundred-weight bales of fine merino wool destined for a local carding mill.

---

[34] Arndt, *Harmony on the Connoquenessing*, pg. 917

Precisely for that reason, Shields may have incorporated the Washington Steam Mill & Manufacturing Company. Capitalized at $50,000 to a limited class of shareholders,[35] the facility stood four-stories high on Chartiers Creek at the southern edge of town. Washington County in 1812 led every other county in southwestern Pennsylvania in wool production except Butler, owing to the interests of the Reed family there. Other prominent town leaders, like John Hoge Ewing, Thomas Baird, and Dr. Francis LeMoyne, also had significant interests in raising local sheep, but Alexander Reed was known to have exported raw wool directly to eastern markets as early as 1810.[36] Precisely how much David Shields invested in the steam mill is unrecorded, but a tenth share, or $5,000, would seem consistent with similar ventures.

Whatever plans, whatever hopes, whatever designs Shields might have penned in a business plan to operate the modern mill, however, went the way of the steam that powered it. All expectations evaporated within the year. The mill was sold to Thomas Baird who, although having installed larger wool-carding wheels, also advertised to the public the availability of both warm and cold baths daily, excluding Sundays.[37] Never profitable, the massive four-story frame structure burned to ashes in 1831.

---

[35] Crumrine, *History of Washington County*, pg. 554

[36] Ibid., pg. 481

[37] Ibid., pg. 554

The Summer That Wasn't

In 1816, Pittsburgh enjoyed a population of about 10,000. Astonishingly, because everyone worked six days a week, as many as eight churches had been organized for the sole purpose of Sunday worship. The town offered three banks, three market houses, a theater, a courthouse, and, for those who apparently did not heed their Sunday sermon, a jail. Already, the town was constantly covered in smoky haze, owing as much to the many factories producing iron and glass as to the mills and industries of all kinds employing steam power generated from plentiful, local coal. That year, too, Pittsburgh was incorporated as a city, electing its first mayor, Ebenezer Denny. The body politic also elected a Select Committee of nine members, a General Council of twelve, and, for superfluous political debate only Pennsylvanians seemed to like, nine aldermen.

News of Pittsburgh's incorporation reached the east coast where the editors of the *Boston Yankee* newspaper, not familiar with the nascent city, placed it in Ohio.

1816 was also a very strange year, not just for Pittsburgh residents or those of Washington, Pennsylvania, but for all human kind. One year earlier, on April 10, the Mount Tambora volcano, rising from the Indonesian island of Sumbawa, erupted. The blast was the single deadliest eruption in recorded history killing 90,000 people within a week and affecting atmospheric conditions for more than a year after. The gases that rose from the 13,000 ft. mountain created a massive plume of sulfuric acid that rained for months. That single event caused the first great potato famine of Ireland 8,000 miles away. Typhus spread throughout the British Isles killing another 100,000. In America, tens of thousands of immigrants crept under ominous clouds, escaping the destitution of America's food-starved coasts to the central "warmer" plains of Indiana and Illinois. So unseasonably cold were the months of May through July, so dark were the skies, 1816 became forever known as the year without a summer.[38]

Kindled for the first time in spring of that year, the hearths of the new farmhouse at Newington roared hot all summer.

---

[38] Evans, "Blast from the Past," *Smithsonian Magazine*, July, 2002

A. Way & Co.

In or around 1817, David Shields and Abishai Way partnered in a new venture wherein Abishai, from his Pittsburgh shop, would sell a variety of Harmonists' goods, and through which David could receive wholesale wares to forward on to Indiana. A.Way & Co. became the premiere import-export shop of Pittsburgh.

A letter from David Shields to Frederick Rapp, dated January 22, 1817, encapsulates a lot of how David served his most important client. The following letters, however, are interesting alone in understanding the complexities of keeping accounts accurate in times when every business person relied on his own ledger to balance with those of trusted, yet remote partners. If disputes arose, there was only the written word of correspondence. Important letters, much like the following, required the writer (or an assistant) to copy them into a bound journal. Still, letters crossed constantly through the mail.

(For some context, of the men identified in the following, know that a Mr. Helveti owed significant mortgage payments on several tracts of the Harmonist lands and that Abraham Ziegler was bonded to purchase all of their settled property. Men like Pastor Schnee or Mr. Glacer, an attorney and financier to Baron Dettmar Basse whose iron foundry was now in serious trouble, seemed to be circling like hyenas.)

Washington Penna. Jan 22nd 1817

"Mr. Frederick Rapp
"Respected Friend,

"Your letter of 6th inst. received yesterday is before me but a former letter of December 3rd alluded to in this,... since which nothing material has occurred relative to your business, further than is stated in the within a/ct. [account] except in the case of Helveti who has become a bankrupt, and his place under the Sherriff's hands for sale... I have employed Mr. John Way to attend to the Sale, and bid up the land untill it would also cover your debt, there are several heavy judgements recorded after yours, some of whom must lose. In my next it is probable I can inform you farther.

"I do not expect that Zeigler can do much toward paying you untill next April, I have this day written him urgently on the subject. You observe I have Credited you for the 150 dol. rc'd in your late letter, as also for the 2 pcs. muslin not received by you although in my bill... I lately rec'd a letter from James Allisson Jr. of Beaver, who informs me, that Basse has so arranged with Mr. Glacer as to have the execution on his furnace &c. [etc.] withdrawn for the present, report says that Basse's wife is rich; how that is I do not know. "Winter only set in with us about 11 or 12 days ago, but has been hard freezing weather Since with Some little snow. You never in-formed me yet, if any or what value should be attached to the notes of what purports to be the "Indiana Manufacturing Company" dated at Lexington, of which there is a good many in this country, but not in any credit. I expect I shall be able to sell your Bank Notes as soon as I receive your power of attorney Sent you in my last, but am not quite certain. I shall speak to [John] Arthurs next time I go to Pitts. of the thick pasteboard of his bill, missing. I will then call with Rosenbaum about your Pianna; you stated in a former letter that you were not in a hurry, and I was waiting untill our treasury should be filled from Zeigler and other Sources... We shall indeed be glad to see you in June next as intimated in your letter. Hereafter your business at and through Pittsburgh, will be done by Abishai Way & Co. if agreeable to you having entered into partnership there with Mr. Way.

We are well, and desire to be remembered to your father and friends generally.

David Shields

The following came about two weeks later.

Feb. 1st 1817

"Mr. David Shields

"In my last of the 6th ult. I advised you in particular in regard to Dettmar Basse since that I recd. Yours of the 3rd by which that I learned his long entertained wish to get a wife at last became fulfilled, whether it will better his present situation we must wait for to know, but is very doubtful to me.

"I recd. Two Bills of loading one for 10 and the other for 11 tin plate stoves of Mr. Hull... I think it best to Credit Dettmar Basse for 21 stoves towards the Judgement of $400, which I have aginst him in Beaver County... I also learned with satisfaction that you have with Abishai Way entered into Partnership in order to open a store in Pittsburgh, which will undoubtedly be advantageous to the firm, and of beneficial convenience to us, as I hope you will be able to keep a more regular whole sale store then ever was kept in Pittsburgh before, and as Mr. Way intended to start next Month in Philad. I have according to your cheerful offer inclosed a order for the most wanted article of Store goods, which are necessary and will suit us early in the spring. Being doubtful you have any fund for me on hand, I wish by no means burdensome to you, and rather do without the goods then to embarrasse your own business. I hope and calculate on it for Certain, that Mr. Ziegler this spring will pay the balance of his bond due last year, as well as the next April without fail, therefore shall wait to make out a General Order for Goods untill then when I expect to bring it myself, the Power of Attorney authorizing you to sell my Bank Stoke in Pittsburgh, I can not sent this time...

"my father and family are well and gives their compliments to Miss [Mrs.] Shields, and the whole Society together enjoy good health and is busy to diffuse its Improvements more and more, but chiefly to embellish their minds with Noble Virtues to obtain a good preparation against the day of Christs coming which will be according to events of this time not far distant."

Frederick Rapp almost immediately followed this letter with another, in which he warns Shields about the Indiana Manufacturing Company.

Febr. 18 1817

"Mr. David Shields

"... Some time ago I have recd. a Letter from Mr. Ziegler in which [he] excused himself and stated in regard to his Neglection in making payment that he had been much disappointed in getting money from his Debtors, but promised firmly to pay this Spring, on which I have also wrote him by last mail. He also informed me that he made Sale of part of old harmony to Revd. Schnee of Pittsburgh for the Sum of $64,000 to be paid in seven years in 8 equal Installments one of which to be paid in hand. Your Letter of the 22nd Jan. says that you never recd. Information concerning the Notes of the Indianna Manufacturing Company, but by Examination of my Letter Book found that on the 1st March 1816 I gave you an account that the[y] are not good, the Banck being errected by Imposters which are no place to be found.

Yours &c."

Last but not least, now came from David a response to the prior letter, dated February 1, sent by Frederick Rapp.

Washington Penna. 28th Feb 1817

"Mr. Frederick Rapp

"Respected Friend, my last letter to you was of the date the 30th Jany. since which I have rec'd. Yours of 1st instant containing an order for Sundry goods... The deed and two rects. for taxes which you sent to me for Mr. Brinker, I enclosed per mail to Mr. Way at Pittsburgh... I regret to say that the mail was robbed at Cannonsburgh, and the presumption is those papers will be entirely lost. What may be necessary to do, I will advise you...

"I have just returned from Pittsburgh, where by appointment I have been to have a personal interview with Mr. Ziegler, in order that we might have as close an understanding as possible as to what may be expected from him. I stated to Mr. Ziegler that your agreements for land &c. would not admit of a delay of the full amounts due next April; and wished him to state, definitely, to what extent we might count on him: to which he replied, that he would promise 10,000 Dollars, the half of it by the middle of April and the other half by the middle of May. ...however he calculates on receiving $8,000 from a Mr. Sneigh [Schnee], a german preacher, that once talked to you about buying Harmony, as a part of the 10,000, which I think may be doubtfull...

"Mr. Ziegler has informed me that he has understood and believed the statement true, that Basse had sold the furnace and all of the land in Beaver county, about 2500 acres, to his wife's brother, a Mr. Rogers; for the sum of 45,000;... he is by common report a man of some wealth...

"...I have also had the heats [?] about Helveti's business, he took the benefit of the insolvent acts and his place was advertised to be sold by the Sherriff 26th instant...

"I spoke to John Arthurs about the thick pasteboards, from what he said I think if you examine the bottom of the box you will find them there. He said the pasteboards so exactly filled the bottom of the box, that they may have been supposed to be the wooden bottom.

"When at Pittsburgh a few days ago, I called on Mr. Rosenbaum, who shewed me the Pianna, intended for you, it is a very handsome piece of Workmanship, but as to its excellence of tone, I am not Sufficiently a judge to say anything. It will be sent with other goods about 1st of April. The chemical glasses and Barometer tubes are not forgotten. I have frequently called about them at the glass works...

"Presenting Mrs. Shields and my own respects to your father and all of our friends, I remain Dr. Sir   Your friend
David Shields"[39]

The overlooked pasteboard was needed, perhaps, to bind more daybooks and journals.

---

[39] Arndt, *A Documentary History of the Indiana Decade*, pgs.307-311

Thomas Visits

Typically brief when writing about personal matters in his hundreds of letters to Frederick Rapp, David Shields made short mention of a significant event. In 1819, his father came to visit.

The journey to Washington would have taken a minimum of twenty days, if passed in good weather. Even with the National Road then connected to Wheeling through the Cumberland Gap by 1818, traveling west by stage coach or wagon from Philadelphia would obviate joining it in Cumberland. Rather, Thomas Shields, in July of 1819, celebrated the opening of the Pennsylvania Turnpike. More than 300 miles long, it "opened" due to the completion of the Laurel Hill Pass earlier that spring.

By traveling the established road to Harrisburg, his coach rolled over the newer stretch due east to Chambersburg, then to Bedford, Somerset, and Greensburg. He paid $20 for the privilege of riding with as many as nine other passengers, straddled three abreast on short leather benches, two facing forward and one aft, with no legroom. Typical to the time, the coach was ornate with brightly painted landscapes or portraits of historic figures. Sometimes called "Turtle-backs" for the shape of their roofs, the cabin was suspended on thick belts of bull hide, swinging back and forth to absorb the constant shock of the early roads.[40] Metal springs were not yet invented. The new turnpike, widened by 25 feet atop an older horse path, was made seasonally passable by stones embedded in the road or morticed into arch bridges crossing the various creeks and streams along the way. The turnpike also provided the convenience of new inns and taverns whose investors had

---

[40] Pickenpaugh, *America's First Interstate*, pg. 94

seen great promise in its several years of laborious construction. Lodging fees were extra, as were meals, but overnight accommodations were regularly available, subject to the coach's schedule, of course, which was hardly dependable. A coach might travel in one day—given a change of horses— twenty miles. Fifteen was considered "a good clip." Yet, realistically, the distance travelled in any one day was determined by the next scheduled stop. Had Thomas Shields travelled alone on horseback, he could not have travelled any faster, dependent as he would have been on the health and stamina of a single horse or two. Of course, the cost would have been much less; the toll for a single rider was $6 total, doled out in smaller amounts at the dozens of swinging pole gates—or "turning pikes"—along the way.

The reason for Thomas's visit was family. In Washington, he had six grandchildren he had never met. David and Eliza's youngest was then Rebecca, born two years earlier. In July of that year, Eliza was four months pregnant with Susan. Less than two years later, Hannah, their last, would arrive.

If Thomas had not spent the preceding two years constructing the first framed buildings at Damascus Manor, he would not have been impressed by the genteel flourishes of Washington's business hub. Here were wooden walkways roofed against inclement weather, large stone houses retrofitted to greet exhausted travelers with food and spirits, and a marketplace bustling with more than a few farmers laying out their midsummer produce. If his son had not met him when first he disembarked at the Golden Swan, a reporter from the Washington paper would have been there to ask and gather the latest news from the east. How bad was the current exchange of specie in Philadelphia? Had he seen the elephant "Columbus" parading in the streets there? Did he stop in Harrisburg and see the new capitol building under construction? What about Bedford? Did he know that Thomas Jefferson was to spend the summer there?[41] Always an extrovert, Thomas was happy to discuss anything, even the most pressing questions a western journalist might like to ask.

Of course, David *was* there to greet him, to inquire about his journey, and point out the sights of a young city with four churches, a newly expanded courthouse (now constructed of stone *and* brick,) two (albeit, foundering) banks, and a new public complex where children attended school in one

---

[41] https://www.monticello.org/site/research-and-collections/visit-bedford-springs-pennsylvania-1819

section, lawyers held their private offices in another, and the Washington Reporter operated its presses in a back room. David loaded his father's bags on a buggy to trot out to his humble homestead.

It's doubtful Thomas had ever met Eliza. Although she surely had visited Philadelphia with her father—if just briefly to see the sights while shopping for a new dress or two—she would have been then a young lady of 13 attending the seminary in Bethlehem. She might have then tagged along to dine at the homes of her father's several acquaintances. But Daniel Leet was a man disposed not to sowing social ties, but to forging practical relationships. With whom would they have dined? If not Robert Morris, perhaps John Nicholson; yet both had no time or need then to further their appreciation of the surveyor's art. If not Levi Hollingsworth—always busy with the breadth of his empire—then perhaps the kindly and entertaining Thomas Shields. He knew that Shields had first bid on the several tracts along the Ohio he had parlayed from Mark Wilcox. He was well aware that Shields still owned three other lots in the Depreciation Lands and, in fact, had owned earlier tracts of land in western Pennsylvania, surveyed then by Dorsey Pentecost about whom Leet had few good things to say. He knew that Shields's business associate, Levi Hollingsworth, was actively trying to sell much of the land the two partners had acquired in Finlay Township and, in fact, had responded personally to Hollingsworth's requests to show off land to prospective buyers, (perhaps because Dorsey Pentecost had thankfully disappeared some years earlier.) He knew, too, that Shields had sons––four, in fact—one of whom was looking to create a mercantile route to Washington where few agents were eager to barter on western goods, but where, too, the son could attend to his father's lands, collecting rents and disposing of squatters. He also knew that Shields was a man of the highest integrity. But, no; even if Eliza might have visited Philadelphia, might have had dinner with an acquaintance of her father, she would not have met Thomas Shields. No, in fact, back then, Daniel Leet might have known the esteemed silversmith by his reputation, but not by his company.

Of course, when the surveyor and the silversmith did meet that summer's day along Chartiers Creek in 1819 they had much to discuss. Social protocol would beg a mutual effusion of compliments about their two children, married now 16 years, with adorable children of their own, grandchildren who had been warned not to interrupt the old men's conversation, the principle topic of which they could only speculate was land.

Had it all been worthwhile? Was it paying out? Were there reasons to think optimistically about the promise of new western states?

Other than family, Thomas also came to see the new Washington Steam Mill and Manufacturing company, then in the process of fulling and dyeing cloth. More significantly, he came to see the Depreciation Lands he had first bid on, sight unseen, some thirty-five years earlier.[42] There, he would visit Newington, now improved with a small brick farmhouse, hundreds of acres of corn, rye and wheat, a blacksmith's shop, mill and barn. (By several accounts, the property then was rented out to one Mrs. Bean.)[43] To Thomas, the property seemed very well suited to agriculture, even if he thought the little brick homestead looked no grander than a city cook house. Yet, he would also see on the Ohio River the frequent passage of steamboats, many now regularly carrying passengers to Cincinnati, the largest of which were bound for New Orleans. Such black clouds of coal-fired steam were sights Thomas Shields might not have seen even in the port of Philadelphia.

*   *   *   *   *

No matter by carriage or wagon, the journey home would have been taxing to anyone. At 76 years of age, Thomas's September return east might have killed him were he not accompanied by David on his annual buying trip to Philadelphia. It may as well have; Thomas Shields died before Christmas.

His death, reported as peaceful "without a sigh or struggle," was mourned by thousands whose tributes and sympathies were expressed in several publications of the Baptist church.

Appearing in the Notices of the Baptist Board of Foreign Missions, of which Thomas was Vice President at his death, were words of abject sorrow. "During the last six months his health gradually declined. The taper of life burnt itself out. He came down to his grave full of days, and as a shock [sic] of corn completely ripened. He would often say, 'I have lived and I must die a beggar to the throne of mercy.'"[44]

---

[42] Crumrine, *History of Washington County*, pg. 534

[43] Possibly the mother or spinster sister of John Bean, a merchant, who married Catherine Leet.

[44] *American Baptist Magazine*, March 1820, Vol. 11

Attributed to him on his deathbed were these personal expressions of faith: "I am a sinner; I can be saved by no righteousness of mine—My only refuge is grace—grace—free and sovereign grace—I know whom I have believed, and that He is able to keep that which I have committed into His hands until that day; I know my Redeemer liveth."

Of observations by others came the following: "Deacon Shields was punctual in sanctuary duties. His house was a house of prayer. He was a vivacious talker, and ever ready to impart information or to relate anecdotes. By industry and an aiding Providence he became quite wealthy, but was always humble, frugal in life, hospitable and liberal. Averse to partisan strife, he was a valiant defender of the truth, and was especially distinguished by the vigorous stand he took against Universalism. His advice was always regarded as valuable, and he especially delighted in proffering it in the character of a peacemaker."[45]

In more words, perhaps expressed by the same writer above, came this. "He passed the term of three score years and ten, with a vigor of constitution exceeded by few. He had once thought that at that period he would relinquish all active and public service; but he soon found, and yielded willingly to the idea, that the christian must continue to labour, content to wait for rest until he enter the portals of paradise."

Thomas Shields passed through those portals on December 8, 1819. He was buried at the Sansom Street Baptist Church, where his wife Hannah had confessed her faith just two years earlier.

---

[45] Ibid.

The Panic of 1819

If his father's rapid decline in the winter of 1819 did not shake him, the economic crisis would rattle David for years.

Although the Treaty of Ghent had resolved the trade embargo with England, it did little to restore the financial losses each country had shared in recent years. Banks continued to suffer staggering debts.

US banks were particularly threatened by imminent losses when loans and mortgages, advanced to tens of thousands of pioneers flooding into the "New West," were not repaid. Not only had the "year with no summer" further propelled western migration, but the once-promised exchange of trade back east found that markets were no longer sustainable. Eastern banks demanded their credit be restored, which meant sending agents into the Ohio and Northwest Territory to lay foreclosure notices on property that, in most cases, had barely benefitted from improvement. Ohio was so poor it passed laws to tax its own banks, and that included taxing the very same federal funds loaned to Ohio banks to shore them up.

If the Bank of the United States had once insisted its holdings were backed exclusively by specie, it was now, if not first intended, a land bank. Two significant events arose from the debacle. First, in the decision of McCulloch vs. Maryland—the complaint of which, like Ohio, was that the Second Bank of the United States sued Maryland for taxing it—the Supreme Court ruled that Federal law trumps state laws. The second outcome was a significant depression of land values in the western territories. This time, the mess was caused not by heavily organized speculation, but by individual aspirations and consumer overreach. Little could be done.

Thomas's Will

Thomas Jr., Robert, and John Shields attested to their father's will on January 30, 1820. David attested to it two weeks later, suggesting he travelled to a Philadelphia probate court as soon as the weather had allowed. Not surprisingly, Thomas's will disclosed considerable assets in the way of property and income.

To his wife Hanna, he left "all that my mansion house where I now dwell and lot of ground thereunto belonging situate on the easterly side of Dock Street." He also provided her an annuity of $900 to be paid out in quarterly installments, commencing within thirty days. But the will gave Hanna a choice. If she chose to relinquish the Dock Street mansion to her four sons, each of whom would share in its sale equally, she could have her husband's Front Street estate, as well as his house and lot on the corner of Eighth and Sansom Streets. In addition, she could have his house at No. 70 North Second Street. And, furthermore, all three properties would be adjoined by an annuity of $1200. Thomas also gave her "absolutely forever all my silver plate, beds and bedding, household goods and kitchen furniture which we now have together in housekeeping."

To his sons, he willed their stepmother's disposed choice of property— either the Dock Street mansion or the bundled three city residences—as well *all* of his *other* properties. "I do also give and devise unto my four sons, Thomas, Robert, John and David Shields all and every of my messuages and lots of ground and ground rents situate lying and being within the city or county of Philadelphia together with all my other messuages, lots, lands, tenements and hereditaments situate lying and being in Wayne County or in any other county within the state of Pennsylvania, and also all that my messuage and lots of ground situate in the city of Baltimore; together with all my other real estate whatsoever and wheresoever."

Indeed, Thomas owned property in Baltimore where his brother Caleb lived. And the extent of his properties in Pennsylvania exceeded well beyond what was "situate" in Philadelphia and Wayne County. Shields owned dozens of tracts in Western Pennsylvania, some in partnership with Levi Hollingsworth, particularly in Findlay Township, but also in Westmoreland, Beaver and Butler Counties. In years past, David had attended to settling delinquent taxes on several of these, yet upon his father's death, even Thomas had no known "schedule" by which one could follow tenant contracts nor even the obligations his estate would owe to respective county tax assessors.

Thomas Shields's last will and testament however demanded two conditions. First, the boys were not to sell off or divide any of their inheritance until two years after Thomas's death. And secondly, each of Thomas, Robert and John were to be compensated for an outstanding loan. "On the tenth day of August one thousand eight hundred and twelve having advanced four thousand dollars to my said son David Shields, I do therefore order and direct that in the division of my estate among my four said sons, my said son David shall account and be chargeable to my estate for the said four thousand dollars with interest."

Whatever life event in 1812 had possessed David to seek an advance from his father's estate was not cited.

Curious, too, is the omission of Mary Shields from her father's will. However, having married Sallows Shewell in 1789, she needed none of her father's wealth—nor, by custom, was she entitled to it. Sallows Shewell, the man whom David suggested his father ask to deliver "the deed for Rapp," was a wealthy Philadelphia merchant, trading in chintz, cotton, silks and linens. His shop was at 126 Front Street, "near the Drawbridge," just several doors down from the Golden Cup and Crown.

The elder Shields created one other lasting document before meeting his Redeemer. At Damascus Manor, he had built the county's first Baptist church which welcomed the faithful as early as 1800.[46] In 1822, a trust Shields created in Wayne County endowed its operation, providing for an organizing "society," as well as an "every Sunday" minister.

---

[46] Mathews, *The History of Wayne, Pike and Monroe Counties*, pg. 465

PART FIVE
(1820-1907)

In which religion takes center stage,
a country takes sides, and
an American family takes root.

The End of Speculation

Grief struck David in many ways. Never as loquacious as his father, nor apparently as warm—signing off letters to his Dad with salutations like, "I remain with Sincere wishes for your welfare and happiness" or "I remain with sentiments of respect…"—David found he had little to say about his loss, indifferent to the needs of his clients, sullen and silent through the remaining winter of his sorrow.

Of course, grief is testament to love. Despite the hard luck economy, the failure of his investment in steam power, or the distant issues of trade with the Rapps, David had had the great privilege to prove himself worthy of a father's love. Becoming orphaned, at any age, begets new responsibilities and, for the wise, opportunity.

In June, he wrote to Frederick Rapp apologizing for absent correspondence, but not explaining immediately why. The letter is the longest of hundreds he wrote to his beloved friend. David, matured by his loss, addressed the current state of his world with a perverse mix of wisdom and woe:

> "It is indeed astonishing to look back at what a time of speculation we have passed through, the whole community seemed as it were infected with a mania, the Delirium has passed by, and sober reason has returned, the paper system, the banking system, the landed speculations, have all vanished, as the 'Baseless fabric of vision" while thousands are left to deplore their own folly. As you are in a new country [Indiana] daily filling up by emigration from our older Settlements, and from Europe, who bring with them a great deal of money, and have much to buy from you, who have much to

sell, and as industry like yours must create prosperity, it is supposable that you cannot well know the situation of things in this country. I will then inform you, money (for there is nothing now bears that name but what is deserving of it, the host banks that could not pay their notes on demand have sunk, irretrievably gone,) is very scarce; all kinds of property real and personal have very much depreciated the prices of grain at this place and Pitts…

"Harmony looks much like what it did when you last saw it, but rather on the decline, particularly in all matters of taste, it was rather a melancholy picture to me, who had known its more prosperous days, I did not stay long there."

At length, David went on to relate the current state of the Harmonists' legal battles in Beaver and Butler counties, offering his account of court appearances for which he had no legal standing (either as lawyer or plaintiff,) but by which his esteemed presence might have rendered some favors. At the least, from his perspective, the glass was seemingly half-full.

He closed his letter with the following admission:

"My father died in Decr. last a loss I feel much, his many excellent qualities had strengthened the natural attachment of child to parent.

"I am preparing a house on our Sewickley bottom farm for to remove to next year, where I hope to realize as the Roman poet said 'Otium cum dignitate.' Remember me to your father and society,

Your fr'd
David Shields"

Leisure with dignity. Cicero had said something like it.

Settling Estates

At least for his three brothers, David's pronouncement was true; the days of speculation were over. What many tracts in Wayne County and western Pennsylvania their father had purchased in pure speculation became something of "a chronic malady," either bringing on sudden migraines or requiring regular "bloodletting" more messy than medicinal.

David collected ground rents or lease payments in his region, sending the monies back to Philadelphia. David had been given to making an annual pilgrimage to his birth city each year in late August, sometimes early September, often not returning until mid-October. When collected funds were otherwise available for disbursement to his brothers, David would forward on bank notes through Abishai Way or some other trusted soul.

The banking system however was complex when third parties intervened. One example sheds some light. Recorded on Tuesday, January 16, 1821, David Shields had given a bank note to Abishai Way to carry with him to Philadelphia. The note had been drafted "in favor of" Abishai on the 20th of December, the month preceding, payable no later than 30 days hence, and only then when once deposited into a secondary account of David's at the Schuykill branch of the Bank of Philadelphia. To deposit the note, Abishai had to endorse it himself and make it payable to the order of David Shields and, then, by David's order to that branch, Abishai had to have a second note written in favor of Robert Shields, "Merch. of 2 St., Phil." with which, once issued and only then, Abishai could make a deposit into Robert's account. For the privilege of transacting funds from one bank to another, Shields would pay a premium of one percent to the originating bank (in this case, the Bank of Pittsburgh.) If and when Robert were to draw from his account at the Bank of Philadelphia to pay his two other brothers, he paid a similar premium for each note drawn. The logic behind such premiums was the protection against insolvency either of the two banks might have feared of the other. Apparently, it mattered not that a stranger, such as Abishai Way, could make the deposit across state; it mattered that the originating bank was known to be legitimate and secure. It decidedly mattered, of course, that the payer was willing to pay a fee. In this instance, a comparatively lenient one percent. David's draft to Robert was for $185.12; the premium he paid was $1.86.

Fortunately for David, his Philadelphia transactions only had to occur two or three times a year. More frequently, David attended to matters more problematic and costly. In March, 1821, efforts to eject squatters on one of his late father's properties in Westmoreland County, incurred the following:

> To arbitrators:...$2
> To surveyors, Fullwood & Crankirk:............... $20
> To attorneys Armstrong (10), Alexander (5):...$15
> To expenses at Robbstown of arbitrators,
>   surveyors and witnesses:............................$6
> For traveling expenses to
>   Robbstown, Greensburgh:........................$4

The matter of the McMillan family's "ejectment" from Thomas Shields's property near Robbstown (now West Newton, Pennsylvania) was not a simple matter—nor did it happen anytime soon. The McMillans chose not to leave their cabin for several years, despite the threat of the courts and local sheriff.

In this particular case, it may be appreciated by some that the surveyors earned more for their work than the attorneys. Others might appreciate, too, the fact that, in all such efforts to defend his father's estate, David Shields charged his time and traveling expenses to his three brothers. He did no such thing when on the road for his own clients.

The same week of March, the estate was credited by payment of a note, "the balance in full," for $27.42. The Reverend Mr. Luse apparently made good on a loan from the late Baptist benefactor.

Likewise, in July, the estate received cash from Charles Scholls on "account of his contract for land" in the amount of $400. That "cash" was comprised of notes drawn on three different banks: the Valley Bank ($200,) the Pittsburgh Bank ($180,) and the Bank of Virginia, Fredericksburg Branch ($20.) Typical of the time, the concept of cash was what one could pay by way of a bank note, not by what one might have hidden under a mattress. Even in 1821, specie was just as rare as it always had been.

In other matters of his father's estate, David attended courts in Greensburg, Waynesburg and Butler, drawing on the advice of his counsel, Parker Campbell, Esq. (whose every bill seemingly cost the estate $5. Never $6 or $3.50; always $5.) The particulars are not noted in his daybook, but in most cases it seems that ground rents were past due or, in happier instances, estate property had sold, relieving David of any future attention. Besides the McMillan family of squatters, another lingering court case was that in which the estate had sued "Sam'l Gregory, Philip Price and And. Johnston" and, for which, David charged the estate $1 to "have judgement *renewed*" against the men.

And then there was an evolving matter back in Philadelphia. By the time of his father's death, Thomas and Hanna had already moved from the Dock Street house to the Sansom Street address at 8th Avenue. The widow chose to keep that house as her dwelling place. She had no desire to own two more houses, and so was amenable to receiving the lesser annuity of $900. Thomas Jr., Robert, and David agreed to the change. But John did not. He knew that rents were steadily declining in the city. And, when the combined rents of the other three houses failed to fully cover his widowed stepmother's annuity, John was damned if he was going to pay his own share out of pocket.

Thomas Shields's estate was hardly David's only family concern. His father-in-law, Daniel Leet, and Daniel's brother Jonathan, appear almost daily in Shields' accounts. Among typical entries for muslin, flannel, camphor, ginger and salt sold to his brother, or to his father, "1 Sett knives & forks, 4 Sett dishes," alum, and indigo, Daniel and Jonathan seemed to have *carte blanche* to purchase any items they wished. For Daniel, orders for tea, coffee and loaf sugar are frequent; for Jonathan, whiskey, "seegars," muslin, ribbon, and pins are regular. David would debit his account for Jonathan also with disbursements of cash, typically $2 or $1, for which he made Jonathan scrawl his signature in his daybook. (Of many cash disbursements to his laborers, Jonathan is the only one from whom David required such proof of payment.) Further, for all of these purchases, there is almost no credit recorded; that is, it seems that Daniel or Jonathan were not required to pay back their debts.

At 73, an age few men ever lived to experience, Daniel Leet had been widowed some seven years. He lived alone. Even if then he was in great health, any child would know that, as a male, he was ill-suited to domestic chores. Cooking, cleaning and laundry were not functions favored by men, least of all those raised on the frontier. David might have been kind. Or, just as likely, Eliza insisted on his generosity. After all, David and Eliza controlled the farm. Of course, it would become Eliza's greatest inheritance. And for the simple rights of first refusal, for the rights to manage the property or to develop its value as he saw fit, David made no qualms about his father-in-law's expenses, his provisions, his care or his comfort.

In fact, David paid for the regular assistance of a one Mrs. Arden. A neighbor living nearby in Washington, she attended to Daniel's everyday needs. Mrs. Arden and her "little girl, Sally," were regularly fawned upon with gifts of household goods, pins and ribbons, sewing needles, cloths and "sundries" for which no credit appears to balance these debts in David's books.

One particular example seems to prove it. David Shields' entry for Friday, June 22, 1821, records the following:

Jonathan Leet ~ Dr. [Debit]
    2 scythes $2.62
Mrs. Arden ~ Cr. [Credit]
    19 3/4 yrds tow linen ~ .25 .... 4.94
Daniel Leet ~ Dr. [Debit]
    2 lbs. Coffee .... .75
    4 1/4 lbs Sugar 1.19
    1 yd. Cotton .... .25
    4 dishes .... .40
    Skirt (for little Sally) .... .44
    1 family Bible (for Mrs. Arden) 6.00
Credit D.S. [David Shields]
    Self 2.59
    Mrch. 6.00
    little girl .... .44

(By this last notation, "D.S. or Self" is "picking up the tab" for Daniel's coffee, sugar, cotton and dishes, as well as for the Bible and Sally's skirt.)

Outside of David's daybook, Mrs. Arden appears in a singular context of small town fame. A year earlier, in the Spring of 1820, the town fathers had agreed to set aside funds "to the establishment of a society for the promotion of agriculture and domestic manufacture" of Washington. Appointed chair of the commission was James Kerr.[1] Thereafter known as the Agriculture Society, the subscribing members organized an annual exhibition at which jurors would award prizes for exceptional work. Daniel Leet won $5 for "best oxen." The very next award went to Jane Arden for "second-best piece of table linen." The prize was $2.50. Oddly, the list of eighteen different winners fails to cite the awardee for "*best* table linen."[2]

Further to the curiosities of David's daybook are the ever repetitive entries for Daniel's weekly wont of coffee, tea, sugar, cotton and the occasional dinner plate. If these items were to be "free of charge," why bother recording them in the first place? David Shields, meticulous in many ways, needed to track his inventory. Only by knowing what he depleted of his wholesale purchases could he derive what profit was made in retailing those items he actually sold.

---

[1] Crumrine, *History of Washington County*, pg. 472

[2] Ibid., pg. 473

A Bigger House

With untold assets from his inheritance, David Shields stepped up his game. No longer bound to the fortunes derived from the Harmonists so far away, no longer active in the failed experiment to master steam power in Washington, and no longer committed to sorting out the insolvency of its banks or the politics of his town hall, David Shields, his wife and six children took a leap of faith and focused their future on a more genteel life at Newington.

There, he intended to build a grand addition, one suited to a higher status, yet practical in all matters of livelihood and lifestyle.

Shields employed many to work on his new project along the Little Sewickley Creek. His daybook lists his early laborers, as well as dozens of local suppliers in the building trade. The names of Cornelius Pascal, Andrew Rupel, George Dilworth, Samuel Sutton, William Gillan, Amos Paxon, Elia Grimes, and Thomas Fisher figure prominently over the course of five years. The daybook makes no note of whether the men were white or Black, farmhand or tradesman. For their labors, each was granted full room and board, living in frame structures around Newington. From David, they regularly ordered necessities such as coffee, sugar, whiskey, and cornmeal, but occasionally they were provided shoes, pickled pork, tobacco, and, of course, tools as necessary. All they needed do was ask. There was no payroll, no regular compensation. Rather, David gave his men cash, usually $1 or $2, whenever they might have asked or needed it.

Only one man was paid a set wage. James Kerr, a Scotsman, was employed as a carpenter, joiner, brick layer, and stone mason. Likely the foreman of the many laborers aforementioned, he earned a full fifty cents a day. Early on, Kerr was paid for months of work at a time; later he was paid weekly. Whether or not he had assisted in constructing the earlier brick kiln on the property, it is apparent he knew something of masonry, laying out stone walls without mortar—as was the Scottish custom—and constructing brick walls *with* mortar. Records indicate a lot of "powder" was purchased for Newington, (so much so that it could not have been the "gun" kind.) So, too, wrought-iron nails, sheet tin, hinges and iron bars were purchased in great quantities.

There is no discerning at what age Kerr was first employed, nor how many years he devoted to the project. His name is a fixture in David's books, clearly predating that which is extant and, no doubt, appearing well later. He was a resident of Washington, PA, married to a Margaret Wherry, and apparently chaired the Agriculture Society of Washington (at least for a year or two.) Likely, he was known to David Shields, as well as Daniel Leet, for earlier work on the courthouse or market house there.

James and Margaret had a son in 1816, the same year the little farm house was completed. That boy himself would later attend to Newington and its Sewickley Bottoms community for many years to come. His name was Joseph W. Kerr.

New Beginnings

The first inkling of the decision came by way of a letter from Frederick Rapp to David Shields in which he inquired about lands he had long ago heard were available at 25 cents an acre. Along Fish Creek, somewhere in West Virginia, south of Elizabeth, had been a large tract under some consideration at the time the Harmonists were heading west. Why Frederick Rapp was asking David about this land nearly ten years later came as something odd.

David replied that he had not seen the land himself but that "my father-in-law Mr. Daniel Leet, who surveyed through that country in early times, speaks of it, as a mountainous broken country, and except the bottoms along the watercourses, a poor country. Indeed from all the information I can collect on the subject I am disposed to recommend you not have anything to do with it." David failed to ask Frederick why he might have been interested.

But David shared two cryptic bits of news of his own. First, the reply letter he wrote was addressed from Sewickley Bottom, dated February 16th, 1824. And secondly, he informed Frederick that "letters may be addressed to me in future, as Postmaster, Sewickley bottom, Allegheny County Penna. And unless as is this present case exceeding half an ounce in wt. will be free of postage."

Beginning in September of the preceding fall, the young Shields family started moving into their new house.

Newington was now a grand estate. Here, to anyone passing by, lived a man of some wealth and determination.

The structure, while not fully finished, enclosed nearly twice the volume of the original farmhouse, joining it at its north face away from the river, and, so now, more prominent to Beaver Road. Its new front door faced Little

Sewickley Creek to the west. With five bays on either side, ten feet wider as a whole than the original, it stood ten feet taller, too, even with its gabled roofline flattened for aesthetic if not practical reasons. Masking dual chimneys on its north face, the brick facade rose to bridge a single, yet impressive chimney cap.

Inside, eight hearths on two floors promised winter comfort. The bottom four hearths, framed and mantled, heated twin sitting parlors; the top hearths, four bedrooms. The design was simple and symmetrical. A central hall separated two large rooms on either side, the most southern ones adjoining the smaller farmhouse which rather seemed now as the "addition." The new front hall however gave grand access to a formidable stairway, its balusters spindled and painted, rising fourteen wide steps to an intermediate landing before turning to rise seven more.

Almost upon the family's arrival, one of the two large sitting parlors served as a trading post, general store and, now evidently, a post office. David Shields was its Postmaster. Ever attentive to his business, Shields opened his house to local commerce from its start.

And, yet, the query that Fred Rapp had posed to David was evidence of another new beginning. In the Spring of 1824, George Rapp decided to remove the entirety of his socialist community from Indiana.

Despite early bouts of malaria, long, hot summers clearing thousands of forested acres, and interminable winters of frost and flu, the Harmonists had prospered well. Some three hundred families had raised a community well more productive and profitable than Zelienople. Of course, there were disputes with local homesteaders and there were still issues of navigable access to the bigger ports of Louisville, Cincinnati, and Pittsburgh—especially when winter months shut down river traffic altogether—but there were no obvious struggles internal to the Harmonists. All were committed in their preparation for the second coming of Christ and all were happy in their work for the Lord. But for George Rapp, what may have spurred his decision to move back eastward was *his* discontent. Seemingly alone, he believed the Harmonists had become all too complacent. Well, if not complacent, lethargic. Like idle hands, he feared what work the devil had in store.

Frederick enlisted David's help in finding new land.

A Steamboat on the Ohio

Nicholas Roosevelt, a partner of Robert Fulton and Robert Livingstone, launched the first steamboat on western waters, in March of 1811. The *New Orleans*, a flat-bottomed craft, 150 feet from bow to stern, paddled by wheels both port and starboard, was built on the Monongahela River. Its first voyage departed Pittsburgh on October 20, 1811, and succeeded in reaching New Orleans on January 10, 1812, 82 days later. While on this historic journey, Roosevelt's wife gave birth to their second child, and the steamboat survived the single most violent earthquake ever recorded in the United States.[3]

That Thomas Shields, 25 years earlier, had invested in the very first steam-powered watercraft, brings little capital—yet some coincidence—to the success of Pittsburgh's role in bringing about a seismic shift in commercial transportation.

Just as nautical designers at Beaver developed an earlier industry for long-haul, keel and flatboats, so, too, did local engineers meet the demand for swift propulsion up and down the Ohio river. Investors and riverboat captains made quick money, their greatest risks being unchartered sandbars, unseen flotsam or winter ice. Pittsburgh industry opened new markets to all points west and south to the port of New Orleans. And, from there,

---

[3] At New Madrid, Missouri, on December 16, 1811, ocean-sized waves on the Mississippi River tossed and smashed untold boats ashore, lifted unseen sandbars and wiped away whole islands from what few maps had ever yet recorded their location. The New Madrid earthquake, attended by two more within the next month, is thought to have been ten times more powerful than the San Francisco earthquake of 1906.

improbably, all the way across the Atlantic. Pittsburgh glassware became a prized possession in the dining rooms of European nobility.[4]

Less obvious, but no less significantly, steamboats opened a new era of social intercourse. News carried faster, southern and northern cultures intermixed, and whole families travelled to meet distant relatives long separated by America's dense forests and sparse economy.

In 1824, Frederick Rapp engaged *The Plough Boy*, a stern wheel paddleboat, to carry the first wave of Harmonists, including 3,000 pounds of furniture and tools, from New Harmony on the Wabash to "Deadman's Ripple," a spot described as 18 miles from Pittsburgh, on the Ohio River.[5] The contracted price, dependent on the boat's success in reaching its final destination, was $1,100.

---

[4] Lorant, *Pittsburgh: The Story of an American City*, pg. 70.

[5] Deadman's Ripple was at the present site of the Dashields Lock and Dam, constructed by the Army Corp of Engineers 1927-29, and posthumously named for David Shields.

David's Offer

Washington, Penn 27th March 1824

"Frederick Rapp Esq.

"Respected friend,

"On parting with you last, I promised that I would, immediately after conferring with my father in law, write you on the subject of the sale of our Sewickley estate. ~ I am at liberty to sell, and now offer it to you for $40,000. ~ It contains about 1,400 acres of patent land."

Just two weeks earlier, David Shields had met with Frederick Rapp, possibly, at Sewickley Bottom. Apparently, they had discussed several opportunities. But, astonishingly, Shields had suggested that the very house into which he had just moved his family might be something Rapp would wish to consider. He described in this letter what the property included, and the terms by which the Harmonists could have it, and have it all.

At Newington was a commercial blacksmith's shop and house, "a garden truck patch," and a leased pasture, which earned Shields $50 dollars per year. There was also a smaller house "with a garden farther up the creek" occupied by one of his laborers. And north of the creek were several more houses, all occupied, but where he intended his laborers to live rent free for two or three years more. "In case of purchase I expect you will give my workmen, if they desire it, employ for 6 or 12 months, there are but 4 or 5 and I can recommend them. My carpenters may be taken at once into your employ, I suppose you will want them."

Leet's Tavern or Halfway House, later known as Larks Inn, and now a private residence, photographed for Charles Stotz's *The Architecture of Western Pennsylvania* in 1930.

Halfway House was also included in the offer. It commanded a rent of $150 per year. In addition, "A lot of about 100 feet by 200 feet [is] conveyed to the Methodist Society, on which they have a meeting house." Further, the letter suggests that there are more houses whose leases are to end the following spring.

Shields laid out a few exclusions clarifying his earlier conversation with Frederick. "All the land South of the Creek except my garden and patch, and pasturage for my horses and cattle the ensuing summer, you may have at once into your possession. My dwelling house I must reserve untill October next, and the landments occupied by my workmen and tenants untill 1 April 1825 ~ I shall go on with my improvements untill you return westward, but shall keep an account of all expenditures made for improvements after the first of April, to be added to the purchase, or paid for by you."

The Harmonists could have all that David offered for a deposit of $5,000 on the first of May next, and $5,000 the following April, at which time interest would begin to accrue while the remaining $30,000 was paid. David was clearly confident in the good credit and wealth of the Society.

He then expressed something more than just the terms he wished to confirm. Either he meant to hype his offer, or perhaps his intent was to "open a back door" on his expectations. "Having while at Sewickley stated to you, that if I sold I would take $40,000, I will not forfeit my word, yet when I come to calculate the items of value and expenditures, I believe I have undervalued the estate, which comprises a body of the best land in Pennsylvania... Should you care not purchase my lands I do feel most highly interested that you should purchase in my neighborhood, for after a period of nearly twenty years, in all our various relations, I have always had the greatest satisfaction, and more than from any other sources ~ It would indeed be agreeable to me to have my residence near to you."

The letter does not include mention of the several other ideas that Shields might have presented to the younger Rapp; he only states that there was more land contiguous to his own that could be made available. Finally, Shields reflected on "next steps."

> "In a matter of this magnitude, there may some lesser points occur hereafter, to be adjusted, but none other now occur to me. ~ Our friend John Way Esq. is I presume engaged in the commission given to him, to which I will give all my aid to him as I return home, which will be in a few days. ~ Write me addressed to Sewickley-bottoms PO Allegheny C. S Pa.
>
> Your friend
>
> David Shields
>
> "I shall write you on my return home, as to Squire Way's and my progress on that Commission there."

The Harmonists' Economy

George Rapp wasted no time in replying to his son about Shields's offer.

> Harmonie April 8, 1824
>
> "Frederich:
>
> "Yesterday the 7th I received your letter, and looked over your discoveries. About Schielt's [Shield's] land, [which] I would have considered mostly good and useful land, I have a dissatisfaction with it, first of all because it gets flooded, secondly because it is too high in price. You leave it to him. I have already forgotten it… I am quite sick of flooded lands."

George did show his interest in property further down the Ohio, some of which he thought might have been owned by Shields or, at least, by some acquaintance of his. This included land that Frederick Rapp identified in part as Legionville for which he noted elevations that obviated any likely flooding.

Expressive of the elder Rapp's calculating mind, he wrote:

> "Of course there would be several questions in my mind. If it would be useful, I will mention only a few, for which you will excuse me: is there a creek or run on the place where the city will be laid out, or could one lead one there, or not far from it; is there per chance a spring nearby, which could be brought in by pipes; does the place also have some fall so that rain and water from the roof can be brought away; how far will the nearest houses be from the river; is

there a convenient place to make a ford, or must one take a long and circuitous path; is there also a landing place of still water, and a secure place to land boats or even a steamboat; or can art and work make something like that…if even by use of pulleys…"

Rapp carried on with a dozen more questions about whether or not there were large stones, suitable wood for building, ground water, etcetera and etcetera. The premise that Frederick would not or might not have determined such things himself suggests that George was either pedantic or surprisingly mistrusting. The many questions also suggest that the elder Rapp was quite anxious to relocate his Society and to do so quickly. In the same letter, he worried about how many people could travel at once on a steamboat.

Frederick pressed on with David, inquiring about the other opportunities he might have posed earlier. And, so, David wrote back from Washington that Frederick, then in Pittsburgh, should meet Ephraim Blaine.

*   *   *   *   *

Actually, there were at the time three Ephraim Blaines living in southwestern Pennsylvania. One was a nephew, and two were grandchildren of the late Commissary General (and food financier) of Valley Forge. One grandson in particular, Ephraim Lyon Blaine, was a partner of John Hoge Ewing who had married Blaine's sister Ellen. Both were graduates of Washington College (later Washington & Jefferson College) and both had settled near Washington on estates each had inherited. John H. Ewing was a direct descendant of both Brigadier General James Ewing (whose troops failed to cross the Delaware to Trenton) and David Hoge who had laid out Washington. The Hoges and the Ewings had later acquired thousands of acres in the region, many directly from the estate of Robert Morris, but, in particular, one thousand acres—specifically, tracts 15 through 19 of Leet's survey— indirectly from Isaac Melcher.[6] In or around 1812, Ephraim's father, James Blaine, had built a large frame house on Ewing land near Beaver Creek where Blaine sometime managed a small, but promising plantation.

---

[6] A Barracks-master of the Revolution, he owned 1,000 acres of what had once been known as Logstown, then Legionville (now Ambridge); in 1787, he had laid out a town he called Montmorin there, but died   before   it   could be built.

David Shields, of course, was his neighbor.

In April of 1824, the deal was cut. For much less than $30,000, George Rapp and his 745 Harmonists purchased the 2,200 acres that would soon become *Oekonomie*. Father George soon moved into Ephraim Blaine's house.

First, however, Frederick would have to get his fellow Harmonists from Indiana to Legionville and, secondly (although ideally first,) he would have to sell the commune at Harmonie on the Wabash. Both challenges were solved expediently, yet at incredible expense. To get the remaining six hundred Rappites to their new home, Frederick commissioned the building of a new steamboat, named *The William Penn*. The 156-ton vessel was crafted in Phillipsburg (now Monaca) at the Phillips and Graham boatyards and launched in late June.[7] The boat cost in excess of $20,000.[8] And to affect the disposal of their former community, Frederick advertised in Philadelphia and London papers. Welsh textile manufacturer Robert Owen, then passionate to settle his experiment in utopian socialism, purchased all of Harmony for $150,000. The village, with 20,000 acres, included six mechanics shops, three barns, a large brick church, two distilleries, and eighty-six log homes. It was worth well more than twice the closing price. Yet, in fact, Owen could have had it all for $125,000 if he would have committed to a five year term.[9]

Frederick's swift actions showed just how wealthy the Harmonist Society had become.

And, still, better days were ahead.

---

[7] *Pittsburgh Weekly Gazette*, October 23, 1832

[8] A price relative to that which the boatyard fetched for similar and larger steam craft.

[9] Arndt, *George Rapp's Harmony Society*, pg. 294

A Farm Mansion

David Shields might have hoped for a quick sale of his estate at Newington to the Harmonists. While his expenses to move into a mostly unfurnished house were significant, the real cost to build the country mansion was extraordinary. Extraordinary, that is, because they amounted to almost nothing. His two greatest costs were labor and time. Quite significantly, materials do not factor into the picture. Consider that all of the lumber, every brick and each roof shingle used to build the two and half story structure was manufactured on site, all from raw materials nearby. Consider that, other than the hourly wages billed by James Kerr, his expense for all other labor was mostly paid in tobacco, coffee, and salted mackerel. Consider, too, that Shields, by profession, could barter for anything wholesale.

From Shields's daybook dated August 2, 1823:

Bill of carpenter work, sawing hewing de[tail?] of house and stable, and roofing Saw-mill at Sewickley as per bill from James Kerr carpenter, who was appointed to measure frame	$1,433.23
Saw-mill, trunks, head gate & boarded himself	213.00
Sleds, windlaps, repairing carts, wheel barrows and sundry other jobs at Sewickley	40.00
Landing the stuff & putting up 90 pannels pails [?] at 62 ½	53.00
Putting up posts and boarding part of fence at the back of garden (Sewickley)	10.00
Gate and posts at barn	4.00
Relaying barn floor and bars for barn doors	7.00

Making screen for lime	1.50
Sawing done in addition to Kerr's bill	9.00
Iron wrench and digger	2.25

By comparison, the cost of nails and mortar and tools apparently were far less expensive than the tastes of his wife and daughters. Just one itemized receipt, for which David reimbursed Abishai Way in January of 1824, reveals the following:

Garden tools	$3.38
Ladies Garden Boots	3.00
Straw Hats (x3)	1.50
Churn	5.00
Fire doggs [anvils]	1.50
Tinware	3.69
Brass knobs	9.00
Ticking [or mattresses]	17.82
Rolled Iron [for bed frames]	16.24
Cloth for Maria	12.19
Misc. Merchandize for Maria	24.57

Maria's miscellaneous expenses suggest the cost of a daughter coming of age. Turning twenty in September, she would need clothing and accoutrement respective of a women entering society. A family situated in a grand house could ill afford to let down appearances and yet serve a community of upward mobility in an age of newfound access to communities far and wide.

A Post Office

As the Victorian Age stratified expectations, when steam boat travel brought family, visitors and new customs to western lands, and while an economy of erstwhile homesteaders met with the ever-expanding opportunities of trade with eastern industry, families like the Shieldses were shaped by meeting the challenges of success. For David, this meant his livelihood would need to be more sedentary, more rooted, more integral to the community in which he, again, had championed great esteem. For David, it meant taking on a new career. He became postmaster of one of the first offices west of Pittsburgh.

Indeed, he was appointed to the task. Yet, by no small effort had he lobbied for that appointment. Postmasters were paid well, upwards of $700 per year. The job required extensive accounting of cash, ensuring security for bank notes received, and meeting deliveries with flexible punctuality. That is, one never quite knew when the next coach would arrive, but when it did, the postmaster's presence was absolutely mandatory, not just for mail coming in, but for that going out, too.

The tools of the trade were few; a balance scale and standardized map were essential. All postage in 1824 was charged by weight as well as by the distance it was to travel. A letter was a single sheet of paper, folded in a clever way, and sealed with wax, to obviate the necessity of a separate envelope. Paper was too expensive then. A letter was expected to weigh less than half an ounce. For that letter to travel less than 30 miles, the cost of postage was six cents. Farther, yet less than 80 miles, ten cents. Up to 150 miles, twelve and half cents. 400 miles; eighteen and three-quarter cents. The maximum was twenty-five cents. Exceptions were many. To mail a newspaper cost just a penny; the grand experiment of the original postal service was to support the ideals of a free press. Letter rates for steam boat delivery, and later by train, however were more favorable. But, despite what might seem like cheap rates, in 1824, twenty cents then was roughly $5 today. The success of the U.S. Post Office was, by 1845, so threatened by financial collapse, Congress decided two things. First, it cut postal rates to just five cents or ten cents, demarcated by a distance of 300 miles. And secondly, Congress directed funds into a newly considered postal "service" to actively subsidize the nation's transportation infrastructure. Only by investing in riverboat navigation and the development of railroad lines could the United States Postal Service command the monopoly it needed to survive. Of course, it would never break even. And never has.

One of many perks David Shields enjoyed as the postmaster of Sewickley Bottom was free postage for himself and his family. Another significant benefit, too, was furnishing his new post office inside his own home where he could also run a general store. One might estimate that his revenues from the sale of flour, tobacco, bolting cloths, and Ol' Mon was twice the income he earned from stamping letters and distributing the mail. Yet again, David discovered a wealth few pioneers had ever experienced.

Maria Leet Shields

Maria Shields did not attend school in the privileged way her mother Eliza had. Washington in its earliest days allowed for the education of young men through the ministry of its several churches of which the Presbyterians took active measures to include even the youngest child, regardless of financial means. But girls were not included. Little women like Maria were mostly educated at the heels of their mothers in all practices of domestic "science," which is to say, cooking, sewing, and cleaning. Religious education was a daily ritual practiced at home by memorizing Bible passages, psalms and common prayer. In Washington, the First Baptist Church, for which David Shields, Hugh Wilson and Daniel Moore served as original trustees, employed the Reverend Charles Wheeler as its first pastor beginning in 1815, but his congregation owned no specific church or meeting house until subscriptions to erect one were drawn up in 1819.[10] A small brick schoolhouse on Belle Street served as the Baptists' first house of worship. Somewhat surprisingly, however, in 1816, the trustees of the church, along with Reverend Wheeler, adopted an unusual initiative to establish a Female Baptist Seminary.[11] There can be some doubt about who might have influenced that progressive measure, but there can be no doubt that Maria Leet Shields, then twelve or thirteen, attended the new Seminary's classes.

Like his fellow trustees, Hugh Wilson was a merchant of Washington. Like David, too, he owned a shop on Main Street and purveyed "a large and general assortment of Dry-Goods." Otherwise competitors, Hugh and

---

[10] Crumrine, *History of Washington County,* pg. 517

[11] Creigh, *History of Washington County,* pg. 197

David were actually first cousins by marriage—Hugh's mother, Rebecca, was Daniel Leet's sister, whose niece, Eliza, David married. Confusing as it may seem, Hugh's brother, John, was also a merchant in town. John and his wife had twelve children. Their tenth-born, John Knox Wilson, also became a merchant and, having bought the house into which he was born, conducted his business on the east side of Main street opposite the new courthouse. It would seem, in these circles, all good men were either merchants or Baptists; the best among them, of course, were both.

At 21 years of age, newly moved to Newington, Maria Leet Shields married John K. Wilson. The wedding was celebrated on March 12, 1825, at Newington. It was likely the first large gathering David and Eliza hosted at their new estate.

In earlier days, weddings on the frontier were more rowdy than religious. Guests travelled unbridled paths of great distances to attend a brief ceremony, sworn on the family Bible and perhaps blessed with a succinct prayer. Good wishes were followed by countless jugs of rye and endless roasts of meat. Surely one guest played a fiddle. Several more might have twanged Jew's harps. The festivities ended only when the last person slumped to the ground, too tipsy or tired to dance. Typically, the newlyweds were promised the cabin's loft for their first night. Yet, only if the father of the bride owned a barn where the revelry might continue, was the young couple afforded any privacy. Guests stayed for days.

In 1825, the occasion of a young merchant's marriage to a more prominent associate's daughter called for a more civilized, respectable and spiritual ceremony. It also called for the men to wear their best Sunday suits and the women to present themselves in a fashion only they, by their own hands, would have created. The adornment of colorful new ribbons would excuse a lady's attendance in some dress she might have worn for other occasions. Dress design aspired to what few women might have seen of French fashions, yet, in 1825, illustrations of the same were rare in western Pennsylvania.[12] Children wore whatever they wore on any other given day; they were not to speak or be seen anyway.

In the Shields's new house, the ceremony was drawn from scripture, delivered by the Reverend John Graham, and attended by only the closest of

---

[12] America's first illustrated women's journal, *Godey's Ladies Book* did not begin publishing until 1830.

friends and family.[13] Unlike celebrations along the frontier, the wedding was solemn, a spiritual union blessed more for its practical value than any ideals of love or lasting devotion. Certainly, Maria's marriage was prearranged, a transaction of the newlyweds' fathers. Young women were given little patience to express their romantic interests. To do so was damningly sinful.

The wedding took place on a Saturday. The last day of the work week, it allowed invited guests to travel up from Washington, partake in the ceremony, enjoy supper and a fruitcake, and return home. Agnes Hays recalled her visit to Newington perhaps on this occasion.[14] She was a little girl, around eight, accompanied by her grandparents, arriving from Washington the day before the ceremony. While she may have been wrong about the date of the wedding, or conflated her visit with another, she described some of the many joys of being with the Shields family. "What good manners we had when we went visiting; one's feet always dangled from the horsehair sofa or chairs; you never volunteered a remark, and always said "Yes, Ma'am" or "No, Ma'am," and by and by grown ups would say something, and a little tray with paradisiac cookies and little cut-glass goblets, just big enough for your doll, would come in, and your grandmother would say, "No wine for Aggie, please.

"Where now-a-days do we see people like Miss Hannah and Miss Rebecca Shields, or Miss Anne or Miss Mary Way, or meet with such gracious hospitality? What a real plantation life was lived here; what a majestic presence was Mrs. Shields; what a Quaker gentleman was Mr. Shields! When we retired he handed my grandmother her silver candlestick from the hall table, just as people in the English novels do."[15]

Apparently, no Jew's harps or jugs of rye gave jubilant rise to jig.

Mr. and Mrs. John Knox Wilson would return to his once-bachelor house in Washington. As a wedding gift, David Shields had arranged for his workers to re-shingle the roof.

---

[13] Washington Examiner transcription noted in Ancestry.com.

[14] Agnes McFadden Hays Gormly was the eldest daughter of General Alexander Hays and his wife, Anne McFadden. Her maternal grandparents lived in Washington, PA, and were close friends of David and Eliza.

[15] Gormly, *Old Penn Street,* pg. 29

News of the Day

The following five items all appeared in the same, four-page issue of The
Pittsburgh Weekly Gazette, dated January 28, 1825:

> "A curious fact has come out—that a treaty concluded with the In-
> dians in Mr. Jefferson's time, and carried into effect—was never sub-
> mitted to the Senate for ratification, and no vestige of it is found in
> the public archives. Mr. Jefferson, in a letter on the subject, recog-
> nizes the copy now produced by the Indians, as genuine, and attrib-
> utes the omission to neglect. It's odd. —*V. Record*"

*   *   *   *   *

> "FOR ST. LOUIS. The New Steam Boat, WILLIAM PENN, will
> be ready by the 1st of February next, and will leave this port, for St.
> Louis, on the opening of the navigation. For freight or passage apply
> to:
>
> > Robert Lindell & Co.
> > Commission Merchants, or to
> > A. Way & Co."

*   *   *   *   *

> "**For the curious.** In digging a cellar on the island opposite this town,
> at the depth of about five feet, several Indian darts [arrowheads]
> were found. These darts are of stone, cut to the same shape with

those that have been found at all Indian encampments in the first settlement of the country, and bear the marks of great antiquity. The quere is, whether they were deposited with the bones of their owners at a period so distant that the bones have become incorporated with their mother earth, so as not to be distinguished from it—or whether the soil that covers them is alluvion. Trees of enormous growth stood a few years ago at the spot where this cellar has been dug. —*Harrisb. Chron.*"

*   *   *   *   *

"Friday, January 22, 1825

Mr. Owen of Lanark, has returned from Indiana. We understand he has purchased Harmony from Mr. Rapp, and that he intends to establish a community there on the plan adopted by him for ameliorating the condition of the working classes of society. On Tuesday last he delivered a Lecture, in explanation of this plan, to a very crowded audience in the First Presbyterian Church of this City."

*   *   *   *   *

"CANAL POLICY.
(Communicated by the Philadelphia Society for promoting Internal Improvements.)

The importance of a connection between the Allegheny and Susquehannah rivers, by means of a canal, and so by improving the beds of the rivers communicating with these great waters, as to make upon them a complete ascending and descending steam-boat navigation, has never been sufficiently considered and appreciated by the citizens of Pennsylvania. To them the accomplishments of these improvements is of the highest consequence; and their influence on the prosperity and wealth of our state, when perfected, would be unbounded. They would enable the western portions of the commonwealth to arrive at the Atlantic markets by an easy, certain and cheap success ..."

A Schoolhouse and More

Newington was much more than a residential estate befitting the status of a young, wealthy family of southwestern Pennsylvania. Even before Maria was married, work had begun on other "necessaries" otherwise available only in the city of Pittsburgh.

With seven children living on the grounds, (the eldest, Leet Shields, was approaching his 18th birthday, and the youngest, Hannah, her fourth,) David and Eliza began construction on a one-room schoolhouse. This, too, was constructed of brick. It had a single chimney and hearth, six windows and one door. Although built on the estate, it was situated across Beaver Road from Newington, presumably to make "more public" its benefits to neighboring children.

But the schoolhouse served another vital purpose. Although a Methodist church had long existed nearby, the schoolhouse became a Friday night meeting house, Sunday school and sometime house of worship. Earlier services, both by the Methodist Society and at John Way's barn, led as early as 1798 by the Episcopalian minister, Dr. Francis Reno, helped establish, if not differentiate, a very small community of faith.[16] If their timing was right, itinerant pastors, of which dozens travelled the Beaver Road each month, had an eager audience on any given Friday night or Sunday morning. The schoolhouse still stands today, its original rafters exposed and charred from a later pot stove elevated there. (The idea, however dangerous, was to generate more ambient heat.)

---

[16] Allison, *Presbyterianism in Sewickley Valley*, pg. 11

Evident from later sales, David built other houses in the area, separating sufficient land from his holdings to accommodate the interest of families moving out from the city to tend more extensive gardens or to serve the growing needs of the nascent neighborhood. He posted regular advertisements in the Pittsburgh Weekly Gazette, promoting, "Several tracts and parts of tracts of Land, improved and unimproved, in Allegheny and Beaver counties." He pushed property "3 miles North of the Ohio river, 2 miles S[outh] of Johnston's mills, 4 miles E[ast] of Economy, and 16 miles NW of Pittsburgh," where there "is a good stand for a Blacksmith's shop, having been occupied as such for several years." He offered for lease his father-in-law's Halfway House, too. "The Stone House and appurtenant buildings, the half-way House between Pittsburgh and Beaver, on the Sewickley Bottom... and also the meadows, pastures, and first rate farming land connected therewith." Even as new houses sprung forth, long held property sold with it. David and Eliza spurred economic development well before anyone would call it that.

Their days were busy and bountiful. The times were pleasant and productive. It would seem that life in their chosen valley teemed with commerce and comforts never before realized. Even Newington saw the addition of an ice house, a summer kitchen and, most importantly, the bounties of a well-cultivated garden.

The benefits of residential gardens to the health and nutrition of family were essential. Gardens were cultivated not just for vegetables, fruits or spices, but for reasons obvious only to early Americans. Author Ann Leighton (a non de plume of Isadore Smith) explained succinctly in her 1986 volume on colonial gardens:

"The garden close to the dwelling, neatly fenced, and bright with "a variety of flowers" was as much her [the housewife's] domain as her kitchen and her still room. Throughout the seventeenth century she must be able to extract from it all she would need for flavorings and seasonings and garnishings, for insect repellents and deodorants, for changing the air in rooms and keeping out moths and rodents and snakes, for dyeing and fulling and 'teasing,' for concocting syrups and cordials and waters, for making plasters and salves and coated pills, for treating wounds and aiding in childbirths and in laying out the dead. And of course, all of these plants, useful and dull though they may sound, were capable of bursting into fragrant bloom to make gardens gay and pleasant spots."

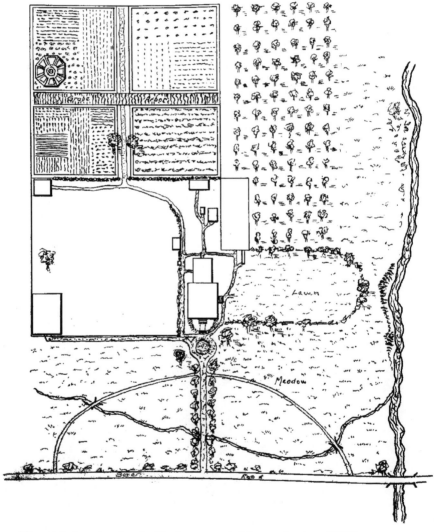

The original garden plan for Newington, copied from a drawing of 1823.
From *Gardens of Colony and State,* published by the Garden Club of America in 1931.

Eliza Shields's garden, indeed, was as much a medicine cabinet, as it was a fruit stand, vineyard, and brilliant ecosystem of fragrant flowers and prized herbs. South of the house, but not more than 100 yards toward the Ohio River, Shields and his laborers had fenced in a garden of about 60,000 square feet, divided into four square, raised beds. A grassy path separated the east and west beds, while a grape arbor ran between the north and south beds. Two cedar trees, well-pruned to encourage dense shade, attracted humming-birds essential to pollination.

Sarah E. Bissell, a Shields descendant, described the early garden in a 1931 publication of the Garden Clubs of America, titled *Gardens of Colony and State*:

> "The garden was outlined by beds of smaller fruits, raspberries, white, pink, and red; gooseberries, strawberries—backed by trellis grapes, white and purple, sharing their sunlight with the herb bed, where grew sage, thyme, and sweet marjoram, rosemary and later tarragon. In the midst of the garden flourished all the old-time flowers, growing in a mass of gorgeous bloom."

Apparently, the Shields family exchanged many seedlings and graft cuttings with the Harmonists who were highly successful arborist and vintners.

The original gardens at Newington grew fox-gloves, jasmine, sweet briar and moss, each cultivated for home health remedies. Besides corn, wheat, rye, and alfalfa grown on larger, open fields, Newington also boasted a significant orchard, in which peaches grew early and apples ripened late into fall.

Sarah Bissell took note of another addition to the grand house: "And then, to fix the garden to ancient times, we find an Indian mound. This has been surmounted by a stone-foundationed summer house strong enough to deter marauding hand from disturbing the Indian grave resting quietly below." Daniel Leet would have seen this earthwork when first he surveyed the well-watered bottoms of the Depreciation Lands. The great mound became his own.

The gardens of Newington would be transformed several times over in future years, prized as they are to the present day.

The Harmonists' Industry

The Harmonists, busy building their new village at Economy, aided neighbors like David Shields in many ways. In addition to sharing the fruits of their vineyards and flowerbeds (apparently, the Harmonists' dahlias were much prized,) Rapp's industrious families also provided wool, flax, and cotton cloths to neighbors, as well as to the wholesale markets of Pittsburgh, Washington and Wheeling. Since their return to Pennsylvania, the Harmonists employed steam power for their manufactories. Seemingly overnight, the town of Economy was booming.

And David Shields was now busier than ever. His partnership with Abishai Way produced sales neither could ever have imagined.

An article in the National Gazette of October 1827 informed the general public of Economy's astounding development:

> "The town is laid out into twelve squares, each being about 15 rods in length and breadth [a rod equaling 16.6 feet], with broad streets intersecting each other at right angles. There are one hundred buildings in the town, eighty of which are dwelling houses; the other buildings are, a large meeting house, with a steeple and town clock; a large and commodious hotel; a four story cotton and woolen factory, built of brick, in which the finest cloths are manufactured; a four story wooden building, for a grist mill; an oil mill; a distillery; a tannery; and several other establishments, for prosecuting mechanical business."[17]

---

[17] Arndt, *George Rapp's Harmony Society,* pg. 384

So extraordinary was the annual production of wool and cotton goods at Economy, Frederick Rapp was invited to speak in Washington, D.C. before the House of Representatives. He could not attend, citing his "bad health of several weeks," but he did later answer the House Committee's detailed subpoena, showing that their "cotton millinery" was highly profitable, and that their woolen lines were stable, despite a glut of foreign wool sitting outside East coast mills.

Of particular note in Rapp's communications with the committee was his inclusion of the Harmonists' interest and early experiments in raising silk. This "scientific art" George Rapp's granddaughter had learned from the Shakers. Even as early as 1826, her silk process outproduced any other in the United States.

Silver & Sorrow

Late in April, 1827, one Erasmus Thomas of Philadelphia appraised the value of goods and chattels belonging to the estate of the deceased widow of Thomas Shields. Hannah Cox Shields died on the 21st of March at the age of 74. The executors of her estate—none of whom were her stepsons—declared that the sum of her belongings did not exceed $1,000, and that her debts were less than $2,000, apparent benchmarks that obviated certain taxes.

Hannah Cox Shields's Last Will and Testament does not account for any real estate then owned by her. The will bequeaths only a few items of some sentimental value to friends and family. To her step-granddaughter, Hannah Shields, then just five years old, she willed "One Silver Coffee Pot, a pair of Silver tea Potts, a Silver Sugar dish and tongs, four Silver Salts with Silver spoons thereto belonging, and four Silver table spoons marked H.S." She gave to David Shields, "Son of my late Husband, the pictures or likenesses of Mr. & Mrs. Shields."

Of the dozens of goods and chattels not bequeathed, the two most valuable items were a set of Silver "pooridgers" at $18, and a feather bed and beddings at $20. The document states she had $105 in cash on hand.

Indeed, the properties in which Hannah Shields once resided had been sold by her step-sons, the brothers now happy to settle down in their respective towns. Robert, his wife Mary Helen Jackson, and five children, established a village in Wayne County, near Damascus, later to be known as Shieldsboro. Thomas Jr. carried forward at his estate in Philadelphia. And John, whom his brother David visited often in Philadelphia, did not venture far from his Chestnut Street home. Several of David's letters to his son Thomas make note of John's chronic ill health.

Matters Now Moot

Political winds changed in 1829 when Inauguration Day that March brought Andrew Jackson to the White House.

All along the Ohio River, a favorable spring brought unusually bountiful crops to July markets.

Midsummer brought Eliza and David to dine "with Mr. Rapp and Society, about 700 in number… an assemblage of healthy and happy faces."

And, the 19th of August brought Daniel Leet to Newington.

Failing in memory and might, conditions apparently too constant for Mrs. Arden's care, Daniel Leet, at long last, came to rest on his Sewickley Bottoms land. Some 45 years had passed since first he surveyed its tracts, then wild and densely forested. Now a plantation of seven hundred fertile acres aided by a small army of farmhands, domestics and craftsmen, Newington was now home. Here he was surrounded by six grandchildren, a devoted and generous son-in-law, and an adoring daughter. The comforts of family had been few and long ago. Now, he could rest. However insecure, introverted or ignoble he might have been about the windfall that became Newington were matters now moot.

Not that many remembered or cared.

*　　*　　*　　*　　*

On November 26, Thanksgiving Day, 1829, Eliza Leet Shields died. She was 15 years old. No cause of death, if ever recorded, is known. A close friend, Catherine Wilson Way, wrote in her journal, "May I die the death of the riteous, and may my last end be like hers."

*   *   *   *   *

In June of the following year, 1830, Daniel Leet breathed his last in his bedroom at Newington.

> "**Died**—on the 17th at his residence with his son-in-law David Shields, Esq. in Sewickley Bottom, Allegheny County, at the advanced age of 82 years, our respected fellow citizen, Major Daniel Leet. Early in the revolutionary struggle he entered the Virginia line of the American forces, was soon promoted to the office of Brigade Major, in which capacity he served many years with much credit to himself. His father having emigrated from Prince William county, Va. to the country in 1779, and the Indians at that early period being troublesome to the settlements of the whites, he was induced by filial piety to come to this county & share with his parents the dangers of a frontier settlement. Soon after his arrival, he opposed manly resistance to the invasions and degradation of the Indians, and in the summer of 1782 distinguished himself as a soldier in the memorable battle with the Indians, best known by the name of Crawford's defeat, on the plains of Sandusky—He then holding a Major's command. ~ For many years before his death, he had retired from the active scenes of life, and now has descended to the grave, ripe in years, and after, it is humbly hoped, having made his peace with God and all mankind. 'Peace be to his ashes.' Washington, June 22, 1830"

~ The Examiner and Farmers' and Mechanics' Repositor,
Vol. XIV, No. 7, Washington, PA June 26, 1830

Daniel Leet was buried at Newington, the second of many souls to rest in peace there. But his body later would be exhumed and moved. His final resting place would be found on familiar ground, yet buried in an edifice unlike any other then erected on western Pennsylvania property.

Partnership Dissolved

Grief took its toll. David and Eliza languished in remorse and sorrow.

David, ever preoccupied with the logistics of postal management, and applying Cicero's ideal to his improved livelihood, ended his long partnership with Abishai Way.

He promoted in the local paper:

"DISOLUTION OF PARTNERSHIP. —

The partnership of the subscribers, late trading under the firm of Abishai Way & Co., has been dissolved by mutual consent. Those indebted to the late firm are requested to call and settle their accounts, and make payment to Abishai Way: those having claim against the concern will present them for payment.

ABISHAI WAY
DAVID SHIELDS
Pittsburgh, April 13, 1831"

As if to defend himself in light of David's professional departure, Abishai posted the following just below the above notice:

"ABISHAI WAY
will continue business at the old stand, No. 47 Market street,
where he is now opening a new stock of Foreign and Domestic
DRY GOODS, suited to the season...
together with a large supply of genuine
"ANKER" BOLTING CLOTHS,

And
Whittemore's Superior Machine Cards.
Also on consignment,
Woollen and Cotton Goods manufactured by the
Harmony Society:
All of which will be sold at the lowest market prices,
On accommodating terms."

Of other notices in the same issue of the Pittsburgh Weekly Gazette were advertisements for the latest attractions at Lambdin's Museum where, for 25 cents admission, patrons could witness "30 taxidermed quadrupeds including a Cougar, or American Brown Tiger; 7 species of monkey; the Emu, from South America, 5 1/2 feet high, and more than 300 Foreign and American Birds, including two living White Crows."

A separate notice promoted the recent exhibit of a scene of "the late murder in Salem, in wax, depicting the murderer Richard [Crowninshield], one hand on the pulse of the victim, and the other arm raised with a dagger. Numbers of ladies, it is said, have been so wrought upon, by looking at this scene, as to faint away." (Never mind that Crowninshield's victim was famously clubbed to death.)

Also to be viewed in Pittsburgh, on a canvas measuring 200 square feet, was William Dunlap's oil depiction of CHRIST REJECTED. "In composition, perspective, coloring, and general effect, it is much superior to any historic production yet exhibited in this city, and merits the reputation and success that have hitherto attended it… Admittance 25 cents."

Frederick Rapp

America was awash with con men in the first half of the nineteenth century; it would seem gullibility was epidemic. Such disease could be cured only by the ruin of its host or the destitution of its victims. Thousands fell prey, for example, to James Jesse Strang and his brazen ascension to the Mormon throne at Beaver Island, Michigan. Tens of thousands flocked to the museés and traveling freak shows staged by P.T. Barnum. Hundreds of thousands more sought immediate relief from gout, pleurisy and ague by purchasing miracle elixirs made of snake oil.

Scholars of George Rapp's Christian commune at Economy concur that the separatist movement by which he had convinced hundreds to depart for America and create their own (and several) "peaceable kingdoms" was not driven by liturgical doctrine nor by the piety of spiritual devotion. The fact is, the Harmonists were never as much a church as they were a congregation. George Rapp had convinced his followers from the beginning that there was one true object to their efforts: to embrace with open arms their savior, Jesus Christ, returning to live among them in a "living heaven" on earth. Their success would come not from collective prayer, but from subjecting personal freedom for the betterment of the whole. How, after thirty years of sweat and toil, they wholeheartedly believed the golden millennium was still so soon to come was not so much the sure promise of their Savior as it was of George Rapp.

Proof of this notion came by way of one Count Leon, a self-professed messiah, who Rapp himself introduced to the Harmonists as "Archduke Maximillian of the Stem of Judah and the Root of David." Late in 1829, Rapp received a number of gilt-edged letters announcing the visit of this "holy man" who, arriving with nearly half a million dollars, was seeking to purchase 100,000 acres to which his own adherents would flock, supposedly by the thousands, and—only if amenable to the Harmonists—join them in their daily devotions to work and prayer. Count Leon was actually one Dr. Samuel Goentgen, an imposter and con man. In addition to his supposed wealth, Count Leon arrived with rare stones for the practice (and assured perfection) of alchemy. He also arrived with such flourish and ceremony no one doubted his legitimacy. Within a year, he proved he was a venerable debater of Christian dogma, but only a handful of his promised followers followed and no new wealth benefited the economy of Economy. Count Leon's only achievement was convincing about a hundred sycophants to separate from the community, reclaim their investments, and follow him to a new "promised land" where they would carve out a new haven. The town was then Phillipsburg which they renamed New Philadelphia. Ultimately, Count Leon proved he was no Father Rapp—and most certainly not the financial manager that Frederick was. After many failed months, he escaped his mutinous followers, fled to New Orleans, and later died in Texas.

The "great secession" instigated by Count Leon created a hole in the heart of the Harmonists that took years to mend. Yet, in shouldering on, the devoted Rappites became ever more productive and profitable than at any time before. Somehow, amidst all the accusations, recriminations, litigations, and ultimate negotiations to rid Economy of its charlatan infection, Frederick Rapp had stayed focused. The steam boat *William Penn* now plied a network of rivers, its paddle wheels churning up profit at every bend. The Harmonists' venture into silk cloths excited a nation of aspiring gentility, and the output of the wool mill at Economy outpaced any other along the Atlantic seaboard.

That is, until November 25, 1833.

Frederick Rapp wrote to Abishai Way the next morning about the terrible fire that burned the wool mill to ashes. The conflagration would set the Society back countless months of steady, predictable income. The younger Rapp became restless, anxious and hypersensitive. By spring, despite a painfully long visit to see physicians in Philadelphia, Frederick returned home and laid in bed, unable to attend to the thousands of decisions he had had to make every day. He died on June 24, 1834. The official cause of death was "dropsy"—edema—of the chest. He was fifty-nine years old.

As if the memory of Frederick Rapp might someday fail him, David Shields wrote in his day book: "FR was… a man of great and strong mind, always noted for his diligence and correct habits. The writer of this has been an intimate acquaintance of the now deceased for thirty years past, and bears testimony to the many excellent traits of character of the dec'd."

Within two years, Abishai Way, too, would die, of unknown cause, at the age of 44, leaving behind his wife and three of seven children. David Shields made no mention of his death in his journal.

Thomas Leet Shields

Odd in many respects, relative to the scores of extant letters that survive as correspondence between David Shields and his sons—evidently, Eliza was more likely to correspond with her daughters—is the absence of his eldest boy, Leet. David's journals say nothing about his first son's schooling, his comings and goings, or his participation in activities in Washington or at Newington. Of course, the most plausible reason for this is that Leet never left home. Census records show he was listed as a resident of Newington even in 1870. Two years older than his brother and three years younger than Maria, he never married.

Thomas L. Shields, on the other hand, is active in his father's journals. He attended Washington College where professor T. M. T. McKennan instructed him in the law. In 1830, two months after his maternal grandfather's death, Thomas was taken by David to board at "Mrs. Fletcher's in Philadelphia." The following summer, he departed on the steamboat *Amulet* for Cincinnati where his maternal grandfather had owned considerable property. Apparently, little of it had been attended to, and in light of sorting out his father-in-law's estate, David sent Thomas to deal with certain matters. One in particular related to the sale of waterfront property at Letart Falls, Ohio. Returning home in the Fall of 1831, Thomas was admitted to the Bar in Washington County and, a month later, on November 3, 1831, the Bar of Allegheny County.[18] In December, he took an afternoon coach to Pittsburgh "to board with Mrs. A., the rent of his office to commence the following day."

---

[18] Twentieth Century Bench and Bar of Allegheny County, Vol. 2, 1903

A January ad appeared in the Pittsburgh Weekly Gazette:

"THOMAS L. SHIELDS
Attorney at Law
Office at the South West corner of
Market Street and the Diamond—
entrance No. 3 in the Diamond."[19]

By spring, promotion of "Valuable Property FOR SALE" appeared in local papers relating to the very opportunity he had attended to the previous fall. "For particulars, respecting the property and the country, inquire of Thomas L. Shields, Esq., or William Semple, of the firm of Bissell & Semple, all of Pittsburgh."

On October 16, 1832, Thomas married Winifred Amelia Neville Chaplin. The wedding was celebrated on Montour's Island at the residence of her aunt, Mrs. Isaac Craig, where the Reverend Dr. Upfold joined the two in holy matrimony. Amelia, as she was known, was born and raised on Neville Island, the homestead of her great-grandfather General John Neville. Amelia was also the granddaughter of Pittsburgh Mayor Isaac Craig.

In 1833, the young couple—he was just 24 and she 20—moved to Batavia, Ohio, a small town outside of Cincinnati. Thomas and his bride would have eight children, all but one born in "that country," before returning twenty years later to Sewickley Bottom.

---

[19] *Pittsburgh Weekly Gazette*, Jan. 10, 1832

The Crash of 1837

Late of an evening on the 17th of November, 1835, David Shields and his laborers rescued one Reverend Leander Kerr and his sister from a terrible accident while riding a coach on Beaver Road. They presumed the pastor had fractured his leg and, so, put the siblings up for the night until a doctor could be summoned the next day. The Reverend convalesced at Newington until the 13th of December, a full four weeks after the incident. David thought it fit to record this odd visit in his journal, but he did not enter it until Christmas Eve that year. Rejoice ye pure in heart.

But, of other blessings, few were to be recorded that holiday. The state of the nation, barely in its sixth decade, was embroiled in financial panic once again. The crisis was sparked when President Jackson vetoed a bill to recharter the country's central bank, which thus gave reason to enact the Specie Circular of 1836, a national mandate requiring that western lands could be purchased only with gold or silver coin. If speculators had any intent to develop land in the new states of Ohio, Louisiana, Indiana, Mississippi, Illinois, Alabama or Missouri, there was no credit to be had. Property values plummeted, mortgages imploded, and banks collapsed everywhere. The panic of 1837 would be felt for ten years, well past Van Buren's indifferent four years, Harrison's 31 days, or Tyler's unelected and unmemorable one term. Seemingly, only when a workman at Sutter's Mill discovered gold in 1847 would the country have reason to hope again.

Of course the absence of specie stopped no one from loading up a wagon with family and tools, and heading west. If land could not be purchased for lack of currency, then squatting was the next best option. And many pioneers did just that. So many, in fact, that Congress recognized the issue by passing the Preemption Act of 1841 whereby squatters were encouraged to purchase their ill-begotten land, upwards of 160 acres, for just $1.25 per acre, a bargain at even twice the price. If not purchased within 14 months of squatting, the land would go to public market.[20] At first, the money would flow to the struggling states. But when eastern states objected, Congress then promised a fairer distribution of the proceeds to all states. (That distribution only took place the following year. The lenient, new squatters rights, however, carried on for years.)

---

[20] *The Columbia Electronic Encyclopedia,* 6th ed.

Batavia, Ohio

Thomas and his young bride could not have arrived in southwest Ohio at a worse time.

Not unlike his father, traveling great distances to do *his* father's bidding, young Thomas and his wife landed in Cincinnati to work for David. There, outside of the booming new city, was property aplenty, much of which had been set aside to serve as bounty for veterans yet not compensated after the Revolution. David Shields wished to claim Daniel Leet's bounty for Eliza. The opportunity for orphans to claim such property, although entirely legitimate, was not actively encouraged. Thus, the legal hoops Eliza, an orphan (and a woman, at that,) might have to jump through decidedly required a lawyer to do the jumping. It was with this challenge in mind that David sent Thomas into Ohio. Of course, the understanding was, if Thomas were to claim such land, he and his family would have it for themselves.

There was also the matter of Daniel Leet's lost claims to hundreds of acres in Scott County, Kentucky, too, not to mention any survey that Thomas's grandfather also had run out on thousands of acres along the Licking River. Indeed, Daniel Leet had retained hundreds of acres awarded to him by commission for his work surveying for George Mason and the Ohio Land Company. 400 acres here, 400 there, such properties had long been leased out and, in certain cases, illegally claimed. Of those still supposed to be under lease, Thomas's father needed a local agent to collect on the rents so assigned. Whether or not Thomas ever knew of the one thousand acres awarded to Leet "on the North Fork" or "along the Elkhorn" east of Frankfort was a matter long since moot. No mention of them survives. But then, too, Virginia's land records, formerly housed in Fincastle, were thought to have been transferred to Clermont County. Surely, Thomas' sleuthing would uncover much.

Ohio's once promised development had proven true. Already, the state powers had deemed that public education for all children was a priority, that slave labor was outlawed, that tax revenues would benefit landowners in measures established by individual county boards (as opposed to the state's general assembly,) and that two state canals would drive an economy never before imagined. The first canal connected Portsmouth on the Ohio River north to Chillicothe and Columbus, then east to Coshocton and Newcomerstown, and north again to Bolivar, Akron and Cleveland. The second great canal connected Cincinnati almost due north to Toledo. Known as the Miami and Erie Canal, construction began in 1825, opening all the way through in 1845. Of course, neither canal would have been viable had not the Erie Canal proved its success before 1825.

Already, Cincinnatians liked to tout their fast-growing city as the "Athens of the West." But, despite the confluence of the Miami River feeding into the Ohio not ten miles from where the Licking fed it, too, Cincinnati's greatest industry was not river oriented. Of all things, it was hog processing. Pigs by the thousands were marched into the city for slaughter and packing. Salted pork and lard then shipped out on steam boats east and south. By the mid-1830s, the industry represented significant revenues of $300,000 annually. And so, to the rest of the world, Cincinnati was better known as "Porkopolis."[21]

Conditions were thus ripe when in 1832 the first of several cholera epidemics descended on American river towns not concerned about what they dumped in their waters. Ohio's river farms were naturally blessed with rich soil. And, so, hog manure was simply dumped along fetid riverbanks, feeding a bacterial ecosystem ideal for human pestilence. Of course, no one knew the origins of cholera, thought at best to come from emanating vapors, strange and mysterious. Indeed, the disease was called Cholera Asphyxia. It could kill in a day. Those afflicted would immediately discharge "rice-water," dehydrating the body with such rapidity as to create a gray-blue skin tone. Muscles naturally contracted with such force as to become horrifically painful. Death typically followed any attempt to rehydrate one's body often

---

[21] Smith, " The Specter of Cholera in 19th Century Cincinnati," *Ohio Valley History*, Vol. 16, No. 2, Summer 2016

because the thirst-quenching water consumed came from the very source in which the bacteria had first thrived.

Young Thomas L. Shields discovered early in his Ohio venture that life would become much harder than he had ever known. Houses for rent were new, but relatively crude. Twenty-five miles southeast of Cincinnati, Batavia was a town of rough means, its few residents scrambling to make ends meet, compromised at all turns by economic conditions that reduced their livelihoods to what could be sowed, cultivated and consumed. But Batavia was also the capital of Clermont County, most of which was central to the Military District granted to Revolutionary veterans of Virginia. Shields spent months clawing for clues in Clermont's crude courthouse. In turn, he built a practice, not surprisingly, on property law. He found as many new clients as there were issues to argue, but for his family, opportunities to settle on a new estate were slim. After months of searching, Thomas found next to nothing; he had arrived too late. Seemingly all the decent property reserved as bounty lands had been claimed; only scraps of rocky or elevated fields were left for the picking. From the start, Thomas was exasperated by his paltry options. Only after some time of deep despair, afraid to admit any failure, he wrote his father.

In response, David wrote back, admonishing his silence:

> "We some time since received three letters from you on the same day, [one] to Rebecca, your mother and my self, and however acceptable they were, it would have been yet more so, had some of them filled the long previous or succeeding gaps of correspondence..."

As if to excuse him, however, David replied with news of alarming conditions in Cincinnati and Sewickley Bottoms.

August 21, 1834

> "We observe that your town [Batavia] has been visited in a slight degree by Cholera, Cincinnatta we suppose has been extensively so, almost all of our towns along the Ohio have been afflicted in a greater or less degree—particularly Wheeling and Pitts. Although not officially announced, Fallston, near Beaver, has been severely

visited, and a few cases have occurred between Beaver and Pitts-burgh, one at Shousetown. There have been several deaths at Wash-ington and it now prevails in the country adjacent to Wash. Our own neighborhood continues healthy and as the weather has be-come cool, I hope it may continue so…"

David closed the letter by throwing his son a bone. "I have observed in a late Pittsburgh newspaper an advertisement for the sale…of some prop-erty…probably belonging to some bankrupt estate, one item of which reads thus: 300 acres on the river Scioto… near the town of Portsmouth… If you think the investigation [worthy,] and if the title and land good, the purchase desirable and time and circumstances suit, I would pay for it…and let the title be made to you."

Like Thomas' many other title searches, the opportunity did not pan out.

Nor did his pursuit of the late James C. Mabin's lands. In multiple coun-ties and on multiple tracts were 2,788 acres, all situated in the prized bounty lands. Like so many other unsettled tracts in and around the flat and fertile Ohio plains, their titles were grossly encumbered with unpaid tax debts. Sheriff sales required lessees to produce surveys and quitrents, or missing heirs to appear, prove their claims and pay up. In the case of James Mabin, deceased, Thomas sought out his children to buy off their tax debts only to learn that a brother, Andrew, residing in Scotland, was the apparent heir. Thomas offered up to his father that he would be happy to go to Edinboro to seek out the lost sibling, but after much time and expense had already been spent to hire an agent overseas, Thomas discovered that he had been duped by the "pettifogging" children's attorney, hoping to have delayed the sale. The saga of clearing that title was conveyed in letters to his father ex-tending from 1839 to 1847. Wrote Thomas to David, "By far the greater portion of lands in that part of the military district are owned by non-resi-dents and are covered, or shingled over, with every variety of encumbrance, heirs, fictitious and fraudulent claims to such an extent indeed that altho it is by far the best part of the country, it is comparatively speaking unsettled and must remain so until their titles are settled." Thomas prophetically added, "This however would be a troublesome business as [ever] we [would] discover by the little experience we have had in this speculation."

And then came a published broadside. Although it was written in German, it promoted a property of many hundreds of acres right in Clermont County. The broadside claimed that one Dr. Daniel DeBenneville, a surgeon of Virginia's 13th (in fact, Daniel Leet's same Regiment,) had been granted 400 acres by military warrant in 1795.[22] Many more acres had been acquired since, but the broadside did not say how many. The doctor's son and heir, Benneville D. Brown, lived in Philadelphia. If Thomas could not strike a deal through correspondence, his father would "close it" surely when next he had business in the big city.

Thomas was driven—he was, in fact, desperate—to find income-yielding property for an entirely different reason; he was now grossly in debt. The misfortune had come swiftly and suddenly. Thomas blamed it all on a former partner, a man with whom he created a short-lived venture selling dry goods. John W. Robinson owned a farm on a "macadamized" road near Maysville, Kentucky, not far from Batavia. Robinson was engaged as the Treasurer for Clermont County. And Thomas was actively representing clients while pursuing land deals. Still, they operated "a stand" at which locals could purchase clothes, hardware, cutlery, parasols, boots and shoes. But times were so hard, cash was so rare, the partnership announced in the local paper that they would gladly accept pork to cover debts owed to the firm.[23] About his ex-partner, Thomas wrote, "I never saw such a change in a man. Six months ago he was esteemed and respected by every one, and his character for honesty, sobriety, propriety of conduct, gentlemanly deportment, stood as fair as that of any man in the country, but he lacked the moral courage to meet and overcome [ad]versity. No sooner did he perceive the approach of embarrassments in his business than he gave up all for lost, and has since taken no measures to relieve himself. He is now I fear a drunkard." Thomas' anger was evidenced by the fact that work the two partners had been conducting were for the benefit of Thomas' cousin, T. F. Shewell, in Philadelphia. Thomas explained to his father, "The situation of the late firm of Robinson and Shields is bad enough. We find it impossible under our claims to collect on our debts in time to satisfy creditors, and have lost several claims which we have set down as good. Our debt of $700 which we had just secured upon an extensive steam sawmill will I suppose be lost in

---

[22] Yoder, "The Pennsylvania German Broadside," Penn State University Press, 2005

[23] *The Clermont Courier*, December 9, 1837

consequence of the destruction of the mill and all the buildings of the owner by fire."[24]

Another promising steam mill had gone to ruin.

Almost a year later, Thomas engaged another lawyer to assist him in getting a lien on two properties owned by Robinson in Maysville and Cincinnati. By forcing them into auction, Thomas would have to offer two-thirds of the total appraised value to win them. He asked his father for $1,700. "If you do so it will remove a weight from my mind that for a long time has tortured me almost beyond expression."

And, as if things could not get worse, one month later, his first-born children, Eliza and Will fell desperately ill. "Eliza…was compelled to take 4 doses of Calomil [mercuric chloride, a purgative] and one blue pill [?] besides other medicines before her fever could be broken. Will has... recovered."

Eight months later, the children got Whooping Cough.

---

[24] Letter from TLS to DS, August 13, 1840, Thomas L. Shields Letter Collection, Univ. of Michigan, Clement Library

John Leet Shields

Back at Newington, however, a sense of normalcy gave definition to ante-bellum life. A few saved letters relate stories of a family's idle pursuits. Thanks to Maria writing to her mother and sisters, a veritable cookbook of delicious cake, crumpet and waffle recipes still survives. From a letter to Susan, Maria encouraged Rebecca to keep up her instructions in oil painting, classes apparently offered at Mrs. Blaine's house. In another letter, Thomas thanked his sister Susan for "the slippers received." And Maria, writing from Washington, commended Susan "on declaring herself a follower of the meek and lovely savior."

In later correspondence, grandmother Eliza took to her bed after a serious illness not disclosed. "Hannah is well," assured Maria, writing from Newington to Washington, "and Mom is getting downstairs again." Leet Shields wrote that his return from Washington to Newington was punctuated by loud cannon fire, apparent afterthoughts of the Fourth of July celebrated two days earlier. David informed his son Thomas, "Your mother and sisters, with the exception of Rebecca who is afflicted with painful affections derivable from her teeth that confines her much to her chamber, are well." Like his sentence structure, David ached to be positive.

In one of the more personal letters to his father, Thomas, now with three children, wrote from Batavia, "Some of our family will probably visit you this summer. I should like to take Will up. He is very wild and mischievous, but withal good natured and affectionate. ~ I took him to "Cin" some weeks ago and having business out in the city, I left him in [the] charge of the landlord with strict instructions to Will not to go outside the room until my return. He contrived to get out however, and was soon lost. He commenced of enquiring every one who would listen to him, for me, and fortunately questioned a gentleman of my acquaintance who, knowing where I usually put up, brought him to the hotel. He was much frightened."

At the time of the incident, William C. Shields had just turned five.

*   *   *   *   *

On May 8, 1840, for no reason recorded or lamented, John Leet Shields, David and Eliza's third son, died at Newington. Maria Shields Wilson wrote to her mother from Washington a full two weeks later to say she "mourns the loss of Brother." Maria does not say anything about the circumstances, does not inquire about a funeral or burial, nor does she even mention her sibling's name. Apparently, none of that information was important.

Of the young man's life, only an account of his travels to Europe in 1837 is known. His companion was Dr. John Dickson, a local friend of the same age, then 25, whom he accompanied to Edinburgh and Dublin to attend lectures on popular medicine. In Rome, they attended to an epidemic of cholera before returning to Sewickley. Dr. Dickson was married the next year to May Ann Way, daughter of John Way, Jr. They had eight children, two of whom were given the middle name Shields.[25]

For his entry in his daybook, David Shields simply recorded: "May 8. John L. Shields, a beloved son, aged 28." He was laid to rest next to his grandfather and sister in the burial ground at Newington.

---

[25] Cushing, *History of Allegheny County*, pg. 238

A Church for Sewickley

Had there been a public service for John Shields, it would have been celebrated at the Edgeworth Ladies Seminary which then served as the temporary Sunday gathering place for local Protestants. In 1836, a Mrs. Mary
Olver relocated the Edgeworth Ladies' Seminary from Braddock's Field to
the Ohio River village. She purchased 40 acres of bottom lands directly from
David Shields at a cost of $30 per acre and there built a two-story rectangle
of bricks in which were fitted classrooms, dormitories, a kitchen, dining
room and downstairs reception hall where local Sunday services were held.
The school for young women was actually founded in Pittsburgh some
eleven years earlier and then named after Maria Edgeworth, Mrs. Olver's
favorite Irish novelist and children's author. So disciplinary was the school,
parents of young ladies from Philadelphia, Baltimore and other points south
held it in the highest esteem. Both Rebecca and Hanna Shields had "ma-
triculated" in Mrs. Olver's classrooms while they were still in Braddock. A
prospectus in 1838 described the new campus as "an eligible location on the
north bank of the Ohio River, near the village of Economy."

Not for another two years would residents of the area decide to name
their town Sewickleyville, a choice much preferred over others then used,
including Fifetown, Contention, and Bowling Green. Boatmen and squatters who were unlikely ever to take up permanent residence referred to the
nascent village as Dogtown. Other transients called it the Devil's Racetrack.
Just west of the town, where the Little Sewickley Creek flowed to the river,
locals called the area Sewickley Bottoms. Not for another decade would the
name Edgeworth refer to anything other than Mrs. Olver's seminary.

Under the pastorate of Reverend Daniel Nevin, ordained just two years earlier, the local presbytery agreed to construct a church of its own. David Shields honored the congregation with a loan to meet the difference between moneys raised and the actual cost of the church, then projected to be $5,400. The church was planned as a simple brick structure with gothic arched windows. Pews were made from planed boards on hewn stumps. In fact, only a few pews were ever seated in the church as there were, at first, too few congregants to warrant more.

Apropos of church foundations, the Rev. Daniel Nevin became a pillar of the early community. Even before the new church opened its doors, he offered sermons to three other congregations regularly, and he conducted weekly Sunday school classes, too. Education, if not just religious instruction, was his forte. By 1848, he became headmaster of the Edgeworth Academy, a second iteration of the Edgeworth Female Seminary. Daniel Nevin however was not the only Nevin to head a school in Sewickley. His brother William (along with John Champ) founded the Sewickley Academy for Boys in 1838. In fact, both brothers had been instructed by their older sibling J. Williamson Nevin who was a professor at the Western Theological Seminary.

David Shields' largesse in offering to cover unsubscribed expenses of the new church was typical of the quiet role he played in many civic endeavors. Following the Crash of 1837, when collecting local commerce taxes was a challenge few government agencies could manage, David Shields and George Rapp loaned a combined $8,000 to Allegheny County.[26]

In 1837, too, upon the completion of the $10,000,000 route connecting the Pennsylvania Canal, via the Portage Railroad, from Philadelphia to Pittsburgh, western Pennsylvanians were all the more excited about the advancement of railroads to Pittsburgh and the west. David Shields was not among them. In the heat of July, he wrote to Frederick Rapp, "We do not want either a canal or a railroad, but a good macadamized turnpike through the valley."[27]

Despite residing in Sewickley Bottom, David became more active on many city boards and committees critical to the region's growth. It could be assumed, too, that his participation was ardently solicited. Volunteering to affect one cause begat his involvement in some other endeavor, and, without the constancy of his former trade, David was now more clearly generous with

---

[26] The Pittsburgh Gazette, Jan. 17, 1837, pg. 2

[27] Hays, *Reminiscences of the Sewickley Valley*, pg. 8

both his time and money. For example, in 1841, he served as a delegate to oppose an act to establish a Poor House in the city. Apparently, he was well aware of the long term stigma such institutions inflict on otherwise law abiding citizens. Shields explained his sentiment, stating "that a Poor House carries with its name something so humiliating and degrading, that numerous instances occur, where poor persons have preferred to suffer in their destitution, rather than resort to a house so obnoxious to their feelings."[28] He audited the Pittsburgh and Greensburg Turnpike Road Company for an annual stipend of just $10.[29] He, in partnership with George Rapp, employing both Harmonists and his own laborers, regularly paid for the repair of Beaver Road, albeit assessing some of the few neighbors it benefitted.

In 1845, David Shields became a Trustee of the new Presbyterian church. He was not, however, a church-goer. David was also elected to the Board of the Bank of Pittsburgh in 1847. That he knew something about bank charters, or dissolving one in times of economic crisis, may have been a consideration secondary to his unblemished and much esteemed character.[30]

David also helped to finance Pittsburgh's first non-denominational hospital. A longtime friend and associate, Judge William Wilkins, solicited David to subscribe to the creation of the Western Pennsylvania Hospital then loosely planned to rise above what would be known as the Strip District. The site would seem a curious location, but even then, it was known that the Pennsylvania Railroad would establish its Pittsburgh yards in the flat lands below. Of course, no passenger train would arrive for another three years, but the promised railroad would be opportune in bringing patients to the hospital.

The campaign took years to reach its goal. More prominent citizens were asked to donate a hefty $100 to its secular mission. David donated $1,000. When at last sufficient funds were raised and the board's plans were made public, a committee interviewed architects to build the four-story, 270 feet long facility. That David Shields was instrumental in awarding that commission is only educated conjecture.[31]

Joseph W. Kerr, the young man whose father had built Newington, was chosen to design the new hospital.

---

[28] Ibid, Sept. 21, 1841, pg. 1

[29] Ibid, Nov. 16, 1847, pg. 2

[30] Ibid.

[31] *Pittsburgh Daily Post*, Aug. 19, 1847, pg. 2

Father Rapp

Since the death of his adopted son Frederick, George Rapp carried on with greater devotion than before. He led his congregation with a strength reinvigorated by his own assessment that all was good, productive and profitable at Economy. Indeed, the work that Frederick had managed for so many years was so complex that it had to be assumed by two men. Father Rapp assigned R.L. Baker and Jacob Henrici to manage the Society's multiple businesses which now included most every commercial manufactory from ladies slippers to iron hinges.

Never active in the politics of the region, Rapp however was keenly aware of the goings-on of Congress and the President. He had few good things to say about Van Buren. In fact, even before the Species Circular of 1836, George Rapp had "called in" his many bank accounts in Pittsburgh and Philadelphia, cashing out the Harmonists' great assets to have it brought to him in gold and silver coins. As if he knew the country would soon crumble for lack of legal tender, George Rapp had it all stored in a secret vault the location of which he would not even share with his two closest associates. It was said in later years that Rapp had more than half a million dollars stashed under his mattress. No doubt, a vault was hidden deeper under his house, but that kind of money then, in that kind of economic crisis, proved what little faith Rapp invested in a secular world of greed and power.

For much of the ensuing decade, Rapp turned his back ever more acutely on the outside world and spoke more frequently to his faithful followers about the promise of the Lord, the duty of devotion and the joy of sacrifice. In fact, Rapp closed his Society to new members, refusing to accept younger pilgrims even newly arrived from Germany. With the decree of celibacy having aged his average congregant, Rapp also took further steps to keep his flock in fold. He annulled the sixth article of the original membership covenant, the one permitting those who might wish to leave the Society with the funds they had first invested. Now all the monies of the Harmonists were to be kept by all of the Harmonists. Share and share alike. Leave at your own discretion, but don't expect a dime for your troubles. Every member of the community was asked to sign the new document and not one refused.[32]

Unlike any leader of a communist society before or after him, George Rapp's patriarchy was both passive and productive. The absolute truth is that his followers did not just adore him, did not just bow to his eminence, they truly liked him.

George Rapp died in his sleep on August 7, 1847. Without alarm or concern for his health at 91 years of age, his congregants were humbled to learn the news. Like all Harmonists, Rapp was laid to rest in an unmarked grave somewhere in the sprawling orchards of the once famous Christian commune.

---

[32] Arndt, *George Rapp's Harmony Society*, pg. 570

Amelia Chaplin Shields

When the sale of Robinson's property in Kentucky finally came to auction, the Sheriff somehow bungled the procedure. The presiding judge consequently had to recuse himself for having authorized the Sheriff's misstep. And the auction was pushed off indefinitely.

Thomas was beside himself. The situation his once errant partner had created for the young attorney in Batavia caused daily anguish. That he could not establish safe title to any kind of property was evident in his more frequent visits east. David had forwarded his son $1,500. Now, Thomas needed to know how to return it, despite his ever-growing debt.

Amelia wasn't having any of it either. She neither liked the frontier town nor the lifestyle. Although her mother often stayed with the young family over long stretches of winter, Amelia found herself alone in the community. It did not help that Thomas travelled days on end to assist clients whose business he much needed. Wrote Thomas to his father, "Owing to a disimularity of tastes, Amelia has little or no intercourse with the female society of the place and as she grows older she feels as I do an increasing solicitude to spend the remainder of her life and to bring up her children in the society of relatives and friends."[33]

In some effort to reconcile their situation, Thomas agreed with Amelia in 1846 to send Eliza to Newington to be educated at the Shields schoolhouse. They hoped that the Edgeworth Seminary would soon reopen—Mrs. Olver had died quite suddenly in 1842—because rumor was that the Reverend Daniel Nevin would take its helm and continue its tradition as a fine

---

[33] Letter from TLS to DS, Dec. 16, 1843, Thomas L. Shields Letter Collection, Univ. of Michigan, Clement Library

English public school.[34] Hope prevailed and, at just ten years of age, Eliza moved to Newington to attend the re-opened seminary. Despite occasional, but painful bouts of homesickness while at Newington, she enjoyed the company of her maiden aunts Rebecca and Hanna, then respectively 29 and 24 years old. Together, they would spend hours collecting the flora of the area and pressing dried specimens in a flower book that still exists today.

Back in Batavia, Thomas also began attending to more idyllic pursuits, including his gardens. He boasted to his mother in a letter that he had grown a tomato weighing one pound, thirteen ounces. And in other letters to his father, he often made note of his peach orchard and vineyards in which he grew new varieties, one he called "cigar-box" grapes "so large" they were "the size of black walnuts."

Presciently, he wrote his father, asking for his brother's assistance, "I hope Leet has a taste for horticulture, in which I include fruits of all kinds. As it is my hobby and I would like much to correspond with him about these things and make occasional exchanges of choice fruits, etc. He will have a fine opportunity of indulging such a taste of Sewickly."

Why Thomas would ask his father about his brother Leet's interest in horticulture is a curious thing. One could only assume that David's eldest son, living at Newington, was active in the farms and gardens of that place anyway. Should one conjecture that Leet was somehow dismissive of his younger brother? Was he indifferent to the role Thomas played for their father? Or was he deeply engrossed in business affairs of his own?

Whichever the case, Thomas directed the notion to his father. "By the way I think you would find raising choice fruits at Sewickly for the Pittsburgh market the most profitable business you could engage in so far as farming is concerned."[35]

---

[34] Nevin, *The Village of Sewickley*, pg. 27

[35] Letter from TLS to DS, March 20, 1845, Thomas L. Shields Letter Collection, Univ. of Michigan, Clement Library

Canals and Trains

It was a sight few people west of the Alleghenies had ever seen. Thousands descended onto the banks of the Ohio river to celebrate its arrival. A wood-fired steam locomotive, billowing huge plumes of thick smoke and hot ash, blew its whistle. Babies wailed and grown men ran for cover. The train from Pittsburgh ran on tracks set back from the northern riverfront, crossing Sewickley Bottoms. Not only was it the first train to depart from Pittsburgh, it was the first train to head west from the city. The event marked two singularly distinct moments in American history. The country's first railroad, the Baltimore and Ohio, would not connect to Wheeling until the following year and the Pennsylvania Railroad would not reach Pittsburgh for another two years. In fact, the train that arrived at Sewickleyville that day in 1851 would go only as far as the village at Economy. Eventually, the line would extend to Crestline, Ohio, where it would meet a later network of tracks reaching as far west as Fort Wayne, Indiana. Aboard a roofless freight car was General William Robinson, Jr., the first mayor of Allegheny City and supposedly the first white child born west of the Allegheny River.[36] A veteran of the Mexican War, General Robinson had formed his company, the Ohio and Pennsylvania Rail Road Company, just three years earlier. Not surprisingly, he was a partner in an early rolling mill whose products were designed chiefly to meet the needs of a country united by trains.

---

[36] Coleman, "Pioneers of Pittsburgh: The Robinsons" *Western Pennsylvania Historical Magazine.* March, 1959, pg. 66-68.

For well more than a year, David had assured his neighbors that no "iron horse" would ever cross his property.[37] In fact, David had only recently opposed the installation of telegraph wires along Beaver Road, always adamant, despite the constant expense of repairs, to keep the road free from tolls.[38] But the railway represented something more promising and profitable than Morse's code. As experienced as David had been in the logistics of shipping, first with teams of wagons and then by steam boat, he also knew how entirely successful the advent of canals had become. Commerce was no longer elevated just by shipping goods, but by transporting the people who needed them. Their aspirations transformed cities in ways never before known. The Pennsylvania Canal aqueduct that ran across the Allegheny River at Pittsburgh had brought wealth and new energy to iron mills operating with greater efficiency in Pittsburgh than any other city. Ironically, the canal brought that first steam locomotive, too. That iron tracks should emanate from a western city with no prior rail connection spoke as much about its capabilities as it did the promise of the new mode of transport. While Pennsylvania engineers struggled to get trains to climb over the Alleghenies, Pittsburgh was already building lines to meet the demands of the west.

That historic day the first train whistle blew was also July 4th, 1851, America's 75th birthday.

---

[37] *History of the Sewickley Presbyterian Church*, pg. 96
[38] *Pittsburgh Daily Post*, Oct. 11, 1848, pg. 2

The Last Straw

The vast majority of the many extant letters between father and son relate to Thomas's fevered pursuit of the DeBenneville lands in Ohio. Despite the coincidence that the doctor served with Daniel Leet at Valley Forge, the letters seem to have been saved for one reason only. So much time and correspondence had been spent in the process of negotiating a deal with Benneville D. Brown the slim chance it might come to some fruition was more precious than the land itself.

The correspondence began as early as 1842 with a registered description of the property, relative to its situation along the Little Miami River, as well as an estimation of the density of its trees and variety of their type, all of which was meant to express the agricultural value of the property (were the trees, of course, to be deadened and cleared.) Early on, before the first winter arrived, Benneville D. Brown wrote to David Shields directly—purposely bypassing Thomas—to offer up a sale. "Be so obliging as to answer this letter by our early frost," pressured Brown. Ten years later, a sale was still pending. In anticipation of the much larger investment, Thomas had purchased several hundred adjacent acres. And now they were as worthless as before.

Insomuch that clearing encumbrances had become the norm, insomuch that courts now adjudicated the process by which heirs could contest first or second generation titles, insomuch that vast acres of unsettled and unproductive land could sit idle in an economy voracious for agriculture and commerce, America's frontier was as perilous as ever. Like Daniel Leet, Thomas L. Shields seemingly stood sentry, alert to wolves of a different kind, armed only with the tools of law, sleepless in the knowledge that he had best fire first or, running to save others, get shot in the back. Thomas's experiment in Ohio was nothing less than exhausting.

Yet, all along, David Shields was adamant that he—or rather his wife––was entitled to Ohio property. He even appealed to his Pittsburgh friend and U.S. Representative, Thomas M. Howe, Esq., "We have been advised that a bill will be presented to your house, to permit such unlocated warrants to be located on any other unallocated lands belong (sic) to the U.S. Permit me dr. Sir to solicit your countenance and aid to the passage in your house of such an (sic) law, as calculated to do justice to an heir of an (sic) Revolutionary officer. With sentiments of respect, Yours, David Shields"

A full year and a half later, Thomas wrote his father, "Our application…for the warranty issued to Daniel Leet has at length been acted upon by the Commissioner of the general land office ~ and I am sorry to add been disallowed."

Never were Daniel Leet's commissioned lands unearthed, never did Thomas Shields find warrants, patents, or proof of former quitrents; never was a claim discovered that offered the least whiff of hope.

At last defeated, Thomas added, "I intend to return to Sewickly to start a market garden."

Indeed, the days of land speculation had come to a long and dismal end.

A Cemetery for Sewickley

Before the winter of 1853, Thomas L. Shields returned to Sewickleyville with his wife and six children: Will, Rebecca, David, Amelia, Lydia, and, not yet three years old, Wilhelmina. Eliza, 18, was already in residence at Newington. An eighth child and namesake, Thomas, would be born in 1856.

Evident since his absence was a town now populated in large part because of the Pittsburgh and Fort Wayne trains that regularly chugged along the Ohio (on the right-of-way, in fact, that would later become Rt. 65.) Sewickleyville enjoyed a population of about 500 residents, a number sufficient in 1853 to call for its incorporation as a borough and, therewith, its own school district. Yet, Sewickleyville already had two distinguished institutions: a seminary for ladies and an academy for boys. Within a decade, the town's population would double. Here, children, mothers and their domestic aides could live on tree-shaded properties, attend church with their peers, and engage in social activities that would best benefit their own preferences of what was civilized and serene. As many as eight trains a day allowed the gentlemen of Sewickleyville the luxury of a mere 27-minute commute into the city of Allegheny (now Pittsburgh's north side.)

Early on, the town's first burgesses, led by the Reverend Robert Hopkins, addressed issues of street improvements and property easements, eager to modernize their village with standards now seemingly ubiquitous in the suburbs of other great American cities. Their plans required the services of an experienced civil engineer and surveyor, and, so it was, that they responded to advertisements of a one Alexander Hays. Of his references, he boasted his affiliation with officers of the Allegheny Valley Railroad as well as the engineers of the Pittsburgh & Steubenville Railroad. In fact, Hays had had a long association with General William Robinson, Jr. when redeveloping Robinson's father's estate in Allegheny City. It is Hays who is credited for naming the Mexican War streets of that popular neighborhood. In fact, both men had served together in the Mexican War; Hays, in particular, was brevetted to Second Lieutenant for his success at the Battle of Atlixco. He was a graduate of West Point and close friend of Ulysses S. Grant. Although something like a local legend for his prior military heroism, Hays was also known to many for his shockingly red hair. In and around Sewickleyville, where he took up the charge to realign the village streets, he was also well known to the Shields family. Married to Annie McFadden in 1846, his bride's parents were longtime friends of David and Eliza Shields.

*　　*　　*　　*　　*

That same year, Thomas built a house on his father's land, above the Beaver Road on "the shelf," elevated to command a view of the Ohio River. At David's suggestion a few years earlier, he had engaged the now renowned architect Joseph Kerr to design a five-bay, two story Federal style house with an interior staircase framed by a Greek Revival arch. The front door with sidelights and a transom allowed for natural light to fill a hallway sixty-feet deep. Tall, mullioned windows testified to the simplicity of the molding, mantels, and doors within.[39] It was said that, over many years, a dining room window was signed by the family, relatives and friends, using a diamond.[40] While there was little of anything fancy about the house, it was a banker's estate compared to their Batavia house. Along with an early barn and a later gardener's cottage, Thomas commanded a full ten acres to grow his specialized fruit trees and imported shrubs. The house was called Chestnut Hill. However, villagers called it the Shields Homestead perhaps in deference to the more noble Shields Mansion across the street.[41]

Seemingly, from his first week back in Sewickley Bottom, Thomas focused on two causes. The first was the welfare of his "old man" who appeared to be slowing down. The second was the foundation of the Grand Old Party.

---

[39] Lowry, "Places," *Pittsburgh Post-Gazette*, Aug. 22, 2002

[40] Smith, *A Guidebook to Historic Western Pennsylvania*

[41] The home was occupied only by direct descendants of the Shields family until it was demolished in 2002.

A staunch adherent to principles Henry Clay had sown in his several presidential bids, most recently in 1848, Thomas attended an "Anti-Administration" convention in Pittsburgh, and was elected a delegate to the first-ever Republican convention held in Philadelphia later that year. In 1856, the GOP nominated John Fremont and William Dayton to their ticket. Abraham Lincoln lost the nod to Dayton as the GOP candidate for Vice President, and of course, Fremont lost the November election entirely to James Buchanan. The central issue was slave labor, outlawed in Ohio and Pennsylvania, but very much a hot topic in the many new western territories whose formal charters the Compromise of 1850 had delayed. Pennsylvania's own James Buchanan subsequently fumbled his presidency and the hopes of all black men, enslaved or not, when, having intervened in Supreme Court matters, the Dred Scott decision shattered the rights of freed slaves everywhere.

Coming from the free state of Ohio, Thomas L. Shields never owned a slave, but he did employ a one William Blankenship who followed the family to Sewickleyville from Batavia. Then, Thomas engaged the man to serve as a nurse companion to his aging father.[42] Many years later, his son David would write about sitting with "Uncle Billy" watching the early trains pass.

In September of 1857, David Shields officially shut down his post office at Newington. It seemed his days were waning. Frail and arthritic, he needed help with every small task.

*   *   *   *   *

Once Sewickley had been designated a borough, Thomas, among other early contributors, hired his friend Hays to help establish a new cemetery and, more specifically, to engineer the road to it.[43] That the idea of a Sewickley Cemetery was then subscribed to by the town's relatively few residents addressed several issues. Although the Presbyterians had started a graveyard sometime after 1840, no church in the area had yet claimed its own soil; rather, families buried their own. Those without property interred their loved ones at the base of Division Street on land shared and "donated" by

---

[42] *The Herald*, Sewickley, 1915?

[43] Hays, *Life & Letters of Alexander Hays*, pg. 114; also, Nevin, *The Village of Sewickley*, pg. 36

Henry Ulery and Thomas Beer for that purpose. Yet, such property (now the Quaker Valley Junior High School) was subject to significant flooding. And so, a new cemetery was laid out on higher ground atop "the shelf" east of Blackburn Road.

With no political premonition did Thomas and his fellow organizers charter their cemetery, although, by 1857, the premise of a civil confrontation was by no means bizarre. The idea of a state's right to self-government––argued at the time as "public sovereignty"—was an anti-federalist ideal lost to the Dred Scott decision. But the notion that Southern states could defend their right to slavery was undermined by Buchanan's Supreme Court when it gave blanket protection to slaveholders wherever they might move and live with their "property." Meanwhile, northern abolitionists fought for the freedom of slaves on purely moral grounds. In 1858, the Lincoln-Douglas debates focused entirely on the issues of slavery, bringing to the forefront of national conversation a topic few had wanted to discuss publicly. The country took firm sides.

Even if the smell of blood was in the air, the fact is rural cemeteries had become quite the rage. Allegheny Cemetery was established in 1844, the sixth-oldest pastoral cemetery in the country. On sprawling green lawns, under canopies of chestnut, oak and maple leaves, the bereaved could come to visit those they mourned and revered. The industrial age had well changed family dynamics in which a newly promised legacy of wealth was to be honored in granite gratitude. The antebellum era also issued in a new understanding of the spiritual world in which angels could watch over the deceased atop ornate columns of alabaster or marble, in which an immortal sphinx would forever guard a stone sarcophagus, or in which finely chiseled sculptures of the dead would stand upon their own graves, posturing not so much in defiance of death as in victory over irrepressible fears now vanquished.

*   *   *   *   *

On November 2, 1857, David Shields enjoyed a similar victory. That he was laid to rest in his own backyard speaks volumes.

A reproduction of David M. Shields's portrait attributed to Thomas Sully. Artist unknown.
Courtesy of the Sewickley Valley Historical Society.

Mournings & Memorials

The final entry in his daybook was written in a hand different from his own: "On this Monday morning at half past two O'clock the owner of this book, and who, for so many years, recorded the memoranda therein—died."

The only surviving obituary of David Shield's death is found in the digital archives of the Mercersburg Journal, a telegraphed reprint of what had appeared in the Pittsburg Chronicle eleven days earlier:

DEATH OF A MILLIONAIRE

"Our obituary column is again charged with the announcement of the death of another worthy citizen of Allegheny county. David Shields, Esq., expired this morning at 2 o'clock, at his residence in Sewickley township, at the advanced age of 78. He was, we believe, the wealthiest man in the county, and his death will be lamented by a large circle of friends, his generous benefactions and inflexible integrity of character."

Tributes to the life, character and generosity of David Shields, Esq., were profuse among the elders and stalwarts of the several congregations that assembled at the Edgeworth Ladies Seminary or the now-crowded Presbyterian Church. Friends and associates in Washington remembered his many contributions of time and talent in leading the community during years of financial crisis and despair. Likewise his closer friends mourned his loss in the face of unsettling times sure to come. David Shields had never placed himself in the political pulpit, but he was clearly opinionated, even if few words were ever put to paper or remembered in speech. Unlike his father—rather, more akin to his father-in-law—he was a man of few words. The trait had served him well.

Even his last will and testament was a simple one. It comprises less than 200 words. Signed and witnessed in October of 1849, his will made his wife one of two executors. That was unusual for the time; women (never mind widows) were not typically entrusted with legal or financial authority. Yet, logically, the appointment of his wife as executor was in deference to *her* father's contributions to their combined wealth. Further to the point, earlier letters received by Thomas in Batavia suggested that, at times, Eliza was reconciling her son's bank accounts. David's first born son, Leet Shields, was named the other executor. David left everything to Eliza with no contingencies should they both have perished together. He excused his executors from the "labor incident to the usual practice of making and filing inventories." Of his many real properties, none were disclosed nor was his financial portfolio revealed. Of course, such information was really not necessary; every asset and debt would have been readily discovered in his neatly organized daybooks. David did however include the following directive: "It is my desire and I would remind my wife in her disposition of my estate to put all our Children on equal footing taking into consideration that some of them have had considerable outfit and donations and others of them have not."

Eliza in mourning, dressed in black crepe daily, welcomed visitors to Newington, a house now seemingly much larger and colder in the weeks that followed a cheerless Christmas. Of her close friends, Mrs. Rebecca Blaine, Mrs. Mary Smith, and the Reverend Daniel Nevin seem to have comforted her most.[44] Of course, Leet, then 50 years old, Rebecca, 40, and Hanna, 35, all lived at Newington to share in their family's grief. .

*   *   *   *   *

The angel of the Lord appeared in the valley soon again. Eliza's second youngest, Susan, died fourteen months later, in February, 1859. She was 37.

Susan had married the Reverend Isaac M. Cook in 1843, raised a young family, and moved to Beaver where, attending to her duties as a pastor's wife, Isaac died suddenly in 1854. A one-time instructor at the Shields

---

[44] The Last Will and Testament of Eliza Shields, direction for gifts

schoolhouse, the Reverend Cook became the first pastor of the West Bridgewater Presbyterian Church and something of a prodigy in clerical circles. Founded by 65 members in 1845, the church had more than 350 congregants upon his death nine years later. Reverend Cook was just 36.

Perhaps the most devout of Eliza's six surviving children—the Shields's daughters were outwardly more spiritual than either surviving son—Susan was her closest child. Thus it was, when just a year and several months after burying her husband, Eliza mourned her second great loss. Orphaned were Susan's children, Eliza Shields Cook, 15, David Shields Cook, 13, and Martha McCracken Cook, 8. Grandmother Eliza took them all under her care.

Eliza, in fact, opened her arms in ways she had not before. Now executor of her late husband's estate—a great portion of which was acquired through her *own* father's estate—Eliza benefitted a number of Sewickley charities for which the only restriction she asserted was her own anonymity. One gift assisted the Reverend James Allison and his trustees in building an entirely new Presbyterian Church. The quiet gesture would honor her late husband. Yet one can also assume that the memory of her devout daughter Susan, the inordinate success of *her* late husband, the Rev. Isaac Cook, and the necessity of a larger church eager to offer a full Sunday school program the Shields schoolhouse could not, was at the forefront of her generosity. Although her contribution to the building fund was no doubt disproportionate to other church members, she exploited her generosity to suggest that Joseph Kerr design the new Gothic Revival edifice. He accepted the commission. Yet, relative to old Presbyterian tastes, it would be a simple and frugal affair, unpretentiously two-stories high, steepled still to reach the heavens.

Within a year of Susan's death, construction was well underway.

Lt. William Shields

The clear glass windows of the new Presbyterian Church had only been installed a few days earlier.[45] Pews were nowhere evident, the altar a mere forethought. But, collected in prayer, mothers and fathers, aunts and uncles, brothers and sisters, hymnals in their outstretched arms, sang softly, choked by fear and foreboding.

"Will" Shields, 23 years of age, stood with his friend John Nevin among forty other "boys" to attend the very first indoor service. The next day they would leave by rail for Pittsburgh, then Philadelphia, onward to Baltimore and then south to the Potomac basin, packed into boxcars with hundreds of other recruits mustered into the 28th Pennsylvania Volunteers, Company G. As the Sewickley Company, those assembled in the new church were comforted by the words of the Reverend James Allison. Each was given a small New Testament. In addition, Captain Conrad Meyer presented William Shields and John Nevin with glistening steel swords. Will was to serve as the company's First Lieutenant, John as its Second.[46] The day was July 6, 1861.

Fort Sumter had fallen less than three months earlier, yet already efforts to tame the ire of southern secessionists had fallen well short of expectations. President Lincoln had ordered the recruitment of 75,000 volunteers to serve a three-month commitment, certain as all northerners were that the mere assemblage of a force that size would quell further southern aggression. The orders were to surround the nation's Capitol where, by September of that

---

[45] *History of the Presbyterian Church of Sewickley*, pg. 19

[46] Ellis, *Lights and Shadows of Sewickley Life*, pg. 248

year, tens of thousands of enlistees—wearing only the ratty clothes they had left home in—settled camps sprawling for miles on the swampy plains of "Washington City." By the end of July, however, the rascal rebels had already waged war on Bull Run at Manassas.

No longer were volunteers recruited for a mere three months but for a full three years. Alexander Hays, who had just served as Major of the Twelfth Regiment, accepted orders to lead the Sixty-Third Regiment of Pennsylvania Volunteers as Colonel, recruiting thousands more from Braddock and Sharpsburg, forming them into two companies. Before departing Camp Wilkins (staged on the Allegheny County Fairgrounds at 28th Street in Pittsburgh,) Hays was feted by friends and family. Any last supper might well have been hosted by Thomas and Amelia Shields, but, if not, the affection between the two men was on display for all to see. Thomas and his older brother, Leet, gave Alexander two horses to take into battle. The largest was named "Leet," the other, "Dan." The gifts were more than just honorific, more than just tokens of esteem; they were, in fact, magnanimous gestures of faith and empowerment. With Will leading his company into three harried years of military service, with heightened fears that a much longer war was inevitable, with no other means by which he and his family could use their wealth so immediately to protect the Union, Thomas furnished Alex with tools of which no other officer could boast. "Leet" and "Dan," by all accounts, were magnificent horses, as well-trained as they were bred, soon to be prized by his troops and fellow officers alike. Remarkable in the many histories of the civil war are the singular letters of Alexander Hays writing to his wife and family about the joy and pride he derived from these prized war horses.

Not surprisingly, Colonel Hays's first settlement of troops venturing out from the staging grounds at Washington was named Camp Shields. Outside of Alexandria, VA, William H. Morrow, a private in Company A of Hays's command, recorded the events there.

> "Camp Shields, named in honor of the Shields family of Sewickley, was situated on the Leesburg Pike, on the farm of Mrs. Powell …When encamped at this place we were visited by the President and Mrs. Lincoln. They drove slowly by while the ragged boys stood in picturesque groups, backed up close to each other to hide

as much as possible, the dilapidated conditions of their wardrobes. This was the first time many of us had seen the President, and we agreed that a more homely man would be hard to find. A Sergeant "Bob" Nesbitt remarked at the time, 'He looked exactly like an old farmer going to a cross-roads church.'" [47]

Lt. William C. Shields had "moved out," too. First stationed at Point of Rocks in Maryland, then on to Knoxville, his company saw no action, training daily for when they would. In October, the 28th Regiment was attached to General Nathaniel Banks's First Brigade along with six other companies. By the time they arrived at Bolivar Heights, WV, near Harper's Ferry, Will learned that his brother had mustered into the 63rd PA Volunteers. David Shields left Pittsburgh on August 26. The regiment to which he was assigned was under the command of Col. Alexander Hays.

Wrote Hays to his wife in December, "The 63rd lies in the extreme left of the "Grand Army," where the first assault of a rebel attack would be met. About a mile beyond, across a magnificent valley, is to be seen the national domain of Mount Vernon. I think, within a week, the 63rd will be in close proximity or perhaps beyond, and then I will write of the Tomb of Washington. Who will refuse to fight with such an incentive near them?

" 'Leet Shields' was on parade and if he had borne a king, he could not have behaved more handsomely. Everybody says 'what a noble horse,' and as I ride though Washington and Alexandria, I overhear the remarks highly complimentary to the rider, who of course is not taken into consideration…

" 'Dave' Shields is duly installed as high private in Capt. Reid's company, and you may assure 'Aunt Beck' [Rebecca B. Shields, a close friend of his wife, Annie] that I will keep the boy in view in return for the high compliment which she pays me in entrusting him to my charge."

Later that month, Hays "detailed Lieut. Brown and Dave Shields as two of the most intelligent young men of my command, to be educated in the 'Signal Service.' They will for a time go to Washington and Georgetown, and when perfect will return to the regiment."

Despite more imminent expectations, it would be a long time until Hays's two companies would see any action. Not until March, after months

---

[47] Hays, *Under the Red Patch*, pg. 35

of guarding the Capitol district, the 63rd Regiment entered the Peninsular Campaign, that is, moving south to the tide water counties of Virginia. Before marching in to "low Dixie," Hays noted to his wife, "Dave Shields paid me a visit today. He is a noble, independent boy, and as soon as I possibly can make him a Lieutenant, I intend to do so on account of his merit, but I do not wish his relatives to know anything of the matter."

By then, Will's 28th Regiment had already crossed the Potomac, in turn, occupying towns like Lovettsville, Wheatland, Leesburg, Upperville, and Ashby's Gap.

In May, Hays and his men moved on from the siege at Yorktown and into the Battle of Williamsburg. General McClellan decried it a Union victory, but the statistics later showed that Southern casualties were 1,682 compared to the Northern's 2,283. As such, that many more Confederates were able to march home to Richmond.

Meanwhile, Will Shields was off in the Appalachian mountains, guarding rail lines in the Blue Ridge or performing reconnaissance on the enemy's movements through the Shenandoahs and the Piedmont. Seemingly in charge of smaller companies, moving nimbly over mountain passes, tactically removed from any larger engagements, Will's participation, compared to his brother's activities, appeared to be safer. The tide would soon turn. Within the year, it would flip entirely.

Shields & Wardrop

The idea, at first, was to cultivate distinctly tolerant fruit trees and unusual varieties of grapes suitable for the gardens and orchards of Pittsburgh's wealthier residents. But Thomas L. Shields learned quickly that the professional gardeners employed by his best customers had no patience to tend vineyards or to defend open orchards from passersby. Instead, Shields's business grew on the merits of ornamental greenery that graced the foyers and parlors of Pittsburgh's ironmongers and bank executives. Still, it was no early success; cultivating an inventory of hearty, extraordinary specimens required years of attention.

And so, Thomas hired a one James Wardrop, a popular gardener and perennial officer of the Allegheny County Horticulture Society. From as early on as 1838, Wardrop operated one of Pittsburgh's most diverse nurseries, situated west of Allegheny City in Manchester, selling fruit trees, asparagus sprouts, rhubarb, dahlias, hyacinths, and roses. In 1850, Wardrop had opened a specialty seed store, and a few years later, he added to his inventory domesticated canaries (for which, of course, he conveniently sold just the right bird seed.) A business partnership with Thomas Bakewell curiously ended about that time.

Perversely, at the outbreak of the war of rebellion, when the decorum of Northerners was to make good and profitable any industrious effort to supply the Grand Army with all due speed and productivity, money was in no short supply. Indeed, as Pittsburgh's skies became that much darker, the paths, porches and gardens of the elite became all the more green. Not coincidentally, Frederick Law Olmstead and Calvert Vaux had won their commissions to create Central Park just two years earlier. And the idea that suburban homeowners could cultivate sweeping lawns, decorated with ornamental curiosities or amusing topiary, was in full sway in Victorian England. Local evidence, too, was the movement of the pastoral cemetery in which Thomas Shields had been so instrumental.

The partnership of Shields and Wardrop established a nursery on Newington land, of course, just south of Beaver Road between Church and Edgeworth Lanes.[48] For many years, Nursery Lane was the only road parallel to Beaver, crossing at Edgeworth.

The Pittsburgh Gazette published what appears to be an early *advertorial*.

> "A recent visit to the Nursery Grounds of Messrs. T.L. Shields & Co. has served to confirm in us the favorable impression which the public has already formed of the extent of these grounds and variety of stock as well as skill and industry employed in the propagation of almost every conceivable kind of fruit trees, vines, shrubs, flowers, evergreens and ornamental plants... Possessing ample means, the house of T.L. Shields & Co. are enabled to employ every appliance which an enlarged experience may deem requisite, whether for the preparation of the soil or the testing of new methods of propagation. The growing of fruit trees is born with Mr. T.L. Shields. To propagate a tree or vine which will yield rich, juicy, melting, golden fruits is the crowning glory of his life...
>
> "A very important adjunct of the nurseries is the gentlemanly Superintendent, James Wardrop. The visitor will always get from him a civil and intelligent answer, and purchasers can rely upon his prompt and skillful filling and packing of their orders...
>
> "W.C. Shields, the junior member of the firm, at the commencement of the slaveholders' rebellion, laid aside the "pruning hook," and took up the sword. When peace will smile once more upon the land, we will hope for his safe return."

---

[48] Hardie, *Sewickley: A History of a Valley Community*, pg. 36

General Alexander Hays

The dawn of June 1, 1862, gave first light to the Battle of Fair Oaks Station, southeast of Richmond, Virginia. Otherwise known to the confederates as Seven Pines, the battle was significant for several reasons. First, after Shiloh, it yielded the highest casualties in the Civil War to date; both forces shared in some 11,000 dead, injured or missing. Secondly, as an early effort of the Peninsular Campaign, it was the closest General George McClellan would ever get to Richmond. Finally, it gave young David Shields his first taste of battle.

Again, William Morrow, a member of the company, captured the fear of the confrontation.

"Calculating upon the swell of the Chickahominy [River], which was holding the two wings of our army apart, the Rebel General Johnston had seized this moment to hurl his army against us in order to annihilate our entire left wing.

"The musketry fire soon deepened into a continuous roar and presently the deep, hollow booming of cannon joined in, and we all knew a battle had begun. Soon an orderly from General Kearney's headquarters was seen galloping to Colonel Hays' tent, and in a few minutes we were hurrying up the railroad to the scene of carnage. Presently the shells from the Rebel cannon began to shriek over our heads, bursting with startling crashes among the treetops, while the zip, zip, zip of the musket balls betokened that we would soon be in the midst of it.

"On our front was a large slashing—that is, the woods had been cut down, the trees being felled so that they lay in every way forming an almost impenetrable mass of trunks and branches. The Rebels had possession of a portion of this slashing, and Jameson's brigade...was ordered in to drive them out. In we went, yelling and cheering like madmen."[49]

What Morrow described underwhelms in detail the overall onslaught that the Union forces committed to victory at the singular battle. Hays and his men, Dave Shields included, dove into the "slashing" with fearless abandon. They won the day.

Of the lesser casualties of the fight was Hays's horse, Dan. His rear left leg was shot, and Hays feared it was his steed's "last." As to his young human charge, Hays wrote his wife " 'Dave' Shields is well and hearty, although his clothes are cut up by bullets, as are the clothes of almost every man in the regiment."[50]

It was said after the battle that McClellan's Union forces took too long to reorganize. Had they acted more swiftly, they might have taken Richmond. But Robert E. Lee had devised multiple strategies to defend the Confederate Capital. By August, McClellan's First Brigade retreated to Bull Run.

Then Hays did it again. At a single battle at Nelson's Farm in Glendale, Virginia, Hays's nimble forces swept in behind the first battery of the engagement. To his superiors who saw the whole melee, Hays's experience and the training of his several companies showed that his men had "what it took."

At the second Battle of Bull Run, Hays, responding to the commands of General Kearney, ordered 357 infantry of the 63rd to rout out rebel forces descending an open railroad bed. They confronted an army of 5,000, yet did not retreat, not at first, not until an hour later, losing half of their men. The 5,000 rebels incurred losses of many more hundred than did Hays.

He wrote to his wife three days later:

"We received there the most terrible fire I have ever experienced, to which the 63rd replied hotly. For some time we were

---

[49] Hays, *Life and Letters of Alexander Hays*, p 223
[50] Ibid., pg. 239

unsupported, but my regiment never wavered. I have telegraphed you of my situation. A large ball struck the main bone between the ankle and the knee, not breaking, but splintering it, glancing off and breaking the smaller bones. The entrance hole is as large as a half dollar. I assure you I have a sore shin, but a quarter of an inch variation would have cost me my leg..."

Hays added, "David Shields was not in battle. I had given him permission to visit the young men lately enlisted at Sewickley for the artillery; he was unable to join the regiment afterwards, but is safe... Both of my horses were shot."

In September, Colonel Alexander Hays was promoted to Brigadier General for his command at Fair Oaks. And along with his greater rank came the opportunity to organize a staff. As had once been "threatened" by Hays, he promoted David Shields to Lieutenant.

Within months, he would make him his aide-de-camp, too. 'Dave' was just 18 years old.

A *Carte de Visite* image of Captain David L. Shields.
Courtesy of the Gilbert Hays Collection, Detre Library, Western Pennsylvania Historical Society.

Will at Antietam

Farther north, just across the Maryland border from West Virginia, ten miles south of Hagerstown and five above Harper's Ferry, Antietam Creek flows south into the Potomac River. On the 16th of September, 1862, Robert E. Lee's rebel forces made their first foray into Union territory. General McClellan's army of 87,000 men pursued 38,000 confederates, yet, for whatever reason, McClellan assumed that Lee commanded twice as many men.

Lt. William C. Shields was in command of his regiment under General Joseph K. Mansfield, newly appointed to lead the XII Corps of the Army of the Potomac. The corps had only recently been assigned from its operations in the Shenandoah Valley to join the Army of Virginia. It was the smallest corps of any, having only two divisions rather than the regular three. At Antietam, the corps numbered 12,300, comprising 22 infantry regiments and three batteries of light artillery. Shields served as a lieutenant to Major Ario Pardee, Jr., who in turn, served under Lieutenant Colonel Hector Tyndale. Shields's exact movements on the battlefield are not known, but from exhaustive studies by civil war buffs the choreography of the 28th PA Infantry is well documented. At 8:40 am the morning of the battle, Shields was commanding his men on the front line. In fact, his regiment was the only one within 200 yards of any rebel team. By 9:30 am the regiment had retreated to the rear of the famed Dunkard Church.[51] At 10:30, Shields again was at the front line, once more leading the closest of any regiment to the enemy at Antietam. This was all the more surprising in the knowledge that General

---

[51] https://antietam.aotw.org/maps.php?map_number=4

Mansfield had just fallen. The man had been in charge of the XII Corps for just two days.

The "bloodiest single day in American history" resulted in the deaths of 5,000 men, yet saw casualties of 24,000. And while McClellan had pursued Lee (and Lee had retreated,) McClellan once again failed to follow through toward likely victory. Famously, upon consideration of McClellan's hesitant response, Lincoln relieved him of his command. Ambrose E. Burnside became Major General of the Army of the Potomac.

William Shields, injured, but not critically, survived. Antietam represented the last great battle of the year. The yanks, as well as the rebels, retreated before winter fell on darker days. Not until May would Lt. Shields see battle again. His younger brother would not be far away.

Fidus Achates

By several accounts, David Shields returned home to his parents, grand-mother and family for a brief respite over the winter holidays of 1862. While his commander convalesced outside Washington, unable to get about with his badly damaged leg, his wife, Annie, visited him in his Alexandria board-ing house shared with other officers mending their wounds. It's not clear if Lt. William C. Shields received the same gift of a holiday leave.

In January of the new year, Abraham Lincoln signed the Emancipation Proclamation, freeing all slaves owned in the Confederate states. The proc-lamation, however, changed nothing for slaves in states that remained loyal to the Union.

By March, David was given the assignment of provost marshal to pro-cess Southern refugees and rebel deserters, neither of whom apparently were treated any differently than prisoners. By this turn he was known to other officers in the regiment as Hays's "fidus achates" (or most trusted friend) and by subordinates (as well as the General) as his aide-de-camp, although that title was also ascribed to Col. George Corts who, despite being Shields's superior, seemed as pleased with 'Dave's' recognition as his own. Both men adored Hays, even if the General might have loved his horses more. In hun-dreds of letters to his wife, he rarely ever left out news or anecdotes about 'Dave's' activities, so close was she to the Shields family—so busy was Dave, otherwise—to share first-hand stories of the war.

Chancellorsville

By early May, the reorganization of Union forces had offered no promotion for First Lieutenant William C. Shields of Company G then still under the captaincy of Conrad Meyer. Known by their more popular name, the Sewickley Rifles, Pennsylvania's 28th Regiment was now assigned to Brigadier General John W. Geary's Second Division of the Twelfth Army Corp. Will Shields, however, still wielded the same glistening sword he received at the Sewickley Church two years earlier.

The Battle of Chancellorsville was waged over three days under the leadership of General Joseph Hooker, who, in February of 1863, was assigned the command of the Army of the Potomac after his predecessor General Ambrose Burnside failed Union efforts at the Battle of Fredericksburg. Hooker, like McClellan before him, also failed to realize the poverty of the rebel forces stationed across the Rappahannock. As seemingly only Robert E. Lee was bold to do, he split his diminished army into two divisions to flank Hooker on either side. Hooker's objective was to control Chancellorsville whose only military asset seemed to be its elevation. Southeast of the town, along the strategic Plank Road, General Geary positioned Company G to repel enemy advances. For their defensive position, they built a series of earthen walls known as "breastworks" to which they could retreat, but from which they could also charge. As such, on the morning of May 3, Lt. William Shields once again found himself on the frontline.

Captain Conrad Meyers reported the events of the day to his superiors:

"On the morning of the 3rd, the regiment still in position along the breastworks at 6 a. m., heavy firing commenced on our right, which was continued until between 8 and 9 a. m., when the troops on our right were forced back, leaving our right exposed to a ranking fire from the enemy's artillery and musketry... After having formed in line, the regiment was again ordered by General Geary to retake the position along the breast-works, which order was promptly executed. We found the enemy intrenching themselves in our breast-works on the right in strong force, when Major L.F. Chapman, commanding the regiment, ordered a change of front perpendicular to the rear. While under a galling fire from the enemy, the dispatch and coolness with which this movement was executed by the few who remained, considering the numerous fires the regiment was exposed to, would have done honor to veterans of a hundred battles. Having formed our line, we again charged upon the enemy, driving them back and capturing a number of prisoners; but we were again repulsed, owing to superiority of numbers and the destructive fire from the enemy's artillery. We again advanced, and in this charge the regiment lost one of the bravest and most efficient officers in the service, Major L.F. Chapman. He fell, while proving his devotion to his country, gallantly leading his men upon the enemy. Here also fell Lieutenant William C. Shields, of Company G, and Lieutenant Peter Kaylor, of Company F. They met death like heroes, while urging the men forward. Here also fell many of our best and bravest men."

Lt. William C. Shields was killed, perhaps instantly. His body, like so many others, was left where it fell and was never recovered. Further, the breastworks had been set on fire after the battle.

Not but forty miles north, at Hays's headquarters at Centreville, Dave Shields anxiously awaited all telegraphs and correspondence for his regiment. The word was grim that Chancellorsville had fared well for the Yanks. The name and rank of Lt. William C. Shields, Company G, sadly appeared on May 8.

The next day, the Pittsburgh Gazette posted:

"LIEUT. SHIELDS KILLED.—Lieut. William Shields, son of Thomas L. Shields, of Sewickley, and a member of the Friend

Rifles, 28th Pennsylvania Regiment. (Formerly Col. Geary) is reported killed in the late battles. One hundred and fifty men were killed and wounded in the regiment."

Wrote General Hays to his wife on May 11:

"We all feel anxious for news. You have the sad news for the Shields family, of the death of William. For two days I made inquiry in Washington, hoping I might be able to secure the body. As I was required here, I sent word for 'Dave' to come down. He is yet in Washington, with permission to remain as long as necessary, but there is no hope of the recovery of the body now…"

The last known image of Lt. William C. Shields.
Courtesy of the Sewickley Valley Historical Society.

Gettysburg

Stephen Crane wrote *The Red Badge of Courage* more than thirty years after the Battle of Chancellorsville on which events the book was based. Henry Fleming, the protagonist, rued his cowardly defection, learning later that courage, and only courage, could make him a man. Indeed, like many a soldier, fearful of war, of blindly charging the enemy, of maiming boys no older and no less wise than he, Dave Shields carried his guilts and grief across battlefields of incomprehensible bloodshed. For his family and for his town, the war had become a dire commitment fueled by an unspoken admission that Northern losses had been too great to betray the very courage young men like Will Shields had demonstrated in the heat of battle. What rallied parents, uncles, aunts, grandparents and siblings to support their local regiments—by organizing Sanitary Fairs, auctioning homemade goods, or simply rolling bandages—was not the sporadic cheer of victory, but the daily death knell of hundreds upon hundreds dead. There was no giving up, even if Southern aggression had advanced farther north and into Pennsylvania.

In early June, Dave Shields was given a week's furlough to return home to Sewickleyville during which time the family held a service for William. Certainly, they remembered the many other local boys who would never return. David arrived back at Centreville on June 12, just two weeks before the Battle of Gettysburg.

Lieut. Colonel S. Duncan Oliphant wrote for the *United States Service Magazine* in September 1864 the account of General Hays at Gettysburg. The two had shared a long period convalescing together. The story is one of the most colorful descriptions of Hays (who himself said very little about the third day of the conflict.) Repeatedly he had written to his wife and father-in-law about the tragedies befalling his horses and the capturing of rebel flags following Pickett's infamous charge. But he rarely spoke about his personal victories.

"On the third day of the Battle of Gettysburg, General Hays commanding the Third Division of the Second Army Corps, found himself opposed to General A.P. Hill with who[m] was Pickett and others of General Hays' schoolmates at West Point and comrades of the Mexican war. Hill had been cannonading the Union lines for some time without effect, then moved his troops across the field, thinking, no doubt, that his veterans would draw these raw militia like chaff before the wind. But they met General Hays and his veterans. He had put fight into them. Behind the slight shelter of a low stone fence he restrained himself and his men until the enemy were at close quarters. Then as one man they arose, and with well-directed volleys sent the head of Hill's column reeling back in confusion upon its rear and center. A hurricane, charged with lead and fire and death, consumed them.

"The battle was won. This was the decisive charge. General Hays was a hero among heroes at Gettysburg. His command captured from the enemy that day twenty banners and battle flags, three thousand stand of arms, and captured and killed about twice the number of his command. Out of twenty mounted orderlies he had but six left. He had lost all of his colonels; lieutenant colonels command[ing] brigades; lieutenants command[ing] regiments. Three of his horses had been killed under him; his entire staff was unhorsed. Their steeds lay dead where they fell or were in their last agonies. His men gathered around their chief to congratulate him. Reeking with dust and sweat, and weary with the toil of battle, they received the commendation they so richly deserved. How proud they were of their commander! How proud was he of his 'boys?' The general took young 'Dave' Shields, his boy lieutenant and aide-de-camp, not then twenty years of age, and who could count as many battles, in his arms, imprinting a kiss upon his cheek while yet his boyish face was aglow with the flush of victory. What youth in the land would not be prouder of that kiss of honor from his general than a hundred from the lips of the fairest maiden in the land?"

Brigadier General Alexander Hays, photographed by Mathew Brady.
Courtesy Brady-Handy Collection, Library of Congress.

Indeed, of the "greater casualties" of the day, according to Hays writing to his wife, "I am untouched, as are also Corts and Shields, which is miraculous, although we all lost our horses. 'Dave' Shields had the shoulder of his coat blown off by a shell. 'Dan' was killed by a cannon ball through the heart just after I had exchanged him for 'Leet.' 'Leet' was shot severely in the breast—three balls. One has been extracted and will be sent to 'Leet' Shields...

"The battle cannot be described except as the most terrible fought between men."

But it wasn't just 'Dave's' coat that was blown away. Shrapnel from the impact had embedded hot lead into torn flesh that would bother him for years. He survived the devastating odds of infection, but the pain would not go away. Nonetheless, Lt. Shields carried on his duties with a regularity that amazed even his mentor. Constant were the notes back home to share with the Shields family that 'Dave' was well.

General Hays, however, suffered issues of sudden blindness, a condition he had had for many years following the Mexican War. It was an ironic one at that—his youngest son, Alden, who attended a special school in Philadelphia during the war, was blind.[52] In the months following Gettysburg, pursuing Lee's forces, Hays also battled issues of hearing loss, and then, increasingly, of rheumatism. He had not been well for several weeks when his wife Annie joined him in camp for Christmas in 1863. Even then, his company advanced toward Morton's Ford. Despite her sister's advice, Annie stayed with his company through early February. That's when things fell apart.

While crossing the Rapidan at Morton's Ford on February 6, Hays and his company, the first to repel the newly discovered rebel advances there, were brutally ambushed. Yet another horse was shot out from under Hays. He was feared drowned in the cold swift current. The casualties to his company were high; 200 men were killed in the course of just one hour. And Hays's "Fidus Achates," Lieutenant David Shields, took a direct hit to the chest. An exploding bullet exited his back, irreparably shredding muscle.

Mrs. Hays wrote to her mother the next day.

"I started for the hospital this morning in an ambulance with blankets and a bed to bring David Shields in. When about a mile from here I met one of our orderlies, who told me that Lieut. Shields was dead and General Hays wounded. Mother, I thought my very heart would break when I listened to his account of our killed and

---

[52] According to biographical notes written by Frederick Way, the toddler apparently stabbed himself with a fork. Clarke Room, Sewickley Library.

wounded. We drove on about a mile, when we met Potter, Shields and an orderly. I came back with them, and have David in my Sibley tent. Dr. Cooper has dressed his wound, and, though a most serious one, there is no immediate danger; the ball entered the left breast, under the nipple, and came out of his back, near the side. During the night he coughed and raised a quantity of blood, besides having great difficulty in breathing. Since he came here he has not coughed at all, and is now sleeping as quiet as a babe. David was also shot in the right foot, the top of his middle toe is cut away, but the wound is very slight. He is as patient as possible and so thankful to have me here. A few minutes ago I was turning him; he looked up and said, 'Oh, Mrs. Hays, what would I have done if Aunt Rachel had taken you home?' The doctor insists upon quiet, so I have a sentinel at the door...

"General Hays is so far uninjured, although his escape is miraculous. His horse 'Solomon' is shot in eight places; he is doing well...

"Ambulances are coming in all the time with the wounded... it would not do for me to leave David, as he will require the most careful nursing..."[53]

One month to the day after his near fatal wound, Lt. David Shields arrived back in the care of his mother, father, and sisters in Sewickleyville. Although there would be much protest about unfulfilled obligations to his General, David would see no more of war.

Many years later, sufficiently mobile and in good health, David devoted a lot of interest, and some intellect, too, in creating a new kind of fertilizer. He spent years testing a theory that if all vegetation eventually turned to carbon, then carbon should be a favored nutrient of healthy plants. The idea proved to be a fruitful pursuit if not a profitable one. He received three patents for his work. But David never again left Sewickley. And he never married. Some said—and David may have concluded, too—he was "damaged goods."[54] Known to neighbors and countless visitors over the year as Captain Shields, he was one of the great characters of Sewickley, revered by all who knew him and many more who wished they did.

---

[53] Hays, *Life and Letters of General Alexander Hays*, pg.539

[54] Frederick Way biographical notes, Clarke Room, Sewickley Library.

The catchphrase held true; "Old soldiers never die." David Shields lived until the age of 97, a full 70 years after the last battle of the Civil War. It was said that the highest award any young Boy Scout in Sewickley could earn was the rare opportunity to meet the grand veteran of Gettysburg, listen to his riveting stories and, if truly deserving, have a good look at the old man's scars of courage.[55]

*　　*　　*　　*　　*

General Alexander Hays did not survive the war. At the Battle of the Wilderness, May 5, 1864, he was mortally wounded and died in transit to a field hospital. He was interred at Allegheny Cemetery on May 14 where his memorial is today surrounded by nine 6-pound cannons buried face down. An oversized statue of the General also stands tall on the Battlefield at Gettysburg. David Shields honored his mentor in 1910 when he commissioned a painting of Hays dragging several of the rebel flags his men had captured in the bloody aftermath of Pickett's charge. The whereabouts of the original oil, painted by Sewickley artist Audley Dean Nicols, are unknown.[56]

Detail of Nicols' commissioned work showing David Shields and General Hays celebrating their victory at Gettysburg. Courtesy Western Pennsylvania Historical Society.

---

[55] Hardie, *Sewickley, A History of a Community Village*, pg. 37

[56] Butko, "The Famous Missing Painting," *Western Pennsylvania History Magazine*, pg.10-25

Eliza's Chapel

In 1864, somehow before the war ended, the new Sewickley Presbyterian Church installed a pipe organ made by George Jardine & Son of New York.[57] Based on the time it might have been ordered and the models then available, the organ had one manual (a single keyboard) with a configuration of eight stops. The unit came in a large vertical console designed appropriately as a tryptic. It would require a company representative and a practiced organist to assemble its multiple trackers (wire rods) and to pitch its 16 (or possibly 24) pipes. The entire instrument, set in carved wood and stained to match the interior of the church, was quite elaborate. Only several churches in Pittsburgh then offered such an affair. It was said to have cost $1,800, $600 more than the cost of the lot on which the new church was erected.[58] The organ was heralded by congregants and curious visitors alike.

But, according to family lore, Eliza Shields would have nothing to do with it. In "her" church, organs, pianos, trumpets or any musical instrument were assuredly and—Eliza would add—*deviously* employed to upstage the choir. The idea of serving God was not to entertain Him, but to adore Him. Anything other than the earnest voice of a pious chorister was dishonest at the least, narcissistic at best. Further, anything more chromatic, louder, tympanic, or shrill was blasphemous theatricality.

The truth may be that other events inspired Eliza to separate from the very church she so earnestly helped to build. In the late winter of 1864, the Reverend James Allison resigned, too. Although he wrote an extensive history

---

[57] Cameron, "Jardine & Son: The Era of Spectacular Organs" *The Tracker*, Volume 47, Number 1, January 2003

[58] Allison, *Presbyterianism in Sewickley Valley*, pg. 28

of Sewickley's Presbytery, he declined to explain his own resignation. At the age of just 41, he was not "called" to another church, and he remained in Sewickley to edit *The Presbyterian Banner*, a much respected, but regional newsletter.

News of the apparent schism appeared in the Pittsburgh Gazette, dated July 30, 1864. "A neat and commodious house of worship will be erected as soon as possible, and will be located immediately west of the grounds of Shields' and Wardrop's nurseries. It will be about one mile distant from the house of the First church of Sewickley; and besides accommodating the Edgeworth Ladies' Seminary and the people of the lower Sewickley valley, it will bring the means of grace within convenient reach of an extensive population lying up the two Sewickley creeks and over the neighboring hills for several miles north of the Ohio river."

In February, 1865, the Edgeworth Seminary burned. Not coincidentally, it was where disaffected congregants had been holding their interim services. Pittsburgh papers, however, reported that the fire was "communicated" by a bake-oven and, while much furniture was lost, none of the fifteen "inmates" then boarding at the schools was harmed.[59]

Fortunately, before summer, a white clapboard edifice stood waiting at the corner of Beaver Road and (what is today) Church Lane. Eliza Shields had donated the land, then estimated to be worth $1,200, and paid the construction costs of $2,300.[60] More than a few like-minded Presbyterians joined her for its first service when, in 1865, the wood frame structure was dedicated, without flourish, "to the worship of God." The "Old White Chapel" stood firmly until 1960.

The chapel, however, almost from its first Sunday service, was woefully insufficient. When the war was "done" and "Johnny" had come marching home, the numbers were too great. If Sewickley's population had doubled in just the ten years between the first train and the fall of Fort Sumter, those seeking the serenity of the suburb tripled after the war.

Eliza Shields again called on Joseph Kerr to design a third Presbyterian church in the Sewickley valley. But the architect was so popular, so swamped with work, he had to beg for time. Then, Kerr was just finishing touches on Reed Hall at the Western Pennsylvania Hospital for the Insane at Dixmont.

---

[59] *The Pittsburgh Gazette*, February 14, 1865
[60] Ellis, *Lights and Shadows of Sewickley*, pg. 149

And no sooner had he finished that than he won the commission for a new City Hall in Pittsburgh. But Kerr found the time to oblige his insistent client.

The style of Eliza Shields' new church would revert back to the more classical forms of Gothic Revival. Made of sandstone, with lancet windows proportioned to a massive equilateral roofline, the new house of worship offered a vaulted ceiling of 40 feet. Two wide columns of pews made from Honduran mahogany allowed for a center aisle which was met at the crossing with semicircular steps ascending to the altar. The church had no centered narthex; its gospel facade offered a side entrance for alternate access to stairs descending into a parish hall and kitchen below. There, also, was a coal burning furnace whose heat ascended through a square iron grate at the crossing. The church boasted no steeple and no spire, but it did feature four crenellated turrets, of which one cleverly served as the building's chimney.

Wrote architectural historian James D. Van Trump many years later about the church design, "the structure is undeniably handsome in a restrained way and as late as it is, it is probably one of the best surviving examples of the archeological phase of the Gothic Revival in Western Pennsylvania."[61]

The cornerstone of the Leetsdale Presbyterian Church was laid on June 23, 1868. Not quite 18 months later, the new church was completed. The Rev. James Allison gave the morning's dedication sermon. The Rev. David R. Kerr (no known relation) gave a sermon in the afternoon, and for the evening's service, the Rev. S. J. Wilson (also no known relation) spoke. Presbyterians were not shy about "being present unto the Lord." Sermons often droned on for hours seemingly to spurn Episcopalians who delighted in short Gospels, musical doxologies, responsively chanted creeds, and other obviously impersonal recitations. In fact, Presbyterians were known to hand out chips to those attending each and every sermon; only those with the requisite sum of tokens were then allowed to receive holy communion.[62]

Leet Shields endowed the church with a donation of $5,000. The building cost $18,000, unfurnished. Of course, when first dedicated, it had no organ and no stained glass. What comforts it did offer were mostly of the spiritual kind. For Eliza Shields, its greatest comfort was its proximity to Newington. Built almost adjacent to the white chapel, the church was a mere five minute

---

[61] Shields, *A Short History of the Shields Presbyterian Church*, pg. 9

[62] Hardie, *Sewickley: A History of a Valley Community*, pg.42

walk from her front door. At 80 years of age, constant knee and joint pain had begun to set in.[63]

Family lore aside, however, the congregation of the Leetsdale Presbyterian Church, Eliza included, soon enjoyed singing to the dulcet tones of a new pump organ. Within two years, Alden Hays, the late General's blind son, became the church's beloved organist. He played every Sunday for more than 17 years.

The design of the Leetsdale Presbyterian Church is attributed to Joseph W. Kerr, a favored architect of the Shields family, but a very popular one, then fully committed to building Pittsburgh's French Renaissance City Hall at the time the Shields Church was completed. Photo courtesy of the Gilbert Hays Collection, Detre Library, Western Pennsylvania Historical Society.

---

[63] *Ibid.*, pg. 38

D. Leet Shields

Seemingly forgotten, Leet Shields died in January, 1871. No obituary, not even a notice of death, appears in any extant newspaper of the day. Curiously, too, the census of 1870 reported him as "retired" and cited his age as 50. The 1860 census had cited his age as 45. In fact, he was 63 upon his death.

An undated daguerrotype of Leet Shields. Courtesy of the Sewickley Valley Historical Society.

If indeed he had a debilitating condition, was born with a defect, or contracted some chronic illness in infancy, there is no mention of his challenges, physical or otherwise, in any family communication or record.

There remains one account of his riding from Washington to Sewickley Bottom in July, 1837, having visited his sister Susan there. The purpose of the letter seems to assure her of his safe return, but he writes about an encounter in which several men outside of a resting stop accuse "a Negro" of having stolen $1.50. Leet writes that he feared for the man's safety, until others confessed that they had misplaced the cash and "nothing came of it." The incident he shares seems to be a telling one; it openly reflects a concern for his own safety. The greater value of the letter, however, is the proof that Leet was educated, could write well, and was able to express empathy and sincere gratitude. Sadly, there is no shred of evidence to suggest he was valued, respected or much loved.

Likewise, of course, there is nothing to suggest otherwise.

Eliza Leet Shields

The crippled, arthritic hands of Eliza, matriarch of the Leet-Shields family, mother of nine children and nineteen grandchildren, were of little use. By the time she added the last codicil to her will, her signature was a shaky, illegible swirl. She was said to have suffered rheumatism in wincing pain. Yet, she made her way around her prized gardens and up to her beloved school-house by the aid of a farmhand who carried her immodestly on his back.[64] In ways never before recognized, "Mrs. Shields" became the most esteemed resident of Edgeworth, and of Sewickley, too. Principled and devout in her commitments to church, the seminary, and her own schoolhouse, she com-manded a respect from a community ever-flourishing with the arrival of young families seeking the very "social security" she and her husband had first endowed in their serene valley. Of course, her considerable wealth may have had something to do with the reverence with which she was treated in her remaining years. Yet stories suggest that her real legacy was born of the triumphs she had survived as a pioneer, and as a devoted mother and wife. No cantankerous old dowager, "Mrs. Shields" was apparently well liked by all who knew her.

A portrait of a much younger Eliza Leet Shields hangs at Newington above one of two fireplaces in the house's large front parlor. It is a charming pose, as if Eliza is playing peek-a-boo with a child behind a window that is the frame of her portrait. She is dressed mostly in black, yet wears a white lace cap on her dark brown hair. Her smile is wholly engaging.

---

[64] Hardie, *Sewickley: A History of a Valley Community,* pg. 38

Another portrait of Eliza is missing. Its whereabouts may be known only by a distant relative or, more likely, by an admirer of fine portraits who knows not who the subject is. Like so many heirlooms inherited by one generation from another—indeed, like Thomas Shields's prized silverware, too——much has been lost to neglect or time.

An undated ambrotype of Eliza Leet Shields. Courtesy of the Sewickley Valley Historical Society.

*   *   *   *   *

On March 21, 1872, Eliza Leet Shields died. She was 88. Only four of her children survived her death.

In her original will, written two years after her husband's death, Eliza Leet Shields left substantial sums of money to her children and grandchildren. It accounted equitably for earlier gifts and advances made to several grandchildren and, most particularly, for assets her late husband and she had left in Thomas's hands. One grandchild, however, seems to have been favored. Wilhelmina Shields, Thomas's youngest daughter, was given all of the silver engraved with the family monogram. In particular, the will stated she was to receive a coffee pot, two tea pots, a sugar bowl and creamer, as well as an extra $500 more than the $1500 most other grandchildren were to receive. The will gave no explanation for this instruction, but of course she was the youngest granddaughter, just 8 years old at the time it was written, and, alone, she shared her great-grandmother's name.

Eliza's will also directed a number of annuities for close friends like Rebecca Blaine and Mary Smith, and more than a handful of one-time gifts of $50 or $100 to friends and neighbors not since identified. Eliza gave $1,000 to the Reverend William Passavant for his work in building an infirmary and orphanage. A later codicil, however, refused to award the once-promised gift of $5,000 her late husband had committed to the Western Pennsylvania Hospital.

Finally, a clause in Eliza's will cited her desire to leave the family's burial ground "now surrounded by a stone wall and located upon the mansion farm where I now reside…to my children and the children of my late daughter Susan Cook, and the heirs of their bodies begotten." That Eliza might have had the foresight to separate the burial lot from the residence seems wise. Rebecca and Hannah would inherit all of Newington. But by protecting them from the responsibility of the burial ground and its maintenance, Eliza oddly left no endowment for the same. It would become a small issue solved in the most unusual way.

Thomas Leet Shields

Thomas Leet Shields died on March 9, 1879. An obituary appeared in several papers, the kindest of which ran in the Highland Weekly of Hillsboro, Ohio, on March 20. It read in part:

> "The whole population of the beautiful Sewickley valley attended the funeral, as Mr. Shields was highly esteemed. Mr. Shields was a lawyer of eminent ability, and a man of the highest order of intellect. He was at one time a resident of Batavia, Clermont County, Ohio, and for years was retained as leading counsel in every case of importance. His oratorical powers were such as to command attention at all times. He was an accomplished scholar, a gentleman in the true sense of the word, and was moreover a public-spirited citizen."

A local paper, however, made seemingly purposeful note of his ill health. The Pittsburgh Daily Post wrote, "Mr. Shields has been an invalid for a long time, and although surrounded by all the comforts that wealth and a devoted family could bestow, he was unable to enjoy them. During his life time he acquired a large and valuable estate, and of its products he was a cheerful and liberal giver..."

Another paper wrote, "Mr. Shields was a man of rare culture, and was gifted with a memory that retained all that was valuable in his intellectual researches. Philanthropic, generous and esteemed in life, he met his death with christian resignation."

Most obituaries addressed his son Will's sacrifice in the war. Even David's wounds were cited in another. Several papers included "the success" of his several daughters, meaning, rather, who they had married. "One daughter is the wife of William Collins, Esq., another of William L. Jones, and another of James Oliver, Esq."

Thomas L. Shields was clearly proud of all of his children. Throughout his life, and particularly during the Batavia years when separated from his larger family, he wrote amusing stories about them, often sharing events of their birthday celebrations. Charmed by her excitement one year, Thomas had written about little Eliza's upcoming "burnt-day."

A retouched daguerrotype said to be of Thomas Leet Shields.

*   *   *   *   *

Winifred Amelia Chaplin Shields died ten years later. Although little is known about her "triumphant return" to society from the boredom of Batavia, Amelia did serve a pivotal role in the Edgeworth community, albeit after her husband's death. The Leetsdale Presbyterian Church, in the years following the close of the Civil War, engaged its several women's committees to serve communities in need. Upon the request of the then pastor's wife, the church established a separate parish in Big Sewickley Creek valley where they constructed the Van Cleve Chapel. Amelia was asked to serve as President of the Leetsdale Missionary Society, and among efforts to furnish their satellite synod, the ladies proactively raised funds for destitute widows, freed slaves and "disabled" ministers of the South.[65]

She died on June 30, 1899, at the age of 87. Said her obituary, she enjoyed "remarkably good health until a year ago."

---

[65] Shields, *A Short History of the Shields Presbyterian Church*, pg. 13

Maria Shields Wilson

Sometime upon the death of her brother Thomas, Maria and her husband John Knox Wilson retired to the Sewickley valley, although not at Newington. In recent years, before his death, Thomas and John had formed a corporation called the Pittsburgh and Economy Railroad, capitalized at $200,000, in partnership with Jacob Henrici of the Harmonist Society, as well as with other local investors like Dr. John Dickson. The intent of the company was to lay down tracks dedicated to the business of the Harmonists and not complicated by the schedule of the adjacent rails. Long before the war, the Harmonists had invested in the Pittsburgh, Chicago and Fort Wayne railroad which made them exponentially more profitable—and evidently influential—in obtaining rights to lay down a secondary, yet shorter, railroad. The demands of forming the company obligated the Wilsons to work closely with the Harmonists and other investors. And, thus, with the passing of Thomas, the responsibility to reestablish roots in Leet Township was all the more important.[66]

In July of 1882, John Knox Wilson died. Always a merchant, he earned great respect and wealth from his turns as a Washington bank incorporator, and early investor in local railways. His son, John Jr., in fact, was employed by the Pennsylvania Railroad at the time of his death.

Maria died the following year on December 19, 1883. She was survived by her son David Shields Wilson, Robert Knox Wilson, Eliza Shields Bissell, John C. Wilson, Catherine E. Way, Rebecca Atwood, and Daniel Leet Wilson. Her youngest daughter, Anne Wilson, had died at the age of three.

---

[66] Formed in 1869, Leet Township comprises Leetsdale, Edgeworth and part of Sewickley Heights.

Rebecca and Hannah Shields

Perhaps only because they never married, the two youngest surviving daughters of David and Eliza Shields seemed to be the closest siblings. Rebecca and Hanna had moved into Newington in 1823 and there remained residents of the country mansion for more than 70 years.

Of their love interests, no diaries or journal reveal any romantic yearnings, hopes or fears. Each was said to have been inordinately beautiful and, of course, they were wealthy beyond comparison. As such, no suitors, local or otherwise, would deem themselves to be deserving. At their father's death, they had reached the ages of 35 and 30, respectively, and he had made no pretenses of arranging suitable partners for their long term welfare. "Financial wherewithal" would not have been necessary anyhow. For these reasons, their prospects for marriage would be forever slim.

Yet, there are no clues that the girls were ever unhappy, except when Rebecca's teeth were "afflicted with painful affections."

A year after their mother's death, they channeled their love into creating a new outdoors for Newington. With help from their brother Thomas, they had engaged the services of Samuel Bowne Parsons, Jr., then an assistant in his father's Flushing, New York, nursery, to design an extraordinary landscape on the immediate grounds of the estate. Parsons would clear acres of original brush and establish a new, yet seemingly natural vista of colorful flora comprising Japanese maples, flowering dogwoods and hundreds of white and purple rhododendrons.[67]

---

[67] Lowry, "Guardians of the Gardens," *Pittsburgh Post-Gazette*, June 17, 2006

One lasting evidence of their common joy is found in a book of pressed flowers collected from the grounds at Newington. It is a marvel of scientific integrity and childlike whimsey, recording both the Latin genus of the specimens as well as the fanciful names used in everyday parlance. Indeed, the Shields family seemingly all shared an interest in gardens and natural landscape design.

Rebecca also enjoyed painting. First instructed by her neighbor and namesake, Rebecca Blaine, she later became a student of George Hetzel. He who founded the Scalp Level School of landscape painting had his own Pittsburgh studio and, from 1865 until 1904, he offered instruction at the Pittsburgh School of Design for Women.

None of Rebecca's paintings survive, but two paintings depicting Rebecca do. First is a portrait of the young woman, attributed to Thomas Sully, called "Sunshine," purportedly painted when she was in her mid-teens. The portrait was said to have been exhibited in London in 1888 to much acclaim. The second is a portrait of both girls together. The pose suggests they are working on their book of pressed flowers. What is particularly intriguing about the canvas is the inclusion of a globe, possibly one of the two owned by their mother Eliza from her days at the Moravian Seminary for Girls in Bethlehem. One globe displays the world's geography as it was known in 1790 and the other lays out the night sky constellations. Both girls may have been "instructed in the globes" when matriculating at Mrs. Olver's Edgeworth Seminary in Braddock. In fact, the globes may have been put to good use in the Shields schoolhouse. That they survive today is remarkable.

*   *   *   *   *

A passport application for Rebecca appears in the records of that office. In 1873 she applied to leave the country to visit "Ireland, England, Scotland and the Continent." The application was "attested to" by her nephew David S. Wilson. No one today can say if she sailed that year or for how long she might have "seen the world."

*   *   *   *   *

This portrait of both Hannah and Rebecca Shields still hangs at Newington.
One of their two globes is depicted above the bookcase. Artist unknown; circa 1850.

Upon their mother's death, the girls inherited everything, except Newington's burial grounds. Hannah, who died first, on March 28, 1895, had an estate then valued at $300,000. Her sister who died September 16, 1899, had an estate estimated in local papers to be in excess of $365,000. Converted to a current valuation in gold, her estate would be as if she had liquid assets of $3.24 million. Neither estate is supported by an investment portfolio or schedule of properties then owned. It would seem that John K. Wilson had attended to such assets as the executor of their mother's estate. In fact, he purchased from Eliza hundreds of acres on the other side of the tracks, land separated from the original estate by the railroads but imminently developable for industrial use. The two sisters' estates, of course, represent just half of the inheritance that descended to the four surviving siblings. And, even considering a depreciation of its considerable value due to earlier advances and loans to Thomas, the wealth that David Shields generated in his life time would seem to be income largely earned. If the days of land speculation had fulfilled any promises, forensic accountants today would be greatly challenged to prove—or deny—any such postulation.

Both women gave to their community generously and similarly, suggesting that each had had her will written at the same time. Hannah's was dated 1893. Each left $1,000 to the Leetsdale Presbyterian Church, $1,000 to a building fund for a parsonage, $500 to the Reverend William A. Passavant for his infirmary, $500 to the Colored Orphans Home in Allegheny and another $500 to the Aged Colored Women's Home in Pittsburgh. Thirty-one bequests were allocated to as many nephews, nieces, grandnephews, and grandnieces (and not all in equal measure) as they believed were then generous. Rebecca, the last survivor, then bequeathed the entire estate of Newington to her late sister Susan's youngest child, Martha McCracken (nee Cook) Williams, who had lived at Newington upon her mother's death some forty years earlier. She had married Luther Halsey Williams in 1876. In 1891, however, a month after returning from a vacation in Bermuda, he died suddenly of nephritis.[68] At the time, Martha and he had three children: Susan Shields (15), Mary Leet (12), and L. Halsey Williams, Jr. (9).

On June 4, 1904, Mary L. Williams married Frank Faber Brooks.

And ever since, one generation of Brookses to the next has attended to the loving care and constant maintenance of the country manse which is Newington.

---

[68] *Pittsburgh Daily Post*, May 27, 1891, pg. 2

Lasting Foundations

In 1892, Rebecca and Hannah Shields did the unthinkable. As if they feared some wrath from beyond the grave, they decided to do away with the family plot. The burial grounds "inside a stone wall" had become a constant thorn of guilt and shame. Their nephew, David S. Wilson, implored the sisters to do something about it.[69] Their solution was a simple, but expensive one.

The mausoleum was completed in 1894. Designed by a local architect, John Upton Barr, it looks more like a church, large enough from the outside to seat a small congregation for worship within. In fact, at its time, it was called a mortuary chapel. The Romanesque stone facade features a large six-petaled rose window and an inviting gothic entrance. The mausoleum, however, is locked and gated. It was designed for the internment of 36 bodies in its floor and walls.

Upon its completion, the Reverend Henry Browne attended to exhuming the bodies of 18 relatives of the family, the most recent death of which was Luther Halsey Williams who died three years earlier. Wilhelmina Leet and Wilhelmina Shields were brought up from Washington. So, too, were Isaac and Rebecca Leet. And, in no particular order recorded, the bodies interred in Newington's burial ground were laid to rest in the new mausoleum. Eliza's first daughter, Maria, was buried with Anne Wilson, her daughter who died in infancy. In fact, Eliza was buried with Wilhelmina, her second-born who had died at birth. And, Daniel Leet was interred in the vault adjacent to his wife, Wilhelmina. Strangely, that same fall, on

---

[69] Kidney, *Pittsburgh's Landmark Architecture*, pg. 260

September 30, 1894, Lydia Hannah Shields, Thomas's daughter and wife of William L. Jones, died in an accident when the carriage she and her husband were riding was struck by an electric trolley. She was interred the afternoon of her funeral.

Wrote the historian James D. Van Trump, "Private mausoleums were by no means uncommon in both England and America in former times, but a mausoleum of this size would be an unusual adjunct of the English country church. It would be even less common in American churchyards and, in Western Pennsylvania, it is probably unique."[70]

A family tree of those interred follows.

In more recent decades, the mausoleum, in fact has been used for Sunday services, once briefly by the Anglican community that now leases the church next door.

*   *   *   *   *

In 1906, Martha C. Williams, who inherited all of Newington from Rebecca and Hannah Shields, asked the trustees of the Leetsdale Presbyterian Church to rename the house of worship in honor of her beloved grandmother, Eliza Leet Shields. In 1907, the congregation heartily agreed to rename it the Shields Presbyterian Church.[71] The decision was nearly unanimous for two reasons: the first having something to do with the proximity of the church to the train stop long since named Shields Station, and the second having everything to do with honoring the church's great benefactor. The truth is, however, the building has little to say about Eliza.

The three large lancet windows of the church pay homage to Daniel and Wilhelmine (sic) Leet. Painted in Germanic-like script, seven different verses descend the panes of glass to read:

A broken and a contrite heart, O God, thou will not despise. (Psalm 51:17)

The Father sent the Son to be the Saviour of the world. (John 4:14)

He was despised and rejected by men, a man of sorrows, and accompanied with grief. (Isaiah 53:3)

---

[70] *Ibid*, pg. 260

[71] Shields, *A Short History of the Shields Presbyterian Church*, pg. 18

This cup may not pass away from me except I drink it. Thy will be done. (Matthew 26:42)

When Jesus had cried with a loud voice, he said, Father, into my hands I commend thy spirit. (Luke 23:46)

Christ hath once suffered for sins, the just for the unjust, that he might bring us to God. (1 Peter 3:18)

God forbid that I should glory, save in the cross of our Lord Jesus Christ. (Galations 6:14)

The Gospel side window pays homage to Lt. William C. Shields with the following inscription:

I have fought a good fight, I have finished my course, I have kept the faith.
In memory of
LIEUT. WILLIAM C SHIELDS
28th Regiment Penn. Volunteers
Killed at the Battle of Chancelorsville (sic) May 3, 1865
AGED 25 YEARS

One of two Epistle side windows honors Luther Halsey Williams, Martha Cook Williams's late husband, with this inscription:

So long Thy power hath blest me, sure it still
Will lead me on.
O'er moor and fen, o'er crag and torrent, till
The night is gone,
And with the morn those angel faces smile,
Which I have loved long since, and lost awhile!

The verse is derived from a poem, and later hymn, *Lead Kindly, Light*, written by Cardinal John Henry Newman in 1834. The poem was written shortly after the young priest fell ill and could not travel.

And yet another Epistle window honors a young girl, Bessie L. Young, who was neither a Leet nor a Shields, but was a congregant whose father served as one of the early trustees. Session minutes, written on August 6, 1892, reflect that "Bessie L. Young died from burns received yesterday."[72]

Not a plaque nor a word is inscribed about Eliza Leet Shields. Of course, she would not have approved of it in her lifetime. Her disdain for the super-fluous, the spectacular, or the boastful seems to have been honored by the congregation through their grieving years and since. Indeed, the church is a simple one, solidly built, having well stood the test of time. If it is a reflection of Eliza's love for her community—for her parents, Daniel and Wilhelmina, for her husband, David, or her grandson, Will—it is a testament then, too, to the pioneer's spirit, to the unbridled determination of the white settler, and to the triumph of those whose trials and tribulations are the very history of western Pennsylvania.

---

[72] *Ibid.*, pg. 16

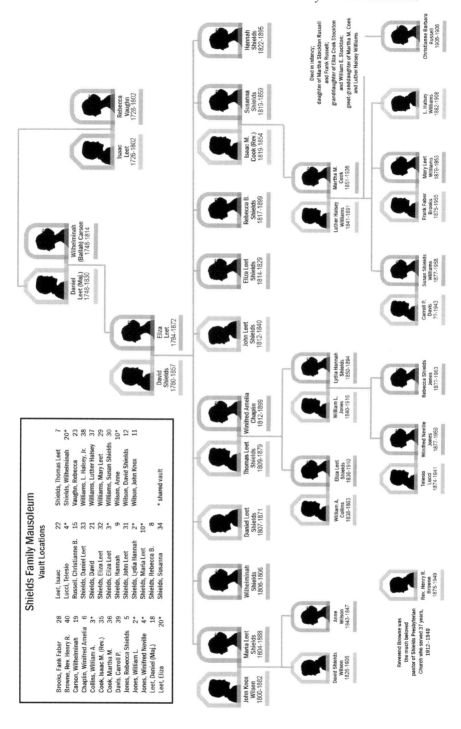

Shields Family Mausoleum

Vault Locations

Brooks, Fank Faber	28	Leet, Isaac		Shields, Thomas Leet	7
Browne, Rev. Henry R.	40	Lucci, Telesio		Shields, Wilhelminah	20*
Carson, Wilhelminah	19	Russell, Christianne B.		Vaughn, Rebecca	23
Chaplin, Winifred Amelia	6	Shields, Daniel Leet		Williams, L. Halsey, Jr.	38
Collins, William A.	3*	Shields, David		Williams, Luther Halsey	37
Cook, Isaac M. (Rev.)	35	Shields, Eliza Leet		Williams, Mary Leet	29
Cook, Martha M.	36	Shields, Eliza Leet		Williams, Susan Shields	30
Davis, Carroll P.	39	Shields, Hannah		Wilson, Anne	10*
Jones, Rebecca Shields	5	Shields, John Leet		Wilson, David Shields	12
Jones, William L.	2*	Shields, Lydia Hannah		Wilson, John Knox	11
Jones, Winifred Neville	4*	Shields, Maria Leet	10*		
Leet, Daniel (Maj.)	18	Shields, Rebecca B.			
Leet, Eliza	20*	Shields, Susanna	34	* shared vault	

Reverend Browne was
the much beloved
pastor of Shields Presbyterian
Church who served 37 years,
1912–1949

Died in infancy;
daughter of Martha Stockton Russell
and Frank Russell;
granddaughter of Eliza Cook Stockton
and William E. Stockton;
great-granddaughter of Martha M. Cook
and Luther Halsey Williams

Epilogue

According to Roy Wilhelm, a forty-year career journalist for the Fremont (Ohio) News-Messenger, the Sandusky plains were once covered with the Indian mounds of both the Aden and Hopewell cultures.[1] Whether or not one of these mysterious earthworks served as the infamous "Battle Island" so critical in the defeat of William Crawford's disastrous expedition into "that country" in 1782, we may never know. Wrote historian Basil Meek in his 1909 chronicle of the region:

> "As to who were the authors of the great earthworks in Sandusky County, written history does not certainly tell, but with such few facts as it has given us, and archaeological investigation offered, and by the aid of some Indian traditions, we are able to determine with some degree of certainty who were their authors. By later researches it has been discovered that Indian traditions have often remarkable foundations in fact — and sometimes none at all."[2]

---

[1] Wilhelm, "Sandusky County Had Dozens of Native American Earthworks," *Fremont News-Messenger*, Oct. 6, 2017

[2] Meek, *Twentieth Century History of Sandusky County, Ohio*, pg. 39

Endnotes: Notables at Newington

Joseph W. Kerr

The Pittsburgh Daily Post for February 28, 1848, reported on the splendor of the newest steamboat *Brilliant.* "Extreme length on deck, 225 feet; 35 feet beam; 29 feet floor, and 6 feet depth of hold. She has five boilers, each 26 feet long, and 40 inches in diameter...The boat was draughted by Joseph W. Kerr, our talented young townsman. Her cabin—built in the Gothic style—is... ornamented with taste, and at great expense."

That a young boat designer would become one of Pittsburgh's preeminent architects seems peculiar, but the fact is Joseph Kerr was a registered architect well before working for the noted boatbuilder Peter Shouse (whose daughter he married.) Joseph's father, James, the much sought-after carpenter and mason from Washington, PA, had sent him to study architecture in Edinburgh several years earlier.

Among his first commissions were Western Pennsylvania Hospital, Passavant Hospital on Reed and Roberts Streets in Oakland, Masonic Hall at Third and Wood Streets, and the Hill-McCallam-Davies House of Evergreen Hamlet, all of which were designed and completed before 1852. The first planned "romantic" suburb in America, Evergreen Hamlet was the mastermind of attorney William Shinn who, along with other early investors, dreamed of a village of exquisite homes, beautifully designed, and built in tight proximity to a school. The concept was something like a modern, gated community but without the gates. Four of Evergreen Hamlet's houses, all different in style, actually still stand. Some have argued that Kerr designed all of them; extant drawings only prove he was responsible for the Hill-McCallam-Davies House.

Sadly, the homestead Kerr designed for Thomas Shields was razed in 2002.

In 1867, Kerr won the commission for a new City Hall in Pittsburgh. Until then, the city's municipal offices were a hodgepodge of public spaces attached to Market Square. They were used as often for public meetings as they were for popular entertainments of the day. And with shoppers creating constant traffic between buildings and arcades, the city's two council bodies voted to purchase a lot at Smithfield Street and Virgin Alley (now Oliver Way) to construct a single building dedicated to the "business of the city." Joseph Kerr was the go-to architect for Gothic Revival, but, in response to the design committee's request for proposals, Kerr drafted a more secular, Second Empire design of astounding detail and French elegance. The eight-story building (five of which were incorporated in its majestic tower pavilion) was constructed of wrought iron beams and arched brick. The tower was faced on four sides with a massive clock, supplied with the correct time from the Allegheny Observatory, and its two-ton bell served as the city's fire alarm for more than 20 years. The building was not completed until May, 1872. Concurrently, he had to have drafted his design for Eliza's new Presbyterian church, for which that cornerstone was laid on June 23, 1868.

Thomas Sully

The prolific Philadelphia portraitist, Thomas Sully (1783-1872) trained under Gilbert Stuart and Benjamin West. Of his vast portfolio, he painted many wealthy Pittsburghers, yet he was not known to have visited the city to do his work. As such, his portrait of David Shields was likely commissioned in Philadelphia during one of many fall visits. But the renowned artist, credited for his much more famous portraits of Thomas Jefferson, John Quincy Adams, Andrew Jackson, and Queen Victoria, also painted Rebecca Leet Shields. Like Eliza's portrait, the work is unsigned and not dated, but local lore attested to it having been presented in an 1888 London exhibition. Noted a magazine of the time, highlighting many attractive women in the Sewickley valley, Rebecca Shields was described as having "melting, large black eyes, perfect features, riotously curling, dark brown hair, a complexion deliciously tinted, an animated expression, changeful, piquant, she was peerless." Further, the article claimed, "Sully, the famous portrait painter of Philadelphia, was secured by the young girl's proud father to depict the charming features of sweet sixteen, the effort proving a gratifying success. The artist, in love with the sweet face, made a copy for himself. Since then it has been exhibited in London as a typical American beauty. Numerous engravings, under the title of 'Sunshine,' have been struck off, and are eagerly sought by lovers of the beautiful all over this country and England."[3] The original oil resides in a private residence in Pittsburgh.

Thomas Sully's portrait of Rebecca Shields. From a private collection.

Samuel Bowne Parsons, Jr.

The son of Samuel Parsons whose nursery in Flushing, New York, provided much of the foliage that went into the design of Frederick Law Olmstead's Central Park, Samuel Jr. became something of an American legend in the history of landscape design. But to understand his legacy, one must be acquainted with his inspiration.

---

[3] Nevin, *The Social Mirror*, pg. 32.

Lancelot "Capability" Brown was an 18th century English gardener who first created landscape designs to mimic all that appeared wholly natural. He is credited as the first landscape architect to have done away with formal gardens and, instead, create man-made lakes, manicure rolling vistas of green lawns, and clear away wholly natural, but sprawling vegetation that would otherwise offend a balanced composition were the landscape to have been painted on canvass. His designs reshaped thousands of acres on hundreds of estates owned by England's richest lords and ladies. (His nickname was thought to have honored his many talents, but, in fact, it sprung from his conviction that every large estate had many capabilities never realized.)

A hundred years later, Samuel Bowne Parsons, Jr., became one of a handful of renowned landscape architects who pursued Capability Brown's design sensitivities. He created dozens of parks like Abingdon Square in Greenwich Village, Albemarle Park in Asheville, North Carolina, and Balboa Park in San Diego. But, at just thirty years of age and not yet a paid associate to his mentor Calvert Vaux (senior partner to Frederick Law Olmstead,) Samuel Parsons Jr. was managing the Flushing nursery when, in 1873, he received an invitation from Thomas Shields. A customer of the young Parsons, Shields sought out landscape architects. Apparently, his sisters, Rebecca and Hannah, the two remaining residents and only caretakers at Newington, wished to enhance the beauty of their natural setting.

Quite separate from the cultivated fields surrounding the "mansion farm," Newington's grounds included ten acres of winding creeks, dense vegetation and massive, "first-growth" trees. One sycamore thought then to be more than 200 years old was 130 feet tall and four meters round. Parsons, with the deafening approval of the sisters, cleared sweeping vistas along Little Sewickley Creek, planting scores of ornamental trees—magnolias, dogwoods, lilacs, and Japanese maples—and rearranging the landscape to burst with spring colors or explode in fall flames. Parsons was largely responsible for planting the hundreds of rhododendrons for which Newington is regionally famous.

John Upton Barr

Only because Joseph Kerr's popularity afforded him little time, architect John Barr was engaged to design another edifice at Newington. Upon inheriting all of Newington as the two surviving residents of the country estate, Rebecca and Hannah Shields, in 1893, decided to honor their family legacy by erecting a mausoleum, one very purposely seated on the property. Erosion affecting the family burial ground, as well as some fear of the succession of ownership, suggested to them that only a large stone edifice would ensure permanency. A Northside architect with recent credentials in cemetery work, Barr offered the sisters a significant stone sanctuary designed in the Richardsonian Romanesque style.

John Barr's architectural legacy is not a deep one. But, among several campus buildings, a Northside church, and High School, he and his partner Henry Moser are credited for the design of Allegheny Cemetery's distinctive Office Building at its entrance on Butler Street in Lawrenceville. The facility, unchanged since its construction in 1870, is on the National Register of Historic Places.

*   *   *   *   *

So, too, is Newington. Nominated in 1975 by James D. Van Trump, architectural historian of the Pittsburgh History and Landmarks Foundation, the estate, begun in 1816, expanded in 1823, and fully "modernized" in 1959, is a rare example of architectural and landscape preservation. Wrote Van Trump in the application for its national recognition, "Estates of this kind were never common during the nineteenth century in the Pittsburgh area. Newington would seem to be the sole survivor of those that were established."

Separate from the estate's recognition by the U.S. Department of the Interior, Shields Presbyterian Church—today known as Grace Anglican Church—is also recognized as an historic landmark by the distinguished Pittsburgh foundation.

Acknowledgements

I am the luckiest man ever to have a wife who has not only tolerated my absences—whether if I'm just in my office above the garage or on a three-day jaunt to Philadelphia—but has supported me in my endless months of research by willingly (and sometimes eagerly) accompanying me to obscure graveyards, empty forts and mice-infested cabins. During these months (but really it's been years) of Covid, she has suffered solitude perhaps more than anyone should, but she has always found interest in my next chapter or my most recent discovery, and has consoled me endlessly when I can't find what I've spent too long searching for or when my computer has decided, completely on its own, to stop working. She knows how much this work has meant to me; more than that, she knows how much she means to me. Thank you, Lulu, for your love, wisdom and strength, always and forever.

While writing this family narrative, I have been awed often by the fact that I have an aunt living in Sewickley who in May of this past year reached her 100th birthday. She's an especially sweet and cheerful woman, much like her mother (my paternal grandmother) was. This one aunt was married into the same Sewickley house in which she still lives. Her groom, who carried her across that threshold more than 75 years ago, was a brother-in-law to a direct descendant of the Shields family. As such, Jay Brooks is my aunt's nephew by marriage. I have known him for many years because he is a first cousin to my first cousins.

Which makes us...well, close family friends. Jay, more than "holding down the fort" for several decades, holds more information, more great stories, more "dirt," and more love for his family and ancestors than any other descendant I have had the pleasure to meet. And, of course, there are many who take pride in their Shields/Leet legacy. The late Betty G.Y. Shields, who actually married into the family, might have known more in her time, but Jay carries the torch and he has kept it burning bright for many, including me. I can never thank Jay enough for the time he spent poring over countless letters (wearing white gloves at all times,) making piles of interesting reading or sketching out genealogies of one family after another. Never have I arrived at his place when he was not in the middle of clearing one room or organizing another, or working the gardens or lawns, rake in hand, boots muddied, and baseball cap pulled down tight. Were it not for Ellen, his ever-productive wife, (and an exceptionally talented interior decorator, too,) Newington would be but his sole life. They have worked magic to keep their "farm mansion" the charming, yet unpretentious home it is.

I owe much to so many more, too. Almost from the beginning, I learned from John Kroeck the countless tales and (mostly true) stories of Major Leet, the Girty brothers, Blaine family, Harmonists and Robert Morris. There can be no source more relevant than someone who can lay down context and, at the same time, question motives and outcomes with a curiosity that is fresh and compelling. John has been incredibly generous with his time and deep knowledge; I am forever indebted to him.

Also, generous beyond words was David Vater, architect and historian who knows more about Pittsburgh than any one person should. It's not just that he knows who designed or built everything in our region, but he knows how and, almost more importantly, why. I suspect, too, from the many photocopies he forwarded to me in the early days of Covid, he owns one of the most extensive libraries of Pittsburgh architecture in the city.

Dan Telep was incredibly helpful in ways I had never expected. He is the regional authority on the US Post Office. Sure, he knows a lot about stamps, but his invaluable collection of local postmarks and cancelled correspondence includes dozens of letters actually written by, or to, David Shields. Dan was as elucidating as were the many letters he proudly shared with me.

Regional history can only be as valuable as the commitment so many volunteers and (woefully underpaid) staff give to preserving it. There are many great historians in our area who offer worlds of rich resources to researchers like me, or to genealogists, high school students and masters candidates who can never repay the contributions these kind people make every day. Sewickley Valley owes a massive debt to Harton Semple and Susan Horton, and, now, Amanda Schaffer, too. Thank you also to SVHS Board Member Mary Beth Pastorius for introducing me to finding obscure land records online. At the Washington County Historical Society, Tom Millholan and Clay Kilgore are incredibly proactive in reaching out to their members. On days when the whole world seemed to be locked down, I would receive happy and valuable info from them. I only wish I could have spent more time visiting their historic headquarters. Likewise, the Beaver Historical Society offered early, safe access to records I had not thought would be there. Thanks goes to Bob Mitchell for following up on some picayune requests, too. Kay Stephenson, who I've not yet met, was extremely helpful in digging into the land records of Thomas Shields at Damascus Manor. I do hope to visit the Honesdale Historical Society when next I get to the northeast region of Pennsylvania. Finally, the Pennsylvania Historical and Museum Commission deserves high praise for providing me access to records and correspondence of the Harmonists that, in normal (and, thus, busier) days, I might have had to dig up in Harrisburg. I cannot thank Sarah Buffington enough for giving up many hours of her restricted work days for my needs.

As always, I am in debt to the Pittsburgh Regional History Center, which really means old friends like Andy Masich, Betty Arenth, Tonia Rose, and Brian Butko who have always encouraged my interests, and, in this particular case, introduced me to Alan Gutchess at the Fort Pitt Museum. Alan knows everything that went on before the Depreciation Lands came to be, and he knows all the characters that roamed these rivers and woods, as well as those that plied the plains of Sandusky.

And thanks to Alan, I was introduced to Steve Fuller who, since he was a young boy, has collected anything and most everything of the indigenous tribes of the Ohio Valley. It is Steve's tomahawk that graces the cover of this book. He believes that this once ubiquitous tool was a gift to Dr. Absalom Baird, perhaps for medical attention rendered (and, we can only hope, not as a result of injury from the same.) Thank you, Steve.

For great help in learning more about General Alexander Hays when he was not on a battlefield, my thanks go to Kit Mueller and his cousin, D.B.

Hays. Both are proud descendants and, like me, wish they knew more about the great man's local exploits.

Of course, none of this work would hold together without the invaluable resources of the library and archives of the Pennsylvania Historical Society. Essential to my research were volumes of letters written by and to Levi Hollingsworth. I thank the staff there for helping me locate the most seemingly obscure files.

Marion Ahlers has been a longtime friend and work associate, yet, most recently, she has been my editor. I owe her for guiding me through dense thickets and seeing the forest for the trees. Even when it seemed I was lost in these woods, she kept an elevated perspective—and a cheerful voice—so that I might heed her good advice. Thank you.

Thanks also to Alex Mysels for the fantastic cover design, as well as for his patience. Thanks also to Josh Snyder of Wooster, Ohio, for the cover photography.

And then there are thanks necessary to dozens of people whom I barged in on, presuming they could offer me help. And, without hesitation, they did, and most graciously, too. Thank you to David Aloe for my impromptu visit to the Shields schoolhouse, to the Reverend James Wilson at the First Baptist Church of Philadelphia whom I interrupted mid-podcast to inquire about silver chalices (and also to Roy Harker who followed up with more info about the same,) to Ed Diener who kindly mailed me (at his own expense) a copy of his late mother's authoritative (and rare) biography of Dorsey Pentecost, to Dolly Ellenberg and Deborah Harding, both at the Carnegie, for searching for weird antiquities like silver shoe buckles and tomahawks that apparently were never there in the first place, and to many members of the DAR who likewise dug around for archives that, alas, never existed.

Finally, I also want to express my respect and deep appreciation for the many indigenous people, including the Seneca Nation, who called the Pittsburgh region Dionde:ga. I wish to acknowledge the members of the Haudenosaunee Confederacy, the Leni Lenape, the Shawnees, and the Wyandots, whose stories have long been lost or neglected, whose lands were stolen, and whose contributions and respect for our one planet can never be repaid.

Select Bibliography

Achenbach, Joel. *The Grand Idea, George Washington's Potomac and the Race to the West.* New York: Simon & Schuster, 2004.

Agnew, Daniel. *History of the region of Pennsylvania north of the Ohio and west of the Allegheny River, of the Indian Purchases, and of the running of the southern, northern, and western State Boundaries.* Pittsburgh: University of Pittsburgh Press, 1887.

A history of the Presbyterian church of Sewickley, Pennsylvania, consisting of certain addresses, delivered February 16-19, 1913, on the occasion of the seventy-fifth anniversary of the permanent organization of the church, together with a compendium of events, photographs and notes, prepared by a committee of the congregation. New York: The Knickerbocker Press, 1914.

"American Baptist Magazine." March 1820, Vol. 11, *Latter-Day Luminary*, Philadelphia

Anderson, David A., Ph.D., Paula Bienenfeld, Ph.D., Elizabeth Fauber, Jonathan Glenn, M.A., Hope Leininger, and Timothy McAndrews, Ph.D. "Phase III Archaeological Investigations at the Leetsdale Site (36AL480) Area 3–South, Leetsdale, PA," US Army Corps of Engineers, April, 2010.

Annual Report of the Secy of Internal Affairs of the Commonwealth of PA, year ending 1892. Part 1. Harrisburg: Edwin K. Meyers, State Printer, 1893.

Arndt, Karl J.R. *A Documentary history of the Indiana decade of the Harmony Society, 1814-1824.* Indianapolis: Indiana Historical Society, 1975.

———. *George Rapp's Harmony Society, 1785-1847.* Cranbury, NJ: Associated University Presses, Inc., Revised Edition, 1972.

Atwood, Craig D. *Community of the Cross, Moravian Piety in Colonial Bethlehem.* University Park, PA: The Pennsylvania State University Press, 2004.

Axtell, James. "Who Invented Scalping?" *American Heritage*, Vol. 28, Iss. 3, 1977.

Bailey, Ron. "A Surveyor for the King," *Colonial Williamsburg Journal,*
https://research.colonialwilliamsburg.org/foundation/journal/
Summer01/Surveyor.cfm

Barbieri, Michael. "How Far is 'Musket-Shot'? Farther Than You Think." *Journal of the American Revolution.* August 26, 2013.

Barr, Daniel P. *A Colony Sprung from Hell.* Kent, Ohio: The Kent State Press, 2014.

Bausman, Joseph H. *History of Beaver County, Pennsylvania and its centennial celebration.* Volume III. New York: Knickerbocker Press, 1904.

Blaine, John Ewing. *The Blaine Family; James Blaine, emigrants and children, Ephraim, Alexander, William, Eleanor.* Cincinnati: Ebbert and Richardson, 1920.

Brackenridge, Hugh Henry. *Narratives of a late expedition against the Indians; with an account of the barbarous execution of Col. Crawford; and the wonderful escape of Dr. Knight and John Slover from captivity, in 1782.* Philadelphia: Francis Bailey, 1783.

Brown, Parker, B. "The Battle of Sandusky: June 4-6, 1782," *Western Pennsylvania History Magazine,* April, 1982.

Bushman, Richard. *The Refinement of America, Persons, Houses, Cities.* New York: Vintage Books, 1992.

Butko, Brian. "The Famous Missing Painting," *Western Pennsylvania History Magazine* Vol. 86, No. 1 (Spring 2003)

Butterfield, Consul Willshire, 1824-1899. *An Historical Account of the Expedition Against Sandusky Under Col. William Crawford in 1782: With Biographical Sketches, Personal Reminiscences, and Descriptions of Interesting Localities; Including, Also, Details of the Disastrous Retreat, the Barbarities of the Savages, and the Awful Death of Crawford by Torture.* Cincinnati, R. Clarke & Company, 1873.

——————. *History of the Girtys: a Concise Account of the Girty Brothers, Thomas, Simon, James And George, And of Their Half-brother John Turner : Also of the Part Taken by Them In Lord Dunsmore's War, In the Western Border War of the Revolution, And In the Indian War of 1790-95: With a Recital of the Principal Events In the West During These Wars...* Cincinnati: R. Clarke, 1890.

Cameron, Peter T. "Jardine & Son, The Era of Spectacular Organs," *The Tracker, Journal of the Organ Historical Society.* Vol. 47, Number 1, January, 2003.

Clock, Lori. "Surveyor's Chain," The Colonial Williamsburg Official History Site, web. October 5, 2011.

Cockrell, W. Brewster. "Joseph W. Kerr (1815-1888)— Architect; and the Building of the Presbyterian Church, Sewickley, PA." Typescript. 2005.

Coleman, Dorothy Smith. "Pioneers of Pittsburgh: The Robinsons." *Western Pennsylvania Historical Magazine.* 42 (1), (March 1959).

Creigh, Alfred, b. 1810. *History of Washington County: from its first settlement to the present time...* 1870.

Cresswell, Nicholas, 1750-1804. *The Journal of Nicholas Cresswell, 1774-1777.* New York: L. MacVeagh, The Dial Press, 1924.

Crumrine, Boyd. 1838-1916. *History of Washington County, Pennsylvania: with biographical sketches of many of its pioneers and prominent men.* Philadelphia: H.L. Everts & Co., 1882.

Cushing, Thomas B., b. 1821. *History of Allegheny County, Pennsylvania, in Two Parts with Genealogy and Biography,* Chicago: A. Warner & Co., 1889.

Cuthbert, Anthony. "Assessment of Damages Done by the British Troops during the Occupation of Philadelphia, 1777-1778." *The Pennsylvania Magazine of History and Biography.* Vol. 25, No. 3, 1901.

Dennis, Stephen Neal. *Historic Houses of the Sewickley Valley.* Sewickley: White Oak Publishing, 1996.

The Diaries of George Washington, vol. 2, *14 January 1766–31 December 1770,* ed. Donald Jackson. Charlottesville: University Press of Virginia, 1976.

Diener, Mary Alice. *The Honorable Dorsey Pentecost, Esquire.* Fresno, CA: Pioneer Publishing Company, 1978.

Doerflinger, Thomas M. *A Vigorous Spirit of Enterprise, Merchants and Economic Development in Revolutionary Philadelphia.* Chapel Hill: University of North Carolina Press, 1986.

Draper, Lyman C. *A 491-volume collection of partially indexed letters, genealogical and historical notes, land records, newspaper clippings, and interview notes pertaining to the frontier history and settlement of the old Northwest and Southwest Territories of the United States from the 1740s to 1830.* Microforms. West Virginia University Library.

Dyke, Samuel E. *The Pennsylvania Rifle.* Lancaster, PA: 1974.

Eckart, Allen. *The Dark and Bloody River.* New York: Bantam Books, 1995.

Elhanan, Winchester. *The Universal Restoration, exhibited in four dialogues between a minister and his friend; comprehending the substance of several real conversations which the author had with various persons, both in America and Europe, on that interesting subject, chiefly designed fully to state, and fairly to answer the most common objections that are brought against it from the Scriptures.* Philadelphia: T. Dobson, 1792.

Ellis, Agnes L. *Lights and shadows of Sewickley life, or, Memories of sweet valley.* Philadelphia: Lippincott, 1893.

Engels, Jeremy. "Equipped for Murder: The Paxton Boys and the Spirit of Killing All Indians in Pennsylvania, 1763-1764." *Rhetoric and Public Affairs* 8, no. 3 (2005): 35581. http://www.jstor.org/stable/41939988.

Fleming, George T., 1855-1928; Hays, Gilbert Adams. *Life and letters of Alexander Hays, brevet colonel, United States army, brigadier general and brevet major United States volunteers.* Pittsburgh, 1919.

Franklin, Benjamin, 1706-1790. *A narrative of the late massacres, in Lancaster County, of a number of Indians, friends of this province, by persons unknown: with some observations on the same.* Library of Congress, 1764.

Furgurson, Ernest B. *Chancellorsville 1863, The Souls of the Brave.* New York: Vintage Books, 1993.

Gallagher, Winifred. *How the Post Office Created America.* New York: Penguin Books, 2017.

Gormly, Agnes M. Hays. *Old Penn Street (The Old Fourth Ward).* Pittsburgh: 1902.

Hardie, Frances C. *Sewickley, A History of a Valley Community.* Pittsburgh: R.R. Donnelly Financial, 1998.

Harper, Rob. "Looking the Other Way: The Gnadenhütten Massacre and the Contextual Interpretation of Violence." *The William and Mary Quarterly.* Vol. 64, No. 3, 2007.

Harpster, John W. *Crossroads, Descriptions of Western Pennsylvania, 1720-1829.* Pittsburgh: University of Pittsburgh Press, 1938.

Harrington, Hugh T. "The Inaccuracy of Muskets." *Journal of the American Revolution.* July 15, 2013.

Hays, George. *Reminiscences of the Sewickley Valley,* Sewickley: Harmony Press, 1968.

Hays, Gilbert Adams. *Under the Red Patch, Story of the 63rd Regiment Pennsylvania Volunteers, 1861-1864.* Pittsburgh: Market Review Publishing Co., 1908.

Heckewelder, John Gottlieb Ernestus, 1743-1823. *A narrative of the mission of the United Brethren among the Delaware and Mohegan Indians : from its commencement, in the year 1740, to the close of the year 1808 ; comprising all the remarkable incidents which took place at their missionary stations during that period ; interspersed with anecdotes, historical facts, speeches of Indians, and other interesting matter.* Philadelphia: McCarty & Davis, 1820.

Hogan, Edmund. "The Pennsylvania state trials : containing the impeachment, trial, and acquittal of Francis Hopkinson, and John Nicholson, esquires ; the former being judge of the Court of Admiralty, and the latter, the comptroller-general of the Commonwealth of Pennsylvania;" *Pennsylvania. General Assembly, 1780.* House of Representatives; Pennsylvania General Assembly, 1793-1794.

Jaffee, David. "Peddlers of Progress and the Transformation of the rural North 1760-1860." *The Journal of American History.* September, 1991.

James, Alfred P. *The Ohio Company, Its Inner History.* Pittsburgh: University of Pittsburgh Press, 1959.

Jennings, Zelie. *Some Account of Dettmar Basse and the Passavant Family and their Arrival in America.* HathiTrust.org. Pittsburgh, 1903

Kauffman, Henry J. *The Colonial Silversmith, His Techniques and His Products.* New York: Galahad Books, 1969.

Kilgore, Clay. "Looking Back at John Julius LeMoyne," *Washington Observer-Reporter,* July 17, 2017.

"Baptist Board of Foreign Missions for the United States." *The Latter-Day Luminary.* Vol. 2. Philadelphia: Anderson & Meehan, 1821.

Le Moyne de Morgues, Jacques, and Theodor de Bry. *Narrative of LeMoyne: An Artist who Accompanied the French Expedition to...* Boston: J.R. Osgood and Co., 1875.

Thomson, Charles, 1729-1824. Broadside from the Continental Congress, July 25th, 1778, regarding the Indian situation in the Ohio country, the construction of forts in the Ohio Country, and the possible attack against the British garrison at Fort Detroit. Continental Congress Broadside Collection (Library of Congress)

Lienhard, John, H. "Engines of Our Ingenuity, No. 285," https://www.uh.edu/engines/epi285.htm

Lindsey, William Thomas, et al. *Notes on the Settlement and Indian Wars of the Western Parts of Virginia and Pennsylvania from 1763 to 1783: Inclusive, Together with a Review of the State of Society and Manners of the First Settlers of the Western Country.* United States, J.S. Ritenour and W.T. Lindsey, 1912.

Lockwood, Alice B. *Gardens of Colony and State.* New York; Scribners & Son. 1931

Lorant, Stefan. *Pittsburgh, The Story of an American City.* Garden City, NY: Doubleday & Company, Inc., 1964.

Loskiel, George Henry, 1740-1814, and Christian Ignatius Latrobe. *The History of the Moravian Mission Among the Indians in North America: From Its Commencement to the Present Time.* London: T. Allman, 1838.

Lowry, Patricia. "Guardians of the Gardens," *The Pittsburgh Post-Gazette.* June 17, 2006.

Marshe, Witham. *Journal of the Treaty at Lancaster in 1744, with the Six Nations.* Lancaster: The New Era Steam Book and Job Print, 1884.

Mathews, Alfred. *The History of Wayne, Pike and Monroe Counties, Pennsylvania.* Philadelphia: R.T. Peck and Co., 1886.

Meek, Basil. *Twentieth Century History of Sandusky County, Ohio and Representative Citizens.* Whipporwill Publications, 1909.

Melish, John, 1771-1822. *Account of a society at Harmony, (twenty five miles from Pittsburg), Pennsylvania, United States of America: taken from "Travels in the United States of America, in the years 1806 and 1807, and 1809, 1810, and 1811."* London: R. and A. Taylor, 1815.

Mishoff, Willard O. "Business in Philadelphia during the British Occupation, 1777-1778." *The Pennsylvania Magazine of History and Biography* 61, no. 2 (1937).

Morris, Robert. *Robert Morris Papers*, from the Collection of the Pennsylvania Historical Society, Philadelphia, PA.

Mulkearn, Lois. *A Traveler's Guide to Western Pennsylvania.* Pittsburgh: University of Pittsburgh Press, 1953.

Munger, Donna Bingham. *Pennsylvania Land Records, A History and Guide for Research.* Lanham, MD: Scholarly Resources, Inc., 1991.

Nevin, Adelaide Mellier. *The Social Mirror: a character sketch of the women of Pittsburg and vicinity during the first century of the county's existence. Society of to-day.* Pittsburgh: T.W. Nevin, 1888.

Nevin, Franklin Taylor. *The Village of Sewickley.* Sewickley: The Sewickley Printing Shop, 1929.

Oyler, John. "Mystery of Catfish Path's Name Solved," *Tribune-Review*, January 5, 2017.

The Papers of George Washington, Colonial Series, vol. 9, *8 January 1772–18 March 1774*, ed. W. W. Abbot and Dorothy Twohig. Charlottesville: University Press of Virginia, 1994.

The Papers of George Washington, Retirement Series, vol. 4, *20 April 1799–13 December 1799*, ed. W. W. Abbot. Charlottesville: University Press of Virginia, 1999, pp. 512–527

Passavant, Dettmar. "A Romantic Story of Baron Basse, Founder of Zelienople," *Western Pennsylvania History*, January 1, 1925.

Pickenpaugh, Roger. *America's First Interstate, The National Road, 1806-1853.* Kent, OH: The Kent State University Press, 2020.

Pitzer, Dr. Donald E. "How the Harmonists Suffered Disharmony: Schism in Communal Utopias." Keynote address presented to Harmony Society Family (descendants) June 28, 2008, Ambridge, PA. Clinton, NY: Hamilton College Digital Commons, 2011.

Randall, Willard Sterne. "Hamilton Takes Command," Smithsonian Magazine, January, 2003.

Reader, F. S. *Some Pioneers of Washington County, PA; A family History.* New Brighton, PA: Press of F.S. Reader & Son, 1902.

Rush, Benjamin, M.D. *An Account of the Bilious remitting Yellow Fever, as it appeared in the City of Philadelphia in the year 1793.* Philadelphia: Thomas Dobson, 1794.

Ryall, Kay. "Man After Whom Butler was Named Slain by Indians," *Pittsburgh Press,* January 21, 1934.

Sakolski, Aaron. *The Great American Land Bubble, The Amazing Story of Land-Grabbing, Speculations, and Booms from Colonial Days to the Present Time.* Mansfield Centre, CT: Martino Publishing, 2011.

Schattschneider, Allen W. and Frank, Albert H. *Through Five Hundred Years and Beyond, A Popular History of the Moravian Church.* Bethlehem, PA: The Interprovincial Board of Education, Moravian Church in America, 1958.

Schwartz, Seymour I. *The French and Indian War, 1754-1763, The Imperial Struggle for North America.* New York: Simon & Schuster, 1994.

Semple, Harton. *Sewickley Cemetery, History of the Sewickley Valley Found in Sewickley Cemetery.* Sewickley: Sewickley Cemetery, 2009.

"Sewickley Centennial: One Hundredth Anniversary of the Naming of the Town 'Sewickleyville,' 1840-1940." [Sewickley, Pa.?]: [publisher not identified], 1940

Shields, Betty G.Y. *A Short History of the Shields Presbyterian Church: 1864-1964,* [Sewickley, Pa.?]: [publisher not identified], 1964

Shields, Thomas L. *Thomas L. Shields Letters, 1839-1847.* William L. Clements Library, The University of Michigan.

Shoemaker, Henry W. "This Morning's Comment," *Altoona Tribune,* Jan 6, 1938.

Sipe, C. Hale. *Fort Ligonier and Its Times.* Ligonier, PA: Fort Ligonier Memorial Foundation, 1975.

Smith, Helene and George Swetnam. *A Guidebook to Historic Western Pennsylvania.* Pittsburgh: University of Pittsburgh Press, 1976.

Smith, Jewel A. *Music, Women and Pianos in Antebellum Bethlehem, Pennsylvania; The Moravian Young Ladies' Seminary.* Bethlehem, PA: Lehigh University Press, 2008.

Smith, Matthew D. "The Specter of Cholera in 19th Century Cincinnati." *Ohio Valley History.* Filson Historical Society and Cincinnati Museum Center. Vol. 16, No. 2, Summer 2016.

Smith, Robert A. et al. *BeaverTown 2002, A Place in History—Then...And Now.* State College, PA: Jostens Printing and Publishing Co., 2002.

Smith, Ryan K. *Robert Morris's Folly, The Architectural and Financial Failures of an American Founder.* New Haven: Yale University Press, 2014.

Spencer, David. *Early Baptists of Philadelphia.* Philadelphia: William Sycklemoore, 1877.

Stark, Peter. *Young Washington, How Wilderness and War Forged America's Founding Father.* New York: Ecco, 2018.

Stephenson, R.S. *Clash of Empires, The British, French & Indian War, 1754-1763.* Pittsburgh: The Senator John Heinz Pittsburgh Regional History Center, 2005.

Stone, William L. "Journal of a Volunteer Expedition to Sandusky from May 24 to June 13, 1782." *Pennsylvania Magazine of History & Biography.* 01-01, 1894.

Stryker, William S. *The Battles of Trenton and Princeton.* 1898.

Thacher, James, 1754-1844. *A military journal during the American revolutionary war, from 1775-1783.* Boston: Cottons & Barnard, 1827.

Thompson, Robert N. *Disaster on the Sandusky, The Life of Colonel William Crawford.* Staunton, VA: American History Press, 2017.

Thompson, William D. *Philadelphia's First Baptists.* Philadelphia: First Baptist Church of Philadelphia, 1989.

Thwaites, Reuben Gold, 1853-1913, Louise Phelps Kellogg, and Sons of the American Revolution, Wisconsin Society. *Frontier Defense On the Upper Ohio, 1777-1778.* Madison: Wisconsin Historical Society, 1912.

US Army Quartermaster Foundation, https://achive.is/20120907233402/ http://www.qmfound.com/MG_Thomas_Mifflin.htm

Van Trump, James D. "Living with Antiques, Newington, the Pennsylvania House of Mr. and Mrs. J. Judson Brooks." *Antiques Magazine*, May, 1968.

Versluis, Arthur. "Western Esotericism and the Harmony Society," Michigan State University http://esoteric.msu.edu/Versluis.html

Wallace, Paul A. W. *Indian Paths of Pennsylvania.* Harrisburg: Pennsylvania Historical and Museum Commission, 1965.

Washington, George. *Washington and the West: Being George Washington's Diary of September, 1784*, Forgotten Books, 2019.

Wetsel, Richard D. *Frontier Musicians on the Connoquenessing, Wabash and Ohio: a history of the music and musicians of George Rapp's Harmony Society (1805-1906).* Athens, OH: Ohio University Press, 1976.

Wilhelm, Roy. "Sandusky County Had Dozens of Native American Earthworks," *Fremont News-Messenger*, Oct. 6, 2017.

Williston, George C. "The 1782 Volunteer Militia from Washington County, Pa., and their Moravian Indian victims," Typescript. http://freepages.rootsweb.com/~gwilli824/genealogy/moravian.html

Winner, John E. "The Depreciation and Donation Lands," *Western Pennsylvania Historical Magazine*, Vol. 8, No. 1, January, 1925.

Woodward, Susan L. *Indian Mounds of the Middle Ohio Valley*. McDonald & Woodward Pub. Co., 2002.

Yoder, Don. *The Pennsylvania German Broadside*. State College, PA: Penn State University Press, 2005

Index

About the Author

Prentiss is the principal author and editor of the popular illustrated reference book, *Pittsburgh Born, Pittsburgh Bred: 500 of the More Famous People Who Have Called Pittsburgh Home*, chosen by the Senator John Heinz History Center as the official publication to celebrate Pittsburgh's 250th anniversary. He has written dozens of Pittsburgh biographies as editor and publisher of Allegheny Cemetery's *Heritage* newsletter, and published two local history books with the late C. Hax McCullough. Prentiss also was an editor of *The Power of Pittsburgh*, published by Towery Books as the centerpiece of a larger economic development campaign he directed for the Allegheny Conference on Community Development. A former theatre marketing professional and advertising creative director for more than 30 years, in 2005, Prentiss also co-founded Pennsylvania Pure Distilleries, the first vodka distillery in Pennsylvania and makers of Boyd & Blair Potato Vodka.

The Surveyor and The Silversmith is his first deep dive into writing an American family's narrative history. He can be reached at *explorditions.com*.

Made in the USA
Columbia, SC
20 June 2022

61972847R00259